CHEROKEE CITIZENSHIP COMMISSION DOCKETS 1880-1884 AND 1887-1889 VOLUME IV

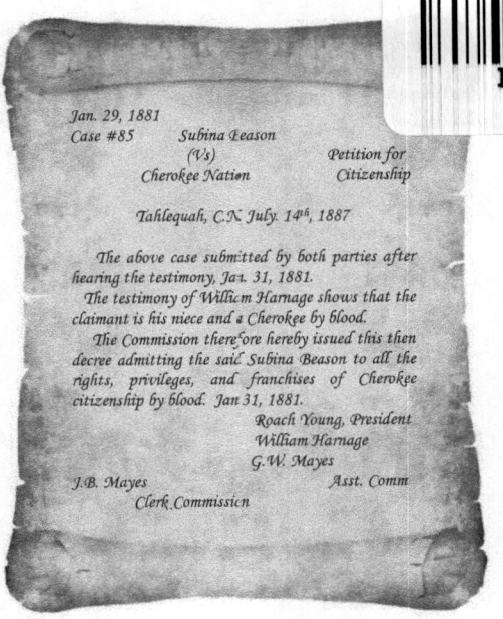

Jan. 29, 1881
Case #85   Subina Beason
                (Vs)   Petition for
                Cherokee Nation   Citizenship

Tahlequah, C.N. July. 14th, 1887

The above case submitted by both parties after hearing the testimony, Jan. 31, 1881.
The testimony of William Harnage shows that the claimant is his niece and a Cherokee by blood.
The Commission therefore hereby issued this then decree admitting the said Subina Beason to all the rights, privileges, and franchises of Cherokee citizenship by blood. Jan 31, 1881.

Roach Young, President
William Harnage
G.W. Mayes

J.B. Mayes   Asst. Comm
Clerk Commission

TRANSCRIBED BY
JEFF BOWEN

NATIVE STUDY
Gallipolis, Ohio
USA

Copyright © 2011
by Jeff Bowen

ALL RIGHTS RESERVED
No part of this publication may be reproduced
or used in any form or manner whatsoever
without previous written permission from the
copyright holder or publisher.

Originally published:
Baltimore, Maryland
2011

Reprinted by:

Native Study LLC
Gallipolis, OH
www.nativestudy.com
2020

Library of Congress Control Number: 2020916859

ISBN: 978-1-64968-061-7

Made in the United States of America.

Other Books and Series by Jeff Bowen

1901-1907 Native American Census Seneca, Eastern Shawnee, Miami, Modoc, Ottawa, Peoria, Quapaw, and Wyandotte Indians (Under Seneca School, Indian Territory)

1932 Census of The Standing Rock Sioux Reservation with Births And Deaths 1924-1932

Census of The Blackfeet, Montana, 1897- 1901 Expanded Edition

Eastern Cherokee by Blood, 1906-1910, Volumes I thru XIII

Choctaw of Mississippi Indian Census 1929-1932 with Births and Deaths 1924-1931   Volume I
Choctaw of Mississippi Indian Census 1933, 1934 & 1937, Supplemental Rolls to 1934 & 1935 with Births and Deaths 1932-1938, and Marriages 1936-1938 Volume II

Eastern Cherokee Census Cherokee, North Carolina 1930-1939 Census 1930-1931 with Births And Deaths 1924-1931 Taken By Agent L. W. Page Volume I
Eastern Cherokee Census Cherokee, North Carolina 1930-1939 Census 1932-1933 with Births And Deaths 1930-1932 Taken By Agent R. L. Spalsbury   Volume II
Eastern Cherokee Census Cherokee, North Carolina 1930-1939 Census 1934-1937 with Births and Deaths 1925-1938 and Marriages 1936 & 1938 Taken by Agents R. L. Spalsbury And Harold W. Foght Volume III

Seminole of Florida Indian Census, 1930-1940 with Birth and Death Records, 1930-1938

Texas Cherokees 1820-1839 A Document For Litigation 1921

Choctaw By Blood Enrollment Cards 1898-1914 Volumes I thru XVII

Starr Roll 1894   (Cherokee Payment Rolls) Districts: Canadian, Cooweescoowee, and Delaware Volume One
Starr Roll 1894 (Cherokee Payment Rolls) Districts: Flint, Going Snake, and Illinois   Volume Two
Starr Roll 1894 (Cherokee Payment Rolls) Districts: Saline, Sequoyah, and Tahlequah; Including Orphan Roll   Volume Three

Cherokee Intruder Cases Dockets of Hearings 1901-1909 Volumes I & II

Indian Wills, 1911-1921 Records of the Bureau of Indian Affairs Books One thru Seven;
 Native American Wills & Probate Records 1911-1921

Other Books and Series by Jeff Bowen

Turtle Mountain Reservation Chippewa Indians 1932 Census with Births & Deaths, 1924-1932

Chickasaw By Blood Enrollment Cards 1898-1914 Volume I thru V

Cherokee Descendants East An Index to the Guion Miller Applications Volume I
Cherokee Descendants West An Index to the Guion Miller Applications Volume II (A-M)
Cherokee Descendants West An Index to the Guion Miller Applications Volume III (N-Z)

Applications for Enrollment of Seminole Newborn Freedmen, Act of 1905

Eastern Cherokee Census, Cherokee, North Carolina, 1915-1922, Taken by Agent James E. Henderson   Volume I (1915-1916)
Volume II (1917-1918)
Volume III (1919-1920)
Volume IV (1921-1922)

Complete Delaware Roll of 1898

Eastern Cherokee Census, Cherokee, North Carolina, 1923-1929, Taken by Agent James E. Henderson   Volume I (1923-1924)
Volume II (1925-1926)
Volume III (1927-1929)

Applications for Enrollment of Seminole Newborn Act of 1905 Volumes I & II

North Carolina Eastern Cherokee Indian Census 1898-1899, 1904, 1906, 1909-1912, 1914 Revised and Expanded Edition

1932 Hopi and Navajo Native American Census with Birth & Death Rolls (1925-1931) Volume 1 - Hopi
1932 Hopi and Navajo Native American Census with Birth & Death Rolls (1930-1932) Volume 2 - Navajo

Western Navajo Reservation Navajo, Hopi and Paiute 1933 Census with Birth & Death Rolls 1925-1933

Cherokee Citizenship Commission Dockets 1880-1884 and 1887-1889 Volumes I, II & III

Visit our website at **www.nativestudy.com** to learn more about these and other books and series by Jeff Bowen

This series is dedicated to Joyce Tranter,
for giving me the inspiration of a lifetime.
And also to Dominick Lane Dugan.
Remember Isaiah 40:31
God bless!

INTRODUCTION

This publication was previously published by another publisher in 2009 and has now been reproduced by Native Study LLC. There are five volumes in this series concerning the Cherokee Citizenship Commission Dockets 1880 to 1889. This is material that was never before transcribed containing 2,288 Cherokee docket decisions.

This is somewhat of an explanation concerning the reasoning behind the proceedings that led the Cherokee tribal courts to take charge of these docket hearings.

The Cherokee relied upon their leaders to guide them but they ended up hanging in the balance after the Civil War, with their loyalties split worse than ever and their country ravished. Fathers and brothers were off fighting a war that didn't even concern them. By the time the war was over the Cherokee people had lost any form of stability. The men fighting the war came back to the same old political hatreds and in-fighting. The Nation was being over run with many that claimed they were Cherokee, hoping to benefit from false claims of citizenship. These people, known as intruders, did nothing but make it more difficult for the Cherokees because of the pressures from the Government to control their boundaries. The blood Cherokees that were seeking their homeland were again in question as to who they were. They found nothing but scrutiny and distrust, the war had made them choose a side, and the U.S. Government didn't care for the choice of the majority.

Intruder after intruder was encroaching on Cherokee land and what was to seem like a never ending battle. Many Cherokee citizens had lost their rights while intruders that didn't belong stayed using up what little resources there were. The government was telling the Cherokee leaders to settle their own intruder problems or else they would have to intercede. In an effort to clarify who were true Cherokee citizens and who were not, or who had been wrongfully taken off of the rolls, was a problem.

There were part-bloods, full-bloods, and no bloods along with mass confusion, prejudice, vendettas, and deceptions. The intruders wanted a free ride and were willing to use the confusion as a camouflage to achieve their purpose and greed.

This was a situation where the government was threatening to come in and turn the Cherokee Nation into a Federal Territory because it appeared to them that the Tribal Council would not be able to organize an effort to control the problem. But this wasn't the issue at hand as far as the Cherokee were concerned. They felt as if, according to their treaty stipulations, the United States was responsible for intruder removal. They felt as if the United States had let things get out of hand and that the government had not lived up to its contractual agreement. According to treaty stipulations this was true, but, they were told to either come up with a solution or lose their rights as a sovereign nation.

From William G. McLoughlin's book, *After the Trail of Tears, The Cherokees Struggle for Sovereignty 1839-1880*, it references on page 354, "Still, the Nation remained very uneasy about the fundamental question of its right to define who were its own citizens and its right to expect the United States to remove those who the Nation judged were not. Ever since 1872, federal agents had refused to expel from the Nation those former slaves whom the Nation considered 'aliens' and since 1874, federal agents had been under instructions from the Bureau of Indian Affairs to compile their own list of black or white persons who, in their opinion, had some claim to citizenship despite previous rulings of the Cherokee Courts on their claims."

On page 355-356, "On the basis of the affidavits and reports submitted, the Secretary of Interior, Zachariah Chandler, sent E.C. Watkins to the Nation in 1875, to investigate the citizenship problem and gather information that Chandler could use to ask Congress to take action on behalf of these 'men without a country'. Watkins reported in February, 1876, that many of those on Ingall's list were 'clearly entitled' to Cherokee citizenship. Oochalata denied it. He counter charged that Ingalls was meddling in Cherokee affairs and wrote to the Bureau of Indian Affairs to complain. Receiving no satisfactory response, he wrote directly to President Grant on November 13, 1876, enclosing a petition from the Cherokees Cooweescoowee District, complaining that the agent had not removed thousands of intruders in their area though ordered to do so by the Council. Some of these intruders were former slaves from the Deep South, but most were white U.S. citizens from Kansas, Missouri, and Arkansas.

Grant referred this letter to Commissioner J.Q. Smith. Annoyed that Oochalata had gone over the head of the Interior Department to the President, on December 8, Smith wrote Oochalata a long, assertive, and highly provocative letter outlining for the first time the department's position on this question. Smith said that from the evidence he had received, both from various federal agents and from the investigations of E.C. Watkins, the Cherokee Nation had failed to deal consistently and impartially with the problems of former slaves and others who claimed Cherokee citizenship. Therefore, the Bureau of Indian Affairs would continue to compile its own list of those who had 'prima facie' evidence for citizenship [whether the Cherokee courts had acted negatively on their claims or not], and it would take no action to remove them until the Cherokees carried four stipulations to resolve the issue. First, the Council must establish a clear, legal procedure providing due process for adjudicating all prima facie claims. Second, the rules by which such cases were decided must be approved by the Secretary of the Interior to ensure their impartiality. Third, he suggested that the Cherokee Circuit Courts be designated as the appropriate bodies for such hearings. Finally, claimants' appeals of the decisions of the Cherokee Circuit Courts must be forwarded to the Secretary of the Interior, and no claimant for citizenship should be removed from the Nation until the Secretary had made his own ruling. In effect, Smith asserted the right of the Bureau of Indian Affairs to decide who was and was not a Cherokee citizen. A crucial decision concerning the issue of the sovereignty of Indian nations was about to be reached.

Oochalata was stunned and wrote a 139-page letter to Smith explaining why this procedure was totally unacceptable and contrary to law, treaties, precedent, and the U.S. Constitution."

On page 357, "Acting on instructions from Oochalata, the Cherokee Delegation sent another letter to President Grant on Jan. 9, 1877, insisting that treaty rights, the Trade and Intercourse Act, and precedent gave the Nation the right 'to determine the question as to who are and who are not intruders.' The president referred their letter to Secretary of the Interior, Carl Schurz, who, on April 21, 1877, told the delegation that he supported Smith's four stipulations for settling the matter. Oochalata ignored this response and in August, 1877, sent to the new Commissioner of Indian Affairs, Ezra A. Hayt, a list of all the intruders whom the Cherokees wished to be immediately removed. On Nov. 7, Hayt replied flatly that the Bureau of Indian Affairs would not do so: 'while the department reserves to itself the right to finally determine who are and are not intruders under the law, **it expects the Cherokee Nation Council to enact some general and uniform law by which the Cherokee courts shall hear and determine the rights of claimants to citizenship,** subject only to the review of the Secretary of Interior after a final adjudication has been reached.'"

On page 358-9, "The department's claim that it had the right to judge intruders was, in Oochalata's opinion, 'a new doctrine for construing treaty or contracts in writing, to add to it verbally, a new clause, after the expiration of 92 years from date of that compact or treaty and without the consent of [one] party. . . . It is a dangerous doctrine to which I can never agree.'

While he urged the Council to send a protest through its delegation, Oochalata also asked it to enact a law that would establish a court to decide citizenship claims in a legal and uniform manner. The Council complied on Dec. 5, 1877, but the compromise was fatally weakened by the Council's failure to address two aspects of the law governing the Citizenship Court's actions.

First, the law provided no guidelines for deciding cases that would meet the demands of the Bureau of Indian Affairs, and consequently, in cases involving former slaves, the Citizenship Court relied, as the Cherokee Supreme Court had in 1870-71, simply on the wording in the Treaty of 1866. Second, the Council explicitly refused to allow the right of the Secretary of the Interior to review the decisions of the Court, stating that the Cherokee Citizenship Court was 'a tribunal of last resort'. The three persons appointed to the court, were John Chambers, O.P. Brewer, and George Downing. Also referred to as the Chamber's Commission, the Court began to hold hearings early in 1878. All persons claiming to have grounds for citizenship were required to present them or be declared intruders."

On pages 359-360, McLoughlin continues, "By the end of 1878, Oochalata struggling to find some new approach to the problem. On Dec. 3, he went over the head of the Bureau of Indian Affairs again, and wrote to Pres. Rutherford B. Hayes, forwarding a complete account of all of the cases adjudicated by the Citizenship Court and asking him to order the expulsion of those rejected and all other intruders. He told Hayes that the Cherokee Nation had an 'inherent national right' to define its own citizens, while the United States had a well-established obligation to expel non-citizens. Suspecting that Hayes would reject this request, Oochalata approached Commissioner Ezra A. Hayt and tried to work out a compromise. He said that the Cherokees would stop confiscating the property of those former slaves judged to be intruders pending the appointment of a joint commission of Cherokees and members of the Bureau to review the rejected claims. Hayt agreed only on the condition that decisions of this commission must be unanimous or the Bureau would retain the right to make its own decision in each case. Oochalata and the delegation could not accept such a condition, and the negotiations broke down. Finally, as a last resort, the council decided to submit a series of questions to the Secretary of Interior, Carl Schurz, about their right to determine citizenship and the obligation of the United States to accept their determinations. They asked Schurz to present their questions to Attorney General Charles Devens for his opinion. They sent the letter on March 3, 1879, and after Hayt informed Devens of his views on the matter, Devens held hearings at which both sides presented their views. Realizing the importance of the decision, the Cherokees spent the money necessary to hire the best lawyers they could find to assist them. Hayt said that the status of at least one-thousand persons was at issue, the Council argued that there were over twice that many intruders whom the Department was refusing to move.

Throughout the dispute, the Bureau of Indian Affairs declined to act against intruding squatters from Kansas who made no pretense to citizenship.

"The three questions that the Council asked Devens to answer were: Did the Cherokee Nation have the right to determine its own citizenship? Did the former slaves who were citizens have any share in the use of Cherokee land or in the money derived from the sale of the Cherokee land? Was it, or was it not, the duty of the Federal government to remove intruders under treaty stipulations and Trade and Intercourse Act? By the time Devens sent his reply, the Citizenship Court had heard 416 claims for citizenship and rejected 338."

Devens' opinion was clearly in the negative as far as the Cherokee Nation's sovereignty and decision processes were concerned. On page 364, McLoughlin observes, "Clearly, as since the days of Andrew Jackson, Federal refusal to honor the requirement of removing intruders was to be the means of forcing the Indian nations to do what they did not want to do." Ochalata would not run again as the election of August 1879 neared and Dennis W. Bushyhead became the new chief on August 4, 1879 but in the end it didn't matter who was chief the fight to keep Cherokee sovereignty along with self government was all but lost by 1880. On pages 365-366, McLoughlin wrote, "The turning point was reached in 1887 when Congress passed the Dawes Severalty Act. The act expressed what was now the national consensus among white voters (including Indian reformers, railroad magnates, and entrepreneurs) -that the solution to '"the Indian question'" was to denationalize the tribes in the Indian Territory, survey and allot their land in severalty, and establish a white-dominated territorial government over '"Oklahoma'" the Choctaw word for '"red man.'"

The sovereignty of the Western Cherokee tribe was taken, and to this day they still don't have a true land base as a nation. Even though others were able to take away the land that was promised to remain theirs forever; nobody was able to take away their right and ability to choose who was a true citizen and who was not. The dockets transcribed within this series are exactly as they appeared on the microfilm copies from the original court records involving citizenship during the time periods of 1880-1889.

These dockets were referenced and transcribed from microfilm series; 7RA25-0001 (American Genealogical Lending Library), Cherokee Citizenship Commission Docket Books, 1880-1884 and 1887-1889.

Jeff Bowen
Gallipolis, Ohio
NativeStudy.com

Cherokee Citizenship Commission Docket Books
(1880-84, 1887-89) Volume IV
Tahlequah, Cherokee Nation

MATHIS

DOCKET #1344
CENSUS ROLLS 1851

APPLICANT FOR **CHEROKEE CITIZENSHIP**

	POST OFFICE: Carlisle Ga	ATTORNEY: A E Ivey	
NO	**NAMES**	**AGE**	**SEX**
1	Jane Mathis	58	Female
2	Cicero Wilson	12	Male
3	James ? "	10	"
4	John H "	8	"
5	Joseph A "	7	"
6	Samuel "	6	"

ANCESTOR: Thos McDaniel

Office Commission on Citizenship
Cherokee Nation July 2nd 1889

There being no evidence in support of the above named case, the Commission decides that Jane Mathis age 58 years and Cicero Wilson age *(12)* years, James ? Wilson age 10 years, John H Wilson 8 years, Joseph A Wilson age 7 years, and Samuel Wilson age 6 years are not Cherokees by blood.
Attest
    E G Ross
        Clerk Commission
                              J E Gunter Com

MATHIS

DOCKET #1345
CENSUS ROLLS 1852

APPLICANT FOR **CHEROKEE CITIZENSHIP**

	POST OFFICE: Carlisle Ga	ATTORNEY: A E Ivey	
NO	**NAMES**	**AGE**	**SEX**
1	John M Mathis	22	Male
2	Lucinda "	21	Female
3	Louisa J "	3	"
4	Flora B "	1	"

ANCESTOR: Allen Mathis

Rejected Aug 16th 1889

Cherokee Citizenship Commission Docket Books
(1880-84, 1887-89) Volume IV
Tahlequah, Cherokee Nation

Office Commission on Citizenship
Cherokee Nation Ind Ter
Tahlequah Aug 16th 1889

There being no evidence in support of this case the Commission decide that John M Mathis age 22 yrs and Lucinda Mathis 21 yrs and the following children, Louisa J 23[sic] yrs and Flora B Mathis Female age 1 yr are not Cherokees by blood. Post Office Carlisle Ga.

Attest
    D S Williams
    Asst Clk Com

John E Gunter
    Commissioner

MORRIS

DOCKET #1346
CENSUS ROLLS 1835 & 52

APPLICANT FOR **CHEROKEE CITIZENSHIP**

POST OFFICE: Childers Station IT		ATTORNEY: A E Ivey	
NO	NAMES	AGE	SEX
1	James Morris	28	Male
2	Joseph D "	20	"
3	Sarah M "	16	Female
4	Eliza B "	15	"
5	James A "	13	Male
6	Rose E "	11	Female
7	Thomas F "	9	Male

ANCESTOR: *(Name Illegible)*

Office Commission on Citizenship
Cherokee Nation Ind Ter
Tahlequah August *(illegible)*

There being no evidence in support of this case the Commission decide that James Morris aged *(28)* years, Joseph D Morris aged 20 years, Sarah M Morris aged 16 years, Eliza B Morris aged 15 years, James A Morris aged 13 years, Rose E Morris aged 11 years, Thomas F Morris aged 9 years are not Cherokees by blood. Post Office Childers Station IT

Attest
    EG Ross
        Clerk Commission

JE Gunter   Com

Cherokee Citizenship Commission Docket Books
(1880-84, 1887-89) Volume IV
Tahlequah, Cherokee Nation

MATHIS

DOCKET #1347
CENSUS ROLLS 1852

APPLICANT FOR **CHEROKEE CITIZENSHIP**

POST OFFICE: Carlisle Ga		ATTORNEY: A E Ivey	
No	NAMES	AGE	SEX
1	James A Mathis	25	Male
2	Sarah M "	26	Female
3	James T "	5	Male
4	Benjamin "	2	"

ANCESTOR: Allen Mathis

Office Commission on Citizenship
Cherokee Nation Ind Ter
Tahlequah Aug 16th 1889

There being no evidence in support of this case the Commission decide that James A Mathis age 25 years and Sarah M Mathis age 26 years and the following children James T age 5 years and Benjamin age 2 years are not Cherokees by blood.

Attest
   E G Ross
      Clerk Commission

                                  JE Gunter Com

McCOY

DOCKET #1348
CENSUS ROLLS 1851

APPLICANT FOR **CHEROKEE CITIZENSHIP**

POST OFFICE: Mineral Springs Ga		ATTORNEY: A E Ivey	
No	NAMES	AGE	SEX
1	Rosannah McCoy	50	Female
2	(Illegible) "	32	"
3	Betsy E "	21	"
4	Thomas "	14	Male
5	(Illegible) "		Female
6	Sallie "	8	"

Cherokee Citizenship Commission Docket Books
(1880-84, 1887-89) Volume IV
Tahlequah, Cherokee Nation

7	Ida "	5	"

ANCESTOR: Geo W Welch

Now on this the *(illegible)* day of June 1888, comes the above case up for final hearing, and the Commission says, "We the Commission on Citizenship after examining the testimony in the above case, *(illegible...)* and they are hereby re-admitted to all the rights and privileges of Cherokee citizens by blood.

J T Adair, Chairman Commission
John E Gunter   Commissioner
D W Lipe   Commissioner

MOSELY

DOCKET #1349
CENSUS ROLLS 1851

APPLICANT FOR **CHEROKEE CITIZENSHIP**

POST OFFICE: Jasper Ga		ATTORNEY: A E Ivey	
NO	NAMES	AGE	SEX
1	Hester A J Mosely	35	Female
2	Martin "	17	Male
3	Macy "	15	Female
4	Davis "	13	Male
5	John "	10	"
6	Enoch "	7	"
7	Horatio "	6	"
8	Nancy "	4	Female
9	Carter "	1	Male

ANCESTOR: John Talley Sr

Office Commission on Citizenship
Cherokee Nation Ind Ter
Tahlequah August 16th 1889

There being no evidence in support of this case the Commission decide that Hester A J Mosely age 35 years and the following children Martin age 17 years, Macy age 15 years, Davis age 13 years, John age 10 years, Enoch age 7 years, Horatio age 6 years, Nancy age 4 years and Carter Mosely age 1 year are not Cherokees by blood.

Cherokee Citizenship Commission Docket Books
(1880-84, 1887-89) Volume IV
Tahlequah, Cherokee Nation

Attest
    E G Ross
        Clerk Commission

                      J E Gunter   Com

McCUTCHIN

DOCKET #1350
CENSUS ROLLS 1851

APPLICANT FOR CHEROKEE CITIZENSHIP
ATTORNEY: A E Ivey

No	POST OFFICE: NAMES	AGE	SEX
1	James R McCutchin	37	Male
2	James "	15	"
3	Alphia "	13	Female
4	John C "	12	Male
5	Flora ? "	10	Female
6	William "	8	Male
7	Mollie "	6	Female
8	Modare "	5	"
9	Louis "	2	Male

ANCESTOR: Mary Atwood

                      Office Commission on Citizenship
                          Cherokee Nation Ind Ter
                            Tahlequah Aug 16th 1889

There being no evidence in support of this case the Commission decide that James R McCutchin age 37 yrs and the following named children, James now age 15 yrs, Alphia Female age 13 yrs, John C male age 12 yrs, Flora Female age 10 yrs, William male age 8 yrs, Mollie Female age 6 yrs, Modare Female age 5 yrs and Louis McCutchin Female[sic] age 2 yrs are not Cherokees by blood. Post Office *(Illegible)* Ark.

Attest
    D S Williams
    Asst Clk Com   John E Gunter   Com

Cherokee Citizenship Commission Docket Books (1880-84, 1887-89) Volume IV
Tahlequah, Cherokee Nation

MITCHEL

DOCKET #1351
CENSUS ROLLS 1835

APPLICANT FOR CHEROKEE CITIZENSHIP

POST OFFICE: Van Buren Ark		ATTORNEY: A E Ivey	
NO	NAMES	AGE	SEX
1	Wm A Mitchel	32	Male
2	Walter L "	7	"
3	Wallace A "	5	"
4	Alonzo W "	3	"
5	William "	1	"

ANCESTOR: *(Illegible)* Franklin

Office Commission on Citizenship
Cherokee Nation Ind Ter
Tahlequah Aug 16th 1889

There being no evidence in support of this case the Commission decide that Wm A Mitchel age thirty two years and the following children Walter L age seven years, Wallace A age five years, Alonzo W age three years and William ? Mitchel age one year are not Cherokees by blood.
Attest
    E G Ross
        Clerk Commission   JE Gunter Com

DOCKET #1352   *(All names illegible)*

DOCKET #1353   *(All names illegible)*

MARSHALL

DOCKET #1354
CENSUS ROLLS 1845-48-51&52

APPLICANT FOR CHEROKEE CITIZENSHIP

POST OFFICE: Dardanelle Ark		ATTORNEY: Boudinot & Rasmus	
NO	NAMES	AGE	SEX
1	Sarah A Marshall	46	Female
2	John S "	19	Male

Cherokee Citizenship Commission Docket Books
(1880-84, 1887-89) Volume IV
Tahlequah, Cherokee Nation

3	R E "	17	"
4	Allie N "	15	Female
5	Sarah A "	14	"
6	Myrtle O "	11	"
7	Don T "	6	Male
8	Thomas W "	3	"

ANCESTOR: Nathan Thomas

Office Commission on Citizenship
Cherokee Nation Ind Ter
Tahlequah Aug 17th 1889

There being no evidence in support of this case the Commission decide that Sarah A Marshall age 46 years and the following children John S male 19 yrs, R C male 17 yrs, Allie N Female 15 yrs, Sarah A Female 14 yrs, Myrtle O Female 11 yrs, Don T male 6 yrs, & Thomas W Marshall male age 3 yrs are not Cherokees by blood. Post Office Dardanelle Ark.

Attest
    D S Williams   John E Gunter
    Asst Clk Com   Commissioner

MATHIS

DOCKET #1355
CENSUS ROLLS 1835-48-51&2

APPLICANT FOR **CHEROKEE CITIZENSHIP**

POST OFFICE: North View Mo		ATTORNEY: Boudinot & Rasmus	
NO	NAMES	AGE	SEX
1	Sarah M Mathis	30	Female
2	Nora J "	infant	"

ANCESTOR: Barsheba Goodrich

Office Commission on Citizenship
Cherokee Nation Tahlequah IT
June 20th 1889

There being no evidence in support of the above named case the Commission decide that Sarah M Mathis aged 30 years and Nora J Mathis Female Infant are not Cherokees by blood.

Cherokee Citizenship Commission Docket Books
(1880-84, 1887-89) Volume IV
Tahlequah, Cherokee Nation

Attest
    E G Ross
        Clerk Commission

                                JE Gunter Com

MOORE

DOCKET #1356
CENSUS ROLLS

APPLICANT FOR CHEROKEE CITIZENSHIP

POST OFFICE: Richmond Ind		ATTORNEY: L B Bell	
NO	**NAMES**	**AGE**	**SEX**
1	Mary Moore		Female

ANCESTOR: Ann Crews

The Commission decide against claimant. See decision in case of Andrew Meredith Docket 2180 Book E, Page 26 and case John Henly Docket 1250, Book C, Page 346.

                                  J.E. Gunter Com

MOUNT

DOCKET #1357
CENSUS ROLLS 1835

APPLICANT FOR CHEROKEE CITIZENSHIP

POST OFFICE: Vinita CH		ATTORNEY: H L Landrum	
NO	**NAMES**	**AGE**	**SEX**
1	W.J.L. Mount	31	Male
2	M C Washam	24	Female
3	Walter "	18 mo	Male

ANCESTOR: Annie Forman

Rejected Aug 17th 1889

                      Office Commission on Citizenship
                          Cherokee Nation Ind Ter
                          Tahlequah Aug 17th 1889

There being no evidence in support of this case the Commission decide that W J L Mount age 31 yrs and M.C. Washam Female 24 years, a Sister, Walter Washam male 18 months a nephew are not Cherokees by blood. Post Office Vinita C.N.

Cherokee Citizenship Commission Docket Books
(1880-84, 1887-89) Volume IV
Tahlequah, Cherokee Nation

Attest
    D S Williams   John E Gunter
    Asst Clk Com   Commissioner

MEADORS

DOCKET #1358
CENSUS ROLLS 1835 & 52

APPLICANT FOR CHEROKEE CITIZENSHIP

POST OFFICE: Belmont Arks		ATTORNEY: A E Ivey	
No	NAMES	AGE	SEX
1	Nancy D Meadors	34	Female
2	Drusilla "	7	"
3	Jessie "	6	Male
4	A J "	3	"

ANCESTOR: John Rogers

Now on this the 17th day of March 1888, comes the above case for a final hearing, the parties having made application pursuant to the provisions of an Act of the National Council approved December 8th 1886, and all the evidence being duly considered and found to be insufficient and unsatisfactory, it is adjudged and declared by the Commission that

Nancy D Meadors, Drusilla Meadors, Jessie Meadors and A.J. Meadors are not Cherokees and are not entitled to the rights, privileges and immunities of Cherokee Citizens by blood.

                         J.T. Adair   Chairman Commission
                         John E Gunter   Commissioner
                         D. W. Lipe   Commissioner

Attest
    C C Lipe
        Clerk Com

The decision in the James C.C. Rogers case found in Book C, page 627, and testimony on Journal pages 325 to 333 governs this case.

Cherokee Citizenship Commission Docket Books
(1880-84, 1887-89) Volume IV
Tahlequah, Cherokee Nation

MEADORS

DOCKET #1359
CENSUS ROLLS 1835 & 52

APPLICANT FOR CHEROKEE CITIZENSHIP

POST OFFICE: Belmont Arks		ATTORNEY: A E Ivey	
NO	NAMES	AGE	SEX
1	Martha J Meadors		
2	Charles "	7	Male
3	Cary "	5	Female
4	John D "	2	Male

ANCESTOR: John Rogers

Now on this the 17th day of March 1888, comes the above case for a final hearing, and the parties having made application pursuant to the provisions of an Act of the National Council approved December 8th 1886, all the evidence being duly considered and found to be insufficient and unsatisfactory, it is adjudged and declared by the Commission that

Martha J Meadors, Charles Meadors, Cary Meadors and John D Meadors are not Cherokees and they are not entitled to the rights, privileges and immunities of Cherokee citizens by blood.

                         J.T. Adair   Chairman Commission
                         John E Gunter   Commissioner
                         D. W. Lipe   Commissioner

Attest
       C.C. Lipe
           Clerk Com

The decision in the James C.C. Rogers case found in Book C, page 627, and testimony on Journal pages 325 to 333 governs this case.

DOCKET #1360   *(All names illegible)*

Cherokee Citizenship Commission Docket Books
(1880-84, 1887-89) Volume IV
Tahlequah, Cherokee Nation

MEREDITH

DOCKET #1361
CENSUS ROLLS 1835 to 1852

APPLICANT FOR CHEROKEE CITIZENSHIP

POST OFFICE: Buffalo Kans		ATTORNEY: A E Ivey	
No	NAMES	AGE	SEX
1	Soloman J Meredith	36	Male
2	Lillie ? "	10	Female
3	Rosa E "	8	"
4	Gracie V "	6	"
5	Myrtle M "	? mo	"

ANCESTOR: Mary Crews

The Commission decide against claimant. See decision in the case of Andrew Meredith Docket 2180 Book E, Page 26 and John Henly Docket 1250, Book C Page 346.

JE Gunter   Com

MEREDITH

DOCKET #1362
CENSUS ROLLS 1835 to 1852

APPLICANT FOR CHEROKEE CITIZENSHIP

POST OFFICE: Oskaloosa Iowa		ATTORNEY: A E Ivey	
No	NAMES	AGE	SEX
1	Alonzo F Meredith	41	Male
2	Baby "	?	"

ANCESTOR: Mary Crews

The Commission decide against claimant. See decision in the case of Andrew Meredith Docket 2180 Book E, Page 26 and John Henly Docket 1250, Book C Page 346.

J. E. Gunter   Com

Cherokee Citizenship Commission Docket Books
(1880-84, 1887-89) Volume IV
Tahlequah, Cherokee Nation

MEREDITH

DOCKET #1363
CENSUS ROLLS 1835 to 1852

APPLICANT FOR CHEROKEE CITIZENSHIP

POST OFFICE: Searsboro Iowa		ATTORNEY: A E Ivey	
No	NAMES	AGE	SEX
1	Wm W Meredith	66	Male
2	Leslie "	17	"

ANCESTOR: Mary Crews

The Commission decide against claimant. See decision in the case of Andrew Meredith Docket 2180 Book E, Page 26 and John Henly Docket 1250, Book C Page 346.

J.E. Gunter Com

MORGAN

DOCKET #1364
CENSUS ROLLS 1835 and 52

APPLICANT FOR CHEROKEE CITIZENSHIP

POST OFFICE: Mulberry Arks		ATTORNEY: A.E. Ivey	
No	NAMES	AGE	SEX
1	Margaret L Morgan	26	Female
2	Martha A "	3	"
3	Malissa "	2	"
4	William "	8 mo	Male

ANCESTOR: *(Name Illegible)*

Rejected Aug 17th 1889

Office Commission on Citizenship
Cherokee Nation Ind Ter
Tahlequah Aug 17th 1889

There being no evidence in support of this case the Commission decide that Margaret L Morgan age 26 yrs and the following children Martha A Morgan Female 3 yrs, Malissa Female age 2 yrs and William Morgan male age 8 mos are not Cherokees by blood. Post Office Mulberry

Attest
    D.S. Williams
    Asst Clk Com

John E Gunter
Commissioner

Cherokee Citizenship Commission Docket Books
(1880-84, 1887-89) Volume IV
Tahlequah, Cherokee Nation

MARTIN

DOCKET #1365
CENSUS ROLLS 1835 & 1852

APPLICANT FOR CHEROKEE CITIZENSHIP

POST OFFICE: Kilgore Tex		ATTORNEY: J M Bell	
NO	NAMES	AGE	SEX
1	Martha Martin	58	Female

ANCESTOR: *(Name Illegible)*

Office Commission on Citizenship
Cherokee Nation Ind Ter
Tahlequah Aug 17th 1889

There being no evidence in support of this case the Commission decide that Martha Martin age 58 yrs is not a Cherokee by blood. Post Office Mulberry Ark.

Attest
    D.S. Williams   John E Gunter
    Asst Clk Com   Commissioner

MAYHEW

DOCKET #1366
CENSUS ROLLS 1835

APPLICANT FOR CHEROKEE CITIZENSHIP

POST OFFICE: Chetopa Kans		ATTORNEY: C H Taylor	
NO	NAMES	AGE	SEX
1	H Mayhew	64	Male

ANCESTOR: John Mayhew

Rejected April 19th 1889

    H. Mayhew the applicant for Citizenship alleges that he is the son of John Mayhew whose name he *(illegible)* was duly enrolled upon the rolls of Cherokees by blood, citizens of the Cherokee Nation taken and made in the year 18835[sic] *(illegible)* no evidence accompanies this application and as the name of John Mayhew does not appear on the rolls of 1835.

Cherokee Citizenship Commission Docket Books
(1880-84, 1887-89) Volume IV
Tahlequah, Cherokee Nation

The Commission decrees that H. Mayhew is not a Cherokee by blood and is not entitled to citizenship in the Cherokee Nation, April 17th 1889. Post Office address Oct. 5, 1889 was Chetopa Kansas.

Will.P.Ross
Chairman
John E Gunter   Com

Attest
    D.S. Williams
       Clk Com.

MAYFIELD

DOCKET #1367
CENSUS ROLLS 1835 to 1852

APPLICANT FOR **CHEROKEE CITIZENSHIP**

POST OFFICE: Van Buren Ark		ATTORNEY: L S Sanders	
No	NAMES	AGE	SEX
1	Wm L Mayfield	31	Male
2	Niter[sic] "	5	Female
3	Pearl "	2	"

ANCESTOR: Pearson Mayfield

Rejected Aug 17th 1889

Office Commission on Citizenship
Cherokee Nation Ind Ter
Tahlequah Aug 17th 1889

There being no evidence in support of this case the Commission decide that Wm L Mayfield age 31 yrs and the following children Niter Female age 5 yrs and Pearl Mayfield age 2 yrs are not Cherokees by blood. Post Office Van Buren Ark.

Attest
    D S Williams
    Asst Clk Com

John E Gunter
Commissioner

Cherokee Citizenship Commission Docket Books
(1880-84, 1887-89) Volume IV
Tahlequah, Cherokee Nation

MAYFIELD

DOCKET #1368
CENSUS ROLLS 1835 to 1852

APPLICANT FOR CHEROKEE CITIZENSHIP

Post Office: Van Buren Ark		Attorney: L S Sanders	
No	NAMES	AGE	SEX
1	Joseph H Mayfield	35	Male
2	Jennie B "	4	Female
3	Earl "	1	Male

ANCESTOR: Pearson Mayfield

Rejected Aug 17th 1889

Office Commission on Citizenship
Cherokee Nation Ind Ter
Tahlequah Aug 17th 1889

There being no evidence in support of this case the Commission decide that Joseph H Mayfield age 35 yrs and his children Jennie B Female age 4 and Earl Mayfield male are not Cherokees by blood. Post Office Van Buren Ark.

Attest
    D S Williams   John E Gunter
    Asst Clk Com   Commissioner

MAYFIELD

DOCKET #1369
CENSUS ROLLS 1835 to 1852

APPLICANT FOR CHEROKEE CITIZENSHIP

Post Office: Van Buren Ark		Attorney: L S Sanders	
No	NAMES	AGE	SEX
1	South M Mayfield	27	Male

ANCESTOR: Pearson Mayfield

Rejected Aug 17th 1889

Office Commission on Citizenship
Cherokee Nation Ind Ter
Tahlequah Aug 17th 1889

There being no evidence in support of this case the Commission decide that South M Mayfield age 27 years is not a Cherokee by blood.
Post Office Van Buren Ark.

Cherokee Citizenship Commission Docket Books
(1880-84, 1887-89) Volume IV
Tahlequah, Cherokee Nation

Attest
    D S Williams   John E Gunter
    Asst Clk Com   Commissioner

MEAD

DOCKET #1370
CENSUS ROLLS 1835 to 1852

APPLICANT FOR CHEROKEE CITIZENSHIP

POST OFFICE: Siloam Springs Ark		ATTORNEY: L S Sanders	
NO	NAMES	AGE	SEX
1	Mary Ellen Mead	32	Female
2	Edna E "	7	"
3	Elmo M "	5	Male

ANCESTOR: Margaret Walker

Rejected Aug 17th 1889

                         Office Commission on Citizenship
                         Cherokee Nation Ind. Ter
                         Tahlequah Aug. 17th 1889

There being no evidence in support of this case the Commission decide that Mary Ellen Mead age 32 yrs and the following children Edna E Female age 7 yrs and Elmo M Mead male age 5 yrs are not Cherokees by blood. Post Office Siloam Springs Ark.

Attest
    D S Williams   John E Gunter
    Asst Clk Com   Commissioner

MARONEY

DOCKET #1371
CENSUS ROLLS 1835-48-51&2

APPLICANT FOR CHEROKEE CITIZENSHIP

POST OFFICE: Marbley[sic] NC		ATTORNEY: C H Taylor	
NO	NAMES	AGE	SEX
1	Martha Maroney	50	Female
2	Florence "	22	"
3	John L "	20	Male
4	Baily R "	19	"

Cherokee Citizenship Commission Docket Books
(1880-84, 1887-89) Volume IV
Tahlequah, Cherokee Nation

5	Louiza "	14	Female
6	William H "	7	Male
7	Elizabeth W "	6	Female

ANCESTOR: *(Name Illegible)*

Now on this the 11th day of February 1888, comes the above case for final hearing, and having made application pursuant to the provisions of an Act of the National Council approved December 8th 1886, and all the evidence being duly considered and found to be sufficient and satisfactory to the Commission, it is adjudged and determined by the Commission that and determined by the Commission that Martha Maroney, Florence Maroney, John L Maroney, Baily R Maroney, Louiza Maroney, William H. Maroney and Elizabeth W Maroney are Cherokees by blood and they are hereby re-admitted to all the rights, privileges and immunities of Cherokee citizens by blood and a certificate of said decision of the Commission and of re-admission was made and furnished said parties accordingly and certificate issued.

        J T Adair
         Chairman Commission
Cornell Rogers   D W Lipe
 Clerk   John. E. Gunter
         Commissioners

MILLSAPS

DOCKET #1372
CENSUS ROLLS 1835 & 1852

APPLICANT FOR CHEREOKEE CITIZENSHIP

POST OFFICE: Siloam Springs Ark		ATTORNEY: L S Sanders	
NO	NAMES	AGE	SEX
1	Marinda F Millsaps	53	Female
2	Adelade "	33	"
3	Desdimony H "	30	"
4	Nancy T "	28	"
5	Francis M "	26	"
6	Benjamin K "	22	Male
7	Mary "	20	Female
8	Malina J "	18	"
9	Wesley G "	14	Male
10	William H "	8	"

ANCESTOR: Benjamin Hide

Cherokee Citizenship Commission Docket Books
(1880-84, 1887-89) Volume IV
Tahlequah, Cherokee Nation

Office Commission on Citizenship
Cherokee Nation Ind Ter
Tahlequah May 23, 1889

In the above named case the Commission today decide that Marinda F Millsaps age 53 years and her children named as follows, Adelade aged 33, Desdimony H aged 30 years, Nancy T aged 28 years, F M aged 26 years, Benjamin K aged 22 years, Mary aged 20 years, Malina J aged 18 years, Wesley G 14 years, William H aged 8 years are not of Cherokee blood. See Decision in case of Nancy Ann Thompson *(Illegible)* 2008 Book D Page 494.

J E. Gunter   Com

McGARRAH

DOCKET #1373
CENSUS ROLLS 1835

APPLICANT FOR CHEROKEE CITIZENSHIP

POST OFFICE: McKinney Tex		ATTORNEY: W.A. Thompson	
NO	NAMES	AGE	SEX
1	J C McGarrah	51	Male
2	Lorance "	19	"
3	W D "	14	"
4	George Henry "	11	"
5	Walter "	8	"
6	Julia "	4	Female
7	Lucy "	2	"

ANCESTOR: Jack McGarrah

Rejected June 26th 1889

Office Commission on Citizenship
Cherokee Nation
Tahlequah June 26th 1889

The above named case having been submitted this day without evidence the Commission decide that J.C. McGarrah aged 51 years and Mary McGarrah aged 40 years (his wife) and their children Lorance aged 9[sic] years, W.D. McGarrah aged 14 years, George Henry McGarrah aged 11 years, Walter McGarrah aged 8 years *(illegible)*, and Julia McGarrah aged four years and Lucy McGarrah aged two years of McKinney Texas, are not of Cherokee blood and not entitled to citizenship in the Cherokee Nation.

Cherokee Citizenship Commission Docket Books
(1880-84, 1887-89) Volume IV
Tahlequah, Cherokee Nation

Attest
    D.S. Williams
    Asst Clk Com   J.E. Gunter   Com

DOCKET #1374   *(All names illegible)*

MARCUM

DOCKET #1375
CENSUS ROLLS 1835-48-51&2

APPLICANT FOR CHEROKEE CITIZENSHIP

POST OFFICE: Fort Smith Ark		ATTORNEY: Boudinot & Rasmus	
No	NAMES	AGE	SEX
1	Thomas Marcum	44	Male

ANCESTOR: Susan Brock

Rejected Aug 17th 1889

Office Commission on Citizenship Cher. Nat Ind Ter. Tahlequah Aug. 17th 1889
Application for Cherokee Citizenship

    The above application was filed on the 5th day of October 1887, and on this day the case coming up for final hearing the Commission find after examing[sic] the papers submitted by claimant that he claimed to derive his Cherokee blood through his great great grand mother one Susan Brock whose name Plaintiffs believe appears upon one of the census rolls of Cherokees taken in the years 1835, 48, 51, & 52. *(Illegible)* of claimants' claim of Cherokee blood he submitts[sic] as evidence the affidavits of Alfred Marcum, John A Duff Sr, William Strong, James B Gay and Plaintiffs own affidavit, after examing[sic] these affidavits we find that they do not come within the rule of this Commission in regard that all affidavits taken by an official outside of this Nation must have a certificate attached certifying to the credibility of affiants by said official – but waving this defect in the affidavits referred to an examination of the rolls named fails to show the name of Susan Brock or other ancestor from whom the applicant claims to have derived his Cherokee blood. The Commission therefore decide that Thomas Marcum is not of Cherokee blood and not entitled to Citizenship in the Cherokee Nation.

Attest
    D S Williams   John E Gunter
    Asst Clk Com   Commissioner

Cherokee Citizenship Commission Docket Books
(1880-84, 1887-89) Volume IV
Tahlequah, Cherokee Nation

MAST

DOCKET #1376
CENSUS ROLLS 1835 to 1852

APPLICANT FOR CHEROKEE CITIZENSHIP

POST OFFICE: Chetopa Kans		ATTORNEY: A E Ivey	
No	NAMES	AGE	SEX
1	M Mast	39	Male

ANCESTOR: James Smith

Rejected Aug 17th 1889

Office Commission on Citizenship
Cherokee Nation Ind Ter
Tahlequah Aug 17th 1889

There being no evidence in support of this case the Commission decide that M. Mast age 39 yrs is not Cherokee by blood. Post Office Chetopa Kans

Attest
    D S Williams   John E Gunter
    Asst Clk Com   Commissioner

MEALER

DOCKET #1377
CENSUS ROLLS 1851

APPLICANT FOR CHEROKEE CITIZENSHIP

POST OFFICE: Ellijay Ga		ATTORNEY: A E Ivey	
No	NAMES	AGE	SEX
1	Miles P Mealer	21	Male

ANCESTOR: Kindness Mealer

Rejected Aug 17th 1889

Office Commission on Citizenship
Cherokee Nation Ind Ter
Tahlequah Aug 17th 1889

There being no evidence in support of this case the Commission decide that Miles P Mealer age 21 yrs is not a Cherokee by blood.
Post Office Ellijay Ga.

Cherokee Citizenship Commission Docket Books
(1880-84, 1887-89) Volume IV
Tahlequah, Cherokee Nation

Attest
    D S Williams   John E Gunter
  Asst Clk Com   Commissioner

MUSGRAVES

DOCKET #1378
CENSUS ROLLS 1835 to 1852

APPLICANT FOR CHEROKEE CITIZENSHIP

POST OFFICE: Galena Ark		ATTORNEY: A E Ivey	
No	NAMES	AGE	SEX
1	Milly Musgraves	24	Female
2	James "	9	Male
3	Nancy "	5	Female

ANCESTOR: Jno Thompson

Rejected Aug 17th 1889

                       Office Commission on Citizenship
                             Cherokee Nation Ind Ter
                              Tahlequah Aug 17th 1889

There being no evidence in support of this case the Commission decide that Milly Musgraves age 24 yrs and the following children James Musgraves male 9 yrs and Nancy Musgraves Female 5 yrs are not Cherokees by blood.
Post Office Galena Ark.

Attest
    D S Williams   John E Gunter
  Asst Clk Com   Commissioner

McCOY

DOCKET #1379
CENSUS ROLLS 1835 to 1852

APPLICANT FOR CHEROKEE CITIZENSHIP

POST OFFICE: Claremore IT		ATTORNEY: A E Ivey	
No	NAMES	AGE	SEX
1	M E McCoy	28	Female
2	S M "	9	
3	H A "	4	

Cherokee Citizenship Commission Docket Books
(1880-84, 1887-89) Volume IV
Tahlequah, Cherokee Nation

4	L B "	1

ANCESTOR: Mrs Bradson

Rejected Aug 17th 1889

Office Commission on Citizenship
Cherokee Nation Ind Ter
Tahlequah Aug 17th 1889

There being no evidence in support of this case the Commission decide that M E McCoy age 28 yrs and the following children S.M. McCoy 9 yrs, H A McCoy age 4 yrs and L B McCoy age 1 yr are not Cherokees by blood.
Post Office Claremore I.T.

Attest
    D S Williams   John E Gunter
    Asst Clk Com   Commissioner

MELTON

DOCKET #1380
CENSUS ROLLS 1835 to 1852

APPLICANT FOR **CHEROKEE CITIZENSHIP**

POST OFFICE: Claremore IT		ATTORNEY: A E Ivey	
No	NAMES	AGE	SEX
1	Jackson T Melton	30	Male

ANCESTOR: Mrs Bradson

Office Commission on Citizenship
Cherokee Nation Ind Ter
Tahlequah Aug 17th 1889

There being no evidence in support of this case the Commission decide that Jackson T Melton age 30 yrs is not a Cherokee by blood.
Post Office Claremore I.T.

Attest
    D S Williams   John E Gunter
    Asst Clk Com   Commissioner

Cherokee Citizenship Commission Docket Books
(1880-84, 1887-89) Volume IV
Tahlequah, Cherokee Nation

MOSS

DOCKET #1381
CENSUS ROLLS 1835 to 1852

APPLICANT FOR CHEROKEE CITIZENSHIP

POST OFFICE: Dyer Station Arks		ATTORNEY: A E Ivey	
No	NAMES	AGE	SEX
1	Mary Catherine Moss	39	Female
2	James B "	16	Male
3	(Illegible) "	14	"
4	Geo H "	12	"
5	Nancy E "	10	Female
6	(Illegible) M "	6	"
7	Alice "	5	"
8	John T "	3 mo	Male

ANCESTOR: *(Name Illegible)*

(All information illegible)

MOORE

DOCKET #1382
CENSUS ROLLS 1835 to 1852

APPLICANT FOR CHEROKEE CITIZENSHIP

POST OFFICE: Evansville Ark		ATTORNEY: A E Ivey	
No	NAMES	AGE	SEX
1	Mary E Moore	40	Female
2	Dora "	17	"
3	Sarah "	15	"
4	Ira G "	10	Male
5	Landan N "	3	"
6	Addie "	9	Female

ANCESTOR: Mrs Mayfield

Office Commission on Citizenship
Cherokee Nation Ind Ter
Tahlequah August 19th 1889

There being no evidence in support of this case the Commission decide that Mary E Moore age 40 years and the following children Dora age 17 years,

Cherokee Citizenship Commission Docket Books
(1880-84, 1887-89) Volume IV
Tahlequah, Cherokee Nation

Sarah age 15 years, Ira G age 10 years, Landon N age 3 years and Addie age 9 years are not Cherokees by blood.

Attest
    E G Ross   JE Gunter   Com
        Clerk Commission

MAYSON

DOCKET #1383
CENSUS ROLLS 1835

APPLICANT FOR CHEROKEE CITIZENSHIP

POST OFFICE: Republic Mo		ATTORNEY: A E Ivey	
No	NAMES	AGE	SEX
1	Rebecca Mayson	33	Female
2	Dora Mason	13	"
3	Rhoda "	11	"
4	Arnold "	9	Male
5	Lotta "	7	Female
6	Arch "	2	"

ANCESTOR: Silas Hilton

Rejected Aug 17th 1889

                      Office Commission on Citizenship
                           Cherokee Nation Ind Ter
                                Tahlequah Aug 17th 1889

There being no evidence in support of this case the Commission decide that Rebecca Mayson age 33 yrs and the following children Dora Female 13 yrs, Rhoda Female 11 yrs, Arnold male 9 yrs, Lotta Female 7 yrs, and Arch Mayson Female age 2 yrs are not Cherokees by blood. Post Office Republic Mo.

Attest
    D S Williams   John E Gunter
    Asst Clk Com   Commissioner

Cherokee Citizenship Commission Docket Books
(1880-84, 1887-89) Volume IV
Tahlequah, Cherokee Nation

MELTON

DOCKET #1384
CENSUS ROLLS 1835 & 52

APPLICANT FOR **CHEROKEE CITIZENSHIP**

POST OFFICE: Claremore IT		ATTORNEY: A E Ivey	
No	NAMES	AGE	SEX
1	E L Melton	21	Male
2	J H "	17	"
3	Vivian "	12	Female
4	Lauriny "	9	"

ANCESTOR: Mrs Bradson

Rejected Aug 17th 1889

Office Commission on Citizenship
Cherokee Nation Ind Ter
Tahlequah Aug 17th 1889

There being no evidence in support of this case the Commission decide that E L Melton age 21 yrs and the following children J.H. Melton male age 17 yrs, Vivian Female 12 yrs and Lauriny Melton age 9 yrs Female are not Cherokees by blood. Post Office Claremore I.T.

Attest
    D S Williams   John E Gunter
    Asst Clk Com   Commissioner

McDONALD

DOCKET #1385
CENSUS ROLLS 1835 - 52

APPLICANT FOR **CHEROKEE CITIZENSHIP**

POST OFFICE: Neosho Falls Kans		ATTORNEY: A E Ivey	
No	NAMES	AGE	SEX
1	W W McDonald		Male

ANCESTOR: James Smith

See decision in this case in that of Margaret A Puffer Book *(Illegible)*, Page 434 – Adverse to claimant.

                                 Cornell Rogers
                                 Clk Com on Citizenship

Cherokee Citizenship Commission Docket Books
(1880-84, 1887-89) Volume IV
Tahlequah, Cherokee Nation

Office Com on Citizenship
Tahlequah I.T. Sept 24th 1888

McDONALD

DOCKET #1386
CENSUS ROLLS 1835 to 1852

APPLICANT FOR **CHEROKEE CITIZENSHIP**

POST OFFICE: *(Illegible)* Kans		ATTORNEY: A E Ivey	
No	NAMES	AGE	SEX
1	Thomas K McDonald		Male

ANCESTOR: James Smith

See decision in this case in that of Margaret A Puffer this Book on Page 434 – Adverse –

                                              Cornell Rogers
                                              Clk Com on Citizenship

Office Com on Citizenship
Tahlequah I.T. Sept 24th 1888

MOORE

DOCKET #1387
CENSUS ROLLS 1835 & 1852

APPLICANT FOR **CHEROKEE CITIZENSHIP**

POST OFFICE: Parsons Kans		ATTORNEY: A E Ivey	
No	NAMES	AGE	SEX
1	Louisa Moore	25	Female

ANCESTOR: James Smith

Rejected Aug 17th 1889

                                Office Commission on Citizenship
                                     Cherokee Nation Ind Ter
                                     Tahlequah Aug 17th 1889

There being no evidence in support of this case the Commission decide that Louisa Moore age 25 yrs is not a Cherokee by blood. Post Office Parson[sic] Kans.
Attest
    D S Williams   John E Gunter
    Asst Clk Com   Commissioner

Cherokee Citizenship Commission Docket Books
(1880-84, 1887-89) Volume IV
Tahlequah, Cherokee Nation

MOURNGER

DOCKET #1388
CENSUS ROLLS 1835 & 1852

APPLICANT FOR CHEROKEE CITIZENSHIP

POST OFFICE: Van Alstyne Tex		ATTORNEY: A E Ivey	
NO	NAMES	AGE	SEX
1	R B Mourngcr	28	Male

ANCESTOR: John Mournger

Rejected Aug 17th 1889

Office Commission on Citizenship
Cherokee Nation Ind Ter
Tahlequah Aug 17th 1889

There being no evidence in support of this case the Commission decide that R.B. Mounger[sic] age 28 yrs is not a Cherokee by blood.
Post Office Van Alstyne Tex

Attest
    D S Williams   John E Gunter
    Asst Clk Com   Commissioner

MYERS

DOCKET #1389
CENSUS ROLLS 1835 - 52

APPLICANT FOR CHEROKEE CITIZENSHIP

POST OFFICE: *(Illegible)* Tex		ATTORNEY: A E Ivey	
NO	NAMES	AGE	SEX
1	Mrs O.T. Myers		Female

ANCESTOR: K.W. Hargrove

We the Commission on Citizenship after examining the testimony in this case together with the rolls mentioned in the 7th Sec of the Act of Dec. 8th 1886 find that Mrs. O.T. Myers *(remainder illegible)*.

Cherokee Citizenship Commission Docket Books
(1880-84, 1887-89) Volume IV
Tahlequah, Cherokee Nation

MUNSON

DOCKET #1390
CENSUS ROLLS

APPLICANT FOR CHEROKEE CITIZENSHIP

POST OFFICE: Coffeyville Kan		ATTORNEY: A E Ivey	
No	NAMES	AGE	SEX
1	Wm P Munson		Male

ANCESTOR:

CHEROKEE NATION, IND. TER.

Tahlequah, September 29th 1888

Wm P Munson
   (vs)
Cherokee Nation

    In the matter of the claim for citizenship in the Cherokee Nation of Wm P. Munson applicant. The the[sic] Commission on Citizenship find that the name of Mrs Rosa from whom the applicant claims a Cherokee descent or that of himself fails to appear on the rolls of Cherokees mentioned in the 7th Sec of the Act of Dec. 8th 1886. In relation to Citizenship, in the absence of which not withstanding, any testimony that may be filed, and its *(illegible)*, this Commission cannot grant citizenship. In this case however there is no evidence outside of Mr Munson's own declaration. Therefore: Wm P Munson is not a Cherokee by blood and is ~~therefor~~ not entitled to any of the rights and privileges of such on account of his blood, and is an intruder upon the public domain of the Cherokee Nation.

                       J T Adair   Chairman Commission
                       H C Barnes Commissioner

McQUINN

DOCKET #1391
CENSUS ROLLS 1835 & 52

APPLICANT FOR CHEROKEE CITIZENSHIP

POST OFFICE:		ATTORNEY: A E Ivey	
No	NAMES	AGE	SEX
1	Louisa McQuinn		Female

Cherokee Citizenship Commission Docket Books
(1880-84, 1887-89) Volume IV
Tahlequah, Cherokee Nation

2		Catherine "		17	"
3		Jessie "		15	"
4		Olive "		9	"
5		James P "		7	Male
6		Lora E "		5	Female
7		Ivy V "	grand child	2 mo	"

ANCESTOR: John McQuinn

Rejected Aug 17th 1889

Office Commission on Citizenship
Cherokee Nation Ind Ter
Tahlequah Aug 17th 1889

There being no evidence in support of this case the Commission decide that Louisa McQuinn and the following children Catherine McQuinn Female age 17 yrs, Jessie Female age 15 yrs, Olive Female 9 yrs, James P male 7 yrs, Lora E Female 5 yrs, Ivy V Female 2 months (grand child) are not Cherokees by blood.

Attest
    D S Williams   John E Gunter
    Asst Clk Com   Commissioner

MOUNGER

DOCKET #1392
CENSUS ROLLS 1835 & 52

APPLICANT FOR CHEROKEE CITIZENSHIP

POST OFFICE: Van Alstyne Tex		ATTORNEY: A E Ivey	
No	NAMES	AGE	SEX
1	H R. Mounger	56	
2	M P "	17	Male
3	E J "	14	Female
4	I A "	11	Male

ANCESTOR: James Haines

Rejected Aug 17th 1889

Office Commission on Citizenship
Cherokee Nation Ind Ter
Tahlequah Aug 17th 1889

Cherokee Citizenship Commission Docket Books
(1880-84, 1887-89) Volume IV
Tahlequah, Cherokee Nation

There being no evidence in support of this case the Commission decide that H R Mounger age 56 yrs and the following children M.P. Mounger male age 17 yrs, E J Female 14 yrs, and I A Mounger male 11 yrs are not Cherokees by blood. Post Office Van Alstyne Tex.

Attest
    D S Williams   John E Gunter
    Asst Clk Com   Commissioner

MARSHALL

DOCKET #1393
CENSUS ROLLS 1835 & 52

APPLICANT FOR CHEROKEE CITIZENSHIP

No	POST OFFICE: Lancaster Ark	ATTORNEY: A E Ivey	
	NAMES	AGE	SEX
1	Geo W Marshall	29	Male
2	Ellen F "	1	Female

ANCESTOR: Lawrance Slaughter

Rejected Aug 17th 1889

                      Office Commission on Citizenship
                            Cherokee Nation Ind Ter
                              Tahlequah Aug 17th 1889

There being no evidence in support of this case the Commission decide that Geo W. Marshall age 29 yrs and Ellen F Marshall Daughter age 1 yr are not Cherokees by blood. Post Office Lancaster Ark.

Attest
    D S Williams
    Asst Clk Com   John E Gunter
                                                                Commissioner

Cherokee Citizenship Commission Docket Books
(1880-84, 1887-89) Volume IV
Tahlequah, Cherokee Nation

CHASTIAN

DOCKET #1394
CENSUS ROLLS 1835 & 52

APPLICANT FOR CHEROKEE CITIZENSHIP

POST OFFICE: Dyer, Crawford Co Ark		ATTORNEY: A.E. Ivey	
No	NAMES	AGE	SEX
1	Harvey Mc Chastian[sic]	21	Male
2	Jessie E. "	Infant	"

ANCESTOR: John Rogers

Now on this the 17th day of March 1888, comes the above case for a final hearing, the parties having made application pursuant to the provisions of an Act of the National Council approved December 8th 1886. All the evidence being duly considered and found to be insufficient and unsatisfactory to the Commission, it is adjudged and determined by the Commission that and declared by the Commission that

Harvey Mc Chastian and Jesse[sic] E Chastian are not Cherokees and are not entitled to the rights and privileges of Cherokee Citizens by blood.

       J T Adair   Chairman Commission
       John E Gunter Commissioner
       D W Lipe   Commissioner

Attest
  C.C. Lipe
    Clerk Com

The decision in the James C.C. Rogers case found in Book C, page 627, and testimony on Journal pages 325 to 333 governs this case.

MEADOWS

DOCKET #1395
CENSUS ROLLS 1835 & 52

APPLICANT FOR CHEROKEE CITIZENSHIP

	POST OFFICE:	ATTORNEY:	
No	NAMES	AGE	SEX
1	Mary E Meadows	19	Female
2	Delohema "	Infant	"

ANCESTOR: John Rogers

Cherokee Citizenship Commission Docket Books
(1880-84, 1887-89) Volume IV
Tahlequah, Cherokee Nation

Now on this the 17th day of March 1888, comes the above case for a final hearing. The parties having made application pursuant to the provisions of an Act of the National Council approved December 8th 1886. And all the evidence being duly considered and found to be insufficient and unsatisfactory, it is adjudged and declared by the Commission that

Mary E Meadows and Delohema Meadows are not Cherokees and are not entitled to the rights, privileges and immunities of Cherokee citizens by blood.

                       J T Adair   Chairman Commission
                       John E Gunter   Commissioner
                       D W Lipe   Commissioner

Attest
    C.C. Lipe
        Clerk Com

The decision in the James C.C. Rogers case found in Book C, page 627, and testimony on Journal pages 325 to 333 governs this case.

EDWARDS

DOCKET #1396
CENSUS ROLLS 1835, 1846, 1852 & 1852

APPLICANT FOR **CHEROKEE CITIZENSHIP**

POST OFFICE: Alma Ark		ATTORNEY: A E Ivey	
No	NAMES	AGE	SEX
1	Silas McDonald Edwards	27	Male

ANCESTOR: Benjamin Franklin Edwards

Rejected Aug 17th 1889

                       Office Commission on Citizenship
                       Cherokee Nation Ind Ter
                       Tahlequah Aug 17th 1889

There being no evidence in support of this case the Commission decide that Silas McDonald Edwards age 27 yrs is not a Cherokee by blood. Post Office Alma Ark.

Attest
    D.S. Williams   John E Gunter
    Asst Clk Com   Commissioner

Cherokee Citizenship Commission Docket Books
(1880-84, 1887-89) Volume IV
Tahlequah, Cherokee Nation

McRAY

DOCKET #1397
CENSUS ROLLS 1851

APPLICANT FOR CHEROKEE CITIZENSHIP

POST OFFICE: Marietta Ga		ATTORNEY: A.E. Ivey	
No	NAMES	AGE	SEX
1	Nancy M McRay	20	Female
2	Ulin L. "	1	"

ANCESTOR: Mandie Tidwell

We the Commission on Citizenship after examining the evidence in the above case, find that the applicant and her child are Cherokees by blood deriving their Cherokee blood from John Tidwell *(illegible)* who was the grandfather of the applicant. *(Illegible...)* satisfaction of the Commission that he was a half-breed Cherokee. Therefore under an Act creating this Commission dated Dec. 8th 1886, *(illegible...)* and are hereby re-admitted to all the rights and privileges of Cherokee citizens by blood.

J T Adair, Chairman Commission
John E Gunter   Commissioner
D W Lipe   Commissioner

Office Com on Citizenship
Tahlequah I.T. Sept 24th 1888

MAXIE

DOCKET #1398
CENSUS ROLLS 1835 & 46

APPLICANT FOR CHEROKEE CITIZENSHIP

POST OFFICE: Alma Ark		ATTORNEY: A.E. Ivey	
No	NAMES	AGE	SEX
1	Hulda L Maxie	26	Female

ANCESTOR: *(Name Illegible)*

Rejected Aug 17th 1889

Office Commission on Citizenship
Cherokee Nation Ind Ter
Tahlequah Aug 17th 1889

Cherokee Citizenship Commission Docket Books
(1880-84, 1887-89) Volume IV
Tahlequah, Cherokee Nation

There being no evidence in support of this case the Commission decide that Hulda L Maxie age 26 yrs is not a Cherokee by blood. Post Office Alma Ark.

Attest
    D.S. Williams
    Asst Clk Com   John E Gunter
                                               Commissioner

McDONALD

DOCKET #1399
CENSUS ROLLS 1835 & 52

APPLICANT FOR **CHEREKEE CITIZENSHIP**

POST OFFICE: Harris IT		ATTORNEY: A E Ivey	
NO	NAMES	AGE	SEX
1	Martha McDonald		Female
2	Mary H. "	12	"
3	Joohes T. "	10	"
4	Lina M. "	8	"
5	Geo P "	4	Male
6	Joles "	6	"
7	Mattie S. "	1	Female

ANCESTOR: Rogers

Rejected Aug 17th 1889

                     Office Commission on Citizenship
                          Cherokee Nation Ind Ter
                             Tahlequah Aug 17th 1889

There being no evidence in support of this case the Commission decide that Martha McDonald and the following children Mary H Female age 12 yrs, Joohes T Female 10 yrs, Lina M Female 8 yrs, Geo. C[sic] male 4 yrs, Joles male 6 yrs and Mattie S McDonald Female age 1 yr not Cherokees and are not entitled to the rights, privileges and immunities of Cherokee citizens by blood. Post Office Harris I.T.

Attest
    D.S. Williams
    Asst Clk Com   John E Gunter
                                         Commissioner

Cherokee Citizenship Commission Docket Books
(1880-84, 1887-89) Volume IV
Tahlequah, Cherokee Nation

MORRIS

DOCKET #1400
CENSUS ROLLS 1835 & 52

APPLICANT FOR **CHEROKEE CITIZENSHIP**

POST OFFICE: Childers Station I.T.		ATTORNEY: A.E. Ivey	
No	NAMES	AGE	SEX
1	Wm H. Morris	40	Male
2	James D. "	13	"
3	Andrew F "	11	"
4	Caledonia A "	6	Female
5	Wm O. "	11m	Male

ANCESTOR: Letitia Little

Rejected Aug 17th 1889

Office Commission on Citizenship
Cherokee Nation Ind Ter
Tahlequah Aug 17th 1889

There being no evidence in support of this case the Commission decide that Wm H Morris age 40 yrs and the following children, James D Morris male 13 yrs, Andrew F male age 11 yrs, Caledonia A Female age 6 yrs, and Wm O Morris male age 11 months, Post Office Childers Station I.T. not Cherokees by blood.
Attest
   D.S. Williams   John E Gunter
   Asst Clk Com   Commissioner

MASSEY

DOCKET #1401
CENSUS ROLLS 1851

APPLICANT FOR **CHEROKEE CITIZENSHIP**

POST OFFICE: Hickory Flat Ga		ATTORNEY: A E Ivey	
No	NAMES	AGE	SEX
1	James C. Massey	34	Female
2	Rosie D "	12	"
3	Mary E "	10	"
4	John R "	8	Male
5	Thomas J "	6	"
6	Jackson "	2	"

ANCESTOR: *(Name Illegible)*

Rejected Aug 17th 1889

Cherokee Citizenship Commission Docket Books
(1880-84, 1887-89) Volume IV
Tahlequah, Cherokee Nation

Office Commission on Citizenship
Cherokee Nation Ind Ter
Tahlequah Aug 17th 1889

There being no evidence in support of this case the Commission decide that James C Massey age 34 yrs and the following children Rosie D Female age 12 yrs, Mary E Female age 10 yrs, John R male age 8 yrs, Thomas J male age 6 yrs, and Jackson Massey male 2 yrs. are not Cherokees by blood. Post Office Hickory Flat Ga.

Attest
    D.S. Williams
    Asst Clk Com

    John E Gunter
    Commissioner

VAUGHN

DOCKET #1402
CENSUS ROLLS 1835

APPLICANT FOR **CHEROKEE CITIZENSHIP**

POST OFFICE: Huntsville Ark		ATTORNEY: C.H. Taylor	
No	NAMES	AGE	SEX
1	George W Vaughn	74	Male

ANCESTOR: Feraby Vaughn

Office Commission on Citizenship
Cher Nat July 2nd 1889

There being no evidence in support of the above named case the Commission decide that George W Vaugh[sic] age 74 male is not a Cherokee by blood.
Post Office Huntsville Ark.

    DS Williams
    Clk Commission

    JE Gunter   Com

Cherokee Citizenship Commission Docket Books
(1880-84, 1887-89) Volume IV
Tahlequah, Cherokee Nation

VAUGHN

DOCKET #1403
CENSUS ROLLS 1835

APPLICANT FOR CHEROKEE CITIZENSHIP

POST OFFICE: Clifty Ark		ATTORNEY: C H Taylor	
No	NAMES	AGE	SEX
1	James D Vaughn	41	Male
2	Nancy V "	13	Female
3	Cordelia "	11	"
4	John D "	9	Male
5	Molly "	7	Female
6	Cora "	5	"
7	Martha "	4	"
8	Sallie "	2	"
9	Willie F "	1	"

ANCESTOR: Feraby Vaughn

Rejected July 2nd 1889

Office Commission on Citizenship
Cher Nat July 2nd 1889

There being no evidence in support of this case the Commission decide that James D Vaughn age 41 yrs and the following children Nancy Female 13, Cordelia female age 11, John D male age 9, Nancy[sic] female 7, Cora female 5, Martha female 4, Sallie female 2, Willie Female, are not Cherokees by blood. Post Office Clifty Ark.

D.S. Williams
Clk Commission

JE Gunter Com

YOUNG

DOCKET #1404
CENSUS ROLLS 1835 & 52

APPLICANT FOR CHEROKEE CITIZENSHIP

POST OFFICE: Mineral Springs Ark		ATTORNEY: A E Ivey	
No	NAMES	AGE	SEX
1	Elisha Young	50	Male
2	Henry C "	20	"
3	Jeremiah "	18	"
4	Mandy "	16	Female

Cherokee Citizenship Commission Docket Books
(1880-84, 1887-89) Volume IV
Tahlequah, Cherokee Nation

5	James "	14	Male
6	Felix R "	14	"
7	David "	12	"
8	John "	8	"

ANCESTOR: John Thompson

Rejected Aug 20th 1889

Office Commission on Citizenship
Cherokee Nation Ind Ter
Tahlequah Aug 20th 1889

In the above case the applicant alleges that he is the son of John Young and Millie Young who *(illegible)* Millie Thompson daughter of John Thompson a half breed Cherokee whose name should be enrolled on census rolls of Cherokees by blood taken and *(illegible)* in the year 1835 and 1852 by the United States. The witnesses in this case are James Young age 76 brother of claimant and Benjamin Stephen 74 yrs of Howard County Arkansas. In their affidavits taken exparte they swear to the allegation set forth but do not state *(illegible)* ground of their knowledge of the blood of John Thompson and as the name of said John Thompson can not be found on the rolls named, the Commission decide that Elisha Young age 50 yrs and children Henry C age 20 yrs, Jeremiah 18 yrs, James and twin brother Felix age 14 yrs, David 12 yrs, John 8 yrs, & Mandy (daughter) age 16 yrs are not of Cherokee blood.
Mineral Springs Ark.

Attest
D S Williams   Asst Clk Com   J E. Gunter   Com

YOUNG

DOCKET #1405
CENSUS ROLLS 1835 & 52

APPLICANT FOR **CHEROKEE CITIZENSHIP**

POST OFFICE: Lewisville Texas		ATTORNEY: A E Ivey	
NO	NAMES	AGE	SEX
1	Thomas G Young	44	Male
2	Maggie "	13	Female

ANCESTOR: Ward

Rejected Aug 20th 1889

Cherokee Citizenship Commission Docket Books
(1880-84, 1887-89) Volume IV
Tahlequah, Cherokee Nation

Office Commission on Citizenship
Cherokee Nation Ind. Ter.
Tahlequah August 20th 1889

The application in this case was filed on the 3rd day of Oct, 1887, and there being no evidence in support of said case the Commission decide that Thomas G Young age 44 yrs and Maggie Young female age 13 yrs are not Cherokees by blood. P.O. Lewisville Texas.

Attest
    D S Williams
    Asst Clk Com   J E Gunter   Com

YOUNG

DOCKET #1406
CENSUS ROLLS 1835 & 52

APPLICANT FOR CHEROKEE CITIZENSHIP

POST OFFICE: Galina[sic] Ark		ATTORNEY: A E Ivey	
No	NAMES	AGE	SEX
1	Wm A Young	24	Male
2	Larkin "	6	"
3	Deily "	4	"
4	Francis "	2	Female

ANCESTOR: John Thompson

Rejected Aug 20th 1889

Office Commission on Citizenship
Cherokee Nation Ind Ter
Tahlequah Aug 20th 1889

In the above named case the Commission decide that the claimant William A Young 24 yrs of age and his sons Larkin Young 6 yrs, Deily 4 yrs and daughter Francis Young age 2 yrs are not of Cherokee blood because there is no evidence in support of the claim and of reason set forth in the case of Elisha Young claiming through same ancestor.
See Docket 1404 B.C. Page 530.
P.O. Galina Arkansas.
Attest
    D.S. Williams
    Asst Clk Com   J E Gunter   Com

Cherokee Citizenship Commission Docket Books
(1880-84, 1887-89) Volume IV
Tahlequah, Cherokee Nation

YOUNG

Docket #1407
Census Rolls 1835 & 52

Applicant for **CHEROKEE CITIZENSHIP**

Post Office: Galena Ark		Attorney: A E Ivey	
No	NAMES	Age	Sex
1	John Young	62	Male
2	Dill "	20	"

Ancestor: John Thompson

Rejected Aug 20th 1889

Office Commission on Citizenship
Cherokee Nation Ind. Ter.
Tahlequah Aug 10th 1889

In the above case the Commission decide that applicant John Young aged 62 years and son Dill Young age 20 yrs are not of Cherokee blood because there is no evidence filed with the application and because of reason set forth in case of Elisha Young. See Docket 1404 B.C. Page 530.
P.O. Galena Ark.

Attest
    D.S. Williams   J E Gunter   Com
    Asst Clk Com

YOUNG

Docket #1408
Census Rolls 1835 & 52

Applicant for **CHEROKEE CITIZENSHIP**

Post Office: Galena Ark		Attorney: A E Ivey	
No	NAMES	Age	Sex
1	Micheal[sic] Young	28	Male
2	Ida "	8	Female
3	Manin "	6	Male
4	Eddie "	4	"
5	Anderson "	2	"
6	Infant	3 wks	Female

Ancestor: John Thompson

Cherokee Citizenship Commission Docket Books
(1880-84, 1887-89) Volume IV
Tahlequah, Cherokee Nation

Rejected Aug 20th 1889

>Office Commission on Citizenship
>Cherokee Nation Ind Ter
>Tahlequah Aug 20th 1889

In the above named case the Commission decide that applicant Micheal[sic] Young age 28 yrs and his daughters Ida Young age 8 yrs and Infant age 3 weeks and sons Manin age 6 yrs, Eddie age *(illegible)* and Anderson Young age 2 yrs are not of Cherokee blood for reasons stated in the case of Elisha Young Docket 1404 B.C. Page 530.
P.O. Galena Ark

Attest
    D.S. Williams
    Asst Clk Com   J E Gunter   Com

YOUNG

DOCKET #1409
CENSUS ROLLS 1835 & 52

APPLICANT FOR CHEROKEE CITIZENSHIP

POST OFFICE: Lewisville Texas		ATTORNEY: A E Ivey	
NO	NAMES	AGE	SEX
1	Joseph S Young	40	Male
2	Annie B "	17	Female
3	Lillian M "	14	"
4	Georgia B "	12	"

ANCESTOR: Ward

>Office Commission on Citizenship
>Cherokee Nation Ind Ter
>Tahlequah August 20th 1889

There being no evidence in support of this case the Commission decide that Joseph S Young age 40 years and the following children Annie B female age 17 years, Lillian M female age 14 years, and Georgia B Young female age 12 years are not Cherokees by blood. Post Office Lewisville Texas.
Attest
    E G Ross
        Clerk Commission   J E Gunter   Com

Cherokee Citizenship Commission Docket Books
(1880-84, 1887-89) Volume IV
Tahlequah, Cherokee Nation

YOUNG

DOCKET #1410
CENSUS ROLLS 1824, 1835 & 1852

APPLICANT FOR CHEROKEE CITIZENSHIP

POST OFFICE: Mountainburg Ark		ATTORNEY: A.E. Ivey	
NO	NAMES	AGE	SEX
1	Cordelia Young	23	Female

ANCESTOR: Caroline Bell

Rejected Aug 20th 1889

Office Commission on Citizenship
Cherokee Nation Ind Ter
Tahlequah Aug 20th 1889

Application for Cherokee Citizenship

The above applicant claims that she is the grand daughter of Caroline Bell whose name she alleges should appear upon the census rolls of Cherokees taken in the year *(illegible...)* & 1852. The name of Caroline Bell does not so appear on either of the rolls refered[sic] to by plaintiff. Therefore we decide that claimant Cordela[sic] Young age 23 yrs is not a Cherokee by blood.

Attest
  D.S. Williams
  Asst Clk Com   J E. Gunter   Com

UNDERWOOD

DOCKET #1411
CENSUS ROLLS 1835 & 52

APPLICANT FOR CHEROKEE CITIZENSHIP

POST OFFICE:		ATTORNEY: A.E. Ivey	
NO	NAMES	AGE	SEX
1	Martha Underwood	34	Female
2	James "	11	Male
3	Sarana "	9	Female
4	Luster "	7	Male

ANCESTOR: *(Name Illegible)*

Cherokee Citizenship Commission Docket Books
(1880-84, 1887-89) Volume IV
Tahlequah, Cherokee Nation

Office Commission on Citizenship
Cherokee Nation Ind Ter
Tahlequah Sept 17th 1889

The above case was called once and *(illegible)* for Sept 17th and being called and no one responding and there being no evidence on file in support of claim the Commission decide that Martha Underwood age 34 years and the following children James Underwood male 11 years, Sarah[sic] female age 9 years, Luster Underwood male age 7 years are not Cherokees by blood.
Attest
    E G Ross
        Clerk Commission   *(No other signature is seen)*

VAUGHN

DOCKET #1412
CENSUS ROLLS

APPLICANT FOR CHEROKEE CITIZENSHIP

POST OFFICE: Galena Kansas		ATTORNEY: C H Taylor	
No	NAMES	AGE	SEX
1	Martha C Vaughn	32	Female
2	Romulus "	9	Male

ANCESTOR: *(Name Illegible)*

Rejected July 2nd 1889

Office Commission on Citizenship
Cher Nat July 2nd 1889

There being no evidence in support of the above named case the Commission decide that Martha C Vaughn age 32 years and her child Romulus male age 9 are not Cherokees by blood. Galena Kans.

D.S. Williams
Clk Commission   J E Gunter   Com

Cherokee Citizenship Commission Docket Books
(1880-84, 1887-89) Volume IV
Tahlequah, Cherokee Nation

VAUGHN

DOCKET #1413
CENSUS ROLLS 1835

APPLICANT FOR **CHEROKEE CITIZENSHIP**

POST OFFICE: *(Illegible)* Ark		ATTORNEY: C.H. Taylor	
NO	NAMES	AGE	SEX
1	Adison M Vaughn	36	Male
2	Andrew J "	12	"
3	John F "	10	"
4	Columbus "	8	"
5	Catherine "	4	Female
6	George "	1	Male

ANCESTOR: Feraby Vaughn

Rejected July 2nd 1889

Office Commission on Citizenship
Cher Nat July 2nd 1889

There being no evidence in support of the above named case the Commission decide that Adison M Vaughn age 36 yrs and the following children Andrew J Vaughn age 12 male, John F Vaughn age 10 male, Columbus male age 8, Catherine Female age 4, George male age 1 yr are not Cherokees by blood.
Post Office Hindsville Ark.

D.S. Williams
Asst Clk Commission

JE Gunter Com

VAUGHN

DOCKET #1414
CENSUS ROLLS 1835

APPLICANT FOR **CHEROKEE CITIZENSHIP**

POST OFFICE: Hindsville Ark		ATTORNEY: C.H. Taylor	
NO	NAMES	AGE	SEX
1	Christener Vaughn	40	Male
2	Grandville "	14	"
3	Dolly "	12	Female
4	Christener "	10	Male
5	George "	8	"
6	Manda E. "	2	Female

ANCESTOR: Feraby Vaughn

Cherokee Citizenship Commission Docket Books
(1880-84, 1887-89) Volume IV
Tahlequah, Cherokee Nation

Rejected July 2nd 1889

                                     Office Commission on Citizenship
                                           Cher Nat July 2nd 1889

There being no evidence in support of the above named case the Commission decide that Christener Vaughn age 40 and the following children Grandville male age 14, Dolly female age 12, Christener male age 10, George male age 8, Manda E female age 2 years are not Cherokees by blood. Post Office Hindsville Ark.

       D.S. Williams
       Clk Commission   J E Gunter   Com

VAUGHN

DOCKET #1415
CENSUS ROLLS 1835

APPLICANT FOR CHEROKEE CITIZENSHIP

POST OFFICE:		ATTORNEY: C H Taylor	
NO	NAMES	AGE	SEX
1	Mark A Vaughn	26	Male
2	Washington "	10	"
3	Joseph "	9	"
4	Benjamin "	8	"
5	Kate "	7	Female
6	George "	1	Male

ANCESTOR: Feraby Vaughn

                                     Office Commission on Citizenship
                                         Cherokee Nation Ind Ter
                                         Tahlequah July 2nd 1889

There being no evidence in support of this case the Commission decide that Mark A Vaughn age 26 yrs and the following children Washington Vaughn male 10 yrs, Joseph male 9 yrs, Benjamin male 8 yrs, Kate Female age 7 yrs, and George Vaughn male age 1 yr are not Cherokees by blood. Post Office Hindsville Ark.

Attest
     D.S. Williams
     Asst Clerk Commission   J E Gunter   Com

Cherokee Citizenship Commission Docket Books
(1880-84, 1887-89) Volume IV
Tahlequah, Cherokee Nation

USRAY

DOCKET #1416
CENSUS ROLLS 1835, 48, 51 & 52

APPLICANT FOR **CHEROKEE CITIZENSHIP**

POST OFFICE: Osage Ark		ATTORNEY: Boudinot & Rasmus	
NO	NAMES	AGE	SEX
1	Louisa Usray	42	Female
2	Lana "	18	"
3	Winnie "	16	"
4	*(Illegible)* "	14	Male
5	Barton "	12	"
6	Margaret "	9	Female
7	Hugh "	6	Male

ANCESTOR: Rachel Coplin Copeland

Commission on Citizenship.

CHEROKEE NATION, IND. TER.

Tahlequah, September 3rd 1889

Louisa Usray
    vs   Application for Cherokee Citizenship
The Cherokee Nation

    The applicant in the above case Louisa Usray 42 years old at the date of filing her application, Oct. 1st 1887, alleges that she if the granddaughter of one Rachael Coplin or Copeland whose name she believes will be found on the census rolls of Cherokees by blood taken in the years 1835, 48, 51, 52. In her petition to the National Council for admission to citizenship 16th November 1885, she represents that she gets her Cherokee blood from her father Wm Morris who was the son of Rachael Coplin who was recognized as of Cherokee blood. Affidavits (Exparte) of J.S. Douglas 60 yrs of age taken before H.H. Moore, Clerk Circuit Court of Carroll County State of Arkansas, the 21st day of December 1885, states that he knew applicant well and that she was the daughter of Wm Morris who was related to one *(Illegible)* Jack Copelin who claimed Cherokee descent and that they lived in Overton County, Tennessee, and was from the "Georgia purchase" in the Old Nation. Rebecca Morris 72 yr old in an

Cherokee Citizenship Commission Docket Books
(1880-84, 1887-89) Volume IV
Tahlequah, Cherokee Nation

affidavit before Allen Ross, Clerk of Tahlequah District, Cherokee Nation, *(illegible)* 1885, knows applicant well and also her father Wm Morris and grandfather Joe Copelin who was half Cherokee. Witness resides in Carroll County, State of Arkansas. Thompson Gardenhire in an affidavit before J.H. Bohannon, Clerk Circuit Court for Madison County, State of Arkansas, *(Illegible)* 18, 1885, knows applicant only by character but knew Wm Morris son of Rachael Copelin who was the daughter of Joseph Coplin from 1833 to 1837 in Overton County Tennessee.

Dr. I P. *(Illegible)* of Carroll County Arkansas swears before H.H. Moore, Clk of Circuit Court that he is acquainted with applicant and that it was his understanding that she is of Cherokee blood which she claims Cherokee derived from the Copelin family and knows well & intimately. James Copelin nephew of Joe Copelin and his boys who were always called the Cherokee boys by the people where they lived and that he first got acquainted with James Copelin in Pope County Arkansas in the year 1847. The evidence as above sketched while of a hear-say character as to the Indian descent of the applicant shows that her alleged Indian ancestors lived in the Cherokee Country East of the Mississippi River or near its *(illegible)* in Tennessee at the date of the taking the census of Cherokees by blood by the United States in 1835. The reasonable presumption is that if they were of Cherokee Indian blood they would have been enrolled with other Cherokees and that they would have claimed and participated in the rights and privileges enjoyed in lands and money by other Cherokees. But such has not been shown to be the case or that they at any time heretofore presented any claim to citizenship in the Cherokee Nation and as neither the name of Louisa Usray of William Morris nor of Rachael Morris nee Rachael Copelin can be found on the rolls of Cherokees *(illegible)* to, the Commission decide that Louisa Usray age 42 yrs and her sons *(Illegible)*, age 18[sic] yrs and Barton 12 yrs and Hugh 6 yrs and her daughters Lana Usray 18 yrs, Winnie 16 yrs and Margaret Usray 12 years are not of Cherokee blood and not entitled to citizenship in the Cherokee Nation.

          Will.P.Ross
           Chairman
        J.E. Gunter Com

Cherokee Citizenship Commission Docket Books
(1880-84, 1887-89) Volume IV
Tahlequah, Cherokee Nation

YORK

DOCKET #1417
CENSUS ROLLS 1835, 51 & 52

APPLICANT FOR CHEROKEE CITIZENSHIP

POST OFFICE: Sherman Texas		ATTORNEY: L B Bell	
No	NAMES	AGE	SEX
1	M.V. York		

ANCESTOR: *(Illegible)*

Office Commission on Citizenship
Cherokee Nation Ind Ter
Tahlequah Aug 19th 1889

There being no evidence in support of this case, the Commission decide that M V York is not a Cherokee by blood. Post Office Sherman Texas.
Attest
   E G Ross
      Clerk Commission   J E Gunter Com

VESTAL

DOCKET #1418
CENSUS ROLLS

APPLICANT FOR CHEROKEE CITIZENSHIP

POST OFFICE: *(Illegible)* Kans		ATTORNEY: L B Bell	
No	NAMES	AGE	SEX
1	David Vestal		

ANCESTOR:

Commission on Citizenship.

CHEROKEE NATION, IND. TER.

Tahlequah, August 22nd 1889

David Vestal, et. al.
    vs   Application for Cherokee Citizenship
The Cherokee Nation

    The applicant in the above case one David Vestal, Benjamin Vestal, Sarah H Wilson, John H. Vestal., James M Vestal and Nathan Vestal. The

Cherokee Citizenship Commission Docket Books
(1880-84, 1887-89) Volume IV
Tahlequah, Cherokee Nation

witness Rhoda Johnson 70 years old and Eli Johnson same age in affidavit affirmed to 22 day of *(Illegible)* timber A.D. 1884 before Wm. R. McClelland, Clerk of Circuit Court for Hendricks County, State of North Carolina. State severally the same facts that the above named persons are the children of Jemima Vestal who is of Cherokee descent and who was said to have been born on or about the 25th day of February A.D. 1805 in Guilford County State of North Carolina and died in Johnson County, Kansas the 29th day of May 1883. And that she was the daughter of one Sarah Hubbard a person of Cherokee descent said to have been born in Guilford County, North Carolina in 1781 and died in same county and state in 1825 and that said Sarah Hubbard was daughter of Howard Patterson nee Elnora who was said to be of Cherokee descent. These affidavits are of marked similarity and are insufficient, being <u>exparte</u>, to show that the applicants are of Cherokee blood. There is also no proof that they they[sic] at any time resided in the Cherokee Nation or have *(illegible...)* themselves of any right or *(illegible)* fits belonging to persons of Cherokee descent while it is admitted that neither their own names nor that of any ancestor appears on either of the census rolls of Cherokees by blood taken and made by the United States in the years 1835-48-51-52 referred to in the 7th Section of the Act of Dec 8th 1886 creating a Commission on Citizenship and *(illegible...)*. The Commission therefore decide that applicants are not of Cherokee blood. P.O. Prairie Center, Kan.

Will.P.Ross
Chairman

Attest
    E G Ross
           Clk Com

John E. Gunter Com

DOCKET #1419   *(All names illegible)*

DOCKET #1420   *(All names illegible)*

YARDEN

DOCKET #1421
CENSUS ROLLS 1835,48,51 & 52
    or Old Settlers   APPLICANT FOR CHEROKEE CITIZENSHIP

POST OFFICE: Union Town Ark		ATTORNEY: Boudinot & Rasmus	
NO	NAMES	AGE	SEX
1	Elizabeth Yarden	50	Female

Cherokee Citizenship Commission Docket Books
(1880-84, 1887-89) Volume IV
Tahlequah, Cherokee Nation

2	Sallie Birchfield	17	"
3	Richard B Yarden	11	Male

ANCESTOR: Wm Moton

Office Commission on Citizenship
Cherokee Nation Ind Ter
Tahlequah August 28th 1889

The above case having been submitted by applicants' attorney Mr. Boudinot without evidence we decide that claimant Elizabeth Yarden age fifty years and children Sally Birchfield age seventeen years and Richard B Yarden age eleven years are not Cherokees by blood.
Attest
    EG Ross
        Clerk Commission
                                  JE Gunter   Com

YEARBERRY

DOCKET #1422
CENSUS ROLLS E or W

APPLICANT FOR **CHEROKEE CITIZENSHIP**

POST OFFICE: Trident, Benton Co Ark		ATTORNEY: L.S. Sanders	
NO	NAMES	AGE	SEX
1	Cynthia M. R Yearberry	32	Female
2	Martha E. "	13	"
3	Walter C. "	11	Male
4	John G. "	9	"
5	Lottie A. "	7	Female
6	Roger E. "	5	Male
7	Fannie M. "	3	Female
8	Thos N. "	1	Male

ANCESTOR: *(Illegible)* or *(Illegible)*
Rejected Aug 20th 1889

Office Commission on Citizenship
Cherokee Nation Ind Ter
Tahlequah August 20th 1889

There being no evidence in support of this case the Commission decide that Cynthia M.R. Yearberry age 32 yrs. and the following children Martha E.

Cherokee Citizenship Commission Docket Books
(1880-84, 1887-89) Volume IV
Tahlequah, Cherokee Nation

female age 13 yrs, Walter C male 11 yrs, John G male 9 yrs, Lottie A Female 7 yrs, Roger E. male 5 yrs, Fannie M Female 3 yrs. and Thos N Yearberry male age 1 yr. are not Cherokees by blood. P.O. Tredent[sic] Benton Co Ark.

Attest
    D.S. Williams
    Asst Clk Com   J E Gunter   Com

YOUNG

DOCKET #1423
CENSUS ROLLS 1835, 48, 51 & 52

APPLICANT FOR CHEROKEE CITIZENSHIP

POST OFFICE: Scottsville Ark		ATTORNEY: Boudinot & Rasmus	
No	NAMES	AGE	SEX
1	Margaret J Young	48	Female
2	John McCune	18	Male
3	Mary McCune	16	Female

ANCESTOR: Bashiba Goodrich

Office Commission on Citizenship
Cherokee Nation Ind Ter
Tahlequah Aug 28th 1889

The above application was submitted without evidence by claimants' attorney Mr. Boudinot.

Therefore we decide that applicant Margaret J Young age 48 years and nephew John McCune age 18 years and niece Mary McCune age 16 years are not Cherokees by blood and not entitled to Citizenship in the Cherokee Nation.
Attest
    E G Ross
        Clerk Commission   JE Gunter   Com

Cherokee Citizenship Commission Docket Books
(1880-84, 1887-89) Volume IV
Tahlequah, Cherokee Nation

YOUNG

DOCKET #1424
CENSUS ROLLS 1835

APPLICANT FOR **CHEROKEE CITIZENSHIP**

POST OFFICE:		ATTORNEY: J.S. Stapler	
No	NAMES	AGE	SEX
1	Malinda Young		Female
2	John Webster "	19	Male
3	James Lester "	15	"
4	Robert Andrew "	13	"
5	Nannie May "	11	Female

ANCESTOR: ~~William~~ George Wilson

We the Commission on Citizenship after carefully examining the ... in the above case and also the Old Settler pay rolls of 1851 and the above case having come up for final hearing and the amendment thereto *(illegible...)* we find the above applicant, Malinda Young and her four children, viz: John Webster, James Lester, Robert Andrew, and Nannie May Young to be Cherokees by blood and are hereby re-admitted to all the rights, privileges and immunities of Cherokee citizens by blood and a certificate of said decision of the Commission and of re-admission was made and furnished said parties accordingly and certificate issued.

       D.W. Lipe   Acting Chairman Commission
       John E Gunter Commissioner
Office Com on Citizenship.
Tahlequah I.T. July 13th 1888

Gunter's name was signed by D.W. Lipe, *(remainder illegible).*

VAUGHN

DOCKET #1425
CENSUS ROLLS 1835

APPLICANT FOR **CHEROKEE CITIZENSHIP**

POST OFFICE: Whitney Ark		ATTORNEY: C.H. Taylor	
No	NAMES	AGE	SEX
1	George W Vaughn	38	Male
2	Cora "	12	Female
3	Andrew J "	9	Male

Cherokee Citizenship Commission Docket Books
(1880-84, 1887-89) Volume IV
Tahlequah, Cherokee Nation

4	Charles J "	7	"

ANCESTOR: Feraby Vaughn

Rejected July 2nd 1889

Office Commission on Citizenship
Cherokee Nation Ind. Ter.
Tahlequah July 2nd 1889

There being no evidence in support of this case the Commission decide that George W. Vaughn age 38 yrs and the following children Cora Female age 12 yrs, Andrew J. male age 9 yrs, and Charles J. Vaughn male age 7 yrs. are not Cherokees by blood. Post Office Whitney Ark.

Attest
    D.S. Williams
    Asst Clk Commission   JE Gunter   Com

VAUGHN

DOCKET #1426
CENSUS ROLLS 1835

APPLICANT FOR **CHEROKEE CITIZENSHIP**

POST OFFICE: Whitney Ark		ATTORNEY: CH Taylor	
NO	**NAMES**	**AGE**	**SEX**
1	Thomas Vaughn	35	Male
2	James "	17	"
3	Jeff "	15	"
4	Moses "	13	"
5	Daniel "	11	"

ANCESTOR: Feraby Vaughn

Office Commission on Citizenship
Cherokee Nation July 2nd 1889

There being no evidence in support of the above case the Commission decide that Thomas Vaughn age 35 male, James male age 17, Jeff male age ... Moses male age 13, Daniel male age 11 yrs are not Cherokees by blood. Post Office Whitney Ark.

Cherokee Citizenship Commission Docket Books
(1880-84, 1887-89) Volume IV
Tahlequah, Cherokee Nation

D.S. Williams
Asst Clerk Commission

J.E. Gunter   Com

DOCKET #1427   *(All names illegible)*

VAUGHN

DOCKET #1428
CENSUS ROLLS 1835

APPLICANT FOR CHEREOKEE CITIZENSHIP

POST OFFICE: Cliftey[sic] Ark		ATTORNEY: CH Taylor	
No	NAMES	AGE	SEX
1	Allen W. Vaughn	39	Male
2	Leroy "	16	"
3	Margaret E "	13	Female
4	Mary A "	11	"
5	B. F. "	9	Male
6	O. D. "	4	"
7	Jennie Ann "	2	Female

ANCESTOR: Feraby Vaughn

Rejected July 2nd 1889

Office Commission on Citizenship
Cherokee Nation Ind Ter
Tahlequah July 2nd 1889

The above case having been submitted without evidence the Commission decide against the applicant Allen W. Vaughn aged 39 yrs and his sons Leroy aged 16 yrs, B.F. Vaughn aged 9 yrs, and O.D. Vaughn aged 4 yrs and his daughters Margaret aged 13 yrs, Mary A. aged 11 yrs and Jennie Ann aged 2 yrs. P.O. address Cliftey[sic] Ark
Attest
    D.S. Williams
    Asst Clerk Commission   J.E. Gunter   Com

Cherokee Citizenship Commission Docket Books
(1880-84, 1887-89) Volume IV
Tahlequah, Cherokee Nation

VAUGHN

DOCKET #1429
CENSUS ROLLS 1835

APPLICANT FOR CHEROKEE CITIZENSHIP

POST OFFICE: Cliftey[sic] Ark		ATTORNEY: CH Taylor	
NO	NAMES	AGE	SEX
1	Benjamin Vaughn	72	Male

ANCESTOR: Feraby Vaughn

Rejected July 2nd 1889

Office Commission on Citizenship
Cherokee Nation Ind. Ter.
Tahlequah July 2nd 1889

There being no evidence in support of this case the Commission decide that Benjamin Vaughn age 72 yrs is not a Cherokee by blood. Post Office Clifty Ark

Attest
    D.S.Williams
    Asst Clk Com   J.E. Gunter   Com

VAUGHN

DOCKET #1430
CENSUS ROLLS 1835

APPLICANT FOR CHEROKEE CITIZENSHIP

POST OFFICE: Whitney Ark		ATTORNEY: C.H. Taylor	
NO	NAMES	AGE	SEX
1	John P Vaughn	27	Male
2	Gilford "	6	"

ANCESTOR: Feraby Vaughn

Rejected July 2nd 1889

Office Commission on Citizenship
Cher. Nat July 2nd 1889

There being no evidence in support of this case the Commission decide that John P Vaughn age 73[sic] yrs and his son Gilford male age 6 yrs are not Cherokees by blood. Post Office Whitney Ark.

Cherokee Citizenship Commission Docket Books
(1880-84, 1887-89) Volume IV
Tahlequah, Cherokee Nation

D.S. Williams
Clk Commission

J.E. Gunter   Com

VAUGHN

DOCKET #1431
CENSUS ROLLS 1835

APPLICANT FOR CHEROKEE CITIZENSHIP

POST OFFICE: Whitner[sic] Ark		ATTORNEY: C.H. Taylor	
No	NAMES	AGE	SEX
1	Isaac Vaughn, Jr.	27	Male
2	Emma "	7	Female
3	Thomas "	5	Male

ANCESTOR: Feraby Vaughn

Rejected July 2nd 1889

Office Commission on Citizenship
Cherokee Nation Ind Ter
Tahlequah July 2nd 1889

There being no evidence in support of this case the Commission decide that Isaac Vaughn age 27 yrs and his children Emma female age 7 yrs and Thomas Vaughn male age 5 yrs are not Cherokees by blood. Post Office Whitner[sic] Ark.

Attest
    D.S. Williams
Asst   Clerk Commission

J E Gunter   Com

VAUGHN

DOCKET #1432
CENSUS ROLLS 1835

APPLICANT FOR CHEROKEE CITIZENSHIP

POST OFFICE: Whitney Ark		ATTORNEY: C H Taylor	
No	NAMES	AGE	SEX
1	Isaac Vaughn, Sr.	69	Male

ANCESTOR: Feraby Vaughn

Rejected July 2nd 1889

Cherokee Citizenship Commission Docket Books
(1880-84, 1887-89) Volume IV
Tahlequah, Cherokee Nation

Office Commission on Citizenship
Cherokee Nation In. Ter.
Tahlequah July 2nd 1889

There being no evidence in support of this case the Commission decide that Isaac Vaughn, Sr age 69 yrs is not a Cherokee by blood. Post Office Whitney Ark.

Attest
    D.S. Williams
Asst Clerk Commission   J.E. Gunter   Com

VAUGHN

DOCKET #1433
CENSUS ROLLS 1835

APPLICANT FOR CHEROKEE CITIZENSHIP

POST OFFICE: Whiting[sic] Ark		ATTORNEY: CH Taylor	
No	NAMES	AGE	SEX
1	Jimmi Vaughn	43	Male
2	Henry Sr "	16	"
3	George S "	12	"
4	Susan M.B.H. "	9	Female
5	Watkins "	6	Male
6	Wassey "	1	"

ANCESTOR: Feraby Vaughn

Rejected July 2nd 1889

Office Commission on Citizenship
Cherokee Nation July 2nd 1889

There being no evidence in support of the above named case the Commission decide that Jimmi Vaughn age 43 male and the following children Henry Sr male age 16, George male age 12, Susan M.B.H. Female age 9, Watkins male age 6, Wassey male age 1 yr are not Cherokees by blood. Post Office Whitney Ark

D.S. Williams
Clk Commission   J.E. Gunter   Com

Cherokee Citizenship Commission Docket Books
(1880-84, 1887-89) Volume IV
Tahlequah, Cherokee Nation

VAUGHN

DOCKET #1434
CENSUS ROLLS 1835

APPLICANT FOR **CHEROKEE CITIZENSHIP**

POST OFFICE: Whitney Ark		ATTORNEY: CH Taylor	
NO	NAMES	AGE	SEX
1	Samuel H Vaughn	40	Male
2	Emily "	19	Female
3	Sissie "	16	"
4	Isaac "	11	Male

ANCESTOR: Feraby Vaughn

Rejected July 2nd 1889

Office Commission on Citizenship
Cherokee Nation Ind Ter
Tahlequah July 2nd 1889

There being no evidence in support of this case the Commission decide that Samuel H Vaughn age 40 yrs and the following children Emily Vaughn Female 19 yrs, Sissie Female 16 yrs & Isaac Vaughn male age 11 yrs are not Cherokees by blood. Post Office Whitney Ark.

Attest
    D.S. Williams
Asst Clerk Commission   J.E. Gunter   Com

HEILMS

DOCKET #1435
CENSUS ROLLS 1835 or Old Settler

APPLICANT FOR **CHEROKEE CITIZENSHIP**

POST OFFICE: McKinney Texas		ATTORNEY: WA Thompson	
NO	NAMES	AGE	SEX
1	Maggie Heilms	29	Female

ANCESTOR: Mary *(No last name given)*

Rejected Aug 20th 1889

Office Commission on Citizenship
Cherokee Nation Ind Ter
Tahlequah Aug 20th 1889

Cherokee Citizenship Commission Docket Books
(1880-84, 1887-89) Volume IV
Tahlequah, Cherokee Nation

There being no evidence in support of this case the Commission decide that Maggie Heilms age 29 yrs and her daughter Maggie Heilms age 4 yrs are not Cherokees by blood.   P.O. McKinny[sic] Texas

Attest
    D.S. Williams
    Asst Clk Com

                                    J.E. Gunter   Com

HUFF

DOCKET #1436
CENSUS ROLLS

APPLICANT FOR CHEROKEE CITIZENSHIP

POST OFFICE: Delutt[sic] Min		ATTORNEY: LB Bell	
NO	NAMES	AGE	SEX
1	R. B. Huff		

ANCESTOR: Ann Crews

The Commission decide against claimant. See decision in case Andrew Meredith Docket 2180 Book E, Page 26 and case John Henly Docket 1250, Book C Page 346.

                                    J.E. Gunter   Com

HUBBARD

DOCKET #1437
CENSUS ROLLS

APPLICANT FOR CHEROKEE CITIZENSHIP

POST OFFICE: Knightstown Ind		ATTORNEY: LB Bell	
NO	NAMES	AGE	SEX
1	Ellen Hubbard	40	Female

ANCESTOR: Ann Crews

The Commission decide against claimant. See decision in the case of Andrew Meredith Docket 2180 Book E, Page 26 and John Henly Docket 1250, Book C Page 346.

Attest
    E.G. Ross
        Clerk Com   John E. Gunter   Com

Cherokee Citizenship Commission Docket Books
(1880-84, 1887-89) Volume IV
Tahlequah, Cherokee Nation

HOUSE

DOCKET #1438
CENSUS ROLLS

APPLICANT FOR CHEROKEE CITIZENSHIP

POST OFFICE: Cassville Mo		ATTORNEY: C.H. Taylor	
NO	NAMES	AGE	SEX
1	John House	35	Male
2	William T "	8	"
3	Hogosther "	5	"
4	Lanattia "	3	Female
5	*(Illegible)* "	1	Male
6	Martha "	5 d	Female

ANCESTOR: Mansfield House

Rejected Aug 20th 1889

Application for Citizenship

Office Commission on Citizenship
Cherokee Nation Ind. Ter.
Tahlequah August 20th 1889

In the above case the Commission decide that John House age 35 years and his sons William T. House age 8 years, Hogosther House age 5 years, *(Illegible)* House 1 year and daughters Lanattia House 3 years, and Martha House five days old are not of Cherokee blood for reasons set forth in the case of George House. See Docket 485 Book B, Page 198. Post Office Cassville Mo.
Attest
    D.S. Williams
Asst Clk Com   J.E. Gunter   Com

HOUSE

DOCKET #1439
CENSUS ROLLS

APPLICANT FOR CHEROKEE CITIZENSHIP

POST OFFICE: Cassville Mo		ATTORNEY: C.H. Taylor	
NO	NAMES	AGE	SEX
1	Wm H House	48	Male
2	A. B. "	20	"
3	F. M. "	19	"
4	C. P. "	17	"
5	Neley E "	6	Female
6	M. F. "	13	"

Cherokee Citizenship Commission Docket Books
(1880-84, 1887-89) Volume IV
Tahlequah, Cherokee Nation

| 7 | E. E. " | 11 | " |

ANCESTOR: Mansfield House

Rejected Aug 20th 1889

Office Commission on Citizenship
Cherokee Nation Ind Ter
Tahlequah Aug 20th 1889

Application for Citizenship

The Commission decide adverse to claimant in the above case and to his children A. B. House (male) 20 years, F. M. House male age 19 yrs, C. P. House male 17 yrs, Neley E. House female 6 yrs, M. F. House female 13 yrs, E. E. House female 11 yrs for reasons set forth in the case of George House In Docket 485, Book B, Page 198 – P.O. Cassville Mo.

Attest
   D.S. Williams
Asst Clk Com   J.E. Gunter   Com

DOCKET #1440   *(All names illegible)*

DOCKET #1441   *(All names illegible)*

HENSLEY

DOCKET #1442
CENSUS ROLLS 1851

APPLICANT FOR **CHEROKEE CITIZENSHIP**

POST OFFICE: Carlisle Ga		ATTORNEY: A.E. Ivey	
No	NAMES	AGE	SEX
1	Emma Jane Hensley	23	Female
2	Luebar E "	5	"
3	John W "	3	Male
4	Estella M "	1	Female

ANCESTOR: *(Name Illegible)*

Office Commission on Citizenship
Cherokee Nation Ind Ter
Tahlequah Sept 17th 1889

Cherokee Citizenship Commission Docket Books
(1880-84, 1887-89) Volume IV
Tahlequah, Cherokee Nation

The above case was called and set for Sept 17th 1889 for a hearing and was again called according to the time set and no one responding and there being no evidence on file in support of claim the Commission decide that Emma Jane Hensley age 23 years and the following children Leubar E. Hensley age 5 years, John W Hensley age 3 yrs and Estella M Hensley age 1 year are not Cherokees by blood.
Attest
    EG Ross
        Clerk Commission
                                    JE Gunter Com

HUCKLEBERRY

DOCKET #1443
CENSUS ROLLS 1835, 48, 51 & 52

APPLICANT FOR CHEROKEE CITIZENSHIP

POST OFFICE: Van Buren Ark		ATTORNEY: A.E. Ivey	
NO	NAMES	AGE	SEX
1	Emily M Huckleberry	34	Female
2	James A "	12	Male
3	Eva W "	8	Female
4	David W "	5	Male
5	Jessie W "	3	"
6	Lettie M "	5 mo	Female

ANCESTOR: Mobley & Ashley

Rejected July 5th 1889

                Office Commission on Citizenship
                    Cherokee Nation Ind. Ter.
                    Tahlequah July 5th 1889

~~There being no evidence in support of this case the Commission decide that~~

                    Application for Cherokee Citizenship
This case having been submitted without evidence by the Attys the Commission decide that Emily M Huckleberry and her children James A age 12 years, Eva W, David age 5 years, Jesse Wage 3 years, and Lettia M Huckleberry age five months are not Cherokees by blood and are not entitled to Cherokee Citizenship. P.O. Van Buren Ark.

Cherokee Citizenship Commission Docket Books
(1880-84, 1887-89) Volume IV
Tahlequah, Cherokee Nation

Attest
    D.S. Williams   J.E. Gunter   Com
    Asst Clk Com

HOWELL

DOCKET #1444
CENSUS ROLLS 1835 & 1846

APPLICANT FOR CHEROKEE CITIZENSHIP

POST OFFICE: Union Town Ark		ATTORNEY: A E Ivey	
No	NAMES	AGE	SEX
1	Sarah A Howell	33	Female
2	Rosa Lee "	16	"
3	Armento "	11	"
4	Wm H "	10	Male
5	Ida "	9	Female
6	Martha "	6	"

ANCESTOR: Vaughn

Office Commission on Citizenship
Cherokee Nation Ind Ter
Tahlequah October 3rd 1889

    There being no evidence introduced in support of the above application and the case having been called in due order without answer from claimant or Attorney the Commission decide that Sarah A Howell 33 years of age and her son William H Howell 10 years and daughters Rosa Lee Howell 16 years, Armento Howell 11 years, Ida Howell 9 years and Martha Howell 6 years are not of Cherokee blood. Post Office Union Town Arkansas

Attest
    E G Ross
        Clerk Commission

                                             J E Gunter   Com

Cherokee Citizenship Commission Docket Books
(1880-84, 1887-89) Volume IV
Tahlequah, Cherokee Nation

HOUSE

DOCKET #1445
CENSUS ROLLS 1835 to 52

APPLICANT FOR **CHEROKEE CITIZENSHIP**

POST OFFICE: Childers Station IT		ATTORNEY: B.H. Stone	
No	NAMES	AGE	SEX
1	B. F. House	50	Male
2	John D House	20	"
3	Wm T "	15	"
4	Lee T "	12	"
5	Calafornia "	9	Female

ANCESTOR: *(Name Illegible)*

Rejected August 30th[sic]1889

Office Commission on Citizenship
Cherokee Nation Ind. Ter.
Tahlequah August 20th 1889

Application for Citizenship

The application in the above case which was filed the 26th of September A.D. 1887, being supported by no evidence the Commission decide that B.F. House age 50 years and his daughter Calafornia House age 9 years, and sons John D House age 20 years, William T. House age 15 years and Lee T House age 12 years are not of Cherokee blood and not entitled to Citizenship in the Cherokee Nation. P.O. Childers Station Ind. Ter.
Attest
    D.S. Williams
  Asst Clk Com   J.E. Gunter   Com

HARKNESS

DOCKET #1446
CENSUS ROLLS 1835

APPLICANT FOR **CHEROKEE CITIZENSHIP**

POST OFFICE: Grape Creek N.C.		ATTORNEY: C.H. Taylor	
No	NAMES	AGE	SEX
1	Edwin L Harkness	25	Male
2	Lester "	5	"
3	Benjamin "	1	"

ANCESTOR: *(Name Illegible)*

Rejected Aug 20th 1889

Cherokee Citizenship Commission Docket Books
(1880-84, 1887-89) Volume IV
Tahlequah, Cherokee Nation

Office Commission on Citizenship
Cherokee Nation Ind Ter
Tahlequah Aug 20th 1889

The Commission in the above named case decide that Edwin L Harkness age 25 yrs and his sons Lester Harkness age 5 years and Benjamin Harkness age one year are not of Cherokee blood for reasons set forth in the decision of the Commission in the case of Marion Harkness. See Docket 1449, Book C, Page 575. P.O. Grape Creek N.C.

Attest
    D.S. Williams
  Asst Clk Com

                                         J E Gunter Com

HAYDEN

DOCKET #1447
CENSUS ROLLS 1835, 48, 51 & 52

APPLICANT FOR **CHEROKEE CITIZENSHIP**

POST OFFICE: Fort Smith Ark		ATTORNEY: Boudinot & Rasmus	
No	NAMES	AGE	SEX
1	Caroline Hayden	55	Female
2	Cassie "	17	"
3	Alfey "	14	Male
4	Etty Mahone "	13	Female
5	Cecil Brown	12	Male

ANCESTOR: Barsheba Goodrich

Rejected June 20th 1889

                Office Commission on Citizenship
                          Cherokee Nation
                      Tahlequah June 20th 1889

There being no evidence in support of the above named case the Commission decide that Caroline Hayden age 55 years and the following children Cassie Female age 17 years Alfey Hayden male age 14 years, Etty Mahone Female 13 yrs, Grand daughter and Cecil Brown Grand son are not Cherokees by blood. Post Office Fort Smith Ark.

Cherokee Citizenship Commission Docket Books
(1880-84, 1887-89) Volume IV
Tahlequah, Cherokee Nation

Attest
    D.S. Williams
    Asst Clk Com

                              J.E. Gunter   Com

HERNDON

DOCKET #1448
CENSUS ROLLS 1835

APPLICANT FOR CHEROKEE CITIZENSHIP

POST OFFICE: McKinney Texas		ATTORNEY: Wm A Thompson	
NO	NAMES	AGE	SEX
1	James R Herndon	39	Male
2	Ula F "	16	Female
3	Geo Henry "	?	Male
4	M.E. "	14	Female
5	Sallie B "	9	"
6	Wm B. "	8	Male
7	Hattie "	7	Female
8	Dora "	5	"
9	Edward D. "	3	Male

ANCESTOR: Jack McGarrah

Rejected June 26th 1889

                Office Commission on Citizenship
                        Cherokee Nation
                Tahlequah June 26th 1889

There being no evidence in support of the above named case the Commission decide that Jas R Herndon age 39 yrs and children Ula F female age 16 yrs, M.E. female age 14 yrs, Geo Henry male age 11 yrs, Sallie B female age 9 yrs, Wm B. male age 8 yrs, Hattie female age 7 yrs, Dora female age 5 yrs and Edward D. Herndon male age 3 yrs are not Cherokees by blood. Post Office McKinney Texas.

Attest
    D.S. Williams
    Asst Clk Com   JE Gunter   Com

Cherokee Citizenship Commission Docket Books
(1880-84, 1887-89) Volume IV
Tahlequah, Cherokee Nation

HARKNESS

DOCKET #1449
CENSUS ROLLS 1848

APPLICANT FOR **CHEROKEE CITIZENSHIP**

POST OFFICE: Tahlequah C.N.		ATTORNEY: *(Illegible)*	
No	NAMES	AGE	SEX
1	Marion Harkness	46	Male
2	William H "	22	"
3	Joseph M "	20	"
4	Sallie T. "	18	Female
5	Malissie L "	14	"
6	Lucinda "	12	"
7	Benjamin "	10	Male
8	Acy "	9	"
9	Elija "	3	"
10	Maud "	2	Female

ANCESTOR: Felix Panther

Now on this the 12th day of February 1889, comes the above case to wit: Marion Harkness et-al for a final hearing. They having made application pursuant to the provisions of an Act of the National Council approved December 8th 1886. From an examination of the roll enumerated in the 7th Section of said Act, it appears that the name of Felix Panther, from whom descent is claimed by Plaintiff, appears as a halfbreed on Mully[sic] roll of 1848, as a white man on the Sila[sic] roll of 1851 and not at all on the Chapman pay roll of 1852, Along with those of his family. The application is supported by no evidence while the testimony of John Taylor, brother-in-law, and Octavia Harkness, daughter of Felix Panther proves conclusively that he was a white man and that applicant did not pretend to be of Cherokee descent until after he had been sometime in this country under *(illegible)* as a citizen of the United States. It is therefore adjudged and declared that Marion Harkness and William H, Joseph M, Sallie T, Hattie L, Lucinda, Benjamin, Acy, and Maud Harkness not Cherokees and are not entitled to any of the rights and privileges of Cherokee citizens by blood.

       Will. P. Ross Chairman
       John E. Gunter Com
       (Cherokee letters) (R Bunch)

Attest
  D.S. Williams Asst Clk

Cherokee Citizenship Commission Docket Books
(1880-84, 1887-89) Volume IV
Tahlequah, Cherokee Nation

HANCOCK

DOCKET #1450
CENSUS ROLLS 1835, 48, 51 & 52

APPLICANT FOR CHEROKEE CITIZENSHIP

POST OFFICE: Farmer Ark		ATTORNEY: Boudinot & Rasmus	
NO	NAMES	AGE	SEX
1	Leah M. Hancock	22	Female
2	Elbert C. "	1	Male

ANCESTOR: Leah Ross

Office Commission on Citizenship
Cherokee Nation Ind Ter
Tahlequah Aug 28th 1889

The above case having been submitted without evidence by claimants Attorneys Boudinot & Rasmus we decide that applicant Leah M Hancock age twenty two years and son Elbert C Hancock age one year are not Cherokees by blood. Post Office Farmer Ark.
Attest
    E G Ross
        Clerk Commission
                      J E Gunter   Com

HERNDON

DOCKET #1451
CENSUS ROLLS 1835

APPLICANT FOR CHEROKEE CITIZENSHIP

POST OFFICE: McKinney Texas		ATTORNEY:	
NO	NAMES	AGE	SEX
1	James Herndon	33	Male
2	Merle "	6	"
3	Maggie "	5	Female
4	Norah "	3	"
5	Loa "	1	"

ANCESTOR: Jack McGarrah

Rejected June 26th 1889

Office Commission on Citizenship
Cherokee Nation
Tahlequah June 26th 1889

Cherokee Citizenship Commission Docket Books
(1880-84, 1887-89) Volume IV
Tahlequah, Cherokee Nation

There being no evidence in support of this case the Commission decide that James Herndon aged thirty three years and his son Merle Herndon six years, and daughters Maggie Herndon five years, Noah[sic] Herndon three years, and Loa Herndon one year are not of Cherokee blood. P.O. McKinny[sic] Texas.

Attest
    D.S. Williams
    Asst Clk Com

                                  J E Gunter Com

HENSON

DOCKET #1452
CENSUS ROLLS 1835

APPLICANT FOR CHEROKEE CITIZENSHIP

POST OFFICE: Branchville Texas		ATTORNEY: R. M. Wolfe	
NO	NAMES	AGE	SEX
1	Henry Henson	60	Male

ANCESTOR: Elizabeth Henson

                    Office Commission on Citizenship
                          Cherokee Nation Ind Ter
                            Tahlequah Sept 23rd 1889

The above case was submitted by Attorney without evidence. The Commission there decide that Henry Henson age 60 years is not a Cherokee by blood.
Attest
    E.G. Ross
        Clerk Commission

                                  J. E. Gunter Com

HIDER

DOCKET #1453
CENSUS ROLLS 1835

APPLICANT FOR CHEROKEE CITIZENSHIP

POST OFFICE: Gibson Station I.T.		ATTORNEY: C.H. Taylor	
NO	NAMES	AGE	SEX
1	Mary Hider	27	Female

Cherokee Citizenship Commission Docket Books (1880-84, 1887-89) Volume IV
Tahlequah, Cherokee Nation

2	Mable "	3	"
3	Berty "	1½	Male

ANCESTOR: Mary Cole

Office Commission on Citizenship
Cherokee Nation Ind Ter
Tahlequah Sept 13th 1889

The above case was called three times and no response from applicant or by Attorney and there being no evidence on file in support of claim the Commission decide that Mary Hider age 27 years, Mable Hider age 3 years and Berty Hider age 1½ years are not Cherokees by blood. Post Office Gibson Station I.T.
Attest
    E G Ross
        Clerk Commission

J.E. Gunter   Com

HERALD

DOCKET #1454
CENSUS ROLLS 1835 & 52

APPLICANT FOR **CHEROKEE CITIZENSHIP**

POST OFFICE: Vinita IT		ATTORNEY: LS Sanders	
No	**NAMES**	**AGE**	**SEX**
1	Sarah Jane Herald	40	Female
2	Joseph I Candery	21	Male
3	James R Herald	15	"
4	Andrew "	10	"
5	Fuller M "	8	"
6	Robert "	6	"
7	Kile "	4	"
8	Louisa "	2	Female

ANCESTOR: John Beamer

Rejected Aug 20th 1889

Office Commission on Citizenship
Cherokee Nation Ind Ter
Tahlequah Aug 20th 1889

Cherokee Citizenship Commission Docket Books
(1880-84, 1887-89) Volume IV
Tahlequah, Cherokee Nation

There being no evidence in support of this case the Commission decide that Sarah Jane Herald age 40 years and the following children Joseph I Candery male 21 yrs, Son James R Herald male age 15 yrs, Andrew male 10 yrs, Fuller M male 8 yrs, Robert male 6 yrs, Kile male 4 yrs, and Louisa Herald Female 2 yrs are not Cherokees by blood. P.O. Vinita I.T.

Attest
    D.S. Williams
    Asst Clk Com   J E Gunter   Com

HURNDEN

DOCKET #1455
CENSUS ROLLS 1835

APPLICANT FOR CHEROKEE CITIZENSHIP

No	POST OFFICE: McKinney Texas	ATTORNEY: Wm A Thompson	
	NAMES	AGE	SEX
1	W. S. Hurnden	30	Male
2	Georgia "	9	Female
3	Leola "	6	"
4	Mack "	4	Male
5	Lucy "	1	Female

ANCESTOR: Jack McGarrah

Rejected June 26th 1889

                              Office Commission on Citizenship
                                       Cherokee Nation
                                 Tahlequah June 26th 1889

There being no evidence in support of this case the Commission decide that W.S. Hurnden age 30 yrs and his children Georgia female age 9 yrs, Leola girl 6 yrs, Mack male 4 yrs and Lucy female age yr are not Cherokees by blood. P.O. McKinny[sic] Texas.

Attest
    D S Williams
    Asst Clk Com

                                      J.E. Gunter   Com

Cherokee Citizenship Commission Docket Books
(1880-84, 1887-89) Volume IV
Tahlequah, Cherokee Nation

HANN

DOCKET #1456
CENSUS ROLLS 1835

APPLICANT FOR CHEROKEE CITIZENSHIP

POST OFFICE: McKinney Texas		ATTORNEY: Wm A Thompson	
NO	NAMES	AGE	SEX
1	Cynthia Ann Hann	43	Female
2	Kate E "	18	"
3	Clay F "	17	Male
4	Florence C "	14	Female
5	Lee F "	10	Male
6	James T "	8	"
7	Wood "	6	"
8	Bennett "	4	"
9	Joe "	2	"

ANCESTOR: Jack McGarrah

Rejected June 26th 1889

Office Commission on Citizenship
Cherokee Nation
Tahlequah June 26th 1889

There being no evidence in support of the above named case the Commission decide that Cynthia Ann Hann age 43 yrs, Kate E female 18 yrs, Clay F male 17 yrs, Sallie M. female age 14 yrs, Florence C female age 12 yrs, Lee F. male age 10 yrs, James F. male age 8 yrs, Wood male age 6 yrs, Bennett H. male age 4 yrs, and Joe W. Hann male age 2 yrs are not Cherokees by blood. P.O. McKinny[sic] Texas.

Attest
    D.S. Williams
    Asst Clk Com

J. E. Gunter   Com

Cherokee Citizenship Commission Docket Books
(1880-84, 1887-89) Volume IV
Tahlequah, Cherokee Nation

HERNDON

DOCKET #1457
CENSUS ROLLS 1835 or Old Settlers

APPLICANT FOR **CHEROKEE CITIZENSHIP**

POST OFFICE: McKinney Texas		ATTORNEY: Wm A Thompson	
No	NAMES	AGE	SEX
1	Benj Z. Herndon	36	Male
2	Felix "	11	"
3	Ben "	6	"
4	Lee "	8	"
5	Mack "	4	"
6	Mary "	2	Female

ANCESTOR: Jack McGarrah

Rejected June 26th 1889

Office Commission on Citizenship
Cherokee Nation
Tahlequah June 26th 1889

The above named case having been submitted by Attorney without evidence the Commission decide against Applicant Benj Z. Herndon aged 36 yrs and his daughter Mary Herndon aged 2 yrs and his sons, Felix Herndon aged 11 yrs, Lee Herndon 8 yrs, Ben Herndon 6 yrs and Mack Herndon 4 yrs. P.O. McKinny[sic] Texas.

Attest
   D.S. Williams
   Asst. Clk. Com   J E Gunter   Com

HERNDON

DOCKET #1458
CENSUS ROLLS 1835 or Old Settler

APPLICANT FOR **CHEROKEE CITIZENSHIP**

POST OFFICE: McKinney Texas		ATTORNEY: Wm A. Thompson	
No	NAMES	AGE	SEX
1	John D Herndon	39	Male
2	Nat "	11	"
3	Harry "	9	"
4	Willie "	5	"
5	(Illegible) '	13	Female

Cherokee Citizenship Commission Docket Books
(1880-84, 1887-89) Volume IV
Tahlequah, Cherokee Nation

| 6 | Lizzie " | 3 | " |

ANCESTOR: Jack McGarrah

Rejected June 26th 1889

Office Commission on Citizenship
Cherokee Nation
Tahlequah June 26th 1889

The above named case having been submitted without evidence the Commission decide that applicant John D Herndon aged 39 yrs, Nat Herndon eleven years, Harry Herndon nine years, Willie Herndon five years sons and *(Illegible)* Herndon thirteen years and Lizzie Herndon three yrs daughters of McKinny[sic] Texas are not of Cherokee blood.

Attest
    D.S. Williams
    Asst Clk Com

                              J.E. Gunter   Com

HENLY

DOCKET #1459
CENSUS ROLLS

APPLICANT FOR **CHEROKEE CITIZENSHIP**

POST OFFICE: Lebo Kansas		ATTORNEY: L.B. Bell	
No	NAMES	AGE	SEX
1	John R. Henly		

ANCESTOR: Sarah Elmore
Adverse. See decision of Commission
in case Z. R. Henly Docket 653, Book B
Page 266.

                              JE Gunter   Com

HUDSON

DOCKET #1460
CENSUS ROLLS 1835 to 52

APPLICANT FOR **CHEROKEE CITIZENSHIP**

POST OFFICE: Van Buren Ark		ATTORNEY: A E Ivey	
No	NAMES	AGE	SEX
1	Martha Hudson	65	Female

Cherokee Citizenship Commission Docket Books
(1880-84, 1887-89) Volume IV
Tahlequah, Cherokee Nation

2	Amanda J "	20	"
3	Edward "	18	Male

ANCESTOR: Wm Wade

Rejected Aug 20th 1889

> Office Commission on Citizenship
> Cherokee Nation Ind Ter
> Tahlequah Aug 20th 1889

There being no evidence in support of this case the Commission decide that Martha Hudson age 65 yrs and her children Amanda J. Daughter 20 yrs and Edward Hudson male 18 yrs are not Cherokees by blood. Post Office Vanburen Ark.

Attest
    D.S. Williams   J.E. Gunter   Com
    Asst Clk Com

HUDSON

DOCKET #1461
CENSUS ROLLS 1835 to 52

APPLICANT FOR CHEROKEE CITIZENSHIP

POST OFFICE: Van Buren Ark		ATTORNEY: A E Ivey	
No	NAMES	AGE	SEX
1	David Hudson	25	Male
2	Walter "	2	"

ANCESTOR: Wm Wade

Rejected Aug 20th 1889

> Office Commission on Citizenship
> Cherokee Nation Ind Ter
> Tahlequah Aug 20th 1889

There being no evidence in support of this case the Commission decide that David Hudson age 25 yrs and his son Walter Hudson age 2 yrs are not Cherokees by blood. P.O. Van Buren Ark.

Attest
    D.S. Williams
    Asst Clk Com   J.E. Gunter   Com

Cherokee Citizenship Commission Docket Books
(1880-84, 1887-89) Volume IV
Tahlequah, Cherokee Nation

HUDSON

DOCKET #1462
CENSUS ROLLS 1835 to 52

APPLICANT FOR CHEROKEE CITIZENSHIP

POST OFFICE: Rudy Ark		ATTORNEY: A E Ivey	
NO	NAMES	AGE	SEX
1	Joseph C Hudson, Jr	30	Male

ANCESTOR: Wm Wade

Rejected Aug 20th 1889

Office Commission on Citizenship
Cherokee Nation Ind Ter
Tahlequah Aug 20th 1889

There being no evidence in support of this case the Commission decide that Joseph C Hudson age 30 yrs is not a Cherokee by blood.
Post Rudy Ark

Attest
    D.S. Williams
    Asst Clk Com

JE Gunter Com

HUDSON

DOCKET #1463
CENSUS ROLLS 1835 & 52

APPLICANT FOR CHEROKEE CITIZENSHIP

POST OFFICE: Van Buren Ark		ATTORNEY: A E Ivey	
NO	NAMES	AGE	SEX
1	Joseph C Hudson. Sr.	42	Male
2	Hamilton "	18	"
3	Monroe "	16	"
4	James "	14	"
5	Gideon "	12	"
6	Elmore "	10	"
7	Argal "	9	"
8	Cleveland "	6	"

ANCESTOR: Wm Wade

Rejected Aug 20th 1889

Cherokee Citizenship Commission Docket Books
(1880-84, 1887-89) Volume IV
Tahlequah, Cherokee Nation

Office Commission on Citizenship
Cherokee Nation Ind Ter
Tahlequah Aug 20th 1889

There being no evidence in support of this case the Commission decide that Joseph C Hudson Sr. age 42 yrs and the following children Hamilton Hudson male 18 yrs, Monroe male 16 yrs, James male 14 yrs, Gideon male 12 yrs, Elmore male 10 yrs, Argal male 8 yrs, and Cleveland Hudson male 6 yrs. are not Cherokees by blood. P.O. Van Buren Ark.

Attest
    D.S. Williams
    Asst Clk Com   JE Gunter   Com

HIGDON

DOCKET #1464
CENSUS ROLLS 1835 & 52

APPLICANT FOR CHEROKEE CITIZENSHIP

POST OFFICE: Grapevine Texas		ATTORNEY: A E Ivey	
NO	NAMES	AGE	SEX
1	Mrs. Hidgon	37	Female

ANCESTOR: Mike Waters

Rejected Aug 20th 1889

Office Commission on Citizenship
Cherokee Nation Ind Ter
Tahlequah Aug 20th 1889

There being no evidence in support of this case the Commission decide that Mrs. Higdon age 27[sic] yrs is not a Cherokee by blood. Post Office Grapevine Tex.

Attest
    D.S. Williams   JE Gunter   Com
    Asst Clk Com

Cherokee Citizenship Commission Docket Books
(1880-84, 1887-89) Volume IV
Tahlequah, Cherokee Nation

HUDSON

DOCKET #1465
CENSUS ROLLS 1835 & 52

APPLICANT FOR CHEROKEE CITIZENSHIP

POST OFFICE: Rudy Ark		ATTORNEY: AE Ivey	
No	NAMES	AGE	SEX
1	Andrew J Hudson	27	Male
2	Andrew J " Jr.	6	"
3	Jas F "	5	"
4	Ada B "	3	Female
5	Mary A. "	1	"

ANCESTOR: Wm Wade

Rejected Aug 20th 1889

Office Commission on Citizenship
Cherokee Nation Ind Ter
Tahlequah Aug 20th 1889

There being no evidence in support of this case the Commission decide that Andrew J Hudson age 27 yrs and the following children Andrew J Hudson male age 6 yrs, Jas. F. male 5 yrs, Ada B female age 3 yrs and Mary A Hudson female age 1 yr are not Cherokees by blood. Post Office Rudy Ark.

Attest
    D.S. Williams
    Asst Clk Com   JE Gunter   Com

HUDSON

DOCKET #1466
CENSUS ROLLS 1835 to 52

APPLICANT FOR CHEROKEE CITIZENSHIP

POST OFFICE: Van Buren Ark		ATTORNEY: A E Ivey	
No	NAMES	AGE	SEX
1	Washington L Hudson	28	Male
2	Edward "	5	"

ANCESTOR: William Wade

Rejected Aug 22nd 1889

Office Commission on Citizenship
Cherokee Nation Ind Ter
Tahlequah Aug 22nd 1889

Cherokee Citizenship Commission Docket Books
(1880-84, 1887-89) Volume IV
Tahlequah, Cherokee Nation

Application for Citizenship.

This case having been submitted by the Attorneys without evidence the Commission decide that Washington L Hudson age 28 years and his son Edward Hudson age 5 years are not Cherokees by blood. Address Van Buren Ark.

Attest
    D.S. Williams
    Asst Clk Com   JE Gunter Com

HUGHS

DOCKET #1467
CENSUS ROLLS 1835 to 1852

APPLICANT FOR CHEROKEE CITIZENSHIP

POST OFFICE: Wee-woo-lea I.T.		ATTORNEY:	
NO	NAMES	AGE	SEX
1	Mary Hughs	27	Female

ANCESTOR: John Sanders

Rejected Aug 22nd 1889

                              Office Commission on Citizenship
                                  Cherokee Nation Ind Ter
                                  Tahlequah Aug 22nd 1889

Application for Citizenship.

This case having been submitted by the Attorneys without evidence the Commission decide that Mary Hugh[sic] age 27 years is not of Cherokee blood. Address Wee-woo-lea I.T.

Attest
    D.S. Williams
    Asst Clk Com   JE Gunter Com

Cherokee Citizenship Commission Docket Books
(1880-84, 1887-89) Volume IV
Tahlequah, Cherokee Nation

HALE

DOCKET #1468
CENSUS ROLLS 1835 to 52

APPLICANT FOR CHEROKEE CITIZENSHIP

POST OFFICE: Little River Texas		ATTORNEY: A E Ivey	
No	NAMES	AGE	SEX
1	N J Hale	21	Male

ANCESTOR: *(Name Illegible)*

Rejected Aug 22nd 1889

                               Office Commission on Citizenship
                               Cherokee Nation Ind Ter
                               Tahlequah Aug 22nd 1889

Application for Citizenship.

This case having been submitted by the Attorneys without evidence the Commission decide that N.J. Hale age 21 years is not of Cherokee blood. Address Little River Tex.

Attest
    D.S. Williams   J E Gunter   Com
    Asst Clk Com

HIGHLAND

DOCKET #1469
CENSUS ROLLS 1835 to 52

APPLICANT FOR CHEROKEE CITIZENSHIP

POST OFFICE: Logan Ark		ATTORNEY: A E Ivey	
No	NAMES	AGE	SEX
1	Wm H Highland	12	Male
2	Chas E "	9	"
3	Minnesota "	8	Female

ANCESTOR: Snodgrass

Rejected Aug 22nd 1889

                               Office Commission on Citizenship
                               Cherokee Nation Ind Ter
                               Tahlequah Aug 22nd 1889

Application for Citizenship.

Cherokee Citizenship Commission Docket Books
(1880-84, 1887-89) Volume IV
Tahlequah, Cherokee Nation

This case having been submitted by the Attorneys without evidence the Commission decide that Willie H Highland age 12 years, Charles E Highland and Minnesoto[sic] Highland are not Cherokees by blood. Address Logan Ark.

Attest   J E Gunter   Com
    D.S. Williams
   Asst   Clk Com

HALE

DOCKET #1470
CENSUS ROLLS 135 to 52

APPLICANT FOR CHEROKEE CITIZENSHIP

POST OFFICE: Little River Texas		ATTORNEY: A E Ivey	
NO	NAMES	AGE	SEX
1	Mrs. T. E. Hale	48	Female
2	W.D.C. "	20	Male
3	A.E. "	18	Female
4	W.E.W. "	11	"
5	W.F. "	16	Male

ANCESTOR: *(Name Illegible)*

Rejected Aug 22nd 1889

                         Office Commission on Citizenship
                               Cherokee Nation Ind Ter
                               Tahlequah   Aug 22nd 1889

Application for Citizenship.

This case having been submitted without evidence by the Attorneys the Commission decide that Mrs. T.E. Hale age 48 years and her children D.W.C.[sic] Hale age 20 years, W.F. Hale age 16 years, A.E. Hale age 18 years & W.E.W. Hale age 11 years are not Cherokees by blood. Address Little River Tex.

Attest
    D.S. Williams   JE Gunter   Com
   Asst Clk Com

Cherokee Citizenship Commission Docket Books
(1880-84, 1887-89) Volume IV
Tahlequah, Cherokee Nation

HENRY

DOCKET #1471
CENSUS ROLLS 1835 & 52

APPLICANT FOR **CHEROKEE CITIZENSHIP**

POST OFFICE:		ATTORNEY: A E Ivey	
No	NAMES	AGE	SEX
1	Mary Jane Henry	35	Female
2	Addie M "	14	"
3	Chas C "	12	Male
4	Wm "	10	"
5	Rillie F "	8	"
6	Dolph "	6	"
7	Mary J. "	4	Female
8	Ruby L "	1	Male[sic]

ANCESTOR: Nancy Jane Henry

Office Commission on Citizenship
Tahlequah IT Aug 21st 1889

This case having been submitted by the Attorneys without evidence the Commission decide that Mary Jane Henry aged 35 and her children Addie M, Chas C, William, Rillie, Dolph, Mary J. and Ruby L Henry aged respectfully 14, 12, 10, 8, 6, 4, and 1 year are not Cherokees by blood.
Attest
  E G Ross
    Clerk Commission   J E Gunter   Com

HOWELL

DOCKET #1472
CENSUS ROLLS 1835 & 52

APPLICANT FOR **CHEROKEE CITIZENSHIP**

POST OFFICE: Lavaca Sebastian Co Ark		ATTORNEY: AE Ivey	
No	NAMES	AGE	SEX
1	Andrew Jackson Howell	45	Male
2	Robert E Lee "	18	"
3	George Washington "	13	"
4	Wm Oscar "	14	"
5	Wm Halbert "	11	"
6	Joseph Mathew "	10	"

Cherokee Citizenship Commission Docket Books
(1880-84, 1887-89) Volume IV
Tahlequah, Cherokee Nation

7	*(Illegible)* B.	"	5	"
8	Wm Edward	"	6	"
9	Edna Olly	"	18	Female
10	Doly *(Illegible)*	"	8	"
11	Maggie	"	1	"

ANCESTOR: Mima Franklin

Now on this the 9th day of January 1888, comes the above case up for a final hearing, the applicants having made application pursuant to the provisions of an Act of the National Council approved December 8th 1886, and all the evidence being duly considered in the Mary A Couch case which was made *(illegible...)* to govern all other cases claiming *(illegible...)*

The decision in the Mary A Couch case found on Docket "A", page 100, governs this case.

        J T Adair   Chairman Commission
        D W Lipe   Commissioner

HENDERSON

DOCKET #1473
CENSUS ROLLS 1835 & 52

APPLICANT FOR CHEROKEE CITIZENSHIP

POST OFFICE: Huntsville Ark		ATTORNEY: A E Ivey	
No	NAMES	AGE	SEX
1	James Henderson	36	Male

ANCESTOR: James Smith

        Office Commission on Citizenship
        Cherokee Nation Ind Ter
        Tahlequah Sept 13 1889

The above applicant was called three times and no answer and there being no evidence on file in support of the application the Commission decide against claimant James Henderson age thirty six years. Post Office Huntsville Ark.
Attest
    E G Ross
    Clerk Com   JE Gunter   Com

Cherokee Citizenship Commission Docket Books
(1880-84, 1887-89) Volume IV
Tahlequah, Cherokee Nation

HARP

DOCKET #1474
CENSUS ROLLS 1835 & 52

APPLICANT FOR CHEROKEE CITIZENSHIP

POST OFFICE: Huntsville Ark		ATTORNEY: A E Ivey	
No	NAMES	AGE	SEX
1	Isabella Harp	34	Female

ANCESTOR: James Smith

Office Commission on Citizenship
Tahlequah I T August 21st 1889

This case having been submitted by the Attorneys without evidence the Commission decide that Isabella Harp age 34 years is not a Cherokee by blood. Post Office Huntsville Ark.
Attest
    E G Ross
        Clerk Commission   JE Gunter Com

HAUKS

DOCKET #1475
CENSUS ROLLS 1835, 48, 51 & 52

APPLICANT FOR CHEROKEE CITIZENSHIP

POST OFFICE: Uz[sic] Texas		ATTORNEY: Boudinot & Rasmus	
No	NAMES	AGE	SEX
1	Lizzie Hauks	18	Female

ANCESTOR: Moton

Office Commission on Citizenship
Tahlequah IT Aug 28th 1889

The above case was called for a hearing and submitted by E.C. Boudinot Atty without evidence. The Commission therefore decide that Lizzie Hauks aged 18 years is not a Cherokee by blood.
Attest
    E G Ross Clerk Commission   JE Gunter Com

Cherokee Citizenship Commission Docket Books
(1880-84, 1887-89) Volume IV
Tahlequah, Cherokee Nation

HOSKINS

DOCKET #1476
CENSUS ROLLS

APPLICANT FOR CHEROKEE CITIZENSHIP

POST OFFICE:		ATTORNEY: L B Bell	
No	NAMES	AGE	SEX
1	Marion Hoskins		Male

ANCESTOR: Ann Crews

The Commission decide against claimant. See decision in the case of Andrew Meredith Docket 2180 Book E, Page 26 and John Henly Docket 1250, Book C Page 346.

John E. Gunter   Com

HUDSON

DOCKET #1477
CENSUS ROLLS 1835 & 52

APPLICANT FOR CHEROKEE CITIZENSHIP

POST OFFICE: Van Buren Ark		ATTORNEY: A E Ivey	
No	NAMES	AGE	SEX
1	Chas F Hudson	22	Male
2	Laura "	5	Female
3	Fannie "	3	"
4	Edward "	1	Male

ANCESTOR: Wm Wade

Commission on Citizenship
Tahlequah Ind Ter Aug 21st 1889

This case having been submitted by the Attorneys without evidence the Commission decide that Chas F Hudson age 22 years and his children Laura, Fannie and Edward Hudson are not Cherokees by blood.
Attest
    E G Ross
        Clerk Commission   JE Gunter   Com

Cherokee Citizenship Commission Docket Books
(1880-84, 1887-89) Volume IV
Tahlequah, Cherokee Nation

HUDSON

DOCKET #1478
CENSUS ROLLS 1835 & 52

APPLICANT FOR CHEROKEE CITIZENSHIP

POST OFFICE: Van Buren Ark		ATTORNEY: AE Ivey	
NO	NAMES	AGE	SEX
1	James T Hudson	36	Male
2	Barbary A "	20	Female

ANCESTOR: Wm Wade

Office Commission on Citizenship
Cherokee Nation Ind Ter
Tahlequah August 21st 1889

This case having been submitted by the Attorneys without evidence the Commission decide that James T Hudson age 36 years and his daughter Barbary A Hudson age 20 years are not Cherokees by blood.
Attest
    EG Ross
        Clerk Commission   J E Gunter Com

HUBBARD

DOCKET #1479
CENSUS ROLLS

APPLICANT FOR CHEROKEE CITIZENSHIP

POST OFFICE: Chetopa Kas		ATTORNEY: Boudinot & Rasmus	
NO	NAMES	AGE	SEX
1	Jane Hubbard	53	Female
2	George "		Male
3	Anna "		Female
4	Mattie "		"
5	Lizzie "		"

ANCESTOR:

Commission on Citizenship.

CHEROKEE NATION, IND. TER.

Tahlequah, August 27th 1889

Cherokee Citizenship Commission Docket Books
(1880-84, 1887-89) Volume IV
Tahlequah, Cherokee Nation

Jane Hubbard
vs
The Cherokee Nation

The applicant for readmission to Citizenship in the Cherokee Nation in the above case made her declaration before T. Caldwell a Notary Public in Labette County State of Kansas, on the 29th day of August 1887 and filed her application before the Commission on Citizenship on the 5th day of October A.D. 1887. From her declaration it appears that she is the daughter of one John Reese who it is said was part Cherokee Indian and of one Sally Thomas, a quadroon who was owned and held as a slave by one Nathan Thomas of Williamson County State of Tennessee and that in 1844 her reputed father John Reese endeavored to purchase her recognizing her as his daughter, from her owner, but failing to do so tried to *(illegible)* to kidnap her and was forced to leave the state and was not again seen. *(Illegible...)* by one Mary Rucker and Philip Rucker who resided in Williamson County at the time of her birth. The affidavit an exparte and do not show state how they knew John Reese to be a Cherokee, or that he ever lived in the Cherokee Country or yet engaged any of the rights and privileges of Cherokee Citizenship. John Reese her alleged father was alive according to the statement of the from claimant in 1844 and if a bona fide citizen of the Cherokee Nation his name should appear on the census roll of Cherokees by blood taken and made by the United States in the year 1835 but it does is not found there. The Commission therefore decide that the above named Jane Hubbard age 53 years and her children George Hubbard (male), Anna Hubbard, Mattie Hubbard and Lizzie Hubbard ages not given are not of Cherokee blood and and not entitled to citizenship in the Cherokee Nation.

Will. P. Ross
Chairman
J E Gunter Com

HUFF

DOCKET #1480
CENSUS ROLLS

APPLICANT FOR CHEROKEE CITIZENSHIP

POST OFFICE: Chicago Ills		ATTORNEY: L B Bell	
NO	NAMES	AGE	SEX
1	Atwood Huff	26	Male

ANCESTOR: Ann Crews

Cherokee Citizenship Commission Docket Books
(1880-84, 1887-89) Volume IV
Tahlequah, Cherokee Nation

The Commission decide against claimant. See decision in the case of Andrew Meredith Docket 2180 Book E, Page 26 and John Henly Docket 1250, Book C Page 346.

           John E Gunter Com

HANNAH

DOCKET #1481
CENSUS ROLLS 1835 & 52

APPLICANT FOR CHEROKEE CITIZENSHIP

POST OFFICE: *(Illegible)* I.T.		ATTORNEY: AE Ivey	
NO	NAMES	AGE	SEX
1	M. A. Hannah	32	Female

ANCESTOR: *(Name Illegible)*

          Office Commission on Citizenship
             Tahlequah August 21st 1889

This case having been submitted by the Attorneys without evidence, the Commission decide that M. A. Hannah age 32 years is not of Cherokee blood.
Attest
  E G Ross
    Clerk Commission   JE. Gunter Com

HANNAH

DOCKET #1482
CENSUS ROLLS 1835

APPLICANT FOR CHEROKEE CITIZENSHIP

POST OFFICE: Tahlequah Ind Ter		ATTORNEY: Ivey & Welch	
NO	NAMES	AGE	SEX
1	Mary J Hannah	23	Female
2	W. L. "	12	"
3	George Ann "	10	"
4	James A "	8	Male
5	B. F. "	4	"

ANCESTOR: George Welch

Cherokee Citizenship Commission Docket Books
(1880-84, 1887-89) Volume IV
Tahlequah, Cherokee Nation

Office Commission on Citizenship
Cherokee Nation Ind Ter
Tahlequah August 21st 1889

This case having been submitted by the Attorneys without evidence the Commission decide that Mary J Hannah age 23 years and her children M.[sic] L. Hannah age 12 years, George Ann Hannah age 10 years, James A. Hannah age 8 years and B. F. Hannah age 4 years are not Cherokees by blood. Post Office Tahlequah I.T.
Attest
    E G Ross
        Clerk Commission   JE Gunter Com

RAPER

DOCKET #1483
CENSUS ROLLS 1835, 48, 51 & 52 or Old Settler

APPLICANT FOR CHEROKEE CITIZENSHIP

	POST OFFICE: Davis Tenn	ATTORNEY: Boudinot & Rasmus	
No	NAMES	AGE	SEX
1	Nathaniel Raper	34	Male
2	James P "	12	"
3	Thos H. "	10	"
4	Mora E "	6	Female
5	Pearl M. "	4	"
6	Samuel D. "	2	Male

ANCESTOR: Charles Raper & Jane & Polly Raper

Now on this the 23rd day of April 1888, comes the above case up for final hearing, they having made application pursuant to the provisions of an Act of the National Council approved Dec 8th 1886, and all the evidence being duly examined and found to be sufficient and satisfactory to the Commission, it is adjudged and determined by the Commission that Nathaniel Raper, James P Raper, Thos H. Raper, Mora E. Raper, Pearl M. Raper and Samuel D. Raper are Cherokees by blood, and they are hereby re-admitted to all the rights, privileges and immunities of Cherokee citizens by blood and a certificate of the Commission and of re-admission was made and furnished said parties accordingly.

                J T. Adair   Chairman Commission
                John E Gunter   Commissioner

Cherokee Citizenship Commission Docket Books
(1880-84, 1887-89) Volume IV
Tahlequah, Cherokee Nation

The evidence in this case will be found in the Charles Raper Jr. case.

RYE

DOCKET #1484
CENSUS ROLLS 1835, 48, 51 & 52

APPLICANT FOR CHEROKEE CITIZENSHIP

POST OFFICE: *(Illegible)* Ark		ATTORNEY: Boudinot & Rasmus	
No	NAMES	AGE	SEX
1	Treshram M Rye	27	Male

ANCESTOR: Hannah Thomas

See decision the this case in the William T. Rye case in Docket "D" Page 8 – Adverse.

          Cornell Rogers
          Clerk Com. on Citizenship

Office Com on Citizenship
Tahlequah, I.T. July 9th '88.

ROLAND

DOCKET #1485
CENSUS ROLLS 1835

APPLICANT FOR CHEROKEE CITIZENSHIP

POST OFFICE: Kansas City Mo		ATTORNEY:	
No	NAMES	AGE	SEX
1	Mary Ann Roland	51	Female

ANCESTOR: *(Names Illegible)*

        Office Commission on Citizenship
         Cherokee Nation Ind Ter
         Tahlequah Aug 21 1889

  This case having been submitted by the Attorneys without evidence the Commission decide that Mary Ann Roland aged 51 years and her three children whose names are not given are not Cherokees by blood.
Attest
  EG Ross
    Clerk Commission   JE Gunter Com

Cherokee Citizenship Commission Docket Books
(1880-84, 1887-89) Volume IV
Tahlequah, Cherokee Nation

RUSHING

DOCKET #1486
CENSUS ROLLS 1835, 48, 51 & 52

APPLICANT FOR **CHEROKEE CITIZENSHIP**

POST OFFICE: Cabbin Creek Ark		ATTORNEY: Boudinot & Rasmus	
No	NAMES	AGE	SEX
1	James W Rushing	35	Male
2	Lena May "	9	Female
3	Anna Bell "	2	"

ANCESTOR: Barsheba Goodrich

Rejected June 20th 1889

Office Commission on Citizenship
Cherokee Nation
Tahlequah June 20th 1889

There being no evidence in support of this case the Commission decide that James W Rushing aged thirty five years and his daughters Lena May Rushing aged nine years and Anna Bell Rushing aged two years of Cabin Creek Arkansas are not of Cherokee blood.

Attest
    D.S. Williams   JE Gunter   Com
    Asst Clk Com

RUSHING

DOCKET #1487
CENSUS ROLLS 1835, 48, 51 & 52

APPLICANT FOR **CHEROKEE CITIZENSHIP**

POST OFFICE: Dover Ark		ATTORNEY: Boudinot & Rasmus	
No	NAMES	AGE	SEX
1	David H Rushing	45	Male
2	J. W "	19	"
3	Henrietta "	17	Female
4	Maggie "	15	"
5	Nancy Mc "	7	"
6	Mary T. "	5	"
7	Delva C "	1	"

ANCESTOR: Barsheba Goodrich

Cherokee Citizenship Commission Docket Books
(1880-84, 1887-89) Volume IV
Tahlequah, Cherokee Nation

Office Commission on Citizenship
Cherokee Nation Ind Ter
Tahlequah June 20th 1889

There being no evidence in support of this case the Commission decide that David H Rushing aged 45 years and the following children J.W Male aged 19 years, Henrietta Female aged 17 years, Maggie Female aged 15 years, Nancy Mc Female aged 7 years, Mary T Female aged 5 years and Delva C Rushing Female aged 1 year are not of Cherokee blood. Post Office Dover Ark.
Attest
   E G Ross
     Clerk Commission

                              J E Gunter Com

RUSHING

DOCKET #1488
CENSUS ROLLS 1835, 48, 51 & 52

APPLICANT FOR **CHEROKEE CITIZENSHIP**

POST OFFICE: Russellville Ark		ATTORNEY: Boudinot & Rasmus	
NO	NAMES	AGE	SEX
1	Geo W Rushing	50	Male
2	Mary F "	18	Female
3	James H. "	17	Male
4	Robt T. "	15	"
5	Geo W. "	13	"
6	Henry A "	9	"
7	Myrtle M "	6	Female
8	Thomas L "	2	Male

ANCESTOR: Barsheba Goodrich

Office Commission on Citizenship
Tahlequah C N June 20th 1889

The above named case was submitted without evidence the Commission decide that George W Rushing aged 50 years and the following named children Mary F Female age 18 years, James H Male aged 17 years, Robt T Male aged 15 years, Geo W. Male aged 13 years, Henry A Male aged 9 years, Myrtle M Female aged 6 years, Thomas L Male aged 2 years are not Cherokees by blood. Post Office Russellville Ark.

Cherokee Citizenship Commission Docket Books
(1880-84, 1887-89) Volume IV
Tahlequah, Cherokee Nation

Attest
    EG Ross
        Clerk Commission   JE Gunter Com

ROREY

DOCKET #1489
CENSUS ROLLS 1835, 48, 51 & 52

APPLICANT FOR CHEROKEE CITIZENSHIP

POST OFFICE: Russellville Ark		ATTORNEY:	
NO	NAMES	AGE	SEX
1	James W Rorey	43	Male
2	George L. "	19	"
3	John F. "	17	"
4	Samuel I "	15	"
5	Sarah E. "	12	Female
6	Lee "	6	"
7	Sidney "	4	Male

ANCESTOR: Polly Kays

                          Adversely.
                See book "B" Page 467

Attest
    EG Ross
        Clerk Commission

RAMSEY

DOCKET #1490
CENSUS ROLLS 1835

APPLICANT FOR CHEROKEE CITIZENSHIP

POST OFFICE: Union Town Ark		ATTORNEY: A E Ivey	
NO	NAMES	AGE	SEX
1	Martha Ramsey	16	Female

ANCESTOR: Tina Ramsey

Rejected Aug 22nd 1889

                    Office Commission on Citizenship
                         Cherokee Nation Ind Ter
                           Tahlequah Aug 22nd 1889

Application for Citizenship.

Cherokee Citizenship Commission Docket Books
(1880-84, 1887-89) Volume IV
Tahlequah, Cherokee Nation

This case having been submitted by the Attorneys without evidence the Commission decide that Martha Ramsey age 16 years is not of Cherokee blood. Address Union Town Ark.

Attest
    D.S. Williams   JE Gunter   Com
    Asst   Clk Com

RIFE

DOCKET #1491
CENSUS ROLLS 1835

APPLICANT FOR **CHEROKEE CITIZENSHIP**

POST OFFICE: Van Buren Ark		ATTORNEY: AE Ivey	
No	NAMES	AGE	SEX
1	Zeda Rife	26	Female
2	Infant "	2 da	"

ANCESTOR: Tandy Critenden

Rejected Aug 22nd 1889

                                       Office Commission on Citizenship
                                       Cherokee Nation Ind Ter
                                       Tahlequah   Aug 22nd 1889

Application for Citizenship

This case having been submitted by the Attorneys without evidence the Commission decide that Zeda Rife age 26 and her infant daughter 2 days old are not Cherokees by blood. Address Van Buren Ark.

Attest
    D.S. Williams   J. E Gunter   Com
    Asst Clerk Com

RANDOLPH

DOCKET #1492
CENSUS ROLLS 1835

APPLICANT FOR **CHEROKEE CITIZENSHIP**

POST OFFICE: Mulberry Ark		ATTORNEY: A E Ivey	
No	NAMES	AGE	SEX
1	Benjamin K Randolph	38	Male

Cherokee Citizenship Commission Docket Books
(1880-84, 1887-89) Volume IV
Tahlequah, Cherokee Nation

2		Mary B. "	12	Female
3		Birdie C "	9	"
4		Myrtle R. "	6	"

ANCESTOR: Randolph

Office Commission on Citizenship
Tahlequah IT Aug 21st 1889

There being no evidence in support of this case the Commission decide that Benjamin K Randolph age 38 years and his children Mary B Randolph 12 years of age, Birdie C Randolph age 9 years, and Myrtle R Randolph age 6 years are not Cherokees by blood and not entitled to Cherokee citizenship in the Nation.
Attest
    EG Ross
        Clerk Commission   JE Gunter Com

REDDEN

DOCKET #1493
CENSUS ROLLS 1835

APPLICANT FOR CHEROKEE CITIZENSHIP

POST OFFICE: Read land I.T.		ATTORNEY: A E Ivey	
No	NAMES	AGE	SEX
1	Ruth Redden	32	Female
2	Stella "	6	"
3	Clifford "	4	Male

ANCESTOR: Tandy Crittenden

Office Commission on Citizenship
Cherokee Nation Ind Ter
Tahlequah August 21st 1889

This case having been submitted without evidence by the Attorneys the Commission decide that Ruth Redden age thirty two years and her children Stella Redden and Clifford Redden are not Cherokees by blood.
Attest
    E G Ross
        Clerk Commission   JE Gunter Com

Cherokee Citizenship Commission Docket Books
(1880-84, 1887-89) Volume IV
Tahlequah, Cherokee Nation

RAPER

DOCKET #1494
CENSUS ROLLS 1851

APPLICANT FOR CHEROKEE CITIZENSHIP

POST OFFICE: Craytia[sic] Ga		ATTORNEY: AE Ivey	
No	NAMES	AGE	SEX
1	Jack Raper	34	Male
2	Hattie "	10	Female
3	Georgia A. "	9	"
4	John H "	6	Male
5	William "	2	"

ANCESTOR: Alexander Raper

Office Commission on Citizenship
Cherokee Nation Ind Ter
Tahlequah Sept 14th 1889

The above case was filed on the 5th day of October 1887 and being called was set for September 16th 1889 for a hearing and according to the time set. The case was again called but no response from applicant or by attorney and there being no evidence on file in support of applicant the Commission decide that Jack Raper age 34 years and the following children Hattie age 10 years, Georgia A age 9 years, John H age 4 years and William Raper age 2 years are not of Cherokee blood.
Attest
    EG Ross
        Clerk Commission   J.E. Gunter   Com

RICKER

DOCKET #1495
CENSUS ROLLS 1835 & 52

APPLICANT FOR CHEROKEE CITIZENSHIP

POST OFFICE: Van Buren Ark		ATTORNEY: A.E. Ivey	
No	NAMES	AGE	SEX
1	Frank Ricker	38	Male
2	George "	13	"
3	Margaret "	13	Female
4	Martha "	11	"
5	Thomas "	8	Male

Cherokee Citizenship Commission Docket Books
(1880-84, 1887-89) Volume IV
Tahlequah, Cherokee Nation

6	Celia "	1	Female

ANCESTOR: Sam'l & Hulda Moton

Rejected Aug 22 1889

Office Commission on Citizenship
Tahlequah I.T. Aug 22 1889

This case was filed on the 5th day of Oct 1887 and was submitted without evidence the Commission therefore decide that Frank Ricker age 38 years and the children George, Margaret, Martha, Thomas & Celia Ricker are not Cherokees by blood. Post Office Van Buren Ark.

D.S. Williams
Asst Clerk Commission

JE Gunter Com

RICKEY

DOCKET #1496
CENSUS ROLLS 1835 & 52

APPLICANT FOR **CHEROKEE CITIZENSHIP**

POST OFFICE: Van Buren Ark		ATTORNEY: A E Ivey	
NO	NAMES	AGE	SEX
1	Dora Rickey	25	Female

ANCESTOR: John Edgly

Rejected Aug 22 1889

Office Commission on Citizenship
Tahlequah I.T. Aug 22 1889

The application in this case was filed on the 5th day of Oct 1887 and was submitted by Atty A.E. Ivey without evidence the Commission therefore decide that Dora Rickey age 25 years is not a Cherokee by blood. Post Office Van Buren Ark.

D.S. Williams
Asst. Clk Com

JEGunter Com

Cherokee Citizenship Commission Docket Books
(1880-84, 1887-89) Volume IV
Tahlequah, Cherokee Nation

RICKS

DOCKET #1497
CENSUS ROLLS 1835 & 52

APPLICANT FOR **CHEROKEE CITIZENSHIP**

POST OFFICE: Van Buren Ark		ATTORNEY: AE Ivey	
NO	NAMES	AGE	SEX
1	Grand Ricks	22	Male

ANCESTOR: Sam & Hulda Moton

                      Office Commission on Citizenship
                      Cherokee Nation Ind Ter
                      Tahlequah August 22nd 1889

The above case was filed on the 5th day of October 1887 and was submitted by Attorney A E Ivey without evidence.

Therefore we the Commission decide that Grand Ricks age 22 years is not a Cherokee by blood. Post Office Van Buren Ark.
Attest
    EGRoss
        Clerk Commission   JE Gunter   Com

RICKS

DOCKET #1498
CENSUS ROLLS 1835 & 52

APPLICANT FOR **CHEROKEE CITIZENSHIP**

POST OFFICE: Van Buren Ark		ATTORNEY: A E Ivey	
NO	NAMES	AGE	SEX
1	Mrs Elizabeth Ricks	60	Female
2	Charles "	18	Male

ANCESTOR: Sam & Hulda Moton

                      Office Commission on Citizenship
                      Cherokee Nation Ind Ter
                      Tahlequah August 22nd 1889

This case having been submitted by the Attorneys without evidence the Commission decide that Mrs. Elizabeth Ricks age 60 years and her son Chas

Cherokee Citizenship Commission Docket Books
(1880-84, 1887-89) Volume IV
Tahlequah, Cherokee Nation

Ricks age 18 years are not Cherokees by blood and not entitled to Cherokee Citizenship.
Attest
    EG Ross
        Clerk Commission   JE Gunter   Com

RICKS

DOCKET #1499
CENSUS ROLLS 1835 & 52

APPLICANT FOR CHEROKEE CITIZENSHIP

POST OFFICE: Van Buren Ark		ATTORNEY:	
No	NAMES	AGE	SEX
1	Silas Ricks	27	Male
2	Henryetta "	8	Female
3	Lena "	3	"

ANCESTOR: Sam & Hulda Moton

Rejected Aug 22nd 1889

                Office Commission on Citizenship
                      Cherokee Nation Ind Ter
                      Tahlequah Aug 22nd 1889

Application for Cherokee Citizenship

    There is no evidence filed in support of the above application. Therefore we decide that applicants Silas Ricks age 27 yrs and his children Henryetta Ricks age 8 yrs and Lena Ricks age 3 yrs are not Cherokees by blood.
Post Office Van Buren Ark.

Attest
    D.S. Williams
    Asst Clk Com   J.E. Gunter   Com

RUSSELL

DOCKET #1500
CENSUS ROLLS 1835 & 52

APPLICANT FOR CHEROKEE CITIZENSHIP

POST OFFICE:		ATTORNEY: A E Ivey	
No	NAMES	AGE	SEX
1	William C Russell	57	Male

Cherokee Citizenship Commission Docket Books
(1880-84, 1887-89) Volume IV
Tahlequah, Cherokee Nation

2	James "	34	"
3	Brinkley "	32	"
4	Nathan "	30	"
5	John "	20	"

ANCESTOR: John Henderson

Rejected Aug 22 1889

Office Commission on Citizenship
Tahlequah I T Aug 22 1889

No evidence filed in support of the above application. Therefore we decide that applicant William C. Russell age 57 and his children James Russell age 34 yrs, Brinkey[sic] Russell age 30[sic] yrs, John Russell age 20 yrs are not Cherokees by blood.
Roff Post Office

D.S. Williams
Asst Clk Com   JEGunter   Com

ROGERS

DOCKET #1501
CENSUS ROLLS 1835 & 52

APPLICANT FOR CHEREKEE CITIZENSHIP

No	POST OFFICE: Alma Ark	ATTORNEY: AE Ivey	
	NAMES	**AGE**	**SEX**
1	James C.C. Rogers	40	Male
2	Ham C. "	20	"
3	Rosa "	18	Female
4	Lillie May "	16	"
5	John C "	15	Male
6	William E. "	12	"
7	Chas W. "	10	"
8	Daisy B. "	8	Female
9	Mary M. "	3	"
10	Pink "	1	"

ANCESTOR: John Rogers

Cherokee Citizenship Commission Docket Books
(1880-84, 1887-89) Volume IV
Tahlequah, Cherokee Nation

James C.C. Rogers, et al
    vs   Application for Cherokee Citizenship
Cherokee Nation

Now on this the 17th day of March A.D. 1888, comes the above entitled case for final dispositions.

This is an important case, as by this decision rests the claims of 113 of applications for citizenship in this Nation

By an agreement of Attorneys on both sides in this case, this was made a test one and that the findings of the Commission in the *(illegible)* shall govern all cases who claim to draw their Cherokee blood through this ancestor, John Rogers.

The evidence was duly and impartially weighed in all of its points and bearings upon this case.

The evidence of John S. Chastian, a nephew of the applicant shows that John Rogers, father of the applicant, lived in Hall County, Georgia, and removed from thence to Walker County of the same state, near Chattanooga, Tenn. It also shows that the applicant's father, John Rogers, lived in Georgia in the counties mentioned above, from his first *(illegible)*, and that the affiant is 54 years old. It also shows that John Rogers came to Arkansas in the year 1844, but has no knowledge that they emigrated west of the Mississippi river as Cherokees at that time, nor that they ever drew monies or subsistence as Cherokees did, it further shows that John Rogers was living in the state of Georgia previous to the year 1835, and if a Cherokee should appear upon the census Rolls of Cherokees taken in that year. The evidence further shows that the applicant is 45 years old, and lived East of the Mississippi river in Georgia in Hall & Walker Counties, of that state up to the year 1843, about the date of his birth when his father, John Rogers, moved into Arkansas, near Van Buren, from Georgia. The statement of Mr. Chastian further shows that Enoch Rogers was the grand father of applicant.

The testimony of J.W. Lacket shows that he was ~~both~~ acquainted with both the applicant and his father, but did not know who John Rogers' wife was, but had heard that she was a Petitt. Mr. Chastian says that he thinks that she was a Teague. Mr. Lacket winds up with these words; "Of my own personal knowledge I do not know that the applicants are Cherokees". The Commission

Cherokee Citizenship Commission Docket Books
(1880-84, 1887-89) Volume IV
Tahlequah, Cherokee Nation

looks upon this kind of evidence as being of a weak nature, and not entitled to the same *(illegible)* as if it had been conclusive and corroborated by other important facts in the premises. The testimony of Sarah Lacket, wife of J.W. Lacket, is in every way the same as that of Mr. Lacket, and is entitled to the same credit. She concludes: "I do not know of my own personal knowledge that these parties, the applicants, are Cherokees, other than what I have been told".

The evidence of Hon. John T. Adair shows that he was born in what is not Habersham County in the state of Georgia, and that he is 75 years old, and that he left his old home in Georgia in 1837, and also that he was well acquainted with the half breed Cherokee that lived along the border of the Old Cherokee Nation and says that he has no "knowledge of any white persons by the name of Rogers' unconnected in some way to-with the Cherokee Indians". His testimony further shows that Hall and Habersham Counties now in Georgia, were *(illegible)* to the U.S. Government, by the Cherokees in the year 1817, and that there were some Cherokees who remained in these counties as Reserves, but upon litigation affidavits, the Indians were in every case beaten, and compelled to remove into the Nation. There was one reservation in Hall County taken by Walter S. Adair, with this exception, the conclusion would nationally be that there were no Cherokees allowed to reside on the tract of country cided[sic] under the treaty of 1817. (Hall & Habersham Cos)

The testimony of Mrs. Susan Harris, shows that she was raised on the Chattahoochee river in now what is Milton County, Ga, it further shows that she knew a John Rogers, a white man, who married her Aunt, Sally Cordery, a one half breed Cherokee woman, and that by this marriage, there were, Robert, William, Jackson K, Joseph, Lovely, George, Henry C. and John P. Rogers. It further shows that John P Rogers came to this country and went to the Cherokee Nation and died. There is no evidence *(illegible)* in the testimony that shows that John P. Rogers was one and the same person as the ancestor of the applicant, nor is it so. It further shows that she knew one Enoch Rogers, a white man, who lived near her in the Old Nation, but that he nor any of his family were known to be Cherokees; that they never claimed to be Cherokees. She had forgotten the names of the sons of Enoch Rogers, but says that if he was alive that he would be an old man, the inference, if a Cherokee, would appear upon some of the Census Rolls of Cherokees taken in the Old Nation, which they do not. There is considerable documentary evidence filed in this case by the Plaintiff's Atty, that we have fully and *(illegible)* examined, Marked Document "A", "B", "C", "D", & "E".

Cherokee Citizenship Commission Docket Books
(1880-84, 1887-89) Volume IV
Tahlequah, Cherokee Nation

Therefore, we the Commission on Citizenship, after a careful investigation of the evidence, and all the Census Rolls of Cherokees in determining this case, find: that James C.C. Rogers, Ham L, Rose, Lillie May, John C, William E, Charles W, Daniel B, Mary M, and Pink Rogers in application No 1: Nancy M, Chastian in application No 2: William M, William A.J, Joseph E, Lucinda E, and John E.B. Chastian in application No. 3: John S, John B, Edward D, James B, Leona C, and Milton B. Chastian in application 4: James M, R.B, S.C, J.C, F.C, and Joseph Oceola Rogers in application No 5: Joseph C, William H, John E, Mary O, Roder[sic] L, Henry W, Charles, Walter W, and Ulyses G. Chastian in application No 6; Amanda C, William M, John B.F, James A, W.B, and A.J. Darley in application No 7; B.F, T.E, N.M, M.H, G.W, M.E, M.C, and R.F. Chastian in application No 8; M.E, M.T, E.M, M.A, W.R, & J.C. Creekmore in application No 9; Elizabeth Lipscomb, W.M.A. and Hallie Hays, (grand children) in application No 10; Nancy M. Dousilla, Jesse and A.J. Meadows in application No 11; William, John W, Rosa n, and Mary E. Losson in application No 12; Lucinda E, Walter L, E.B, Mary M, Leonard J, and Charles F. Abel in application No 13; Lafayette G, Benjamin L, Laura O.L, and Mary E Chastian in application No 14; Thomas H Wills in application No 15; Mary F, Florence, Mundamby Wallace in application No 16; A.J, Martha L, Lillian, Milo, and William Leonard Chastian in application No 17; Lucinda M, John J, Cynthia C, Cordey, and Martha C. Fox in application No 18; J.E. and Wm J.J. Darley in application No 19; Harvy Mc and Jesse E. Chastian in application No 20; Nancy E.S. Rhoads in application No 21; Benton B, James C.C, Mary C, Linsey Ann E Rogers in application No 22; John C. and Charles R. Rogers in application No 24; Mary E and Delohena Meaders in application No 25; Columbus F. and Monroe L. Nelson in application No 26; Eliza R. and Joseph Rogers in application No 27; Martha J, Charles, Cary and John D. Meadors are <u>not</u> entitled to any rights and privileges of Cherokee citizens by virtue of such blood.

                                                  J.T. Adair   Chairman Commission
                                                  John. E. Gunter Commissioner
                                                  D.W. Lipe   Commissioner

Cherokee Citizenship Commission Docket Books
(1880-84, 1887-89) Volume IV
Tahlequah, Cherokee Nation

RUSSELL

DOCKET #1502
CENSUS ROLLS 1835 & 52

APPLICANT FOR CHEROKEE CITIZENSHIP

POST OFFICE: Chalk Valley Ark		ATTORNEY: A.E. Ivey	
NO	NAMES	AGE	SEX
1	Samuel Russell	40	Male

ANCESTOR: Mary S. Bell

Rejected Aug 23rd 1889

Office Commission on Citizenship
Tahlequah I.T. Aug 23rd

The above case was filed on the 5th day of *(illegible)* 1889 and was submitted by Atty A.E Ivey without evidence. Therefore the Commission decide that Samuel Russell age 40 years is not a Cherokee by blood. Post Office Chalk Valley Ark.

D.S. Williams
Asst Clerk Commission

JE Gunter Com

RIGGS

DOCKET #1503
CENSUS ROLLS 1835 & 52

APPLICANT FOR CHEROKEE CITIZENSHIP

POST OFFICE: Carterville Mo		ATTORNEY: AE Ivey	
NO	NAMES	AGE	SEX
1	Andrew J Riggs	31	Male

ANCESTOR: Mrs. Mayfield

Rejected Aug 22 1889

Office Commission on Citizenship
Tahlequah I.T. Aug 22 1889

This case was filed on the 23rd day of Sept 1887 and was submitted by Atty AE Ivey without evidence. Now the Commission decide that Andrew J Riggs age 31 years is not a Cherokee by blood.
Post Office Carterville Mo.

JE Gunter Com

D.S. Williams
Asst Clk Com

Cherokee Citizenship Commission Docket Books
(1880-84, 1887-89) Volume IV
Tahlequah, Cherokee Nation

RIGGS

DOCKET #1504
CENSUS ROLLS 1835 & 52

APPLICANT FOR **CHEROKEE CITIZENSHIP**

POST OFFICE: Ashly[sic] Ills		ATTORNEY: A E Ivey	
NO	NAMES	AGE	SEX
1	Addison Riggs	33	Male
2	Lewis R. "	4	"

ANCESTOR: Mrs. Mayfield

Rejected Aug 22nd 1889

Office Commission on Citizenship
Tahlequah Aug 22nd 1889

The above case was filed on the 23rd day of Sept 1887 and submitted by Atty A.E. Ivey without evidence. Now the Commission decide that Addison Riggs and Lewis Riggs male 4 years are not Cherokees by blood.
Post Office Ashley Ill.

D.S. Williams
   Asst Clerk
      Commission

JE Gunter   Com

RIGGS

DOCKET #1505
CENSUS ROLLS 1835 & 52

APPLICANT FOR **CHEROKEE CITIZENSHIP**

POST OFFICE: San Angelo Texas		ATTORNEY: A E Ivey	
NO	NAMES	AGE	SEX
1	James W. Riggs	39	Male

ANCESTOR: Mrs. Mayfield

Rejected Aug 22nd 1889

Office Commission on Citizenship
Cherokee Nation Ind Ter
Tahlequah Aug 22nd 1889

Application for Cherokee Citizenship

The above application was filed on the 23rd day Sept. 1887, and on this day the case coming up for final hearing, we find no evidence filed in support of

Cherokee Citizenship Commission Docket Books
(1880-84, 1887-89) Volume IV
Tahlequah, Cherokee Nation

Applicants claim of Cherokee blood. Therefore we decide that applicant James W Riggs age 39 yrs is not a Cherokee by blood.
Post Office San Angelo Texas.

Attest   J E Gunter   Com
     D.S. Williams
     Asst Clk Com

RIGGS

DOCKET #1506
CENSUS ROLLS 1835 & 52

APPLICANT FOR CHEROKEE CITIZENSHIP

POST OFFICE: Carterville Mo		ATTORNEY: A E Ivey	
No	NAMES	AGE	SEX
1	Samuel N Riggs	29	Male
2	Addie May "	3	Female
3	Rubie L "	1	"

ANCESTOR: Mrs. Mayfield

Rejected Aug 22nd 1889

                               Office Commission on Citizenship
                               Tahlequah I.T.   Aug 22nd 1889

This case was filed on the 23 day of Sept and was submitted by Atty A E Ivey without evidence. The Commission therefore, decide that Samuel N. Riggs age 29 years and *(Illegible)* L Riggs Female 1 year are not Cherokees by blood. Post Office Carterville Mo.

D.S. Williams
Asst Clerk Commission   J E Gunter   Com

RIGGS

DOCKET #1507
CENSUS ROLLS 1835 & 52

APPLICANT FOR CHEROKEE CITIZENSHIP

POST OFFICE: Carterville Mo		ATTORNEY: A E Ivey	
No	NAMES	AGE	SEX
1	John M Riggs	35	Male
2	Josephine "	6	Female

Cherokee Citizenship Commission Docket Books
(1880-84, 1887-89) Volume IV
Tahlequah, Cherokee Nation

3	Nellie M. "	3	"
4	John "	1	Male

ANCESTOR: Mrs Mayfield

Rejected Aug 22nd 1889

Office Commission on Citizenship
Cherokee Nation Ind Ter
Tahlequah 22nd of Aug 1889

Application for Cherokee Citizenship

There is no evidence filed in the above case. Therefore we decide that applicant John M Riggs age 35 yrs & children Josephine Riggs age 6 yrs, Nellie M Riggs age 3 yrs and John Riggs age 1 yr are [sic] Cherokees by blood. Post Office Carterville Mo.

Attest
    D.S. Williams
    Asst Clk Com

J E Gunter   Com

RIGGS

DOCKET #1508
CENSUS ROLLS 1835 & 52

APPLICANT FOR CHEROKEE CITIZENSHIP

POST OFFICE: Carterville Mo		ATTORNEY:	
No	NAMES	AGE	SEX
1	Landon C.H. Riggs	26	Male
2	Walter A "	2	"
3	Lundon L "	5 mo	"

ANCESTOR: Mrs Mayfield

Office Commission on Citizenship
Cherokee Nation Ind Ter
Tahlequah Aug 22nd 1889

This case having been submitted by the Attorneys without evidence the Commission decide that Landon C H Riggs age 26 years and his children Walter A Riggs age 2 years and Lundon L Riggs age 5 months are <u>not</u> Cherokees by blood and are not entitled to Citizenship.

Cherokee Citizenship Commission Docket Books
(1880-84, 1887-89) Volume IV
Tahlequah, Cherokee Nation

Attest
    EG Ross   JE Gunter   Com
        Clerk Commission

RIGGS

DOCKET #1509
CENSUS ROLLS 1835 & 52

APPLICANT FOR CHEROKEE CITIZENSHIP

POST OFFICE:		ATTORNEY: A E Ivey	
No	NAMES	AGE	SEX
1	Charles A Riggs	23	Male

ANCESTOR: Mrs. Mayfield

                                    Office Commission on Citizenship
                                          Cherokee Nation Ind Ter
                                          Tahlequah August 22, 1889

This case having been submitted by the Attorney without evidence the Commission decide that Charles A Riggs age twenty three years is not of Cherokee blood and not entitled to Cherokee Citizenship. Address Carterville Mo.

Attest
    EG Ross
        Clerk Commission   J.E. Gunter   Com

ROE

DOCKET #1510
CENSUS ROLLS

APPLICANT FOR CHEROKEE CITIZENSHIP

POST OFFICE: Barrettsville Ga		ATTORNEY: A E Ivey	
No	NAMES	AGE	SEX
1	Annie Roe	32	Female
2	Harriett "	9	"
3	Frank "	7	Male
4	Mary T "	4	Female
5	Lewis A "	2	Male
6	Sol*(illegible)* B "	3 mo	Female

ANCESTOR: *(Name Illegible)*

Cherokee Citizenship Commission Docket Books
(1880-84, 1887-89) Volume IV
Tahlequah, Cherokee Nation

Now on this the 17th day of May, 1888, comes the above case up for final hearing, and the Commission says, "We the Commission on Citizenship after "carefully examining into the above case find that the Commission has no "jurisdiction over this case. The law creating this Court or Commission has no "jurisdiction over cases other than those claiming Cherokee citizenship by virtue "of their Cherokee blood and the application in the above case shows that the "parties are of African descent, and if they claim any rights to Cherokee "citizenship, they should have complied with the 9th Article of the Treaty of "1866.

"This Court or Commission claims no jurisdiction over such cases, so in "the matter of Annie Rowe [sic] and her five children, Harriett – Frank – Mary T "– Lewis A – and *(Illegible)* B. Rowe for Cherokee citizenship is hereby "dismissed from this Docket.

         J T Adair   Chairman of the Commission
         D W Lipe   Commissioner

ROBINSON

DOCKET #1511
CENSUS ROLLS 1835 & 52

APPLICANT FOR CHEROKEE CITIZENSHIP

POST OFFICE: Anisworth Town		ATTORNEY: A E Ivey	
NO	NAMES	AGE	SEX
1	Nancy Robinson	50	Female

ANCESTOR: John Cowan

Rejected Aug 22nd 1889

        Office Commission on Citizenship
         Cherokee Nation Ind Ter
         Tahlequah Aug 22nd 1889

Application for Cherokee Citizenship

   No evidence filed in support of the above application. Therefore we decide that Applicant Nancy Roberson[sic] age 50 yrs and her children are not Cherokees by blood. Post Office Anisworth Town

Attest
   D.S. Williams   JE Gunter   Com
   Asst Clk Com

Cherokee Citizenship Commission Docket Books
(1880-84, 1887-89) Volume IV
Tahlequah, Cherokee Nation

ROGERS

DOCKET #1512
CENSUS ROLLS 1835 & 52

APPLICANT FOR CHEROKEE CITIZENSHIP

POST OFFICE: *(Illegible)* Ark		ATTORNEY: A E Ivey	
No	NAMES	AGE	SEX
1	Benton B. Rogers	19	Male
2	James C C. "	17	"
3	Mary C "	15	Female
4	L. E. "	13	"

ANCESTOR: Jon Rogers

Now on this the 17th day of March 1888, comes the above case for a final hearing, the parties having made application pursuant to the provisions of an Act of the National Council approved December 8th 1886. All the evidence being duly considered and found to be insufficient and unsatisfactory, it is adjudged and declared by the Commission that

Benton B Rogers, James C.C. Rogers, Mary C. Rogers and L.E. Rogers are not Cherokees. And they are not entitled to the rights, privileges and immunities of Cherokee Citizens by blood.

        J T Adair   Chairman Commission
        John E Gunter Commissioner
        D W Lipe   Commissioner

Attest
  C.C. Lipe
   Clerk Com

The decision in the James C.C. Rogers case found in Book C, page 627, and testimony on Journal pages 325 to 333 governs this case.

ROGERS

DOCKET #1513
CENSUS ROLLS 1835

APPLICANT FOR CHEROKEE CITIZENSHIP

POST OFFICE: Clarksville Ark		ATTORNEY: Boudinot & Rasmus	
No	NAMES	AGE	SEX
1	James R Rogers	35	Male

Cherokee Citizenship Commission Docket Books (1880-84, 1887-89) Volume IV
Tahlequah, Cherokee Nation

2	Cynthia M "	7	Female
3	Nancy E. "	3	"

ANCESTOR: Barsheba Goodrich

Office Commission on Citizenship
Tahlequah I.T. Aug 22, 1889

This case was submitted by the Attorneys without evidence. The Commission decide that James R Rogers aged 35 years and his daughter Cynthia M aged 7 years and Nancy E. Rogers age 3 years are not Cherokees by blood.
Attest
    EG Ross
        Clerk Commission   JE Gunter   Com

RALSTON

DOCKET #1514
CENSUS ROLLS 1835

APPLICANT FOR CHEROKEE CITIZENSHIP

POST OFFICE: Salmon City Texas		ATTORNEY: J M Bell	
No	NAMES	AGE	SEX
1	John T Ralston	60	Male

ANCESTOR: Elizabeth Ralston

The evidence in this case will be found with the application of Zachariah P Ralston.

The application not bearing Signature of Mr Ralston the case is not considered by the Commission Aug 22- 1889
                W.P.R.
                JE Gunter   Com

Cherokee Citizenship Commission Docket Books
(1880-84, 1887-89) Volume IV
Tahlequah, Cherokee Nation

RUSHING

DOCKET #1515
CENSUS ROLLS 1835, 48, 51 & 52

APPLICANT FOR CHEROKEE CITIZENSHIP

POST OFFICE: Dover Ark		ATTORNEY: Boudinot & Rasmus	
NO	NAMES	AGE	SEX
1	W H. Rushing		Male

ANCESTOR: Barsheba Goodrich

Office Commission on Citizenship
Cherokee Nation Tahlequah
June 20th 1889

There being no evidence in support of the above named case the Commission decide that W.H. Rushing is not a Cherokee by blood.
Attest
    EG Ross   Will. P. Ross
       Clerk Commission   Chairman
                                         J E Gunter   Com

ROSS

DOCKET #1516
CENSUS ROLLS 1835

APPLICANT FOR CHEROKEE CITIZENSHIP

POST OFFICE: Locust Grove I.T.		ATTORNEY: C H Taylor	
NO	NAMES	AGE	SEX
1	Malinda Ross	26	Female

ANCESTOR: Robin Taylor

Rejected Aug 23rd 1889

Office Commission on Citizenship
Cherokee Nation Ind Ter
Tahlequah Aug 23rd 1889

There is no evidence on file in support of the above application. Therefore in view of this fact, we decide that applicant Malinda Ross is not a Cherokee by blood and not entitled to citizenship in the Cherokee Nation. P.O. Locust Grove I.T.

Cherokee Citizenship Commission Docket Books
(1880-84, 1887-89) Volume IV
Tahlequah, Cherokee Nation

Attest

D.S. Williams   Asst Clk Com

Will. P. Ross   Chairman
J.E. Gunter   Com

RUSK

DOCKET #1517
CENSUS ROLLS

APPLICANT FOR CHEREOKEE CITIZENSHIP

POST OFFICE: Siloam Springs Ark		ATTORNEY: L.S. Sanders	
NO	NAMES	AGE	SEX
1	America E Rusk	46	Female
2	William L Smith	28	Male
3	James S. "	26	"
4	John W. "	23	"
5	Adair Elizabeth Rusk	12	Female
6	Lula "	9	"
7	Wm D. "	25	Male
8	John M. "	22	"
9	Eliza E. "	19	Female
10	Mary P "	16	"

ANCESTOR: *(Name Illegible)*

See decision in this case in the Dicey Llewellyn case in Book "B" page 221. Adverse.

Cornell Rogers
Clerk Com.

August 29 – '88

ROBARDS

DOCKET #1518
CENSUS ROLLS 1835 & 52

APPLICANT FOR CHEROKEE CITIZENSHIP

POST OFFICE: Coal Hill Johnson Co Ark.		ATTORNEY: R.M. Wolfe	
NO	NAMES	AGE	SEX
1	C. C. Robards	40	Male

ANCESTOR: Bask Foreman

Re-admitted Sept 25th 1889

Cherokee Citizenship Commission Docket Books
(1880-84, 1887-89) Volume IV
Tahlequah, Cherokee Nation

Office Commission on Citizenship Cher Nat I.T.
Tahlequah Sept 25th 1889

The applicant in the above case alleges that he derives his Cherokee blood from his Mother Jennie Foreman, and she from her Father Bask Foreman, and it having been proven that such is the fact and the name of Bask Foreman being enrolled on the census roll of Cherokees by blood taken by the United States in the year 1835, the Commission decide that the before named C.C. Robards aged 40 years is of Cherokee blood and is entitled to re-admission to citizenship in the Cherokee Nation in accordance with the Constititian[sic] and laws thereof. P.O. Coal Hill Johnson County Arkansas.

Will. P. Ross   Chairman

Attest
   D.S. Williams
   Asst Clk Com.

J.E. Gunter   Com

RIGGLES

DOCKET #1519
CENSUS ROLLS 1835

APPLICANT FOR CHEROKEE CITIZENSHIP

POST OFFICE: Fort Smith Ark		ATTORNEY: Boudinot & Rasmus	
No	NAMES	AGE	SEX
1	Joe H Riggles	7	Male
2	Frank "	5	"

ANCESTOR: Jake West & Martha Hill

Rejected Sept 6th 1889

Office Commission on Citizenship
Cherokee Nation Ind Ter
Tahlequah Sept 6th 1889

The above case was submitted by Atty without evidence. The Commission therefore decide that Joe H Riggles & Frank Riggles are <u>not</u> Cherokees by blood.
Post Office Fort Smith Ark.

Attest
   D.S. Williams
   Asst Clk Com

Will. P. Ross
Chairman
J.E. Gunter   Com

Cherokee Citizenship Commission Docket Books
(1880-84, 1887-89) Volume IV
Tahlequah, Cherokee Nation

RIGGLE

DOCKET #1520
CENSUS ROLLS 1835

APPLICANT FOR **CHEROKEE CITIZENSHIP**

POST OFFICE: Fort Worth Texas		ATTORNEY:	
NO	NAMES	AGE	SEX
1	Jefferson Riggle	45	Male
2	Henry "	20	"

ANCESTOR: Jake West and Martha Hill

Rejected Sept 6th 1889

>Office Commission on Citizenship
>Cherokee Nation Ind Ter
>Tahlequah Sept 6th 1889

The above case was submitted without evidence. The Commission therefore decide that Jefferson Riggle age 45 yrs and his son Henry Riggle male 20 yrs are not Cherokees by blood and are not entitled to citizenship in the Cherokee Nation. P.O. Forth[sic] Worth Tex.

>Will.P. Ross   Chairman

Attest
   D.S. Williams   J.E. Gunter   Com
   Asst Clk Com

RHEA

DOCKET #1521
CENSUS ROLLS 1835

APPLICANT FOR **CHEROKEE CITIZENSHIP**

POST OFFICE: McKinney Texas		ATTORNEY: W.A. Thompson	
NO	NAMES	AGE	SEX
1	Mrs. Ella Rhea	38	Female
2	James F. "	19	Male
3	Emojean "	15	Female
4	W. A. " Jr	14	Male
5	J. L. "	10	"
6	Mary E "	7	Female
7	J. E. "	5	Male

ANCESTOR: Jack McGarrah

Cherokee Citizenship Commission Docket Books
(1880-84, 1887-89) Volume IV
Tahlequah, Cherokee Nation

Office Commission on Citizenship
Cherokee Nation June 26 1889

There being no evidence in support of the above named case the Commission decide that Ella Rhea aged 38 years and the following children James F. male aged 19 years, Emojean Rhea Female aged 15 years, W.A. Male aged 14 years, J.L. Male aged 10 years, Mary E Female aged 7 years and J.E. Rhea male aged 5 years are not Cherokees by blood.
Attest

E.G. Ross   Will.P. Ross
Clerk Commission   Chairman
     J.E. Gunter   Com

RYE

DOCKET #1522
CENSUS ROLLS 1835, 48, 51 & 52

APPLICANT FOR CHEROKEE CITIZENSHIP

POST OFFICE: Fort Smith Ark		ATTORNEY: Boudinot & Rasmus	
No	NAMES	AGE	SEX
1	William T. Rye	54	Male
2	John W. "	19	"
3	Robert L. "	18	"
4	Russell "	11	"

ANCESTOR: Hannah Thomas

The above case coming up for final hearing, it having been submitted by Plaintiff's Atty. This case embraces the application of William T. Rye, Jr, Eugene H Rye and Tresham M Rye, all claiming a Cherokee descent from one Hannah Thomas, whose name they allege appears upon the rolls of Cherokees of the years 1835, '48, '51, & '52. In summary of the evidence in this case, as well as others, the first thing done after a case has been submitted is to ascertain whether or not the applicant, or their ancestors, do appear upon any of the rolls mentioned in Sec. 7 of the Act, defining how applicants for citizenship shall obtain the same entitled, "An Act providing for the appointment of a Commission to try and determine applications for Cherokee Citizenship", approved Dec. 8th 1886.

The names of these applicants, nor the name of Hannah Thomas, their alleged Cherokee ancestor in this case, do not appear upon any of the rolls of

Cherokee Citizenship Commission Docket Books
(1880-84, 1887-89) Volume IV
Tahlequah, Cherokee Nation

Cherokees of 1835, 1848, 1851, and 1852. Therefore, William T. Rye, and his family, viz: John W. – Robert L. – and Russell Rye and Eugene H. Rye and William T. Rye, Jr. and Tresham M. Rye are <u>not</u> Cherokees by blood and are not entitled to any of the rights and privileges of Cherokee citizens by virtue of such blood.

                        J.T. Adair   Cherokee Commission
                        D.W. Lipe   Commissioner

Office Com on Citizenship
Tahlequah I.T. July 9th '88.

RYE

DOCKET #1523
CENSUS ROLLS 1835, 48, 51 & 52

APPLICANT FOR CHEROKEE CITIZENSHIP

POST OFFICE: Fort Smith Ark		ATTORNEY: Boudinot & R.	
NO	NAMES	AGE	SEX
1	John C. Rye	59	Male
2	Minnie M "	18	Female
3	Clarence "	8	Male
4	George W. "	2	"

ANCESTOR: Barsheba Goodrich

                        Office Commission on Citizenship
                        Tahlequah I.T. June 20th 1889

There being no evidence in support of the above named case the Commission decide that John C. Rye aged 59 years and the following named children, Minnie M aged 18 years, Clarence aged 8 years and George W. Rye aged 3 years are not Cherokees by blood
Attest
    EG Ross   Will. P. Ross
        Clerk Commission   Chairman
                                    J. E. Gunter Com

Cherokee Citizenship Commission Docket Books
(1880-84, 1887-89) Volume IV
Tahlequah, Cherokee Nation

RYE

DOCKET #1524
CENSUS ROLLS 1835, 48, 51 & 52

APPLICANT FOR **CHEROKEE CITIZENSHIP**

POST OFFICE: Fort Smith Ark		ATTORNEY: Boudinot & R.	
NO	NAMES	AGE	SEX
1	Wm T. Rye, Jr.	24	Male

ANCESTOR: Hannah Thomas

See Decision in this case on page 8 in the William T. Rye case in this Docket and No. 1522. Adverse.

Cornell Rogers
Clerk Com. on Citizenship

Office Com on Citizenship
Tahlequah I.T. July 9th '88

RAY

DOCKET #1525
CENSUS ROLLS 1835

APPLICANT FOR **CHEROKEE CITIZENSHIP**

POST OFFICE:		ATTORNEY: C H Taylor	
NO	NAMES	AGE	SEX
1	J. W. Ray, Sr.	47	Male
2	J. W. " Jr.	25	"
3	Wm J. "	20	"
4	B. H. "	14	"
5	Sallie "	16	Female
6	Lillie B. "	12	"
7	C.A. "	6	Male

ANCESTOR: Wm Ray

Rejected Sept 16th 1889

Office Commission on Citizenship
Cherokee Nation Ind Ter
Tahlequah Sept 16th 1889

The above case was called three times and no response from applicant or by Atty and there being no evidence on file, the Commission therefore decide that J.P[sic] Ray, Sr., and J.W. Ray male 25 yrs, William J. Ray male 20 yrs, B.H.

Cherokee Citizenship Commission Docket Books
(1880-84, 1887-89) Volume IV
Tahlequah, Cherokee Nation

Ray male 14 yrs, Sallie Ray Female 16 yrs, Lillie B. Ray Female 12 yrs and C.A. Ray male 6 yrs are not Cherokees by blood. P.O. Rule Ark.

                         Will. P. Ross   Chairman
Attest   J. E. Gunter   Com
   D.S. Williams
   Asst Clk. Com.

RYE

DOCKET #1526
CENSUS ROLLS 1835, 48, 51 & 52

APPLICANT FOR CHEROKEE CITIZENSHIP

POST OFFICE: Fort Smith Ark.		ATTORNEY: Boudinot & R.	
No	NAMES	AGE	SEX
1	Eugene H. Rye	22	Male

ANCESTOR: Hannah Thomas

See Decision in this case in the William T. Rye case. Docket No 1522. Adverse.

                         Cornell Rogers
                         Clerk Com. on Citizenship

Office Com on Citizenship
Tahlequah I.T. July 9th 1888

RANDALL

DOCKET #1527
CENSUS ROLLS 1835, 48, 51 & 52

APPLICANT FOR CHEROKEE CITIZENSHIP

POST OFFICE: Alluwe I.T.		ATTORNEY: Boudinot & R.	
No	NAMES	AGE	SEX
1	Yett Randall	27	Male

ANCESTOR: Mary Sanders

Rejected Sept 6th 1889

                         Office Commission on Citizenship
                         Cherokee Nation Ind Ter
                         Tahlequah Sept 6th 1889

Cherokee Citizenship Commission Docket Books
(1880-84, 1887-89) Volume IV
Tahlequah, Cherokee Nation

The above case was submitted by Atty without evidence. The Commission therefore decide that Yett Randall age 27 yrs is not a Cherokee by blood. P.O. Alluwe I.T.

Attest
    D.S. Williams
    Asst Clk Com.

Will.P. Ross
Chairman
J.E. Gunter   Com

RATCLIFF

DOCKET #1528
CENSUS ROLLS

APPLICANT FOR **CHEROKEE CITIZENSHIP**

POST OFFICE: New Castle Inda		ATTORNEY: L.B. Bell	
No	NAMES	AGE	SEX
1	Anna M Ratcliff		Female

ANCESTOR: Ann Crews

The Commission decide against claimant. See decision in the case of Andrew Meredith Docket 2180 Book E, Page 26 and John Henly Docket 1250, Book C Page 346.

Will.P.Ross
Chairman
John. E. Gunter   Com

RAY

DOCKET #1529
CENSUS ROLLS

APPLICANT FOR **CHEROKEE CITIZENSHIP**

POST OFFICE: Bridgeport Texas		ATTORNEY: C. H. Taylor	
No	NAMES	AGE	SEX
1	Andrew J Ray	58	Male
2	Franie L "	18	"
3	John "	16	"
4	Brown "	12	"
5	George F. "	6	"
6	Katy J. "	8	Female
7	Sis "	1	"

ANCESTOR: Mary Ray formerly Taylor

Cherokee Citizenship Commission Docket Books
(1880-84, 1887-89) Volume IV
Tahlequah, Cherokee Nation

Office Commission on Citizenship
Cherokee Nation Ind Ter
Tahlequah Aug 26th 1889

This case being called three several times and no response from applicant or by Attorney the Commission therefore decide that Andrew J Ray aged 58 years, Franie L. aged 18 years, John aged 16 years, Brown aged 12 years, George F. aged 6 years, Katy J aged 8 years and Sis Ray aged 1 year are not Cherokees by blood. Post Office Bridgeport Texas.

Attest
    EG Ross
        Clerk Commission

Will.P. Ross
Chairman
J.E. Gunter   Com

DOCKET #1530   *(All names illegible)*

RAY

DOCKET #1531
CENSUS ROLLS 1835

APPLICANT FOR **CHEROKEE CITIZENSHIP**

	POST OFFICE: Sanders I.T.	ATTORNEY: C.H. Taylor	
No	NAMES	AGE	SEX
1	J. T. Ray	22	Male
2	Callen "	1	"

ANCESTOR: William Ray

Rejected Aug 26th 1889

Office Commission on Citizenship
Cherokee Nation Ind Ter
Tahlequah Aug 26th 1889

No evidence on file in support of the above application. Therefore we decide that applicant J.T. Ray age 22 yrs and child Callen Ray age 1 yr are not Cherokees by blood. P.O. Sanders I.T.

Will.P. Ross
Chairman
J.E. Gunter   Com

Attest
    D.S. Williams
    Asst Clk Com

Cherokee Citizenship Commission Docket Books
(1880-84, 1887-89) Volume IV
Tahlequah, Cherokee Nation

ROBERTS

DOCKET #1532
CENSUS ROLLS 1835

APPLICANT FOR **CHEROKEE CITIZENSHIP**

POST OFFICE: Decatur Texas		ATTORNEY: C.H. Taylor	
NO	NAMES	AGE	SEX
1	Elijah Roberts	50	Male
2	Allen "	12	"
3	Martha Jane "	10	Female
4	Tom "	8	Male
5	Joe "	5	"

ANCESTOR: William & Absolum Chisolow[sic]

Office Commission on Citizenship
Cherokee Nation Ind Ter
Tahlequah Aug 26th 1889

This case being called three several times and no response from applicant or by Attorney the Commission therefore decide that Elijah Roberts aged 50 years, Allen aged 12 years, Martha Jane aged 10 years, Tom aged 8 years, and Joe Roberts aged 5 years are not Cherokees by blood. Post Office Decatur Texas.

Attest   Will.P. Ross
    EG Ross   Chairman
        Clerk Commission   J.E. Gunter   Com

ROBERTS

DOCKET #1533
CENSUS ROLLS 1835

APPLICANT FOR **CHEROKEE CITIZENSHIP**

POST OFFICE:		ATTORNEY: C.H. Taylor	
NO	NAMES	AGE	SEX
1	Joe Robertson Sr	55	Male
2	Jim "	29	"
3	Joe " Jr	26	"
4	John "	21	"
5	Bill "	21	"

ANCESTOR: Wm & Solomon Chisolom

Rejected Aug 26th 1889

Cherokee Citizenship Commission Docket Books
(1880-84, 1887-89) Volume IV
Tahlequah, Cherokee Nation

Office Commission on Citizenship
Cherokee Nation Ind Ter
Tahlequah Aug 26th 1889

There is no evidence on file in support of the above application. Therefore the Commission decide that applicant Joe Roberts Sr age 55 yrs and children Jim Roberts age 29 yrs, Joe Roberts Jr age 26 yrs, John Roberts age 21 yrs, and Bill Roberts 21 yrs, are not Cherokees by blood. P.O. Decatur Texas.

Will.P. Ross
Chairman

Attest
D.S. Williams
Asst Clk Com

J. E. Gunter   Com

RUSH

DOCKET #1534
CENSUS ROLLS 1835 & 52

APPLICANT FOR CHEROKEE CITIZENSHIP

POST OFFICE: Siloam Springs Ark		ATTORNEY: L.S. Sanders	
No	NAMES	AGE	SEX
1	Calvin Rush	64	Male
2	Cornelia Wilson	25	Female
3	Sarah Warsan	23	"
4	Susan Roxanna Rush	20	"
5	Calvin H. Rush	18	Male
6	Luella Rush	16	Female

ANCESTOR: *(Illegible)* Miller

Rejected Sept 6th 1889

Office Commission on Citizenship
Cherokee Nation Ind Ter
Tahlequah Sept 6th 1889

The above case was submitted without evidence by Atty. The Commission therefore decide that Calvin Rush age 64 yrs. and the following children Cornelia Wilson Female 25 yrs. daughter, Sarah Warsan Female 23 yrs, Susan Roxanna Rush 20 daughter, Calvin H. Rush male 18 yrs, Luella Rush Female 16 yrs. daughter are not Cherokees by blood Cherokees by blood. P.O. Siloam Springs Ark.

Cherokee Citizenship Commission Docket Books
(1880-84, 1887-89) Volume IV
Tahlequah, Cherokee Nation

Attest
    D.S. Williams
    Asst Clk Com

Will.P. Ross   Chairman

J. E. Gunter   Com

RUTHERFORD

DOCKET #1535
CENSUS ROLLS E or W 1835 or 52

APPLICANT FOR CHEROKEE CITIZENSHIP

POST OFFICE: Benton Co Ark Trident		ATTORNEY: L.S. Sanders	
No	NAMES	AGE	SEX
1	Joseph R Rutherford	59	Male
2	Alfred P "	35	"
3	Lewis W "	33	"
4	Lenora Wright "	30	Female
5	Mary England "	27	"
6	Wm M "	21	Male
7	Elizabeth Hunton	19	Female
8	Simonie Thomason	17	"
9	Alice Rutherford	15	"

ANCESTOR: John Rutherford

Now on this the 4th day of October 1888, comes the above case up for final disposition and all the testimony being duly considered upon which this cause if based as well as the census and pay rolls of Cherokees mentioned in the 7th Sec. of Act of Dec. 8th 1886 in relation to Citizenship. The rolls above recited fail to contain the name of John Rutherford the alleged Cherokee ancestor of the applicants in this case, or themselves hence under the law this Commission cannot grant Citizenship to Joseph R Rutherford and his eight children, viz: Alfred P, Lewis W, Lenora Wright, ne Rutherford, Mary England, nee Rutherford, William M, Elizabeth Hunton nee Rutherford, Simonie Thomason, nee Rutherford and Alice Rutherford and we the Commission on Citizenship do hereby declare that the above named parties are not Cherokees by blood and are not entitled to any of the rights and privileges of Citizens of the Cherokee Nation. These parties are residents of Benton County Arkansas.

                J.T. Adair   Chairman Commission
                H.C. Barnes   Commissioner

Cherokee Citizenship Commission Docket Books
(1880-84, 1887-89) Volume IV
Tahlequah, Cherokee Nation

RANDOLPH

DOCKET #1536
CENSUS ROLLS

APPLICANT FOR CHEROKEE CITIZENSHIP

POST OFFICE: Afton I.T.		ATTORNEY: L.B. Bell	
NO	NAMES	AGE	SEX
1	Ellen Randolph		Female

ANCESTOR: Mary Crews

The Commission decide against claimant. See decision in the case of Andrew Meredith Docket 2180 Book E, Page 26 and John Henly Docket 1250, Book C Page 346.

                      Will.P. Ross
                      Chairman
                      J.E. Gunter   Com

ROARK

DOCKET #1537
CENSUS ROLLS E or W 1835 & 52

APPLICANT FOR CHEROKEE CITIZENSHIP

POST OFFICE: Fayetteville Ark		ATTORNEY: L.S. Sanders	
NO	NAMES	AGE	SEX
1	Martha Roark	55	Female

ANCESTOR: George Cline

Rejected Sept. 6th 1889

                      Office Commission on Citizenship
                      Cherokee Nation Ind Ter
                      Tahlequah Sept. 6th 1889

The above case was submitted by Atty without evidence. The Commission therefore decide that Martha Roark age 55 yrs. is not a Cherokee by blood. Post Office Fayettville[sic] Ark.

                    Will.P. Ross
Attest   Chairman
    D.S. Williams   J.E. Gunter   Com
    Asst Clk Com.

Cherokee Citizenship Commission Docket Books
(1880-84, 1887-89) Volume IV
Tahlequah, Cherokee Nation

RIFE

DOCKET #1538
CENSUS ROLLS E or W 1835 & 52

APPLICANT FOR CHEROKEE CITIZENSHIP

POST OFFICE: Van Buren Ark		ATTORNEY: L.S. Sanders	
No	NAMES	AGE	SEX
1	Zida Rife	26	Female

ANCESTOR: Tho. Crittenden

Rejected Sept. 6th 1889

Office Commission on Citizenship
Cherokee Nation Ind Ter
Tahlequah Sept 6th 1889

The above case was submitted by Atty without evidence. The Commission therefore decide that Zida Rife age 26 yrs is not a Cherokee by blood. Post Office Van Buren Ark.

Attest
   D.S. Williams
   Asst Clk Com

Will.P.Ross   Chairman
J.E. Gunter   Com

REDDEN

DOCKET #1539
CENSUS ROLLS 1835 to 52

APPLICANT FOR CHEROKEE CITIZENSHIP

POST OFFICE: Van Buren Ark		ATTORNEY: L.S. Sanders	
No	NAMES	AGE	SEX
1	Rutha Redden	32	Female

ANCESTOR: Thos. Crittenden

Rejected Sept. 6th 1889

Office Commission on Citizenship
Cherokee Nation Ind Ter
Tahlequah Sept. 6th 1889

The above case having been submitted by Atty without evidence the Commission decide that the claimant Rutha Redden age 32 yrs. is not a Cherokee by blood. Post Office Van Buren Ark.

Cherokee Citizenship Commission Docket Books
(1880-84, 1887-89) Volume IV
Tahlequah, Cherokee Nation

Will.P. Ross Chairman

Attest
  D.S. Williams   J.E. Gunter Com
  Asst Clk Com

RYE

DOCKET #1540
CENSUS ROLLS 1835, 48, 51 & 52

APPLICANT FOR **CHEROKEE CITIZENSHIP**

POST OFFICE: Dover Ark		ATTORNEY: Boudinot & R.	
No	NAMES	AGE	SEX
1	Robert T. Rye	32	Male
2	Seth "	9	"
3	M. A. E. "	7	"
4	Effie M. "	4	Female
5	Maggie "	2	"

ANCESTOR: Barsheba Goodrich

Office Commission on Citizenship
Cherokee Nation June 20th 1889

There being no evidence in support of the above named case the Commission decide that Robert T. Rye aged 32 years and the following named children Seth aged 9 years, Effie M. aged 4 years, Maggie aged 2 years and M.A.E. Rye aged 7 years are not Cherckees by blood.

Attest   Will.P.Ross
  EG Ross   Chairman
    Clerk Commission   J.E. Gunter Com

RYE

DOCKET #1541
CENSUS ROLLS 1835, 48, 51 & 52

APPLICANT FOR **CHEROKEE CITIZENSHIP**

POST OFFICE: Nashville Tenn		ATTORNEY: Boudinot & R.	
No	NAMES	AGE	SEX
1	George M Rye	32	Male
2	Guy Rye	11	"

ANCESTOR: Barsheba Goodrich

Cherokee Citizenship Commission Docket Books
(1880-84, 1887-89) Volume IV
Tahlequah, Cherokee Nation

Office Commission on Citizenship
Tahlequah IT June 20, 1889

There being no evidence in support of the above named case the Commission decide that George M Rye aged 32 years and child Guy Rye aged 11 years are not Cherokees by blood.

Attest   Will.P. Ross
   EG Ross   Chairman
     Clerk Commission   J.E. Gunter Com

REASER

DOCKET #1542
CENSUS ROLLS 1835, 48, 51 & 52

APPLICANT FOR **CHEREKEE CITIZENSHIP**

POST OFFICE: McKinney Texas		ATTORNEY: Wm A. Thompson	
NO	NAMES	AGE	SEX
1	James Reaser	47	Male
2	John "	20	"
3	Sarah E "	16	Female
4	Thos. "	9	Male
5	James "	2	Male
6	Wm M. "	8 mo	"

ANCESTOR: John Rich

Office Commission on Citizenship
Tahlequah I.T. July 3rd 1889

There being no evidence in support of the above named case the Commission decide that James Reaser aged 47 years and the following named children John male aged 20 years, Sarah E. female aged 16 years, Thomas male aged 9 years, James male aged 2 years and William M. Reaser male aged 8 months are not Cherokees by blood. Post Office McKinney Texas.

Attest   Will.P.Ross
   E.G. Ross   Chairman
     Clerk Com.   J.E. Gunter Com

Cherokee Citizenship Commission Docket Books
(1880-84, 1887-89) Volume IV
Tahlequah, Cherokee Nation

REACER

DOCKET #1543
CENSUS ROLLS 1835 or Old Settler

APPLICANT FOR **CHEROKEE CITIZENSHIP**

POST OFFICE: McKinney Tex		ATTORNEY: Wm A. Thompson	
No	NAMES	AGE	SEX
1	John Reacer	50	Male
2	Abraham "	17	"
3	Luke "	15	"
4	J. C. "	12	"
5	Lillie M. "	7	Female
6	Lawrance "	4	Male
7	Willie "	2	"

ANCESTOR: John Rich

Office Commission on Citizenship
Cherokee Nation Ind Ter
Tahlequah August 26th 1889

This case having been called three times not less than one hour apart and no response from applicant or by Attorney the Commission decide that John Reacer aged 50 years and Abraham male aged 17 years, Luke male aged 15 years, J.C. aged 12 years, Lillie M. female aged 7 years, Lawrance aged 4 years, Willie Reacer aged 2 years are not Cherokees by blood.
Attest

EG Ross
    Clerk Commission

Will. P. Ross
    Chairman
    J.E. Gunter Com

REACER

DOCKET #1544
CENSUS ROLLS 1835, 51 or 52

APPLICANT FOR **CHEROKEE CITIZENSHIP**

POST OFFICE: McKinney Texas		ATTORNEY: Wm A. Thompson	
No	NAMES	AGE	SEX
1	Luke Reacer	44	Male
2	Maud "	11	Female
3	Lela "	1	"

ANCESTOR: John Rich

Cherokee Citizenship Commission Docket Books
(1880-84, 1887-89) Volume IV
Tahlequah, Cherokee Nation

Office Commission on Citizenship
Cherokee Nation July 2nd 1889

There being no evidence in support of the above named case the Commission decide that Luke Reaser[sic] aged 44 years and the following children Maud female aged 11 years, Lela Reaser female aged 1 year are not Cherokees by blood.

Attest   Will.P. Ross
    EG Ross   Chairman
       Clerk Commission   J E Gunter   Com

REASER

DOCKET #1545
CENSUS ROLLS 1835 or 51 & 52

APPLICANT FOR **CHEROKEE CITIZENSHIP**

POST OFFICE: McKinney Texas		ATTORNEY: Wm A. Thompson	
NO	NAMES	AGE	SEX
1	Thos Reaser	42	Male
2	John T. "	14	"

ANCESTOR: John Rich

Office Commission on Citizenship
Cherokee Nation July 3rd 1888

There being no evidence in support of the above named case the Commission decide that Thomas Reaser aged 42 years and his son John T. Reaser aged 14 years are not Cherokees by blood.

Attest   Will.P. Ross
    EG Ross   Chairman
       Clerk Commission   J.E. Gunter   Com

Cherokee Citizenship Commission Docket Books
(1880-84, 1887-89) Volume IV
Tahlequah, Cherokee Nation

RIGHTS

DOCKET #1546
CENSUS ROLLS 1835

APPLICANT FOR CHEROKEE CITIZENSHIP

POST OFFICE: Miland[sic] Tenn		ATTORNEY: C.H. Taylor	
No	NAMES	AGE	SEX
1	George A Rights	32	Male

ANCESTOR: John Bryant

Rejected Aug 23rd 1889

Office Commission on Citizenship
Cherokee Nation Ind Ter
Tahlequah Aug 23rd 1889

There being no evidence on file in support of the above named case the Commission decide that George A Rights[sic] age 32 years is not a Cherokee by blood and not entitled to citizenship in the Cherokee Nation. P.O. Miland[sic] Tenn.

Attest
    D.S. Williams
    Asst Clk Com.

Will.P.Ross
Chairman
J.E. Gunter Com

ROBBINS

DOCKET #1547
CENSUS ROLLS

APPLICANT FOR CHEROKEE CITIZENSHIP

POST OFFICE: Afton IT.		ATTORNEY: L.B. Bell	
No	NAMES	AGE	SEX
1	Sarah Robbins	44	Female

ANCESTOR: Ann Crews

The Commission decide against claimant. See decision in the case of Andrew Meredith Docket 2180 Book E, Page 26 and John Henly Docket 1250, Book C Page 346.

Will.P. Ross   Chairman
John E. Gunter   Com

Cherokee Citizenship Commission Docket Books
(1880-84, 1887-89) Volume IV
Tahlequah, Cherokee Nation

ROBINS

DOCKET #1548
CENSUS ROLLS

APPLICANT FOR CHEROKEE CITIZENSHIP

POST OFFICE:		ATTORNEY: LB Bell	
NO	**NAMES**	**AGE**	**SEX**
1	W. E. Robins	28	Male

ANCESTOR: Ann Crews

The Commission decide against claimant. See decision in the case of Andrew Meredith Docket 2180 Book E, Page 26 and John Henly Docket 1250, Book C Page 346.

Attest
    EG Ross
        Clk Com

Will.P. Ross
Chairman
John E Gunter Com

RAY

DOCKET #1549
CENSUS ROLLS

APPLICANT FOR CHEROKEE CITIZENSHIP

POST OFFICE: Decatur Texas		ATTORNEY: C.H. Taylor	
NO	**NAMES**	**AGE**	**SEX**
1	Green T Ray	25	Male

ANCESTOR: Mary Ray formerly Taylor

Rejected Aug 23rd 1889

Office Commission on Citizenship
Cherokee Nation Ind Ter
Tahlequah Aug 23rd 1889

As there is no evidence on file in support of the above application we decide that applicant Green T. Ray age 25 yrs is not a Cherokee by blood & not entitled to citizenship in the Cherokee Nation.

Attest
    D.S. Williams
  Asst Clk Com

Will.P. Ross   Chairman
J.E. Gunter Com

Cherokee Citizenship Commission Docket Books
(1880-84, 1887-89) Volume IV
Tahlequah, Cherokee Nation

ROWCROFT

DOCKET #1550
CENSUS ROLLS

APPLICANT FOR CHEROKEE CITIZENSHIP

POST OFFICE: Elk Creek Col		ATTORNEY: L B Bell	
No	NAMES	AGE	SEX
1	Mary Rowcroft		Female

ANCESTOR: Sarah Elmore

Rejected July 2nd 1889

Adversely

See decision of the Commission in the case of John R. Henly Docket 553, Book B, Page 266.

                                Will.P. Ross   Chairman

Attest
   D.S. Williams   J.E. Gunter   Com
   Asst Clk Com

RAY

DOCKET #1551
CENSUS ROLLS

APPLICANT FOR CHEROKEE CITIZENSHIP

POST OFFICE: *(Illegible)* Tex		ATTORNEY: C.H. Taylor	
No	NAMES	AGE	SEX
1	Solomon T Ray	36	Male
2	Savannah T. "	15	Female
3	Bonnie "	13	"
4	Carle "	9	"
5	Thomas "	5	Male

ANCESTOR: Mary Ray formerly Taylor

Adverse. See decision of the Commission in case John R. Henly Docket 553, Book B, Page 266.

                                  Will.P. Ross
                                      Chairman
                                J.E. Gunter   Com

Cherokee Citizenship Commission Docket Books
(1880-84, 1887-89) Volume IV
Tahlequah, Cherokee Nation

RAY

DOCKET #1552
CENSUS ROLLS

APPLICANT FOR **CHEROKEE CITIZENSHIP**

POST OFFICE: Bridgeport Texas		ATTORNEY: C.H. Taylor	
NO	NAMES	AGE	SEX
1	George W. Ray	30	Male

ANCESTOR: Mary Ray formerly Taylor

                          Office Commission on Citizenship
                          Cherokee Nation July 3rd 1889

There being no evidence in support of the above named case the Commission decide that George W. Ray aged 30 yrs is not a Cherokee by blood. Post Office Bridgeport Texas.

Attest   Will.P. Ross
   EG Ross   Chairman
      Clerk Com   J.E. Gunter Com

RICH

DOCKET #1553
CENSUS ROLLS

APPLICANT FOR **CHEROKEE CITIZENSHIP**

POST OFFICE: Emporia Kansas		ATTORNEY: LB Bell	
NO	NAMES	AGE	SEX
1	Elias C. Rich		

ANCESTOR: Sarah Morgan

Rejected Aug 23rd 1889

                          Office Commission on Citizenship
                          Cherokee Nation Ind Ter
                          Tahlequah Aug 23rd 1889

As there is no evidence filed in support of the above application we decide that applicant Elias C Rich is not a Cherokee by blood and not entitled to citizenship in the Cherokee Nation. Post Office Emporia Kans.

                          Will.P. Ross   Chairman
Attest
   D.S. Williams   J.E. Gunter Com
   Asst Clk Com

Cherokee Citizenship Commission Docket Books
(1880-84, 1887-89) Volume IV
Tahlequah, Cherokee Nation

ROBERTS

DOCKET #1554
CENSUS ROLLS 1835

APPLICANT FOR CHEROKEE CITIZENSHIP

POST OFFICE: Decater[sic] Texas		ATTORNEY: Taylor & Ivey	
NO	NAMES	AGE	SEX
1	Mose B. Roberts	29	Male
2	Mynervia "	6	Female

ANCESTOR: Wm Chysom

Rejected Aug 23rd 1889

        Office Commission on Citizenship
        Cherokee Nation Ind Ter
        Tahlequah Aug 23rd 1889

No evidence on file in support of the above application. Therefore we decide that applicant Moses B. Roberts age 29 yrs and child Mynervia Roberts age 6 yrs are not Cherokees by blood. P.O. Decater[sic] Texas.

        Will.P. Ross
Attest   Chairman
 DS. Williams   J.E. Gunter Com
 Asst Clk Com

ROBERTS

DOCKET #1555
CENSUS ROLLS 1835

APPLICANT FOR CHEROKEE CITIZENSHIP

POST OFFICE: Decater[sic] Tex		ATTORNEY: Taylor & Ivey	
NO	NAMES	AGE	SEX
1	Frank T. Roberts	34	Male
2	Moses B. "	8	"
3	Henry "	6	"
4	Lady B. "	2	Female

ANCESTOR: Wm Chyson[sic]

        Office Commission on Citizenship
        Cherokee Nation Ind Ter

  There is no evidence on file in support of the above application therefore we decide that applicant Frank S. Roberts aged 34 years and children Moses B.

Cherokee Citizenship Commission Docket Books
(1880-84, 1887-89) Volume IV
Tahlequah, Cherokee Nation

Roberts aged 8 years, Henry Roberts aged 6 and lady B Roberts aged 2 years are not Cherokees by blood. Post Office Decatur Tex.

Tahlequah Aug 23rd 1889
   Attest
      E.G. Ross
      Clerk Commission

Will.P. Ross
   Chairman
J.E. Gunter Com

RAMSEY

DOCKET #1556
CENSUS ROLLS

APPLICANT FOR CHEROKEE CITIZENSHIP

POST OFFICE: Union Town Ark		ATTORNEY: A.E. Ivey	
No	NAMES	AGE	SEX
1	Charley Ramsey	19	Male

ANCESTOR: Tom Ramsey

Office Commission on Citizenship
Tahlequah IT Aug 23rd 1889

There being no evidence in support of the above named case therefore the Commission decide that applicant Charley Ramsey aged 19 yrs is not a Cherokee by blood.

   Attest
      EG Ross

Will.P. Ross
   Chairman
J.E. Gunter Com

RAY

DOCKET #1557
CENSUS ROLLS 1835

APPLICANT FOR CHEROKEE CITIZENSHIP

POST OFFICE: Clifty Ark		ATTORNEY: C.H. Taylor	
No	NAMES	AGE	SEX
1	Nancy A Ray	35	Female
2	P. M. "	15	Male
3	John R. "	13	"
4	James W "	10	"
5	C.F. "	8	"

Cherokee Citizenship Commission Docket Books
(1880-84, 1887-89) Volume IV
Tahlequah, Cherokee Nation

6	S. E. "	6	"
7	B. F. "	2	"
8	Joseph "	2	"

Ancestor: Feraby Vaughn

Office Commission on Citizenship
Cherokee Nation Ind Ter
Tahlequah July 2nd 1889

There being no evidence in support [sic] the above case the Commission decide that Nancy A Ray aged 35 years and the following children P.M. Ray aged 15 years, John R Ray aged 13 years, James W Ray age 10 years, C.F. Ray aged 8 years, S.E. Ray aged 6 ears, B.F. Ray aged 2 years, and Joseph Ray aged 2 years are not Cherokees by blood. Post Office Clifty Ark.

Attest   Will.P. Ross
   EG Ross   Chairman
     Clerk Commission   J.E. Gunter   Com

RAGSDALE

Docket #1558
Census Rolls 1835 or Old Settler

APPLICANT FOR **CHEROKEE CITIZENSHIP**

Post Office: Coodys Bluff IT		Attorney: Joe Bean	
No	NAMES	Age	Sex
1	Loretta Francis Ragsdale	27	Female
2	Florence Cullen "	6	"
3	Wm Thomas "	4	Male

Ancestor: Isaac Ragsdale

Rejected Aug 27th 1889

Office Commission on Citizenship
Cherokee Nation Ind Ter
Tahlequah Aug 27th 1889

This case was called 3 several times and no response from applicant or by Atty. the Commission decide that Loretta Francis Ragsdale age 27 years and the following children Florence Cullen Ragsdale Female age 6 yrs Daughter, William Thomas Ragsdale male 4 years son, are not Cherokees by blood. Post Office Coodys Bluff I.T.

Cherokee Citizenship Commission Docket Books
(1880-84, 1887-89) Volume IV
Tahlequah, Cherokee Nation

                              Will.P.Ross   Chairman

Attest
    D.S. Williams   J.E. Gunter   Com
    Asst Clk Com.

ROBERTS

DOCKET #1559
CENSUS ROLLS 1835

APPLICANT FOR CHEROKEE CITIZENSHIP

POST OFFICE: Decater[sic] Texas		ATTORNEY: Taylor & Ivey	
No	NAMES	AGE	SEX
1	William T Roberts	38	Male
2	Mollie "	18	Female
3	Bluford "	20	Male

ANCESTOR: Wm Chysom

Rejected Aug 26th 1889

                      Office Commission on Citizenship
                           Cherokee Nation Ind Ter
                           Tahlequah Aug 26th 1889

The above case coming up for final hearing we find no evidence submitted in support of the application. Therefore we decide that applicant William T. Roberts age 38 yrs and his children Mollie Roberts age 18 yrs and Blueford Roberts age 20 yrs, are not Cherokees by blood and not entitled to citizenship in the Cherokee Nation.

                            Will. P. Ross   Chairman

Attest
    D.S. Williams   J.E. Gunter   Com
    Asst Clk Com

ROGERS

DOCKET #1560
CENSUS ROLLS 1835 or 52

APPLICANT FOR CHEROKEE CITIZENSHIP

POST OFFICE: *(Illegible)* Ark		ATTORNEY: A E Ivey	
No	NAMES	AGE	SEX
1	Eliza R Rogers	14	Female

Cherokee Citizenship Commission Docket Books
(1880-84, 1887-89) Volume IV
Tahlequah, Cherokee Nation

2	Joseph G "	14	Male

ANCESTOR: John Rogers

Now on this the 17th day of March, 1888, comes the above case for a final hearing, the parties having made application pursuant to the provisions of an Act of the National Council approved December 8th 1886. All the evidence being duly considered and found to be insufficient and unsatisfactory, it is adjudged and declared by the Commission that

Eliza R. Rogers and Joseph G. Rogers, not Cherokees and they are not entitled to the rights, privileges and immunities of Cherokee citizens by blood.

J T Adair   Chairman Commission
John E Gunter   Commission
D W Lipe   Commission

Attest
    C.C. Lipe
      Clk Com

The decision in the James C.C. Rogers case found in Book C, page 627, and testimony on Journal pages 325 to 333 governs this case.

ROGERS

DOCKET #1561
CENSUS ROLLS 1835 or 52

APPLICANT FOR **CHEROKEE CITIZENSHIP**

POST OFFICE: Alma Ark		ATTORNEY: A E Ivey	
NO	NAMES	AGE	SEX
1	John C Rogers	19	Male
2	Charles R "	1	"

ANCESTOR: John Rogers

Now on this the 17th day of March 1888, comes the above case for a final hearing. The parties having made application pursuant to the provisions of an Act of the National Council approved December 8th 1886. And all the evidence being duly considered and found to be insufficient and unsatisfactory, it is adjudged and declared by the Commission that

Cherokee Citizenship Commission Docket Books
(1880-84, 1887-89) Volume IV
Tahlequah, Cherokee Nation

John C. Rogers and Charles R. Rogers are not Cherokees by blood and they are not entitled to any rights, privileges and immunities of Cherokee citizens by blood.

        J.T. Adair Chairman Commission
        John E Gunter Commissioner
        D.W. Lipe Commissioner

Attest
  C.C. Lipe
    Clerk Com

The decision in the James C.C. Rogers case found in Book C, page 627, and testimony on Journal pages 325 to 333 governs this case.

ROADS

DOCKET #1562
CENSUS ROLLS 1835 or 52

APPLICANT FOR CHEROKEE CITIZENSHIP

POST OFFICE: *(Illegible)* Ark		ATTORNEY: A E Ivey	
No	NAMES	AGE	SEX
1	Nancy E.S. Roads	20	Female

ANCESTOR: John Rogers

Now on this the 17th day of March, 1888, comes the above case for a final hearing. The parties having made application pursuant to the provisions of an Act of the National Council approved December 8th 1886, and all the evidence being duly considered and found to be insufficient and unsatisfactory, it is adjudged and declared by the Commission that

Nancy E.S. Rhoads[sic] is not a Cherokee by blood and she is not entitled to the rights, privileges and immunities of Cherokee citizens by blood.

        J.T. Adair Chairman Commission
        John E Gunter Commissioner
        D.W. Lipe Commissioner

Attest
  C.C. Lipe
    Clerk Com

Cherokee Citizenship Commission Docket Books
(1880-84, 1887-89) Volume IV
Tahlequah, Cherokee Nation

The decision in the James C.C. Rogers case found in Book C, page 627, and testimony on Journal pages 325 to 333 governs this case.

ROBERSON

DOCKET #1563
CENSUS ROLLS 1835

APPLICANT FOR CHEROKEE CITIZENSHIP

POST OFFICE: Waddell Newton Co Ark		ATTORNEY: A E Ivey	
NO	NAMES	AGE	SEX
1	Sarah Ann Roberson	57	Female
2	Jeremiah Clinton		Male
3	Leaher "		Female
4	Martha Ballard		"
5	Mary Mathis		"

ANCESTOR: John Clinton

Rejected Aug 27th 1889

Office Commission on Citizenship
Cherokee Nation Ind Ter
Tahlequah Aug 27th 1889

The above applicant having been called three times and as there is no evidence on file in support of the application we decide that applicant Sarah Ann Roberson age 57 yrs, her children Jeremiah Clinton, Leaher Clinton, Martha Ballard, and Mary Mathis are not Cherokees by blood and not entitled to citizenship in the Cherokee Nation. Post Office Waddell Newton Co Ark.

       Will.P. Ross
       Chairman

Attest
 D.S. Williams   J.E. Gunter   Com
 Asst Clk Com

RANDOLPH

DOCKET #1564
CENSUS ROLLS 1835 & 46

APPLICANT FOR CHEROKEE CITIZENSHIP

POST OFFICE: Altus Ark		ATTORNEY: A E Ivey	
NO	NAMES	AGE	SEX
1	C. A. Randolph	24	Male

Cherokee Citizenship Commission Docket Books
(1880-84, 1887-89) Volume IV
Tahlequah, Cherokee Nation

2	Charles "	4	"
3	Susan C "	2	Female

ANCESTOR: Payton Randolph

Rejected Aug. 26th 1889

        Office Commission on Citizenship
        Cherokee Nation Ind Ter
        Tahlequah Aug 26th 1889

No evidence on file in support of the above application. Therefore we decide that applicant C.A. Randolph age 24 yrs and his children Charles Randolph age 4 yrs, Susan C Randolph age 2 yrs are not Cherokees by blood and not entitled to citizenship in the Cherokee Nation. Post Office Allus[sic] Ark.

        Will.P. Ross Chairman

Attest
  D.S. Williams   J.E. Gunter Com
  Asst Clk Com

RITTER

DOCKET #1565
CENSUS ROLLS 1835 & 52

APPLICANT FOR **CHEROKEE CITIZENSHIP**

POST OFFICE: Elm Springs Ark		ATTORNEY: A E Ivey	
No	NAMES	AGE	SEX
1	W.R. Ritter	44	Male
2	H.C. "		"
3	R.L "		"
4	J.B. "		"
5	L.A. "		Female
6	S.S. Smith		"
7	Mary Robertson		Female

ANCESTOR: Wm Ritter

Rejected Aug 26th 1889

        Office Commission on Citizenship
        Cherokee Nation Ind Ter
        Tahlequah Aug 26th 1889

There is no evidence on file in support of the above application therefore we decide that applicant W.R. Ritten[sic] and his children H.C. Ritten, R.L. Ritten,

Cherokee Citizenship Commission Docket Books
(1880-84, 1887-89) Volume IV
Tahlequah, Cherokee Nation

J.B. Ritten, also his sisters L.A. Ritten, L.S. Ritten[sic] and Mary Robertson are not Cherokees by blood and not entitled to citizenship in the Cherokee Nation. P.O. Elm Springs Ark.

                              Will.P. Ross   Chairman

Attest
    D.S. Williams   J.E. Gunter   Com
    Asst Clk Com

ROGERS

DOCKET #1566
CENSUS ROLLS 1851

APPLICANT FOR **CHEROKEE CITIZENSHIP**

POST OFFICE: Draketown Ga		ATTORNEY: AE Ivey	
No	NAMES	AGE	SEX
1	Mrs Lucinda Rogers	30	Female
2	Sarah F. "	7	"
3	Samuel M "	5	Male
4	Wm M "	3	"

ANCESTOR: Mancil Tidwell

We the Commission on Citizenship after examining the evidence in this case find the applicant to be a daughter of Mancel[sic] Tidwell and the Granddaughter of John Tidwell, who has proven to be a Cherokee Indian.

Therefore we the Commission unanimously agree and decide that Lucinda Rogers and her three children, Sarah F, Samuel M, and William M. Rogers are Cherokees by blood and are hereby re-admitted to all the rights and privileges of Cherokee citizens by blood.

                          J.T. Adair   Chairman Commission
                          D.W. Lipe   Commissioner
                          H.C. Barnes   Commissioner

Office Com on Citizenship
Tahlequah I.T. Sept 21st 1888

Cherokee Citizenship Commission Docket Books
(1880-84, 1887-89) Volume IV
Tahlequah, Cherokee Nation

ROE

DOCKET #1567
CENSUS ROLLS

APPLICANT FOR CHEROKEE CITIZENSHIP

POST OFFICE: Barrettsville Ga		ATTORNEY: AE Ivey	
No	NAMES	AGE	SEX
1	Henrietta Roe	54	Female

ANCESTOR: Annie McCline

Now on this the 17th day of May, 1888, comes the above case up for final hearing, and the Commission says, "We the Commission on Citizenship after "carefully examining into the above case find that the Commission has no "jurisdiction over cases other than those claiming Cherokee citizenship by virtue "of their Cherokee blood, and the application in the above case shows that the "parties are of African descent, and if they claim any rights to Cherokee "citizenship, they should have complied with the 9th Article of the Treaty of "1866.

"This Court or Commission claims no jurisdiction over such cases, and "the matter of Harriett Roe for Cherokee citizenship is hereby dismissed from "the Docket.

        J T Adair Chairman of the Commission
        D.W. Lipe Commissioner

REEVES

DOCKET #1568
CENSUS ROLLS 1835 & 52

APPLICANT FOR CHEROKEE CITIZENSHIP

POST OFFICE: Bentonville Ark		ATTORNEY: A E Ivey	
No	NAMES	AGE	SEX
1	Mary C Reeves	42	Female
2	Roasa "	18	"
3	William "	15	Male
4	Laura "	13	Female
5	Martha "	11	"

ANCESTOR: Mary S Bell

Rejected Aug 26th 1889

Cherokee Citizenship Commission Docket Books
(1880-84, 1887-89) Volume IV
Tahlequah, Cherokee Nation

                Office Commission on Citizenship
                Cherokee Nation Ind Ter
                Tahlequah Aug 26th 1889

There being no evidence on file in support of the above application we decide that applicant Mary C Reeves age 42 yrs and her children Roasa Reeves age 18 yrs, William Reeves age 15 yrs, Laura Reeves age 13 yrs and Martha Reeves age 11 yrs. are not Cherokees by blood and not entitled to citizenship in the Cherokee Nation. P.O. Bentonville Ark.

                Will.P.Ross
                      Chairman

Attest
    D.S. Williams   J.E. Gunter Com
    Asst Clk Com

RANDALL

DOCKET #1569
CENSUS ROLLS 1835, 46, 51 & 52

APPLICANT FOR **CHEROKEE CITIZENSHIP**

POST OFFICE: Van Buren Ark		ATTORNEY: A E Ivey	
NO	NAMES	AGE	SEX
1	Jane Randall	36	Female
2	Delbirt "	3	Male
3	Walter F "	8 mo	"

ANCESTOR: Sarah Bean

                Office Commission on Citizenship
                Cherokee Nation Ind Ter
                Tahlequah Aug 26th 1889

There being no evidence on file in support of the above application we decide that applicant Jane Randall age 36 yrs and children Delbirt Randall age 3 yrs and Walter F Randall age 8 months are not Cherokees by blood and not entitled to citizenship in the Cherokee Nation. and not entitled to citizenship in the Cherokee Nation. P.O. Van Buren Ark.

                Will.P. Ross
Attest   Chairman
    D.S. Williams   J.E. Gunter Com
    Asst Clk Com

Cherokee Citizenship Commission Docket Books (1880-84, 1887-89) Volume IV
Tahlequah, Cherokee Nation

ROBERTS

DOCKET #1570
CENSUS ROLLS

APPLICANT FOR **CHEROKEE CITIZENSHIP**

POST OFFICE: Daton[sic]		ATTORNEY: A E Ivey	
NO	NAMES	AGE	SEX
1	Nancy Roberts	29	Female
2	Victor J "	8	Male
3	Mary "	6	Female
4	Wm "	4	Male
5	Allice[sic] "	2	Female

ANCESTOR: Rebecca Bliss

Rejected Aug 26th 1889

Office Commission on Citizenship
Cherokee Nation Ind Ter
Tahlequah Aug 26th 1889

The above application was filed on the 5th day of Oct. 1887 and on this day the case coming up for final hearing we find no evidence in support of application Nancy Roberts age 29 yrs and her children, Victor J. Roberts age 8 yrs, Mary Roberts age 6 yrs, William Roberts age 4 yrs and Alice Roberts age 2 yrs are not Cherokees by blood and not entitled to citizenship in the Cherokee Nation. and not entitled to citizenship in the Cherokee Nation. P.O. Dalton.

           Will.P. Ross
              Chairman

Attest
  D.S. Williams   J.E. Gunter Com
  Asst Clk Com

ROUMINE

DOCKET #1571
CENSUS ROLLS 1835 & 52

APPLICANT FOR **CHEROKEE CITIZENSHIP**

POST OFFICE: Pine Hill Texas		ATTORNEY: A.E. Ivey	
NO	NAMES	AGE	SEX
1	Mary L Roumine	39	Female

Cherokee Citizenship Commission Docket Books
(1880-84, 1887-89) Volume IV
Tahlequah, Cherokee Nation

2	Lillie "	16	"
3	John C. "	10	Male

ANCESTOR: Mrs. Dunson nee Vann

Rejected Aug 26th 1889

                         Office Commission on Citizenship
                         Cherokee Nation Ind Ter
                         Tahlequah Aug 26th 1889

The above case was called 3 several times and no response from applicant or by Atty, the Commission decide that Mary L Roumine age 39 yrs and the following children Lillie Roumine Female age 16 yrs, John C. Roumine male age 10 yrs are nor Cherokees by blood. P.O. Pine Hill Texas.

                         Will.P. Ross
                                  Chairman

Attest
     D.S. Williams   J.E. Gunter   Com
     Asst Clk Com

ROGERS

DOCKET #1572
CENSUS ROLLS 1835 & 52

APPLICANT FOR CHEROKEE CITIZENSHIP

POST OFFICE: Belmont Ark		ATTORNEY: A E Ivey	
No	NAMES	AGE	SEX
1	Benton B Rogers	19	Male
2	James C.C. "	17	"
3	Mary C. "	15	Female
4	Linsey Ann E "	13	"

ANCESTOR: John Rogers

Now on this the 17th day of March 1888, comes the above case for a final hearing. The parties having made application pursuant to the provisions of an Act of the National Council approved December 8th 1886, and all the evidence being duly considered and found to be insufficient and unsatisfactory, it is adjudged and declared by the Commission that

     Benton B. Rogers, James C.C. Rogers, Mary C. Rogers, and Linsey Ann Rogers not Cherokees and they are not entitled to the rights, privileges and immunities of Cherokee citizens by blood.

Cherokee Citizenship Commission Docket Books
(1880-84, 1887-89) Volume IV
Tahlequah, Cherokee Nation

J T Adair   Chairman Commission
John E. Gunter   Commissioner
D.W. Lipe   Commissioner

Attest
    C.C. Lipe
        Clerk Com

The decision in the James C.C. Rogers case found in Book C, page 627, and testimony on Journal pages 325 to 333 governs this case.

SCOTT

DOCKET #1573
CENSUS ROLLS 1835, 48, 51 & 52
    or Old Settler   APPLICANT FOR CHEROKEE CITIZENSHIP

POST OFFICE: Van Buren Ark		ATTORNEY: Boudinot & R.	
No	NAMES	AGE	SEX
1	John Scott	54	Male
2	Aloza[sic] "	12	"
3	Zella "	10	Female
4	Mamie "	8	"

ANCESTOR: Micajah Scott

Rejected Aug 28th 1889

      Office Commission on Citizenship Cher Nat Ind Ter
            Tahlequah Aug 28th 1889

The above applicant claims to derive his Cherokee blood through his grand Father Micajah Scott whose name he believes will appear upon the census rolls of Cherokees 1835 to 52. The evidence he submits to sustain these allegations is all "exparte" also the affiants gain their knowledge of applicant through a third person – This evidence is not sufficient to admit applicant and Family to citizenship in this Nation – and further the name of Micajah Scott, applicant's grand Father, does not appear upon any of the Cherokee census rolls mentioned in claimant's application. Therefore we decide that applicant John Scott age 54 yrs and his children, Alonza Scott age 12 yrs, Zella Scott age 10 yrs and Mamie Scott age 8 yrs are not Cherokees by blood and not entitled to citizenship in the Cherokee Nation. and not entitled to citizenship in the Cherokee Nation. P.O. Van Buren Ark.

Cherokee Citizenship Commission Docket Books
(1880-84, 1887-89) Volume IV
Tahlequah, Cherokee Nation

Will.P.Ross
Chairman

Attest
D.S. Williams   J.E. Gunter   Com
Asst Clk Com

SCOTT

DOCKET #1574
CENSUS ROLLS 1835, 48, 51 & 52
or Old Settler   APPLICANT FOR CHEROKEE CITIZENSHIP

POST OFFICE: Van Buren Ark		ATTORNEY: Boudinot & R.	
No	NAMES	AGE	SEX
1	Micajah Scott, Jr	50	Male
2	John " "	19	"
3	Tom "	17	"
4	Jane "	14	Female
5	Susie "	12	"
6	Rebecca "	9	"
7	Adda "	7	"
8	Nannie "	5	"
9	Frank "	4	Male

ANCESTOR: Micajah Scott

Rejected Aug 26th 1889

Office Commission on Citizenship
Cherokee Nation Ind Ter
Tahlequah Aug 26th 1889

The above case was called 3 several times and no response from applicant or by Atty the Commission decide that Micajah Scott Jr. age 50 yrs and the following children John Jr. male 19 yrs, Tom male 17 yrs, Jane Female 14 yrs, Susie Female 12 yrs, Rebecca Female 9 yrs, Adda Female 7 yrs, Nannie Female 5 yrs and Frank Scott male 4 years, are not Cherokees by blood and not entitled to citizenship in the Cherokee Nation. P.O. Van Buren Ark.

Will.P. Ross
Chairman

Attest
D.S. Williams   J.E. Gunter
Asst Clk Com

Cherokee Citizenship Commission Docket Books
(1880-84, 1887-89) Volume IV
Tahlequah, Cherokee Nation

SCOTT

DOCKET #1575
CENSUS ROLLS 1835, 48, 51 & 52
or Old Settler

APPLICANT FOR **CHEROKEE CITIZENSHIP**

POST OFFICE: Childers Station I.T.   **ATTORNEY:** Boudinot & R.

No	NAMES	AGE	SEX
1	Wm C Scott	51	Male
2	John W. "	20	"
3	Eliza "	18	Female
4	Eveline "	17	"
5	Rebecca "	14	"
6	Francis M. "	12	Male
7	Henry "	10	"

ANCESTOR: Micajah Scott

Rejected Aug 27th 1889

Office Commission on Citizenship
Cherokee Nation Ind Ter
Tahlequah Aug 27th 1889

This case being called 3 several times and no response from applicant or by Atty the Commission decide that Wm C. Scott age 51 yrs and the following children John W. Scott male 20 yrs, Eliza E. Scott Female 18 yrs, Eveline Female 17 yrs, Rebecca 2[sic] female 14 yrs, Francis M. male age 12 yrs, and Henry Scott male age 10 yrs are not Cherokees by blood and not entitled to citizenship in the Cherokee Nation. Post Office Childers Station I.T.

Will.P. Ross
Chairman

Attest
   D.S. Williams
   Asst Clk Com

J.E. Gunter   Com

Cherokee Citizenship Commission Docket Books
(1880-84, 1887-89) Volume IV
Tahlequah, Cherokee Nation

SCOTT

DOCKET #1576
CENSUS ROLLS 1835, 48, 51 & 52
or Old Settler

APPLICANT FOR CHEROKEE CITIZENSHIP

POST OFFICE: Van Buren Ark		ATTORNEY: Boudinot & R.	
No	NAMES	AGE	SEX
1	Nancy Scott	53	Female

ANCESTOR: Micajah Scott

Rejected Aug 27th 1889

Office Commission on Citizenship
Cherokee Nation Ind Ter
Tahlequah Aug 27th 1889

The above application was called 3 times & no answer and as there is no evidence on file in support of the application we decide <u>Adversely</u> to claimant age 53 yrs. Post Office Van Buren Ark

Will.P. Ross
Chairman

Attest
 D.S. Williams   J.E. Gunter Com
 Asst Clk Com

SMITH

DOCKET #1577
CENSUS ROLLS 1835, 46, 51 & 52

APPLICANT FOR CHEROKEE CITIZENSHIP

POST OFFICE: Union Town Ark		ATTORNEY: A E Ivey	
No	NAMES	AGE	SEX
1	Mary A Smith	31	Female
2	Emma J. "	10	"
3	Nancy E "	8	"
4	Virgie "	6	"
5	Fleming "	3	Male

ANCESTOR: John Azbell

Rejected Aug 27th 1889

Office Commission on Citizenship
Cherokee Nation Ind Ter
Tahlequah Aug 27th 1889

Cherokee Citizenship Commission Docket Books
(1880-84, 1887-89) Volume IV
Tahlequah, Cherokee Nation

There is no evidence on file in support of the above application Therefore we decide <u>adversely</u> to claimants Mary A Smith age 31 yrs and her children namely Emma J Smith age 10 yrs, Nancy E Smith age 8 yrs, Virgie Smith age 6 yrs, & Fleming Smith age 3 yrs. Post Office Union Town Ark.

Attest
D.S. Williams
Asst Clk Com

Will.P. Ross
Chairman
J.E. Gunter Com

STAGGS

DOCKET #1578
CENSUS ROLLS 1835, 48, 52 & 52
or Old Settler

APPLICANT FOR CHEROKEE CITIZENSHIP

POST OFFICE: Blue Jacket I.T.   ATTORNEY: Boudinot & R.

No	NAMES	AGE	SEX
1	Anderson Staggs	47	Male
2	Luella "	20	Female
3	George "	17	Male
4	Jetty "	15	"
5	Panit "	12	"
6	Elliott "	9	"
7	John "	6	"

ANCESTOR: Kableton Staggs

We the Commission on Citizenship after carefully examining into the matter of Anderson Staggs, applicant in this case, fail to find any proof whatever that he is of Cherokee blood, none of the rolls taken by the U.S. Government East of the Mississippi river from 1835 to the year 1852 show the name of Kableston[sic] Staggs, the alleged ancestor, and from whom the applicants claim to derive their Cherokee blood. From the evidence submitted on part of the claimants, it clearly shows that he is of African descent on his mother's side, and that his father Kableston Stagg[sic] was not a Cherokee.

We the Commission decide that the said applicants Anderson Staggs, and his ~~five~~ six children, ~~are not~~ viz: Luella, George, Jetty, Panit, Elliott and John Staggs are not Cherokees by blood and are hereby declared intruders upon the public domain of the Cherokee Nation.

Cherokee Citizenship Commission Docket Books
(1880-84, 1887-89) Volume IV
Tahlequah, Cherokee Nation

        J.T. Adair   Chairman Commission
        D.W. Lipe   Commissioner
        H.C. Barnes Commissioner

Office Com on Citizenship
Tahlequah I.T. Sept 24th 1888

STICK

DOCKET #1579
CENSUS ROLLS

APPLICANT FOR CHEROKEE CITIZENSHIP

POST OFFICE: Carthage Mo		ATTORNEY: L.B. Bell	
No	NAMES	AGE	SEX
1	Hattie Stick		Female

ANCESTOR: Ann Crews

The Commission decide against claimant. See Docket 2180 Book E, Page 26 and John Henly, Book C Page 346 Docket 1250.

        Will.P. Ross   Chairman

EG Ross
    Clerk Com   John. E. Gunter Com

SMITH

DOCKET #1580
CENSUS ROLLS 1835, 48, 51 & 52
    or Old Settler

APPLICANT FOR CHEROKEE CITIZENSHIP

POST OFFICE: Dardanelle Ark		ATTORNEY: Boudinot & R.	
No	NAMES	AGE	SEX
1	Mahala Smith		Female
2	Frank "		Male
3	George "	13	"

ANCESTOR: John Britton

Rejected Aug 27th 1889

        Office Commission on Citizenship
           Cherokee Nation Ind Ter
           Tahlequah Aug 27th 1889

Cherokee Citizenship Commission Docket Books
(1880-84, 1887-89) Volume IV
Tahlequah, Cherokee Nation

The above application was called three times & no answer and there being no evidence on file in support of the application Mahala Smith and her children Frank Smith and George Smith, age 13 yrs are not Cherokees by blood and not entitled to citizenship in the Cherokee Nation. Post Office Dardanelle Ark.

                                      Will.P. Ross
Attest   Chairman
   D.S. Williams   J.E. Gunter   Com
   Asst Clk Com

SCOTT

DOCKET #1581
CENSUS ROLLS 1835, 48, 51 & 52

APPLICANT FOR CHEROKEE CITIZENSHIP

POST OFFICE: Vinita Ind Tery		ATTORNEY: Boudinot & R.	
NO	NAMES	AGE	SEX
1	Robert Scott	75	Male

ANCESTOR: Silvia Scott

Rejected Aug 27th 1889

                              Office Commission on Citizenship
                                  Cherokee Nation Ind Ter
                                    Tahlequah Aug 27th 1889

The above application having been called 3 times & no answer and as there is no evidence on file in support of the application we decide that applicant Robt S[sic] Scott age 75 yrs is not a Cherokee by blood. Post Office Vinita I.T.

                                  Will.P. Ross
Attest   Chairman
   D.S. Williams   J.E. Gunter   Com
   Asst Clk Com

STEWART

DOCKET #1582
CENSUS ROLLS 1835, 48, 51 & 52

APPLICANT FOR CHEROKEE CITIZENSHIP

POST OFFICE: Dover Ark		ATTORNEY: Boudinot & R.	
NO	NAMES	AGE	SEX
1	Laura A Stewart	28	Female
2	Minnetta "	9	"

Cherokee Citizenship Commission Docket Books
(1880-84, 1887-89) Volume IV
Tahlequah, Cherokee Nation

3	Lizzie N "	7	"
4	William J "	2	Male

ANCESTOR: Barsheba Goodrich

                        Office Commission on Citizenship
                        Tahlequah C.N. June 20 1889

There being no evidence in support of the above named case the Commission decide that Laura A Stewart aged 28 years and the following children Minnetta aged[sic] aged 9 years, Lizzie N. aged 7 years and William J. Stewart aged 2 years are not Cherokees by blood.

Attest

EG Ross   Will.P. Ross
    Clerk Commission   Chairman
                            J.E. Gunter   Com

SUTTON

DOCKET #1583
CENSUS ROLLS

APPLICANT FOR **CHEROKEE CITIZENSHIP**

POST OFFICE: Afton Ark		ATTORNEY: L.B. Bell	
NO	**NAMES**	**AGE**	**SEX**
1	Elizabeth More[sic] Sutton	26	Female

ANCESTOR: Ann Crews

The Commission decide against claimant. See decision Docket 2180 Book E, Page 26 and John Henly Book C Page 346 Docket 1250.

                        Will.P. Ross   Chairman
                        John E. Gunter   Com

SCOTT

DOCKET #1584
CENSUS ROLLS

APPLICANT FOR **CHEROKEE CITIZENSHIP**

POST OFFICE: Valley Mills Inda		ATTORNEY: L.B. Bell	
NO	**NAMES**	**AGE**	**SEX**
1	John Scott		

ANCESTOR: Sarah Morgan

Cherokee Citizenship Commission Docket Books
(1880-84, 1887-89) Volume IV
Tahlequah, Cherokee Nation

The application in the above case is accompanied by no evidence but is one of several filed by L. B. Bell Attorney for claimants who allege their descent from one Mary Crews. It is admitted that neither the name of the applicant nor that of an ancestor is entered upon the census rolls of Cherokees by blood. taken and made by the United States, in the years 1835, 48, 51 & 52. *(Illegible)* on the Act of Dec. 8th 1886 and which governs the decision of this Commission in the provisions. It is therefore decided that the applicant is not of Cherokee blood. See case of John Henly Docket 1250, Book C, Page 376 and Andrew Meredith 2180, Book E, Page 26. P.O. Valley Mills Indiana

Will.P. Ross
Chairman
J.E. Gunter   Com

STOCKSTON

DOCKET #1585
CENSUS ROLLS 1835 & 52

APPLICANT FOR CHEROKEE CITIZENSHIP

POST OFFICE: Siloam Springs Ark		ATTORNEY: L.S. Sanders	
NO	NAMES	AGE	SEX
1	Rosannah Stockston	56	Female
2	E. Catherine Shafer	36	"
3	James C. Stockston	33	Male
4	Daniel "	31	"
5	Rebecca Jane Johnson	28	Female
6	Andrew J. "	26	Male
7	Elizabeth Ellen "	22	Female

ANCESTOR: Francis Martin

Rejected Aug 27th 1889

Office Commission on Citizenship
Cherokee Nation Ind Ter
Tahlequah Aug 27th 1889

There being no evidence in support of the above named application we decide <u>Adversely</u> to claimant Rosannah Stockston age 56 yrs together with her children to wit, E. Catherine Shafer age 36 yrs, James E. Stockston age 33 yrs, Daniel Stockston age 31 yrs, Rebeca[sic] Jane Johnson age 28 yrs, Andrew J. Stockston age 26 yrs, Elizabeth Ellen Stockston 22 yrs.
Post Office Siloam Springs, Ark.

Cherokee Citizenship Commission Docket Books
(1880-84, 1887-89) Volume IV
Tahlequah, Cherokee Nation

Will.P. Ross
Chairman
J.E. Gunter Com

Attest
   D.S. Williams
   Asst Clk Com

SEITZE

DOCKET #1586
CENSUS ROLLS 1835

APPLICANT FOR **CHEROKEE CITIZENSHIP**

POST OFFICE: Densmore[sic] Ark		ATTORNEY: C H Taylor	
NO	NAMES	AGE	SEX
1	J.T. Seitze	45	Male
2	Henry Bell "	19	"
3	Lebron G. "	17	"
4	Baily B. "	15	"
5	William N. "	11	"
6	Frank M. "	5	"
7	Clara Jane "	4	Female
8	Jessie Bryant "	2	"

ANCESTOR: Daniel Coody

Rejected Aug 26th 1889

    Office Commission on Citizenship
    Cherokee Nation Ind Ter
    Tahlequah Aug 26th 1889

The above application was filed on the 4th day of October 1888 and no evidence filed in support of the application we decide that applicant J.T. Seitze age 45 yrs and children Henry Bell Seitze age 19 yrs, Lebron G. Seitze age 17 yrs, Baily B. Seitze age 15 yrs, William N. Seitze age 11 yrs, Frank M. Seitze age 5 yrs, Clara Jane Seitze age 4 yrs, Jessie Bryant Seitze age 2 yrs are not Cherokees by blood. Post Office Densmore[sic] Ark.

              Will.P. Ross
Attest   Chairman
   D.S. Williams   J.E. Gunter Com
   Asst Clk Com

Cherokee Citizenship Commission Docket Books
(1880-84, 1887-89) Volume IV
Tahlequah, Cherokee Nation

SMITH

DOCKET #1587
CENSUS ROLLS 1835

APPLICANT FOR CHEROKEE CITIZENSHIP

POST OFFICE: *(Illegible)* Hill Ark		ATTORNEY: C.H. Taylor	
NO	NAMES	AGE	SEX
1	J. C. Smith	48	Male

ANCESTOR: Sela Brown

Office Commission on Citizenship
Tahlequah Ind Ter July 2nd 1889

No evidence in support of the above case having been presented the Commission decide against the applicant.

Attest
 E G Ross
  Clerk Commission

    Will.P. Ross
     Chairman
    J.E. Gunter Com

SMITH

DOCKET #1588
CENSUS ROLLS 1835

APPLICANT FOR CHEROKEE CITIZENSHIP

POST OFFICE: Lead Hills Ark		ATTORNEY: C.H. Taylor	
NO	NAMES	AGE	SEX
1	William Smith	36	Male

ANCESTOR: Sela Brown

Office Commission on Citizenship
Tahlequah Ind Ter July 2nd 1889

No evidence having been submitted with this case, the Commission decide against the applicant. Post Office Lead Hill Ark.

Attest
 EG Ross
  Clerk Commission

    Will.P. Ross
     Chairman
    J.E. Gunter Com

Cherokee Citizenship Commission Docket Books
(1880-84, 1887-89) Volume IV
Tahlequah, Cherokee Nation

SMITH

DOCKET #1589
CENSUS ROLLS 1835

APPLICANT FOR CHEROKEE CITIZENSHIP

POST OFFICE: Lead Hill Ark		ATTORNEY: C.H. Taylor	
No	NAMES	AGE	SEX
1	C.J. Smith	28	Male

ANCESTOR: Sela Brown

Office Commission on Citizenship
Tahlequah Ind Ter July 2nd 1889

There being no evidence in support of this case the Commission decide against the applicant.

Attest   Will.P. Ross
  EG Ross   Chairman
    Clerk Commission   JE Gunter Com

SWAFORD

DOCKET #1570[sic]
CENSUS ROLLS

APPLICANT FOR CHEROKEE CITIZENSHIP

POST OFFICE: Evansville Ark		ATTORNEY: J.E. Welch	
No	NAMES	AGE	SEX
1	Zorah C Swaford	13	Female

ANCESTOR:

Office Commission on Citizenship

Zora C. Swaford   Oct. 23rd 1889
   v   Application for Cherokee Citizenship
Cherokee Nation

The above case was rejected by the Commission on Aug 26th 1889 on the grounds that applicant was called three times & no answer either in person or by Attorney and no[sic] comes the applicant & asks the Commission to re-open the case for reasons that her Attorney neglected her *(illegible)* by not submitting her evidence for *(illegible...)* In view of these facts we granted the applicant a re-hearing & upon the evidence of Samuel Keys & &[sic] Samuel Price citizens of

Cherokee Citizenship Commission Docket Books
(1880-84, 1887-89) Volume IV
Tahlequah, Cherokee Nation

the Cherokee Nation by blood who swear that applicant Zora C Swaford is realative[sic] of theirs & a Cherokee by blood & *(illegible)* the facts that applicant's ancestor is found upon the Cherokee census rolls we are of the opinion & so decide that applicant Zora C. Swaford should be & she is hereby re-admitted to all the rights & privileges of Cherokee citizenship – The applicant in this case proves her lineal descent from Samuel Keys and his wife Polly Keys whose maiden name was Polly Riley a person of Cherokee blood.

Will.P. Ross
Chairman
J. E. Gunter   Comm

SELSER

DOCKET #1591
CENSUS ROLLS 1851 & 52

APPLICANT FOR CHEROKEE CITIZENSHIP

POST OFFICE:		ATTORNEY: C.H. Taylor	
NO	NAMES	AGE	SEX
1	Martha Selser	54	Female

ANCESTOR: Polly Taylor

The above case being submitted by defendant's Atty. Mr. C.H. Taylor and all the evidence as well as the rolls mentioned in the 7th Sec. of the Act creating this Commission, approved Dec. 8th 1886 it is adjudged and determined by the Commission that and determined by the Commission on Citizenship that the applicant is a Cherokee by blood and is entitled to all the rights and privileges of Cherokee citizens by virtue of such blood and is therefore:

Re-admitted to all the rights and privileges of Cherokee citizens and do hereby so declare.

J T Adair   Chairman Commission
H.C Barnes   Commissioner

Office of Com on Citizenship
July 30 – 1888

Cherokee Citizenship Commission Docket Books
(1880-84, 1887-89) Volume IV
Tahlequah, Cherokee Nation

SWAFORD

DOCKET #1570[sic]
CENSUS ROLLS 1835

APPLICANT FOR CHEROKEE CITIZENSHIP

POST OFFICE: Evansville Ark		ATTORNEY: J E Welch	
No	NAMES	AGE	SEX
1	Zorah C Swaford	13	Female

ANCESTOR: Catharine Price

Rejected Aug 26th 1889

Office Commission on Citizenship
Cherokee Nation Ind Ter
Tahlequah Aug 26th 1889

The above case was called 3 several times not less than one hour apart and no response from applicant or by Atty the Commission decide that Zorah C Swaford age 13 yrs is not a Cherokee by blood. P.O. Evansville Ark.

Will.P. Ross
Chairman

Attest
    D.S. Williams   J.E. Gunter Com
    Asst Clk Com

Reconsidered and Admitted October 22^{nc} 1889

STOCKDALE

DOCKET #1592
CENSUS ROLLS 1835

APPLICANT FOR CHEROKEE CITIZENSHIP

POST OFFICE: Decatur Texas		ATTORNEY: CH Taylor	
No	NAMES	AGE	SEX
1	Martha Stockdale	52	Female
2	Mark "	14	Male
3	Doc "	7	"

ANCESTOR: *(Names Illegible)*

Rejected Aug 26th 1889

Office Commission on Citizenship
Cherokee Nation Ind Ter
Tahlequah Aug 26th 1889

Cherokee Citizenship Commission Docket Books
(1880-84, 1887-89) Volume IV
Tahlequah, Cherokee Nation

The above application was filed on the 5th day October 1887, and on this day the case coming on for final hearing we fail to find any evidence in support of the applicant. Therefore we decide that applicant Martha Stockdale and children Mark Stockdale age 17[sic] and Doc Stockdale age 7 yrs are not Cherokees by blood. Post Office Decatur Texas.

                                            Will.P. Ross   Chairman

Attest
    D.S. Williams   J.E. Gunter   Com
    Asst Clk Com

STEWART

DOCKET #1593
CENSUS ROLLS

APPLICANT FOR CHEROKEE CITIZENSHIP

POST OFFICE: Sanders Station I.T.		ATTORNEY: C.H. Taylor	
NO	NAMES	AGE	SEX
1	G. M. Stewart	45	Male
2	Nealie "	19	Female
3	Sudy "	17	"
4	Lucresy "	10	"
5	Eddie "	8	Male
6	Charley "	5	"
7	*(Illegible)* "	3	"

ANCESTOR: Jane Stewart

Rejected Aug 28th 1889

                          Office Commission on Citizenship
                                Cherokee Nation Ind Ter
                             Tahlequah August 28th 1889

The above case was called for a hearing and submitted by E.C. Boudinot Atty. The Commission therefore decide that G.W[sic] Stewart age 44[sic] yrs and the following children Nealis[sic] Stewart Female 19 yrs. Sudy Female 17 yrs. Lucresy E 10 yrs, Eddie Female[sic] 8 yrs, Charley male 5 yrs and Sue Stewart male 3 yrs are not Cherokees by blood. Post Office Sanders Station I.T.

                                  Will.P. Ross
Attest   Chairman
    D.S. Williams   J.E. Gunter   Com
    Asst Clk Com

Cherokee Citizenship Commission Docket Books
(1880-84, 1887-89) Volume IV
Tahlequah, Cherokee Nation

SPECK

DOCKET #1594
CENSUS ROLLS

APPLICANT FOR CHEROKEE CITIZENSHIP

POST OFFICE: Wilmington Del		ATTORNEY:	
No	NAMES	AGE	SEX
1	Frank Speck		

ANCESTOR: Ann Crews

The Commission decide against claimant. See decision in the case of Andrew Meredith Docket 2180 Book E, Page 26 and John Henly Docket 1250, Book C Page 376.

Will.P. Ross   Chairman
John E Gunter   Com

SANDERS

DOCKET #1595
CENSUS ROLLS

APPLICANT FOR CHEROKEE CITIZENSHIP

POST OFFICE: Genoa Neb		ATTORNEY: L.B. Bell	
No	NAMES	AGE	SEX
1	Milo Sanders		

ANCESTOR: Sarah Morgan

The Commission decide against claimant. See decision in the case of ~~Andrew~~ John ~~Meredith~~ Scott Docket ~~2180~~ 1584 Book ~~E~~ D, Page ~~26~~ 70 and John Henly Docket 1250, Book C Page 376.

Will.P. Ross
Chairman
John E. Gunter   Com

SCOTT

DOCKET #1596
CENSUS ROLLS

APPLICANT FOR CHEROKEE CITIZENSHIP

POST OFFICE: Valley Mills Inda		ATTORNEY: L.B. Bell	
No	NAMES	AGE	SEX
1	Isaac Scott		

ANCESTOR: Sarah Morgan

Cherokee Citizenship Commission Docket Books
(1880-84, 1887-89) Volume IV
Tahlequah, Cherokee Nation

There is no evidence filed in support of the above case. Therefore The Commission decide against claimant. See decision in the case of Andrew Meredith Docket ~~2180~~ 1584[sic] Book ~~E~~ D, Page ~~26~~ 70 and John Henly Docket 1250, Book C Page 376.

        Will.P. Ross
        Chairman
      John E. Gunter Com

SHIBLEY

DOCKET #1597
CENSUS ROLLS 1835 & 52

APPLICANT FOR CHEROKEE CITIZENSHIP

POST OFFICE: Van Buren Ark		ATTORNEY: L.S. Sanders	
NO	NAMES	AGE	SEX
1	Isabelle Shibley	24	Female
2	William Irvin "	5	Male
3	Manervia Emaline "	4	Female
~~4~~	Hettie Myrtle "	2	"

ANCESTOR: Emiline Boatright

Rejected Aug 27th 1889

      Office Commission on Citizenship
      Cherokee Nation Ind Ter
      Tahlequah Aug 27th 1889

The above case was called and submitted by Rasmus Atty without evidence. The Commission therefore decide that Isabelle Shibley age 24 yrs and the following children William Irvin male age 5 yrs, Manervia Everline[sic] Female age 4 yrs, and Hettie Myrtle Shibley Female age 2 yrs are not Cherokees by blood. P.O. Van Buren Ark.

       Will.P. Ross
Attest   Chairman
 D.S. Williams   J.E. Gunter Com
 Asst Clk Com

Cherokee Citizenship Commission Docket Books
(1880-84, 1887-89) Volume IV
Tahlequah, Cherokee Nation

SMITH

DOCKET #1598
CENSUS ROLLS 1835 or 52

APPLICANT FOR **CHEROKEE CITIZENSHIP**

POST OFFICE: Siloam Springs Ark		ATTORNEY: L.S. Sanders	
NO	NAMES	AGE	SEX
1	Hasbard H. Smith	41	Male
2	Minnie L "	10	Female
3	Walter H "	8	Male
4	Ralph N "	3	"

ANCESTOR: Benjamin Hester

Rejected Aug 27th 1889

Office Commission on Citizenship
Cherokee Nation Ind Ter
Tahlequah Aug 27th 1889

The above case was called and submitted by Rasmus Atty without evidence. The Commission therefore decide that Hasbard H. Smith age 41 yrs and the following children Minnie L. Smith Female age 10 yrs, Walter H male 8 yrs son and Randolph[sic] N. Smith son age 3 yrs are not Cherokees by blood. Post Office Siloam Springs Ark.

Attest
D.S. Williams
Asst Clk Com

Will.P. Ross
Chairman
J.E. Gunter Com

SOUTHGATE

DOCKET #1599
CENSUS ROLLS

APPLICANT FOR **CHEROKEE CITIZENSHIP**

POST OFFICE: Topeka Kansas		ATTORNEY: C.H. Taylor	
NO	NAMES	AGE	SEX
1	Malissie Southgate	32	Female
2	Ethel "	3	"

ANCESTOR: Agnes Bain

Rejected Aug 28th 1889

Office Commission on Citizenship
Cherokee Nation Ind Ter
Tahlequah Aug 28th 1889

Cherokee Citizenship Commission Docket Books
(1880-84, 1887-89) Volume IV
Tahlequah, Cherokee Nation

The above case was called Aug 26th for a hearing and laid over to 27th and was then submitted E.C. Boudinot without evidence. The Commission therefore decide that Malissia[sic] Southgate age 32 yrs and Ethel Southgate female age 3 yrs Daughter are not Cherokees by blood. P.O. Topeka Kans.

            Will.P. Ross
Attest   Chairman
  D.S. Williams   J.E. Gunter   Com
  Asst Clk Com

SMITH

DOCKET #1600
CENSUS ROLLS

APPLICANT FOR **CHEROKEE CITIZENSHIP**

POST OFFICE: Afton I.T.		ATTORNEY: L.B. Bell	
NO	NAMES	AGE	SEX
1	Margaret E Smith	24	Female

ANCESTOR: Ann Crews

The Commission decide against claimant. See decision in the case of Andrew Meredith Docket 2180 Book E, Page 26 and John Henly Docket 1250, Book C Page 376.

           Will.P. Ross   Chairman
           John E. Gunter   Com

STEELE

DOCKET #1601
CENSUS ROLLS 1835 & 52

APPLICANT FOR **CHEROKEE CITIZENSHIP**

POST OFFICE: Montrose Montrose Co Colorado		ATTORNEY: Wm A Thompson	
NO	NAMES	AGE	SEX
1	Robert Steele	42	Male

ANCESTOR: Robbie Vann

           Office Commission on Citizenship
             Tahlequah I.T. Aug 22nd 1889

Cherokee Citizenship Commission Docket Books
(1880-84, 1887-89) Volume IV
Tahlequah, Cherokee Nation

The applicant for readmission to citizenship in the above case Robert Steele having proven to the satisfaction of the Commission that he is of Cherokee descent and that his name is found on the census roll of Cherokees by blood taken and made by the United States in the year A.D. 1852 is hereby readmitted to Citizenship in the Cherokee Nation.
Attest
    EG Ross   Will.P. Ross
        Clerk Commission   Chairman
                                            J.E. Gunter   Com

---

SANDERS

DOCKET #1602
CENSUS ROLLS

APPLICANT FOR CHEROKEE CITIZENSHIP

POST OFFICE: Genoa Neb		ATTORNEY: L.B. Bell	
No	NAMES	AGE	SEX
1	Thomas Sanders		Male

ANCESTOR: Sarah Morgan

The Commission decide against the applicant in the above case because it is accompanied by no evidence and for reasons set forth in their decision in the case of John Scott Docket 1584, Book D, Page 70.
                                                 Will.P. Ross
                                                 Chairman
                                                 J.E. Gunter   Com

---

STARBUCK

DOCKET #1603
CENSUS ROLLS

APPLICANT FOR CHEROKEE CITIZENSHIP

POST OFFICE: Erie Kans		ATTORNEY: L.B. Bell	
No	NAMES	AGE	SEX
1	Ann E Starbuck	58	Female
2	Charles E "		Male

ANCESTOR: Mary Crews

Cherokee Citizenship Commission Docket Books
(1880-84, 1887-89) Volume IV
Tahlequah, Cherokee Nation

The Commission decide against claimant. See decision in the case of Andrew Meredith Docket 2180 Book E, Page 26 and John Henly Docket 1250, Book C Page 376.

           Will.P. Ross
                Chairman
          J.E. Gunter Com

STANLEY

DOCKET #1604
CENSUS ROLLS

APPLICANT FOR CHEROKEE CITIZENSHIP

POST OFFICE: Maryville		ATTORNEY: L.B. Bell	
No	NAMES	AGE	SEX
1	Wm C Stanley		Male

ANCESTOR: Ann Crews

The Commission decide against claimant. See decision in the case of Andrew Meredith Docket 2180 Book E, Page 26 and John Henly Docket 1250, Book C Page 376.

           Will.P. Ross Chairman
           John E. Gunter Com

SUTTON

DOCKET #1605
CENSUS ROLLS

APPLICANT FOR CHEROKEE CITIZENSHIP

POST OFFICE: Dakota		ATTORNEY: L.B.B.	
No	NAMES	AGE	SEX
1	Mary B Sutton		

ANCESTOR: Ann Crews

The Commission decide against claimant. See decision in the case of Andrew Meredith Docket 2180 Book E, Page 26 and John Henly Docket 1250, Book C Page 376.

           Will.P. Ross
             Chairman
          J.E. Gunter Com

Cherokee Citizenship Commission Docket Books
(1880-84, 1887-89) Volume IV
Tahlequah, Cherokee Nation

SUTTON

DOCKET #1606
CENSUS ROLLS

APPLICANT FOR CHEROKEE CITIZENSHIP

POST OFFICE:		ATTORNEY: L.B. Bell	
NO	NAMES	AGE	SEX
1	Caroline Sutton		Female
2	Martha "		"

ANCESTOR: Ann Crews

The Commission decide against claimant. See decision in the case of Andrew Meredith Docket 2180 Book E, Page 26 and John Henly Docket 1250, Book C Page 376.

Will.P. Ross   Chairman
John E. Gunter   Com

STANLEY

DOCKET #1607
CENSUS ROLLS

APPLICANT FOR CHEROKEE CITIZENSHIP

POST OFFICE: Charlestown Inda		ATTORNEY: L.B. Bell	
NO	NAMES	AGE	SEX
1	J. C. Stanley		Male
2	Susan F. "	27	Female

ANCESTOR: Ann Crews

The Commission decide against claimant. See decision in the case of Andrew Meredith Docket 2180 Book E, Page 26 and John Henly Docket 1250, Book C Page 376.

Will.P. Ross   Chairman
John E. Gunter   Com

SANDERS

DOCKET #1608
CENSUS ROLLS 1835

APPLICANT FOR CHEROKEE CITIZENSHIP

POST OFFICE: Hudsville Ark		ATTORNEY: C.H. Taylor	
NO	NAMES	AGE	SEX
1	Ada B. Sanders	19	Female

Cherokee Citizenship Commission Docket Books
(1880-84, 1887-89) Volume IV
Tahlequah, Cherokee Nation

2	Claude G "	1	Male
3	*(Illegible)* C. "		Male

ANCESTOR: Feraby Vaughn

Office Commission on Citizenship
Tahlequah I.T. July 2nd 1889

There being no evidence in support of the above case the Commission decide that Ada B Sanders aged 19 years and her child Claude G Sanders aged 1 year are not Cherokees by blood. Post Office Huddsville Ark.

Attest   Will.P. Ross
    EG Ross   Chairman
    Asst Clk Com   J.E. Gunter Com

SMITH

DOCKET #1609
CENSUS ROLLS 1828 or 35

APPLICANT FOR CHEROKEE CITIZENSHIP

POST OFFICE: Childers Station C.N.		ATTORNEY: J.E. Welch	
NO	NAMES	AGE	SEX
1	Thos Smith	47	Male

ANCESTOR: Archiles Smith

Office Commission on Citizenship
Cherokee Nation Ind Ter
Tahlequah August 28th 1889

The above case was called for a hearing and submitted by E.C. Boudinot without evidence. The Commission therefore decide that Thomas Smith age 47 years is not a Cherokee by blood.

Attest   Will.P. Ross
    EG Ross   Chairman
    Clerk Commission   J.E. Gunter Com

Cherokee Citizenship Commission Docket Books
(1880-84, 1887-89) Volume IV
Tahlequah, Cherokee Nation

SHIBLEY

DOCKET #1610
CENSUS ROLLS 1835 & 52

APPLICANT FOR **CHEROKEE CITIZENSHIP**

POST OFFICE: Van Buren Ark		ATTORNEY: L.S. Sanders	
No	NAMES	AGE	SEX
1	Ada Shibley	27	Female
2	Samuel "	6	Male
3	Ada Ann "	4	Female
4	Mary Edna "	2	"
5	Jesse H. "	1	Male

ANCESTOR: Emiline Boatright

Rejected Aug 27th 1889

Office Commission on Citizenship
Cherokee Nation Ind Ter
Tahlequah Aug 27th 1889

The above case was called and submitted by applicants' Atty Rasmus without evidence. The Commission therefore decide that Ada Shibley age 27 yrs and the following children Ada Ann Female age 4 yrs. Daughter, Samuel Son male age 6 yrs, Mary Edna Female 2 yrs Daughter and Jesse H. Shibley Son male 1 yr. are not Cherokees by blood. P.O. Van Buren Ark.

Will.P. Ross
Chairman

Attest
D.S. Williams
Asst Clk Com

J.E. Gunter Com

SMITH

DOCKET #1611
CENSUS ROLLS 1835 & 46

APPLICANT FOR **CHEROKEE CITIZENSHIP**

POST OFFICE: Rudy Ark		ATTORNEY: A E Ivey	
No	NAMES	AGE	SEX
1	Mary F Smith	42	Female
2	Sidena Henryetta "	17	"
3	Mary J. "	13	"
4	Jessie B. "	12	"
5	Sarah Allice "	10	"
6	Augusta W. "	7	"

Cherokee Citizenship Commission Docket Books
(1880-84, 1887-89) Volume IV
Tahlequah, Cherokee Nation

7	Nellie M. "	3	"

ANCESTOR: Henry C Edwards

Now on this the 9th day of January A.D. 1888, comes the above case for final hearing. They having made application pursuant to the provisions of an Act of the National Council approved Dec 8th 1886, and all the evidence being fully considered in the Mary A Couch case, this being and claiming a direct lineage from Mima Edwards, it is adjudged and determined by the Commission that and determined by the Commission that the testimony is insufficient and unsatisfactory, and that they are not Cherokees by blood, and not entitled to the rights, immunities and privileges of such, therefore the Commission decide against applicants. The decision in the Mary A Couch case found on Docket "A", Page 100 and testimony on Journal pages 276 to 278 governs the above case.

        J T Adair Chairman Commission
        D.W. Lipe Commissioner

SPINKLE

DOCKET #1612
CENSUS ROLLS 1835 & 52

APPLICANT FOR CHEROKEE CITIZENSHIP

POST OFFICE: *(Illegible)* Ark		ATTORNEY: A.E. Ivey	
NO	NAMES	AGE	SEX
1	Thomas V Spinkle	22	Male

ANCESTOR: Sarah Thomas

Rejected Aug 27th 1889

       Office Commission on Citizenship
         Cherokee Nation Ind Ter
        Tahlequah Aug 27th 1889

The above application was submitted [sic] applicants Attorney A. E. Ivey without evidence we decide that applicant Thomas V. Spinkle age 22 yrs and his children M Spinkle age 5 yrs & Mary Spinkle age 3 yrs. are not Cherokees by blood. P.O. *(Illegible)* Ark

        Will.P. Ross
Attest   Chairman
  D.S. Williams   J.E. Gunter Com
  Asst Clk Com

Cherokee Citizenship Commission Docket Books (1880-84, 1887-89) Volume IV
Tahlequah, Cherokee Nation

STAUPS

DOCKET #1613
CENSUS ROLLS 1835

APPLICANT FOR CHEROKEE CITIZENSHIP

POST OFFICE: Albequerke[sic] NM		ATTORNEY: A E Ivey	
No	NAMES	AGE	SEX
1	Malvana Staups	33	Female
2	Nancy "	12	"
3	Rachel "	9	"
4	Wm " Twins {	6	Male
5	Gordon "	6	"

ANCESTOR: Hiram Bryant

Now on this the 26th day of June 1388, comes the above case up for final hearing, it being one of eleven cases claiming a descent from Hiram Bryant. Decision governing this case will be found in the Rachel Wilder case in this Book, page 311 – Testimony will be found in the cases of Rachel Wilder, et al. on Record, pages 74 to 81 –

      J T Adair Chairman Commission
      D.W. Lipe Commissioner

STEWART

DOCKET #1614
CENSUS ROLLS 1835 to 52

APPLICANT FOR CHEROKEE CITIZENSHIP

POST OFFICE: Lancaster Ark		ATTORNEY: A E Ivey	
No	NAMES	AGE	SEX
1	Elizabeth J Stewart	46	Female
2	Julia "	23	"
3	Florence "	15	"
4	John "	13	Male
5	Jewell "	11	"[sic]
6	Bolen "	9	"

ANCESTOR: Lawrence Slaughter

Rejected Aug 27th 1889

      Office Commission on Citizenship
      Cherokee Nation Ind Ter
      Tahlequah Aug 27th 1889

Cherokee Citizenship Commission Docket Books
(1880-84, 1887-89) Volume IV
Tahlequah, Cherokee Nation

The above application was called 3 times & no answer & as there is no evidence on file in support of the application we decide the applicant Elizabeth J Stewart age 46 yrs and her children Julia Stewart age 23 yrs, Florence Stewart age 15 yrs, John Stewart age 13 yrs, Jewell Stewart age 11 yrs, & Bolen Stewart are not Cherokees by blood. Post Office Lancaster Ark.

                                          Will.P. Ross

Attest   Chairman
    D.S. Williams   J.E. Gunter   Com
    Asst Clk Com.

SPALE

DOCKET #1615
CENSUS ROLLS 1835

APPLICANT FOR CHEROKEE CITIZENSHIP

POST OFFICE: Alma Ark		ATTORNEY: A.E. Ivey	
NO	NAMES	AGE	SEX
1	John Spale	16	Male
2	Pat "	14	"
3	Wm D. "	11	"
4	Robert B. "	8	"
5	Columbus T. "	6	"

ANCESTOR: Mima Franklin

This case docketed twice, see decision and reference on page 382.

                                        Cornell Rogers
                                        Clerk Commission

HATTEN

DOCKET #1616
CENSUS ROLLS 1835

APPLICANT FOR CHEROKEE CITIZENSHIP

POST OFFICE: Stephensville[sic] Texas		ATTORNEY: A.E. Ivey	
NO	NAMES	AGE	SEX
1	Mary J. Hatten	8	Female
2	H.F. Hatten	5	Male
3	J.S. "	3	"

ANCESTOR: Hiram Bryant

Cherokee Citizenship Commission Docket Books
(1880-84, 1887-89) Volume IV
Tahlequah, Cherokee Nation

Rejected Sept 13th 1889

                        Office Commission on Citizenship
                        Cherokee Nation Ind Ter
                        Tahlequah Sept 13th 1889

The above case was called 3 times and no response from applicant or by Atty and there being no evidence on file in support of claimants. The Commission decide that Mary J Hatten female 8 yrs, J.S. Hatten male 5[sic] yrs and Hiram F. Hatten male 3 yrs are not Cherokees by blood. P.O. Stephensville[sic] Tex.

                    Will.P. Ross
Attest   Chair
  D.S. Williams   J.E. Gunter Com
  Asst Clk Com

SPELD

DOCKET #1617
CENSUS ROLLS 1835

APPLICANT FOR CHEROKEE CITIZENSHIP

POST OFFICE: Alma Ark		ATTORNEY: AE Ivey	
NO	NAMES	AGE	SEX
1	Elizabeth Speld	50	Female
2	Henry T. "	13	Male
3	Delilah E. "	11	Female

ANCESTOR: Mima Franklin

Now on this the 9th day of January 1888, comes the above entitled case up for a final hearing, the applicant having made application pursuant to the provisions of an Act of the National Council approved Dec 8th 1886, and the evidence found to be insufficient and unsatisfactory to the Commission, it is adjudged and determined that Elizabeth Speld, Henry T. – and Delilah E. Speld are not Cherokees by blood and not entitled to the rights and privileges of such, on account claiming the same ancestor, Mima Edwards, as in the Mary A. Couch case.

The decision in the Mary A Couch case found on Docket "A", Page 100 and testimony on Journal pages 276 to 278 governs the above case.

                      J T Adair   Chairman Commission
                      D.W. Lipe   Commissioner

Cherokee Citizenship Commission Docket Books
(1880-84, 1887-89) Volume IV
Tahlequah, Cherokee Nation

SCOTT

DOCKET #1618
CENSUS ROLLS 1835 & 52

APPLICANT FOR **CHEROKEE CITIZENSHIP**

POST OFFICE: Norwalk Mo		ATTORNEY: A E Ivey	
NO	NAMES	AGE	SEX
1	A.L.N. Scott	26	Male

ANCESTOR: Patsy Barnes

Rejected Aug 27th 1889

Office Commission on Citizenship
Cherokee Nation Ind Ter
Tahlequah Aug 27th 1889

The above case was called for a final hearing and now comes A.E. Ivey and submitts without evidence. The Commission decide that A.L.M[sic] Scott age 26 yrs are[sic] not Cherokees by blood. P.O. Norwalk Mo.

                               Will.P. Ross
Attest   Chairman
     D.S. Williams   J.E. Gunter Com
     Asst Clk Com

SCOTT

DOCKET #1619
CENSUS ROLLS 1835 & 52

APPLICANT FOR **CHEROKEE CITIZENSHIP**

POST OFFICE: Norwalk Mo		ATTORNEY: A E Ivey	
NO	NAMES	AGE	SEX
1	A.J. Scott	50	Male
2	Thos J. "	20	"
3	Geo W. "	19	"
4	Mary J. "	17	Female
5	Charles A. "	12	Male
6	Sam M. "	10	"
7	Walter P. "	7	"
8	Eliz V. "	4	"

ANCESTOR: Patsey Barnes

Rejected Aug 27th 1889

Cherokee Citizenship Commission Docket Books
(1880-84, 1887-89) Volume IV
Tahlequah, Cherokee Nation

Office Commission on Citizenship
Cherokee Nation Ind Ter
Tahlequah Aug 27th 1889

The above application have been called 3 times & no answer as there is no evidence filed in support of the application we decide that applicant A.J. Scott age 50 yrs and his children Thomas J. Scott age 20 yrs, Geo. W. Scott age 19 yrs, Mary J. Scott age 17 yrs, Charles A. Scott age 12 yrs, Sam M. Scott age 10 yrs, Walter P. Scott age 7 yrs, Eliza V. Scott age 4 yrs are not Cherokees by blood and not entitled to citizenship in the Cherokee Nation. P.O. Norwalk Mo.

Will.P. Ross
Attest   Chairman
   D.S. Williams   J.E. Gunter   Com
   Asst Clk Com

SCOTT

DOCKET #1620
CENSUS ROLLS

APPLICANT FOR CHEROKEE CITIZENSHIP

POST OFFICE: *(Illegible)*		ATTORNEY: A E Ivey	
No	NAMES	AGE	SEX
1	John Scott	42	Male
2	Georgia E "	13	Female

ANCESTOR: Marcus D. Scott

Rejected Aug 27th 1889

Office Commission on Citizenship
Cherokee Nation Ind Ter
Tahlequah Aug 27th 1889

The above applicant having been called 3 times and no answer & as there is no evidence on file in support of the application we decide <u>Adversely</u> to claimant age 42 yrs and his child Georgia E. Scott age 13 yrs. Post Office Tates Osa.

Will.P. Ross
Attest   Chairman
   D.S. Williams   J.E. Gunter   Com
   Asst Clk Com

Cherokee Citizenship Commission Docket Books
(1880-84, 1887-89) Volume IV
Tahlequah, Cherokee Nation

SMITHERS

DOCKET #1621
CENSUS ROLLS 1835 to 52

APPLICANT FOR **CHEROKEE CITIZENSHIP**

POST OFFICE: Bass		ATTORNEY: A E Ivey	
NO	NAMES	AGE	SEX
1	Eliza Smithers		Female
2	Matilda "	27	"
3	Wm A. "	19	Male
4	Martha A. "	15	Female
5	Asa F. "	10	Male

ANCESTOR: Levi Casten

Rejected Aug 27th 1889

Office Commission on Citizenship
Cherokee Nation Ind Ter
Tahlequah Aug 27th 1889

The above case was called and submitted by Atty A.E. Ivey without evidence. The Commission decide that Eliza Smithers and the following children Matilda J. Female 23 yrs, Wm A. male 19 yrs, Martha A. Female 15 yrs and Asa F. Smithers male 10 yrs are not Cherokees by blood. Post Office Bass.

                                        Will.P. Ross
Attest   Chairman
    D.S. Williams   J.E. Gunter   Com
    Asst Clk Com.

THOMPSON

DOCKET #1622
CENSUS ROLLS 1835 & 52

APPLICANT FOR **CHEROKEE CITIZENSHIP**

POST OFFICE: Gibson Station		ATTORNEY: A.E. Ivey	
NO	NAMES	AGE	SEX
1	Mary Thompson	20	Female

ANCESTOR: Mima Edwards

Now on this the 9th day of January 1888, comes the above case for a final hearing. The parties having made application pursuant to the provisions of an Act of the National Council approved December 8th 1886, and all the evidence being duly examined and found <u>not</u> to be sufficient and satisfactory to the

Cherokee Citizenship Commission Docket Books
(1880-84, 1887-89) Volume IV
Tahlequah, Cherokee Nation

Commission and the name of the ancestor not appearing on the Rolls as claimed in the application.

It is adjudged and determined by the Commission that Mary Thompson is not a Cherokee by blood and is hereby rejected and declared to be intruders.

      J T Adair Chairman Commission
      John E. Gunter Commissioner
            Commissioner

Attest
 C.C. Lipe
  Clerk Commission

WICKED

DOCKET #1623
CENSUS ROLLS 1835, 51 & 52

APPLICANT FOR CHEROKEE CITIZENSHIP

POST OFFICE: Cincinnati Ark		ATTORNEY: Boudinot & Rasmus	
No	NAMES	AGE	SEX
1	Mary Elizabeth Wicked	32	female

ANCESTOR: Charles Wicked

Now on this the 7th day of January, 1888, comes the above case for a final hearing and the parties having made application pursuant to the provisions of an Act of the National Council approved December 8th 1886, and all the evidence being duly examined and found to be sufficient and satisfactory to the Commission, and the name of the ancestor appearing on the rolls of 1835. It is adjudged and determined by the Commission that Mary Elizabeth Wicked is a Cherokee by blood and is hereby readmitted to all the rights, privileges and immunities of a Cherokee by blood.

And a certificate of said decision of the Commission and re-admission were made and furnished to said parties accordingly.

      J T Adair Chairman Commission
      John E. Gunter Commissioner
            Commissioner

C.C. Lipe
 Clerk Commission

Cherokee Citizenship Commission Docket Books
(1880-84, 1887-89) Volume IV
Tahlequah, Cherokee Nation

SULLIVAN

DOCKET #1624
CENSUS ROLLS 1835

APPLICANT FOR CHEROKEE CITIZENSHIP

POST OFFICE: Atwood Tenn		ATTORNEY: C.H. Taylor	
NO	NAMES	AGE	SEX
1	Susan E Sullivan	33	Female
2	May Sullivan	10	"

ANCESTOR: John Bryant

Rejected Aug 28th 1889

Office Commission on Citizenship
Cherokee Nation Ind Ter
Tahlequah Aug 28th 1889

The above case was called for a hearing and submitted by E.C. Boudinot. The Commission therefore decide that Susan E Sullivan age 33 yrs and her Daughter May Sullivan Female age 10 yrs are not Cherokees by blood. Post Office Atwood Tennessee.

Attest
D.S. Williams
Asst Clk Com

Will.P. Ross
Chairman
J.E. Gunter   Com

STIFF

DOCKET #1625
CENSUS ROLLS 1835 or Old Settler

APPLICANT FOR CHEROKEE CITIZENSHIP

POST OFFICE: McKinney Tex		ATTORNEY: Wm A Thompson	
NO	NAMES	AGE	SEX
1	C.N. Stiff	21	Male

ANCESTOR: Jack McGarrah

Office Commission on Citizenship
Cherokee Nation June 26 1889

Cherokee Citizenship Commission Docket Books
(1880-84, 1887-89) Volume IV
Tahlequah, Cherokee Nation

There being no evidence in support of the above named case the Commission decide that C.N. Stiff aged 21 years is not a Cherokee by blood. Post Office McKinney Tex.

Attest   Will.P. Ross
  EG Ross   Chairman
    Clerk Commission   J.E. Gunter   Com

SHERMAN

DOCKET #1626
CENSUS ROLLS 1835 & 52

APPLICANT FOR CHEROKEE CITIZENSHIP

POST OFFICE: Mulberry Ark		ATTORNEY: A.E. Ivey	
No	NAMES	AGE	SEX
1	Nancy E Sherman	31	Female
2	Nettie R. Sherman	8	"
3	Therissa A. Sherman	6	"
4	Cora E Sherman	4	"
5	Lizzie Sherman	2	"
6	Baby Sherman	6 mo	Male

ANCESTOR: Richard Henson

Rejected Aug 27th 1889

                         Office Commission on Citizenship
                               Cherokee Nation Ind Ter
                                   Tahlequah Aug 27th 1889

The above application was called 3 times & no answer & as no evidence is on file in support of the application we decide <u>Adversely</u> to claimant Nancy E Sherman age 31 yrs and her children Nettie R Sherman age 8, Therissa A Sherman age 6 yrs, Cora E Sherman age 4 yrs, Lizzie Sherman age 2 yrs & Baby Sherman age 6 months. P.O. Mulbery[sic] Ark

                                   Will.P. Ross
Attest   Chairman
  D.S. Williams   J.E. Gunter   Com
  Asst Clk Com

Cherokee Citizenship Commission Docket Books
(1880-84, 1887-89) Volume IV
Tahlequah, Cherokee Nation

SHOUSE

DOCKET #1627
CENSUS ROLLS 1835, 51 & 52

APPLICANT FOR CHEROKEE CITIZENSHIP

POST OFFICE: Webbers Falls CN		ATTORNEY: Wm A Thompson	
NO	NAMES	AGE	SEX
1	Elizabeth J Shouse	45	female
2	John Wm Shouse		
3	Maison F. Shouse		
4	Levi L Shouse		
5	Charles A. Shouse		
6	Still H. Shouse		
7	Annie M. Shouse		
8	Scott D. Shouse		

ANCESTOR: Nancy Ross

Rejected May 20th 1889

Office Commission on Citizenship Cher Nat I.T.
Tahlequah May 20th 1889

The application in the above case was filed on the 4th day of October 1887, and is supported by no evidence. The Commission therefore decide that Elizabeth J. Shouse and his[sic] children, John W, Maison F, Levi L, Charles A, Still H, Annie M, Scott D. Shouse whose Post Office at the time of filing was Webbers Falls I.T. are not Cherokees by blood and are not entitled to any rights, privileges and immunities of Cherokee citizens by blood. to Citizenship in the Cherokee Nation.

Will.P. Ross

Attest
    D.S. Williams
    Asst Clk Com

Chairman
J.E. Gunter Com

STUDERVANT

DOCKET #1628
CENSUS ROLLS 1835, 51 & 52

APPLICANT FOR CHEROKEE CITIZENSHIP

NO	NAMES	AGE	SEX
1	Matilda Studervant	38	female

ANCESTOR: Nancy Lucus

Rejected Aug 28th 1889

Cherokee Citizenship Commission Docket Books
(1880-84, 1887-89) Volume IV
Tahlequah, Cherokee Nation

Office Commission on Citizenship
Cherokee Nation Ind Ter
Tahlequah Aug 28th 1889

The above case was called for a hearing and submitted by E.C. Boudinot Atty without evidence. The Commission therefore decide that Matilda Studervant age 38 yrs is not a Cherokee by blood and are[sic] entitled to citizenship in the Cherokee Nation. Post Office Bloomfield Ark.

Will.P. Ross
Attest   Chairman
  D.S. Williams   J.E. Gunter   Com
  Asst Clk Com

STIFF

DOCKET #1629
CENSUS ROLLS 1835, 51 & 52

APPLICANT FOR CHEROKEE CITIZENSHIP

POST OFFICE: McKinney Tex		ATTORNEY: W.A. Thompson	
NO	NAMES	AGE	SEX
1	Mary Stiff	46	female
2	Levi Stiff	19	male
3	Glenn Stiff	20	"
4	Minnie Stiff	17	female
5	Allie Stiff	15	male[sic]
6	Ruby Stiff	13	"[sic]
7	Ezray Stiff	12	female
8	Sallie Stiff	10	"
9	Jessie Stiff	9	"
10	Lou Stiff	7	"
11	Jack Stiff	3	male

ANCESTOR: Jack McGarrah

Office Commission on Citizenship
Cherokee Nation June 26, 1889

There being no evidence in support of the above named case the Commission decide that Mary Stiff age 46 years and the following children Glenn aged 20 years, Minnie aged 17 years, Allie aged 15 years, Ruby aged 13 years, Ezray aged 12 years, Sallie aged 10 years, Jessie aged 9 years, Lou aged 7

Cherokee Citizenship Commission Docket Books
(1880-84, 1887-89) Volume IV
Tahlequah, Cherokee Nation

years, Jack Stiff aged 3 years are not Cherokees by blood. Post Office McKinney Tex.

Attest   Will.P. Ross
   EG Ross   Chairman
     Clerk Com   J.E. Gunter   Com

SLATTON

DOCKET #1630
CENSUS ROLLS 1835

APPLICANT FOR **CHEROKEE CITIZENSHIP**

POST OFFICE: Galena Kansas		ATTORNEY: C. H. Taylor	
No	NAMES	AGE	SEX
1	Elizabeth Slatton	53	female
2	Florence Slatton	23	"
3	Nettie Slatton	21	"
4	James A Slatton	19	male
5	Richard Slatton	17	"
6	Wm Slatton	15	"
7	Charles Slatton	12	"
8	Bessie Slatton	6	female

ANCESTOR: Arch Miller

Rejected April 18th 1889

    Now on this the 18th day of April 1889, comes up for final hearing the case of Elizabeth Slatton verses the Cherokee Nation for readmission to citizenship in the Cherokee Nation. Upon the alleged grounds that she is the grand Daughter of Arch Miller whose name was enrolled upon the census rolls of Cherokees by blood citizens of the Cherokee Nation taken in the year 1835. An examination of the rolls of 1835 shows that no such name as Arch Miller is to be found enrolled upon them. Without refering[sic] to the insufficiency of the exparte affidavits presented by the applicant to establish her Cherokee descent it is therefore adjudged and decreed that Elizabeth Slatton whose application was filed October 1887 and her children Florence Slatton aged 23 yrs, Nettie Slatton aged 21 yrs, James A. Slatton aged 19 yrs, Richard Slatton aged 17 yrs, Wm Slatton aged 15 yrs, Charles Slatton aged 12 yrs, Bessie Slatton aged 6 yrs. are not Cherokees by blood and are not entitled citizenship in the Cherokee Nation. Post Office address Galena Kansas.

Cherokee Citizenship Commission Docket Books
(1880-84, 1887-89) Volume IV
Tahlequah, Cherokee Nation

                    Will.P. Ross
                            Chairman
                John E. Gunter   Com

Attest
    D.S. Williams
        Clk Com

STARBUCK

DOCKET #1631
CENSUS ROLLS

APPLICANT FOR CHEROKEE CITIZENSHIP

POST OFFICE: Center N.C.		ATTORNEY:	
NO	NAMES	AGE	SEX
1	Lucinda Starbuck		female

ANCESTOR: Ann Crews

The Commission decide against claimant. See decision in the case of Andrew Meredith Docket 2180 Book E, Page 26 and John Henly Docket 1250, Book C Page 376.

                    Will.P. Ross
                        Chairman
            J.E. Gunter   Com

SULLIVAN

DOCKET #1632
CENSUS ROLLS

APPLICANT FOR CHEROKEE CITIZENSHIP

POST OFFICE: Center N.C.		ATTORNEY:	
NO	NAMES	AGE	SEX
1	Emily Sullivan		female

ANCESTOR: Ann Crews

The Commission decide against claimant. See decision in the case of Andrew Meredith Docket 2180 Book E, Page 26 and John Henly Docket 1250, Book C Page 376.

                    Will.P. Ross   Chairman
                John E. Gunter   Com

Cherokee Citizenship Commission Docket Books
(1880-84, 1887-89) Volume IV
Tahlequah, Cherokee Nation

SMITH

DOCKET #1633
CENSUS ROLLS

APPLICANT FOR CHEROKEE CITIZENSHIP

POST OFFICE: Rock Springs Ga		ATTORNEY: Boudinot & Rasmus	
NO	NAMES	AGE	SEX
1	Elizabeth F Smith	44	female

ANCESTOR: Wm Burgess, Sr.

(No information given)

SHERMAN

DOCKET #1634
CENSUS ROLLS 1835

APPLICANT FOR CHEROKEE CITIZENSHIP

POST OFFICE: Vinita C.N.		ATTORNEY: L.S. Sanders	
NO	NAMES	AGE	SEX
1	Martha Sherman	25	female
2	Louisa Sherman	1	"

ANCESTOR: John Beamer

Rejected Aug 27th 1889

Office Commission on Citizenship
Cherokee Nation IT
Tahlequah Aug 27th 1889

The above case was called for a final hearing and was answered by Rasmus Atty, he submitted said case without evidence. The Commission therefore decide that Martha Sherman age 25 yrs and her daughter Lucinda Sherman 1 yr of age are not Cherokees by blood. Post Office Vinita I.T.

Attest
   D.S. Williams
   Asst Clk Com

Will.P. Ross
   Chairman
J.E. Gunter Com

Cherokee Citizenship Commission Docket Books
(1880-84, 1887-89) Volume IV
Tahlequah, Cherokee Nation

SANDERS

DOCKET #1635
CENSUS ROLLS

APPLICANT FOR CHEROKEE CITIZENSHIP

POST OFFICE:		ATTORNEY: Boudinot and Rasmus	
NO	NAMES	AGE	SEX
1	Sarah A Sanders	49	female

ANCESTOR: Wm Burgess, Sr.

Rejected Aug 28th 1889

Office Commission on Citizenship
Cherokee Nation Ind Ter
Tahlequah Aug 28th 1889

The above application was submitted by claimant's Attorney Mr. E.C. Boudinot without evidence. Therefore we decide that applicant Sarah A. Sanders age 49 yrs is not Cherokee by blood and not entitled to citizenship in the Cherokee Nation. Post Office. –

Will.P. Ross

Attest
D.S. Williams
Asst Clk Com

Chairman
J.E. Gunter   Com

SHOCKEY

DOCKET #1636
CENSUS ROLLS 1835 & 48

APPLICANT FOR CHEROKEE CITIZENSHIP

POST OFFICE: Coffeyville Kans		ATTORNEY: Boudinot and Rasmus	
NO	NAMES	AGE	SEX
1	Louisa Shockey	39	female
2	Columbus C Wells	18	male

ANCESTOR: Emeline Orvis

Office Commission on Citizenship
Cherokee Nation Ind Ter
Tahlequah August 28th 1889

The above case was called for a hearing and submitted by E.C. Boudinot without evidence. The Commission therefore decide that Louisa Shockey aged

Cherokee Citizenship Commission Docket Books
(1880-84, 1887-89) Volume IV
Tahlequah, Cherokee Nation

39 years and Columbus C Wells aged 18 years are not Cherokees by blood and not entitled to Citizenship in the Cherokee Nation.

Attest   Will.P. Ross
   EG Ross   Chairman
     Clerk Commission   J.E. Gunter   Com

STEELMAN

DOCKET #1637
CENSUS ROLLS 1835, 48, 51 & 52

APPLICANT FOR CHEROKEE CITIZENSHIP

POST OFFICE: Greenwood Ark		ATTORNEY: Boudinot and Rasmus	
No	NAMES	AGE	SEX
1	Martha J Steelman	42	female
2	Carl T Steelman	14	male
3	John A Steelman	12	"
4	Nancy L Steelman	10	female
5	Jesse F Steelman	8	male
6	James M Steelman	6	"
7	Sealey Ella Steelman	4	female
8	Minty B Steelman	2	"
9	Mary E Steelman	infant	"

ANCESTOR: Nancy Reeves

                     Office Commission on Citizenship
                             Cherokee Nation
                          Tahlequah June 20th 1889

There being no evidence in support of the above named case the Commission decide that Martha J Steelman aged 42 years and the following named children Carl F[sic] male aged 14 years, John A. male aged 12 years, Nancy L female aged 10 years, Jesse F. male aged 8 years, James M. male aged 6 years, Sealey Ella female aged 4 years, Minty B. female aged 2 years and Mary E Steelman infant are not Cherokees by blood. Post Office Greenwood Ark.

Attest   Will.P. Ross
   EG Ross   Chairman
     Clerk Commission   J.E. Gunter   Com

Cherokee Citizenship Commission Docket Books
(1880-84, 1887-89) Volume IV
Tahlequah, Cherokee Nation

STEELMAN

DOCKET #1638
CENSUS ROLLS 1835, 48, 51 & 52

APPLICANT FOR CHEROKEE CITIZENSHIP

POST OFFICE: Greenwood Ark		ATTORNEY: Boudinot and Rasmus	
NO	NAMES	AGE	SEX
1	Joel D Steelman	22	male

ANCESTOR: Nancy Reeves

Office Commission on Citizenship
Cherokee Nation Tahlequah
June 20th 1889

There being no evidence in support of the above named case the Commission decide that Joel D Steelman aged 22 years is not a Cherokee by blood.

Attest   Will.P. Ross
  EG Ross   Chairman
    Clerk Commission   J.E. Gunter Com

SMITH

DOCKET #1639
CENSUS ROLLS 1835

APPLICANT FOR CHEROKEE CITIZENSHIP

POST OFFICE: Fort Smith Ark		ATTORNEY: Boudinot and Rasmus	
NO	NAMES	AGE	SEX
1	Lelia Smith	21	female
2	Olan W Smith	1	male

ANCESTOR: Jack West and Martha Hill

Office Commission on Citizenship
Cherokee Nation Ind Ter
Tahlequah August 28th 1889

The above case was called and submitted by Atty without evidence. The Commission decide that Lelia Smith aged 21 years and Olan W Smith and infant are not Cherokees by blood.

Cherokee Citizenship Commission Docket Books
(1880-84, 1887-89) Volume IV
Tahlequah, Cherokee Nation

Attest   Will.P. Ross
    EG Ross   Chairman
        Clerk Commission   J.E. Gunter Com

SANDERS

DOCKET #1640
CENSUS ROLLS

APPLICANT FOR CHEROKEE CITIZENSHIP

POST OFFICE: Vally[sic] Mills Ind		ATTORNEY: L.B. Bell	
NO	NAMES	AGE	SEX
1	Ellis J Sanders		male

ANCESTOR: Sarah Morgan

The Commission decide against claimant. See decision in the case of ~~Andrew Meredith~~ Docket ~~2180~~ 1584 Book D, Page 70 Address Vally[sic] Mills Indiana – 1250, Book C Page 376.[sic]

                                   Will.P. Ross
                                   Chairman
                         John E. Gunter   Com

SANDERS

DOCKET #1641
CENSUS ROLLS

APPLICANT FOR CHEROKEE CITIZENSHIP

POST OFFICE: Vally[sic] Mills Ark		ATTORNEY: L.B. Bell	
NO	NAMES	AGE	SEX
1	Willis Sanders	35	male
2	Florence Sanders	7	female

ANCESTOR: Sarah Morgan

                         Office Commission on Citizenship
                               Cherokee Nation IT
                              Tahlequah June 20th 1889

There being no evidence in support of the above named case the Commission decide that Willis Sanders and Florence Sanders are not Cherokees.

Cherokee Citizenship Commission Docket Books
(1880-84, 1887-89) Volume IV
Tahlequah, Cherokee Nation

Will.P. Ross   Chairman

Attest
   EG Ross   J.E. Gunter   Com
   Clerk Com

DOCKET #1642   *(All names illegible)*

SIZEMORE

DOCKET #1643
CENSUS ROLLS 1835 & 52

APPLICANT FOR CHEROKEE CITIZENSHIP

POST OFFICE: Blue Jacket, C.N.		ATTORNEY: A.E. Ivey	
No	NAMES	AGE	SEX
1	L.D. Sizemore	28	male

ANCESTOR: Joel Sizemore

See decision in this case in that of Sarah A Bonds on Book "A", page 235. Adverse to claimant.

                                                 Cornell Rogers
Office Com on Citizenship   Clerk Com on Citizenship
Tahlequah I.T. Sept 19th 1888.

SIZEMORE

DOCKET #1644
CENSUS ROLLS 1835 & 52

APPLICANT FOR CHEROKEE CITIZENSHIP

POST OFFICE: Blue Jacket C.N.		ATTORNEY: A.E. Ivey	
No	NAMES	AGE	SEX
1	Isom F. Sizemore	35	male

ANCESTOR: Joel Sizemore

See decision in this case in that of Sarah A Bonds on Book "A", page 235. Adverse to claimant.

                                                 Cornell Rogers
                                                 Clerk Com on Citizenship
Office Com on Citizenship
Tahlequah I.T. Sept 19th 1888.

Cherokee Citizenship Commission Docket Books
(1880-84, 1887-89) Volume IV
Tahlequah, Cherokee Nation

SANDERS

DOCKET #1645
CENSUS ROLLS 1835 & 52

APPLICANT FOR CHEROKEE CITIZENSHIP

POST OFFICE: Wau hil leau I.T.		ATTORNEY: A.E. Ivey	
NO	NAMES	AGE	SEX
1	Mary Sanders	20	female
2	Wm Sanders	18	male

ANCESTOR: James & Darcus Sanders

Rejected Aug 28th 1889

Office Commission on Citizenship
Cherokee Nation Ind Ter
Tahlequah August 28th 1889

The above applicant was called 3 times & no answer and there being no evidence in support of the application we decide that applicant Mary Sanders age 20 yrs and her brother Wm Sanders age 18 yrs are not Cherokees by blood and not entitled to citizenship in the Cherokee Nation. P.O. Wau-hil la I.T.

Will.P. Ross
Chairman
J.E. Gunter   Com

Attest
D.S. Williams
Asst Clk Com

SIZEMORE

DOCKET #1646
CENSUS ROLLS 1835 & 52

APPLICANT FOR CHEROKEE CITIZENSHIP

POST OFFICE: Blue Jacket I.T.		ATTORNEY: A.E. Ivey	
NO	NAMES	AGE	SEX
1	Wm Sanford Sizemore		

ANCESTOR: Joel Sizemore

See decision in this case in that of Sarah A Bonds on Book "A", page 235. Adverse to claimant.

Office Com on Citizenship
Tahlequah I.T. Sept 19th 1888.

Cornell Rogers
Clerk Com on Citizenship

Cherokee Citizenship Commission Docket Books
(1880-84, 1887-89) Volume IV
Tahlequah, Cherokee Nation

SIZEMORE

DOCKET #1647
CENSUS ROLLS 1835 & 52

APPLICANT FOR CHEROKEE CITIZENSHIP

POST OFFICE: Blue Jacket I.T.		ATTORNEY: A.E. Ivey	
NO	NAMES	AGE	SEX
1	Alvis Caswell Sizemore	55 ~~male~~	male
2	J Henry Sizemore	29	"
3	A. Reese Sizemore	20	"
4	Wm A. Sizemore	17	"
5	Loving J Sizemore	32	female

ANCESTOR: Isom Sizemore

See decision in this case in that of Sarah A Bonds on Book "A", page 235. Adverse to claimant.

                                                            Cornell Rogers
                                          Clerk Com on Citizenship

Office Com on Citizenship
Tahlequah I.T. Sept 19th 1888.

SPINKLE

DOCKET #1648
CENSUS ROLLS 1835 & 52

APPLICANT FOR CHEROKEE CITIZENSHIP

POST OFFICE: Veneten		ATTORNEY: A.E. Ivey	
NO	NAMES	AGE	SEX
1	Thomas V Spinkle	22	male
2	M Spinkle	5	"
3	May Spinkle	3	female

ANCESTOR: Mrs. T. Thomas

Rejected Aug 27th 1889

                                   Office Commission on Citizenship
                                         Cherokee Nation Ind Ter
                                         Tahlequah Aug 27th 1889

Cherokee Citizenship Commission Docket Books
(1880-84, 1887-89) Volume IV
Tahlequah, Cherokee Nation

The above application was submitted by applicants Attorney A.E. Ivey without evidence. Therefore we decide that applicant Thomas v. Spinkle age 22 is not a Cherokee by blood. P.O. Veneten[sic] Ark.

                                          Will.P. Ross

Attest   Chairman
   D.S. Williams   J.E. Gunter   Com
   Asst Clk Com.

SPANKLE

DOCKET #1649
CENSUS ROLLS 1835 to 1852

APPLICANT FOR CHEREKEE CITIZENSHIP

POST OFFICE: Chester Ark		ATTORNEY: A.E. Ivey	
NO	NAMES	AGE	SEX
1	James J Spankle	38	male
2	Daisy Spankle	6	female
3	Robert Spankle	4	male
4	Henry Spankle	1	"

ANCESTOR: Sarah Thomas

Rejected Aug 28th 1889

                          Office Commission on Citizenship
                                Cherokee Nation Ind Ter
                              Tahlequah August 28th 1889

The above applicant was called 3 times and no answer and there being no evidence on file in support of the application we decide that applicant James J Spankle age 38 yrs, Daisy Spankle age 6 yrs, Robt Spankle age 4 yrs, Henry Spankle age 1 yr are not Cherokees by blood, and not entitled to citizenship in the Cherokee Nation.

                                   Will.P. Ross

Attest   Chairman
   D.S. Williams   J.E. Gunter   Com
   Asst Clk Com.

Cherokee Citizenship Commission Docket Books
(1880-84, 1887-89) Volume IV
Tahlequah, Cherokee Nation

SINCLAIR

DOCKET #1650
CENSUS ROLLS 1835

APPLICANT FOR CHEROKEE CITIZENSHIP

POST OFFICE: Alma Ark		ATTORNEY: E.A.[sic] Ivey	
No	NAMES	AGE	SEX
1	Zephamah Sinclair	33	male
2	Linnie Sinclair	7	male
3	Wm Thomas Sinclair	2	"

ANCESTOR: Hannah Powers

Rejected Aug 28th 1889

Office Commission on Citizenship
Cherokee Nation Ind Ter
Tahlequah Aug 28th 1889

The above applicant was called 3 times and no answer and there being no evidence on file in support of the application we decide that applicant Zephamah Sinclair and children Linnie Sinclair age 7 yrs and William Thomas age 2 yrs are not Cherokees by blood. P.O. Alma Ark.

Attest
D.S. Williams
Asst Clk Com.

Will.P. Ross
Chairman
J.E. Gunter   Com

SAVAGE

DOCKET #1651
CENSUS ROLLS 1835 to 1852

APPLICANT FOR CHEROKEE CITIZENSHIP

POST OFFICE: Cannadaville I.T.		ATTORNEY: A.E. Ivey	
No	NAMES	AGE	SEX
1	Sarah E Savage	34	female
2	Everett A Savage	17	male

ANCESTOR: Moses Lane

Rejected Aug 28th 1889

Office Commission on Citizenship
Cherokee Nation Ind Ter
Tahlequah Aug 28th 1889

Cherokee Citizenship Commission Docket Books
(1880-84, 1887-89) Volume IV
Tahlequah, Cherokee Nation

The above case having been called 3 times and no answer and being no evidence on file in support of the application the Commission decide that applicant Sarah E. Savage age 37 yrs and her child Everett Anderson age 17 yrs are not Cherokees by blood and not entitled to citizenship in the Cherokee Nation P.O. Cannadaville I.T.

Attest
D.S. Williams
Asst Clk Com.

Will.P. Ross
Chairman
J.E. Gunter Com

SMITH

DOCKET #1652
CENSUS ROLLS 1835 to 1852

APPLICANT FOR CHEROKEE CITIZENSHIP

POST OFFICE: Chetopa Kans		ATTORNEY: A.E. Ivey	
No	NAMES	AGE	SEX
1	Harvey Smith	42	male

ANCESTOR: James Smith

See decision in this case in that of Margaret A Puffer this Book on Page 434 – Adverse to claimant.

Cornell Rogers
Clk Com on Citizenship

Office Com on Citizenship
Tahlequah I.T. Sept. 24th 1888

STEPHENS

DOCKET #1653
CENSUS ROLLS 1835 to 52

APPLICANT FOR CHEROKEE CITIZENSHIP

POST OFFICE: Euclid Ark		ATTORNEY: E.A.[sic] Ivey	
No	NAMES	AGE	SEX
1	J.H. Stephens	42	male
2	George L Stephens	21	"
3	Sarah E. Stephens	18	female
4	Mary E. Stephens	16	"
5	Martha Stephens	14	"
6	John Stephens	12	male

Cherokee Citizenship Commission Docket Books
(1880-84, 1887-89) Volume IV
Tahlequah, Cherokee Nation

7	William Stephens	10	"
8	Ada Stephens	8	female

ANCESTOR: John Brown

Rejected Oct 16th 1889

Office Commission on Citizenship C.N. I.T.
Tahlequah Oct. 16th 1889

The applicant alleges that he derives his Cherokee descent from one John Brown whose name he believes was duly enrolled upon the census rolls of Cherokees by blood citizens of the Cherokee Nation taken in the years 1835-52. In support of his application two exparte statements are submitted and which were taken Jno H. Somerville Clerk of the Circuit Court for Howard County State of Arkansas on the 21st day of October 1887. James Young testifies that he has known John H Stephens for 25 years and that he is the son of Benjaman[sic] Stephens and his wife Elizabeth who was daughter of John Brown a half breed Cherokee and was born in Georgia near the North Carolina state line, and claimant has always been considered of Cherokee descent. Benjaman Stephens Father of applicant by his wife Elizabeth Stephens states that he was married to his wife in the state of Alabama in the Cherokee Country that she was the daughter of John Brown who was a half blood Cherokee and was the son of Thomas Brown and Elizabeth Brown both of Cherokee descent and who resided in the Cherokee Country in the state of Georgia, and that Elizabeth Stephens nee Brown was born in 1825. A careful examination of the census rolls of Cherokees taken in 1835-48-52, have failed to show the names of either John or Thomas Brown within the limits of Georgia or Alabama. The names of John Brown appears on the roll of 1835 within the limits of Tennessee, but the statement of Dr. D. D. Thornton of Delaware District aged 70 years and taken by a clerk of the Commission. D.S. Williams on the 9th day of Oct *(illegible)* shows that said Brown had but two daughters and that he (Thornton) married one of them himself and a man named Holmes married the other. The Commission therefore decide that the applicant John H Stephens aged 42 years and William 10 yrs, and his daughters Sarah E. 18 yrs, Mary E. 16 yrs, Martha 14 yrs, and Ada Stephens 8 yrs. are not of Cherokee blood and not entitled to citizenship in the Cherokee Nation.

Attest
   D.S. Williams
   Asst Clk Com.

Will.P. Ross
Chairman
J.E. Gunter   Com

Cherokee Citizenship Commission Docket Books
(1880-84, 1887-89) Volume IV
Tahlequah, Cherokee Nation

SMITH

DOCKET #1654
CENSUS ROLLS 1835 & 52

APPLICANT FOR CHEROKEE CITIZENSHIP

POST OFFICE: Childers Station		ATTORNEY: A.E. Ivey	
NO	NAMES	AGE	SEX
1	Elizabeth Smith	25	female

ANCESTOR: Lettitia Little

Rejected Aug 27th 1889

Office Commission on Citizenship
Cherokee Nation Ind Ter
Tahlequah Aug 27th 1889

The above case was called and submitted by A.E. Ivey Atty without evidence. The Commission therefore decide that Elizabeth Smith age 25 yrs is not a Cherokee by blood. P.O. Childers Station I.T.

Attest
   D.S. Williams
   Asst Clk Com.

Will.P. Ross
                  Chairman
J.E. Gunter Com

SMART

DOCKET #1655
CENSUS ROLLS 1835 to 1852

APPLICANT FOR CHEROKEE CITIZENSHIP

POST OFFICE: Van Buren Ark		ATTORNEY: A.E. Ivey	
NO	NAMES	AGE	SEX
1	Daniel Smart	38	male
2	Roxie Smart	12	female
3	Roxana Smart		"
4	Edward Smart		male

ANCESTOR: Smith

Rejected Sept 13th 1889

Office Commission on Citizenship
Cherokee Nation Ind Ter
Tahlequah Sept 13th 1889

The above case was called 3 times and no response from applicant or by Atty. The Commission decide that Daniel Smith[sic] age 38 yrs and his children,

Cherokee Citizenship Commission Docket Books
(1880-84, 1887-89) Volume IV
Tahlequah, Cherokee Nation

Roxie Smith Female age 12 yrs, Roxana Female 12 yrs (twins) and Edward Smith male 5 yrs are not Cherokees by blood. P.O. Van Buren Ark.

                                          Will.P. Ross
Attest   Chairman
    D.S. Williams   J.E. Gunter   Com
    Asst Clk Com.

DOCKET #1656   *(All names illegible)*

SMITH

DOCKET #1657
CENSUS ROLLS 1835 to 1852

APPLICANT FOR CHEROKEE CITIZENSHIP

POST OFFICE: Siloam Springs Ark		ATTORNEY: A.E. Ivey	
NO	NAMES	AGE	SEX
1	H. Smith	48	male

ANCESTOR: James Hester

Rejected Aug 28th 1889   Office Commission on Citizenship
                                                Cherokee Nation Ind Ter
                                                Tahlequah Aug 28th 1889

The above applicant was called 3 times & no answer and no evidence on file in support of the application we decide that applicant H. Smith is not a Cherokee by blood and not entitled to citizenship in the Cherokee Nation. P.O. Siloam Springs Ark.

                                          Will.P. Ross
Attest   Chairman
    D.S. Williams   J.E. Gunter   Com
    Asst Clk Com.

Cherokee Citizenship Commission Docket Books
(1880-84, 1887-89) Volume IV
Tahlequah, Cherokee Nation

STARNES

DOCKET #1658
CENSUS ROLLS 1835 to 52

APPLICANT FOR **CHEROKEE CITIZENSHIP**

POST OFFICE: Evansville Ark		ATTORNEY:	
No	NAMES	AGE	SEX
1	Josephine Starnes	18	female

ANCESTOR: Wm Lee

Rejected Aug 28th 1889

Office Commission on Citizenship
Cherokee Nation Ind Ter
Tahlequah Aug 28th 1889

The above application was called 3 times & no answer and there being no evidence on file in support of the application we decide that applicant Josephine Starnes age 18 yrs is not a Cherokee by blood and not entitled to citizenship in the Cherokee Nation. P.O. Evansville Ark.

Will.P. Ross

Attest   Chairman
   D.S. Williams   J.E. Gunter   Com
Asst Clk Com.

SHANNON

DOCKET #1659
CENSUS ROLLS 1835 to 52

APPLICANT FOR **CHEROKEE CITIZENSHIP**

POST OFFICE: Evansville Ark		ATTORNEY:	
No	NAMES	AGE	SEX
1	Margaret Shannon	27	female
2	Morgan Shannon	7	male
3	John C. Shannon	2	"

ANCESTOR: William Lee

Rejected Aug 28th 1889

Office Commission on Citizenship
Cherokee Nation Ind Ter

The above applicant was called 3 times and no answer and there being no evidence on file in support of the application we decide that Margaret Shannon

Cherokee Citizenship Commission Docket Books
(1880-84, 1887-89) Volume IV
Tahlequah, Cherokee Nation

applicant age 27 yrs and John C Shannon age 2 yrs are not Cherokees by blood and not entitled to citizenship in the Cherokee Nation. P.O. Evansville Ark.

                                        Will.P. Ross
Attest   Chairman
   D.S. Williams   J.E. Gunter   Com
   Asst Clk Com.

SHANNON

DOCKET #1660
CENSUS ROLLS 1835 to 52

APPLICANT FOR **CHEROKEE CITIZENSHIP**

POST OFFICE: Evansville Ark		ATTORNEY:	
No	NAMES	AGE	SEX
1	Malisa Shannon	33	female
2	Edward Shannon	11	male
3	Annie Shannon	7	female
4	Frank Shannon	5	male
5	Luthia Shannon	6 mo	female

ANCESTOR: William Lee

Rejected Sept 13th 1889

                        Office Commission on Citizenship
                              Cherokee Nation Ind Ter
                              Tahlequah Sept 13th 1889

The above case was called 3 times and no response from applicant or by Atty and there being no evidence on file in support of claim, the Commission therefore decide that Malisa Shannon age 33 yrs and the following children Edward male 11 yrs son, Annie female 7 yrs, Frank male 6 yrs and Luthia C. Shannon female 6 months, are not Cherokees by blood. P.O. Evansville Ark.

                                        Will.P. Ross
Attest   Chairman
   D.S. Williams   J.E. Gunter   Com
   Asst Clk Com.

Cherokee Citizenship Commission Docket Books (1880-84, 1887-89) Volume IV
Tahlequah, Cherokee Nation

STROUP

DOCKET #1661
CENSUS ROLLS 1835

APPLICANT FOR CHEROKEE CITIZENSHIP

POST OFFICE: Seneca Mo		ATTORNEY: J.H. Akins	
No	NAMES	AGE	SEX
1	Clara B. Stroup	20	female

ANCESTOR: Catherine Rowls

Now on this the 18th day of July, 1888, comes the above case up for final hearing. The applicant having complied with the requirements of an Act of the National Council creating this Commission, dated Dec 8th 1886, and the amendment thereto dated Feby. 7th 1888. The Commission after examining all the testimony in the case and also the Old Settler pay rolls of 1851, find the applicant, Clara B. Stroup to be a Cherokee by blood, and as such is hereby re-admitted to all the rights and privileges of a Cherokee citizen by blood.

D.W. Lipe   Actg. Chairman of Commission
John E. Gunter   Commissioner

STIFF

DOCKET #1662
CENSUS ROLLS 1835

APPLICANT FOR CHEROKEE CITIZENSHIP

POST OFFICE: McKinney Tex		ATTORNEY: W.A. Thompson	
No	NAMES	AGE	SEX
1	S.P. Stiff	25	male

ANCESTOR: Jack McGarrah

Office Commission on Citizenship
Tahlequah I.T. June 26, 1889

There being no evidence in support of the above named case the Commission decide that S.P. Stiff aged 25 yrs is not a Cherokee by blood.
Attest   Will.P. Ross
   EG Ross   Chairman
      Clerk Commission   J.E. Gunter   Com

Cherokee Citizenship Commission Docket Books
(1880-84, 1887-89) Volume IV
Tahlequah, Cherokee Nation

SPRINGER

DOCKET #1663
CENSUS ROLLS 1835

APPLICANT FOR CHEROKEE CITIZENSHIP

POST OFFICE: Parris[sic] Tex		ATTORNEY: C.H. Taylor	
NO	NAMES	AGE	SEX
1	Martha Springer	31	female
2	Ema[sic] Springer	7	"
3	Mary Springer	6	"
4	Alexandra[sic] Springer	3	male

ANCESTOR: Ned Christy

Office Commission on Citizenship
Cherokee Nation Ind Ter
Tahlequah Aug 28th 1889

The application in the above case was filed the 3rd day of October A.D. 1887 and this day submitted without evidence. The Commission therefore decide that the applicant Martha Springer aged 31 years and her daughter Emma Springer age 7 years and Mary Springer age 6 years and son Alexander Springer age 3 years are not of Cherokee blood. P.O. Paris Texas.

Attest   Will.P. Ross
  EG Ross   Chairman
     Clerk Commission   J.E. Gunter Com

STAFFORD

DOCKET #1664
CENSUS ROLLS 1835 to 52

APPLICANT FOR CHEROKEE CITIZENSHIP

POST OFFICE: Chester Ark		ATTORNEY: A.E. Ivey	
NO	NAMES	AGE	SEX
1	Rachiel[sic] Stafford	35	female
2	Mary J. Stafford	15	"
3	Caledonia Stafford	13	"
4	Lou Emma Stafford	12	" twins
5	Lou Ella Stafford	12	"
6	Nancy Stafford	10	"
7	Lena Stafford	8	"
8	William Stafford	6	male

Cherokee Citizenship Commission Docket Books
(1880-84, 1887-89) Volume IV
Tahlequah, Cherokee Nation

9	Cricket Stafford	4	female
10	Pete Stafford	2	male

ANCESTOR: Ezekiel Gibson

Office Commission on Citizenship
Tahlequah June 19th 1889

There being no evidence in support of the above named case the Commission decide that Rachiel Stafford aged 35 years and the following named children Mary J Female aged 15 years, Caledonia Female aged 13 years, Lou Emma Female aged 12 years, Lou Ella Female aged 12 years twins, Nancy Female aged 10 years, Lena Female aged 8 years, William Male aged 6 years, Cricket Female aged 4 years and Pete Stafford Male aged 2 years Post Office Chester Ark. are not of Cherokee blood.

Attest   Will.P. Ross
   EG Ross   Chairman
      Clerk Commission   J.E. Gunter   Com

SWAN

DOCKET #1665
CENSUS ROLLS 1835 to 52

APPLICANT FOR CHEROKEE CITIZENSHIP

POST OFFICE: Morehead I.T.		ATTORNEY: A.E. Ivey	
No	NAMES	AGE	SEX
1	William B Swan	34	male

ANCESTOR: Liddie Wofford

Rejected 28th Aug 1889

The above applicant was called three times & no answer and there being no evidence on file in support of the application the Commission decide that applicant William B. Swan age 34 yrs is not a Cherokee by blood and he is hereby rejected. P.O. Morehead I.T.

Attest   Will.P. Ross
   EG Ross   Chairman
      Clerk Com   J.E. Gunter   Com

Cherokee Citizenship Commission Docket Books
(1880-84, 1887-89) Volume IV
Tahlequah, Cherokee Nation

STAFFORD

DOCKET #1666
CENSUS ROLLS 1835

APPLICANT FOR CHEROKEE CITIZENSHIP

POST OFFICE: Hazel Vally[sic] Ark		ATTORNEY: A.E. Ivey	
NO	NAMES	AGE	SEX
1	Rebecca Stafford	36	female
2	Henry H Stafford	18	male
3	Isaac F Stafford	16	"
4	Lougenia Stafford	13	female
5	Martha J Stafford	11	"
6	John M. Stafford	9	male
7	Eddie Stafford	7	"
8	Nancy Stafford	4	female

ANCESTOR: Joel Gibson

Office Commission on Citizenship
Cherokee Nation Tahlequah
June 19th 1889

There being no evidence in support of the above named case the Commission decide that Rebecca Stafford aged 36 years and the following named children Henry H male aged 18 years, Isaac F. male aged 16 years, Lougenia Female aged 13 years, Martha J. Female aged 11 years, John M. male aged 9 years, Eddie male aged 7 years, Nancy Stafford Female are not of Cherokee blood. Post Office Hazel Valley Ark.
Attest   Will.P. Ross
  EG Ross   Chairman
      Clerk Com   J.E. Gunter   Com

STEWART

DOCKET #1667
CENSUS ROLLS 1835 & 52

APPLICANT FOR CHEROKEE CITIZENSHIP

POST OFFICE: Bates Spring Kans		ATTORNEY: A.E. Ivey	
NO	NAMES	AGE	SEX
1	Sarah Stewart	23	female
2	William Stewart	1	male

ANCESTOR: James Smith

Cherokee Citizenship Commission Docket Books
(1880-84, 1887-89) Volume IV
Tahlequah, Cherokee Nation

See decision in this case in that of Margaret A Puffer in Book "C" Page 434 – Adverse to claimant.

                                        Cornell Rogers
                                        Clk Com on Citizenship

Office Com on Citizenship
Tahlequah I.T. Sept 24th 1888

SMITH

DOCKET #1668
CENSUS ROLLS 1835 & 52

APPLICANT FOR CHEROKEE CITIZENSHIP

POST OFFICE: Dixon Mo		ATTORNEY: A.E. Ivey	
NO	NAMES	AGE	SEX
1	John A Smith	56	male

ANCESTOR: James Smith

See decision in this case in that of Margaret A Puffer in Book "C" Page 434 – Adverse to claimant.

                                        Cornell Rogers
                                      Clk Com on Citizenship

Office Com on Citizenship
Tahlequah I.T. Sept 24th 1888

STOKES

DOCKET #1669
CENSUS ROLLS 1835 to 1852

APPLICANT FOR CHEROKEE CITIZENSHIP

POST OFFICE: Mountainburg Ark		ATTORNEY: A.E. Ivey	
NO	NAMES	AGE	SEX
1	Rhoda Stokes	36	female
2	Lyndsy Stokes	7	male
3	Evaline Stokes	5	female
4	Hattie N Stokes	3	"

ANCESTOR: Ezekiel Gibson

                                    Office Commission on Citizenship
                                    Cherokee Nation Tahlequah
                                            June 19th 1889

Cherokee Citizenship Commission Docket Books
(1880-84, 1887-89) Volume IV
Tahlequah, Cherokee Nation

There being no evidence in support of the above named case the Commission decide that Rhoda Stokes aged 36 years, Lyndsy male aged 7 years, Evaline female aged 5 years and Hattie N. Stokes female aged 3 years are not of Cherokee blood. Post Office Mountainburg, Ark.

Attest   Will.P. Ross
   EG Ross   Chairman
      Clerk Commission   J.E. Gunter   Com

SMITH

DOCKET #1670
CENSUS ROLLS

APPLICANT FOR **CHEROKEE CITIZENSHIP**

POST OFFICE: Roy Ga		ATTORNEY: A.E. Ivey	
No	NAMES	AGE	SEX
1	Robert L Smith	49	male
2	Lester Smith	21	"
3	Virginia S Smith	19	female
4	Willie C Smith	17	male
5	Maggie L Smith	16	female
6	Robert E Smith	12	male
7	Nettie Smith	10	female

ANCESTOR: Sintha Smith

The decision in this case can be seen in that of Loucinda Addington's in Book "B" page 5 Docket No 292 – Adverse to the claimant.

                                       C.C. Lipe
                                       Clk Com on Citizenship
Office Commission on Citizenship
Tahlequah I.T. Oct 2 1888

SIZEMORE

DOCKET #1671
CENSUS ROLLS 1835 & 52

APPLICANT FOR **CHEROKEE CITIZENSHIP**

POST OFFICE: Blue Jacket I.T.		ATTORNEY: A.E. Ivey	
No	NAMES	AGE	SEX
1	James H Sizemore	47	male

Cherokee Citizenship Commission Docket Books
(1880-84, 1887-89) Volume IV
Tahlequah, Cherokee Nation

2	H.H. Sizemore	23	"
3	J.R. Sizemore	12	"
4	Noah E. Sizemore	21	"
5	Patience L. Sizemore	19	female
6	Manda J. Sizemore	17	"
7	Margaret R. Sizemore	15	"

ANCESTOR: Isom Sizemore

See decision in this case in that of Sarah A Bonds on Book "A", page 235. Adverse to claimant.

             Cornell Rogers
             Clerk Com on Citizenship

Office Com on Citizenship
Tahlequah I.T. Sept 19th 1888.

SIZEMORE

DOCKET #1672
CENSUS ROLLS 1835 & 52

APPLICANT FOR **CHEROKEE CITIZENSHIP**

POST OFFICE: Blue Jacket I.T.		ATTORNEY: A.E. Ivey	
NO	NAMES	AGE	SEX
1	Percy Ellen Sizemore	6 m	

ANCESTOR: Isom Sizemore

See decision in this case in that of Sarah A Bonds on Book "A", page 235. Adverse to claimant.

             Cornell Rogers
             Clerk Com on Citizenship

Office Com on Citizenship
Tahlequah I.T. Sept 19th 1888.

SHELTON

DOCKET #1673
CENSUS ROLLS 1835 & 52

APPLICANT FOR **CHEROKEE CITIZENSHIP**

POST OFFICE: Hart, McDonnald[sic] Co Mo		ATTORNEY: A.E. Ivey	
NO	NAMES	AGE	SEX
1	William M Shelton	39	male

Cherokee Citizenship Commission Docket Books
(1880-84, 1887-89) Volume IV
Tahlequah, Cherokee Nation

2	Cordelia S Shelton	15	female
3	Amitie V. Shelton	13	"
4	Annie L. Shelton	11	"
5	John R. Shelton	9	male
6	Delphia M Shelton	7	female
7	Cora B Shelton	5	"
8	Laura M. Shelton	3	"

ANCESTOR: Wm Shelton

Rejected Aug 28th 1889

Office Commission on Citizenship
Cherokee Nation Ind Ter
Tahlequah Aug 28th 1889

The above applicant was called 3 times & no answer and there being no evidence on file in support of the application We decide that applicant William M Shelton age 39 yrs and his children, to wit; Cordelia S Shelton age 15 yrs, Amitie V. Shelton age 13 yrs, Anna L. Shelton age 11 yrs, John R. Shelton age 9 yrs, Delphia M. Shelton age 7 yrs, Cora B. Shelton age 5 yrs, Laura M Shelton age 3 yrs are not Cherokees by blood and not entitled to citizenship in the Cherokee Nation. P.O. Hart McDonnald[sic] Co. Mo.

Will.P. Ross
Chairman
Attest
D.S. Williams   J.E. Gunter   Com
Asst Clk Com.

SHEFFIELD

DOCKET #1674
CENSUS ROLLS 1851

APPLICANT FOR CHEROKEE CITIZENSHIP

POST OFFICE: Huntsville		ATTORNEY: A.E. Ivey	
NO	NAMES	AGE	SEX
1	Mary A Sheffield	26	female
2	Martha J Sheffield	6	"
3	Bula J Sheffield	1	"

ANCESTOR: Mancil Tidwell

We the Commission on Citizenship after examining the evidence in the above case and also the rolls taken in 1851 East of the Mississippi river find that

Cherokee Citizenship Commission Docket Books
(1880-84, 1887-89) Volume IV
Tahlequah, Cherokee Nation

John Tidwell, the grandfather of the applicant and the great grand father of the applicant's children, prove himself to be a half breed Cherokee Indian.

Therefore we the Commission on Citizenship agree and decide that Mary A. Sheffield and her two daughters Martha J and Bula J. Sheffield are Cherokees by blood.

        J. T. Adair Chairman Commission
        D.W. Lipe Commissioner
        H.C. Barnes Commissioner

Office Com on Citizenship
 Tahlequah I.T. Sept 28th 1888

SMITH

DOCKET #1675
CENSUS ROLLS 1835 & 52

APPLICANT FOR CHEROKEE CITIZENSHIP

Post Office: Potts Creek Kans		Attorney: A.E. Ivey	
No	NAMES	AGE	SEX
1	Rosa Smith	44	female

ANCESTOR: James Smith

See decision in this case in that of Margaret A Puffer in Book "C" Page 434 – Adverse to claimant.

        Cornell Rogers
        Clk Com on Citizenship

Office Com on Citizenship
 Tahlequah I.T. Sept. 24th 1888

STRASNER

DOCKET #1676
CENSUS ROLLS 1835 to 1852

APPLICANT FOR CHEROKEE CITIZENSHIP

Post Office: Cologne, Ark		Attorney: A.E. Ivey	
No	NAMES	AGE	SEX
1	Emily Strasner	21	female
2	Mary Strasner	6	"
3	Oscar Strasner	2	"[sic]

ANCESTOR: John Thompson

Cherokee Citizenship Commission Docket Books
(1880-84, 1887-89) Volume IV
Tahlequah, Cherokee Nation

Rejected Aug 28th 1889

                        Office Commission on Citizenship
                        Cherokee Nation Ind Ter
                        Tahlequah Aug 28th 1889

The above named applicant was called 3 times & no answer and there being no evidence on file in support of the application we decide that applicant Emily Strasner age 21 years and her children Mary Strasner & Oscar Strasner are not Cherokees by blood and not entitled to citizenship in the Cherokee Nation. P.O. Cologne Ark.

                        Will.P. Ross
Attest   Chairman
   D.S. Williams   J.E. Gunter   Com
   Asst Clk Com.

SPINKLE

DOCKET #1677
CENSUS ROLLS 1835 to 1852

APPLICANT FOR CHEROKEE CITIZENSHIP

POST OFFICE: Alma, Ark.		ATTORNEY: A.E. Ivey	
NO	NAMES	AGE	SEX
1	Moses Spinkle	30	male

ANCESTOR: Sarah Thomas

Rejected Aug 28th 1889

                        Office Commission on Citizenship
                        Cherokee Nation Ind Ter
                        Tahlequah August 28th 1889

The above named applicant was called 3 times & no answer and there being no evidence submitted by claimant in support of the application we decide that applicant Moses Spinkle age 30 yrs is not a Cherokee by blood and not entitled to citizenship in the Cherokee Nation. P.O. Alma Ark.

                        Will.P. Ross
Attest   Chairman
   D.S. Williams   J.E. Gunter   Com
   Asst Clk Com.

Cherokee Citizenship Commission Docket Books
(1880-84, 1887-89) Volume IV
Tahlequah, Cherokee Nation

SIZEMORE

DOCKET #1678
CENSUS ROLLS 1835 to 1852

APPLICANT FOR **CHEROKEE CITIZENSHIP**

POST OFFICE: Blue Jacket I.T.		ATTORNEY: A.E. Ivey	
NO	NAMES	AGE	SEX
1	Sarah Ellen Sizemore	16	female

ANCESTOR: Joel Sizemore

See decision in this case in that of Sarah A Bonds on Book "A", page 235. Adverse to claimant.

Cornell Rogers
Clerk Com on Citizenship

Office Commission on Citizenship
Tahlequah I.T. Sept 19th 1888.

STINNETT

DOCKET #1679
CENSUS ROLLS 1835

APPLICANT FOR **CHEROKEE CITIZENSHIP**

POST OFFICE: Big Vally[sic] Tex		ATTORNEY: A.E. Ivey	
NO	NAMES	AGE	SEX
1	Clay Stinnett	36	Male
2	Alabama Stinnett	14	female
3	Louis Stinnett	10	male
4	Cossa Stinnett	8	female
5	Forest Stinnett	5	male
6	John E. Stinnett	2	"

ANCESTOR: James Stinnett

Office Commission on Citizenship
Cherokee Nation Ind Ter
Tahlequah Sept 2nd 1889

The above case was called three times and no answer and there being no evidence on file in support of the application we decide that claimant Clay Stinnett aged 36 years and children Alabama aged 14 years, Louis aged 10 years, Coosa[sic] aged 8 years, Forest aged 5 years and John E Stinnett aged 2 years are not Cherokees by blood. Post Office Big Valley Texas.

Cherokee Citizenship Commission Docket Books
(1880-84, 1887-89) Volume IV
Tahlequah, Cherokee Nation

Attest   Will.P. Ross
   EG Ross   Chairman
      Clerk Commission   J.E. Gunter   Com

STINNETT

DOCKET #1680
CENSUS ROLLS 1835 to 1852

APPLICANT FOR CHEROKEE CITIZENSHIP

POST OFFICE: Big Valley Tex		ATTORNEY: A.E. Ivey	
NO	NAMES	AGE	SEX
1	E. H. Stinnett	45	male
2	Inice J Stinnett	16	female
3	Thomas O Stinnett	13	male
4	John M Stinnett	11	"
5	M.E.R.A. Stinnett	7	female
6	Rufus Stinnett	4	male
7	Early M Stinnett	5 m	"

ANCESTOR: James Stinnett

Rejected Aug 29th 1889

                         Office Commission on Citizenship
                             Cherokee Nation Ind Ter
                                Tahlequah Aug 29th 1889

The above case was called for a final hearing and submitted by A.E. Ivey without evidence. The Commission decide that E.H. Stinnett age 45 yrs and the following children Inice J. female 16 yrs, Thos O. male age 13 yrs, John M. male 11 yrs, M.E.R.A. female 7 yrs, Rufus male 4 yrs and Early M Stinnett male 5 months are not Cherokees by blood and are not entitled to citizenship in the Cherokee Nation. Post Office Big Valley Texas.

                                    Will.P. Ross
Attest   Chairman
   D.S. Williams   J.E. Gunter   Com
   Asst Clk Com

Cherokee Citizenship Commission Docket Books
(1880-84, 1887-89) Volume IV
Tahlequah, Cherokee Nation

SIZEMORE

DOCKET #1681
CENSUS ROLLS 1835 to 1852

APPLICANT FOR CHEROKEE CITIZENSHIP

POST OFFICE: Blue Jacket I.T.		ATTORNEY: A.E. Ivey	
No	NAMES	AGE	SEX
1	Mary Sizemore	37	female

ANCESTOR: Joel Sizemore

See decision in this case in that of Sarah A Bonds on Book "A", page 235. Adverse to claimant.

           Cornell Rogers
           Clerk Com on Citizenship

Office Com on Citizenship
Tahlequah I.T. Sept 19th 1888.

SIMPSON

DOCKET #1682
CENSUS ROLLS 1835 to 1852

APPLICANT FOR CHEROKEE CITIZENSHIP

POST OFFICE: Lewisville Tex		ATTORNEY: A.E. Ivey	
No	NAMES	AGE	SEX
1	Catherine Simpson	40	female

ANCESTOR: Lewis Gorham

Rejected Aug 28th 1889

         Office Commission on Citizenship
         Cherokee Nation Ind Ter
         Tahlequah Aug 28th 1889

The above was submitted by Attorney for claimant without evidence. The Commission therefore decide that Catherine Simpson is not of Cherokee Indian blood. P.O. Lewisville Texas.

         Will.P. Ross
Attest   Chairman
 D.S. Williams   J.E. Gunter Com
 Asst Clk Com.

Cherokee Citizenship Commission Docket Books
(1880-84, 1887-89) Volume IV
Tahlequah, Cherokee Nation

SETZER

DOCKET #1683
CENSUS ROLLS 1835 to 1852

APPLICANT FOR **CHEROKEE CITIZENSHIP**

POST OFFICE: Chalk Vally[sic] Ark		ATTORNEY: A.E. Ivey	
No	NAMES	AGE	SEX
1	Polona Setzer	35	female

ANCESTOR: Mary S Bell

Rejected Aug 28th 1889

Office Commission on Citizenship
Cherokee Nation Ind Ter
Tahlequah Aug 28th 1889

The above case was submitted by A.E. Ivey Attorney for claimant without evidence. The Commission decide that applicant Polona Setzer and children whose names are not given are not of Cherokee blood. P.O. Chalk Valley Ark.

Attest
   D.S. Williams
   Asst Clk Com.

              Will.P. Ross
              Chairman
              J.E. Gunter Com

WAGNER

DOCKET #1684
CENSUS ROLLS 1835

APPLICANT FOR **CHEROKEE CITIZENSHIP**

POST OFFICE: Mountainburg Ark		ATTORNEY: A.E. Ivey	
No	NAMES	AGE	SEX
1	John C Wagner	18	male

ANCESTOR: Mima Edwards

Now on this the 9th day of January, 1888, comes the above case for a final hearing and the parties having made application pursuant to the provisions of an Act of the National Council approved December 8th 1886, and all the evidence being duly examined and found <u>not</u> to be sufficient and satisfactory to the Commission and the name of the ancestor not appearing on the Rolls as claimed in the application.

Cherokee Citizenship Commission Docket Books
(1880-84, 1887-89) Volume IV
Tahlequah, Cherokee Nation

It is adjudged and determined by the Commission that John C. Wagoner[sic] is not a Cherokee by blood and is is[sic] hereby rejected and declared intruders.

                            J. T. Adair   Chairman Commission
                            John E. Gunter   Commissioner
Attest   Commissioner
    C.C. Lipe
        Clerk Commission

WAGNER

DOCKET #1685
CENSUS ROLLS 1835

APPLICANT FOR CHEROKEE CITIZENSHIP

POST OFFICE: Mountainburg Ark		ATTORNEY: A.E. Ivey	
NO	NAMES	AGE	SEX
1	Henry M Wagner	20	male

ANCESTOR: Mima Edwards

Now on this the 9th day of January, 1888, comes the above case for a final hearing and the parties having made application pursuant to the provisions of an Act of the National Council approved December 8th 1886, and all the evidence being duly examined and found not to be sufficient and satisfactory to the Commission and the name of the ancestor not appearing on the Rolls as claimed in the application.

It is adjudged and determined by the Commission that Henry M Wagner is not a Cherokee by blood and is hereby rejected and declared and[sic] intruder.

                            J. T. Adair   Chairman Commission
                            John E. Gunter   Commissioner
Attest   Commissioner
    C.C. Lipe
        Clerk Commission

Cherokee Citizenship Commission Docket Books
(1880-84, 1887-89) Volume IV
Tahlequah, Cherokee Nation

WAGNER

DOCKET #1686
CENSUS ROLLS 1835

APPLICANT FOR CHEROKEE CITIZENSHIP

POST OFFICE: Mountainburg Ark		ATTORNEY: A.E. Ivey	
No	NAMES	AGE	SEX
1	Andrew Wagoner[sic]	32	male
2	James H Wagner	9	"
3	George A Wagner	7	"
4	Malissa C Wagner	3	female
5	Emory W Wagner	1	male

ANCESTOR: Mima Edwards

Now on this the 9th day of January, 1888, comes the above case for a final hearing and the parties having made application pursuant to the provisions of an Act of the National Council approved December 8th 1886, and all the evidence being duly examined and found not to be sufficient and satisfactory to the Commission and the name of the ancestor not appearing on the Rolls as claimed in the application.

It is adjudged & determined by the Commission that Andrew Wagner, James H Wagner, George A. Wagner, Malissa C. Wagner and Emory W. Wagner are not Cherokees by blood and are hereby rejected and declared intruders.

        J. T. Adair Chairman Commission
        John E. Gunter Commissioner
Attest   Commissioner
 C.C. Lipe
   Clerk Commission

KERBY

DOCKET #1687
CENSUS ROLLS 1835

APPLICANT FOR CHEROKEE CITIZENSHIP

POST OFFICE:		ATTORNEY: A.E. Ivey	
No	NAMES	AGE	SEX
1	Mary Kerby	28	female
2	4 children not named		

ANCESTOR: Mima Edwards

Cherokee Citizenship Commission Docket Books
(1880-84, 1887-89) Volume IV
Tahlequah, Cherokee Nation

Now on this the 9th day of January, 1888, comes the above case for a final hearing and the parties having made application pursuant to the provisions of an Act of the National Council approved December 8th 1886, and the evidence being duly examined and found not to be sufficient and satisfactory to the Commission and the name of the ancestor not appearing on the Rolls as claimed in the application.

It is adjudged & determined by the Commission that Mary Kerby is not Cherokee by blood and is hereby rejected and declared an intruder.

                              J. T. Adair   Chairman Commission
                              John E. Gunter   Commissioner
Attest   Commissioner
    C.C. Lipe
        Clerk Commission

LEVY

DOCKET #1688
CENSUS ROLLS 1835

APPLICANT FOR CHEROKEE CITIZENSHIP

POST OFFICE: Decatur Tex		ATTORNEY: Taylor and Ivey	
NO	NAMES	AGE	SEX
1	Lorena Levy	32	female

ANCESTOR: William Chisolom[sic]

Rejected April 17th 1889

Now on this the 17th day of April, 1889, comes the case of Lorena Levy versus the Cherokee Nation for final hearing. The applicant alleges that she is the great grand child of William Chisholm whose name should appear on the census roll of Cherokees by blood citizens of the Cherokee Nation taken and made in the year 1835. The name of William Chisholm can not be found on the roll of 1835. Mary Ann Roberts the mother of the applicant states that applicant derives her Cherokee blood from her Father Eli Roberts who was her second husband and by whom she has living (October 11th 1887) three boys and two girls, viz: William Tinsley (son), Minerva Tinsley (daughter), Francis (son), Lorena (daughter) and Moses Roberts (son); that Eli Roberts derived his Cherokee blood from his mother Joanna Tinsley and she from her mother who was the daughter of a sister of Absolom and Wm Chisholm whose name should appear on the Old Settler Cherokee rolls west of the Mississippi River. A

Cherokee Citizenship Commission Docket Books
(1880-84, 1887-89) Volume IV
Tahlequah, Cherokee Nation

careful examination of the Old Settler pay roll of 1851 fails to find their names. The testimony fails to establish the fact that Absolom and William Chisholm here refered[sic] to or their sister from whom applicant descended but whose name is not given were Cherokees and that they at any time resided in the Cherokee Nation. The testimony of William Wilson now living in Sequoyah District 78 years old and who married the widow of Tom Chisholm knows nothing of the ancestor claimed by applicant or alleged by her mother. The Commission therefore adjudge that Lorena Levy has failed to establish her right to reside in the Cherokee Nation as a Cherokee by blood and so decree.

                        Will.P. Ross
                        Chairman
                John E. Gunter   Com

Attest
    D.S. Williams
        Clk Com.

LOONEY

DOCKET #1689
CENSUS ROLLS 1835 to 1852

APPLICANT FOR CHEROKEE CITIZENSHIP

POST OFFICE: Dennison[sic] Tex		ATTORNEY: A.E. Ivey	
NO	NAMES	AGE	SEX
1	Charles Looney	23	male
2	Ada May Looney	1	female

ANCESTOR: Allen Looney

Rejected Aug 28th 1889

                    Office Commission on Citizenship
                      Cherokee Nation Ind Ter
                      Tahlequah Aug 28th 1889

The above named case having been submitted by A.E. Ivey Attorney for claimant without evidence the Commission decide that Charles Looney age 23 yrs and his daughter Ada May Looney age 1 year are not of Cherokee blood. P.O. Denison Texas

                      Will.P. Ross
Attest   Chairman
    D.S. Williams   J.E. Gunter   Com
    Asst Clk Com.

Cherokee Citizenship Commission Docket Books (1880-84, 1887-89) Volume IV
Tahlequah, Cherokee Nation

LOWDEN

DOCKET #1690
CENSUS ROLLS 1835 to 52

APPLICANT FOR **CHEROKEE CITIZENSHIP**

POST OFFICE: Cherokee City Ark		ATTORNEY: A.E. Ivey	
NO	NAMES	AGE	SEX
1	Mackey Jane Lowden	36	female
2	George G Lowden	14	male
3	Altha C Lowden	11	female
4	Leslie H Lowden	8	male
5	Raymond M Lowden	6	"
6	Ada Bell Lowden	3	female
7	Lenora V Lowden	7 m	"

ANCESTOR: Richard L Mackey

Rejected Aug 28th 1889

Office Commission on Citizenship
Cherokee Nation Ind Ter
Tahlequah Aug 28th 1889

The above case having been submitted without evidence the Commission decide that Macky[sic] Jane Lowden age 36 yrs and her sons George G age 14 yrs, Leslie H. 8 yrs, Raymond M age 6 yrs and her daughters Altha C age 11 yrs, Ada Bell age 3 yrs and Lenora V Lowden 7 weeks[sic] are not of Cherokee blood. P.O. Cherokee City Ark.

Attest
   D.S. Williams
   Asst Clk Com.

Will.P. Ross
   Chairman
J.E. Gunter   Com

LOCKHART

DOCKET #1691
CENSUS ROLLS 1835 & 52

APPLICANT FOR **CHEROKEE CITIZENSHIP**

POST OFFICE: Claremore, I.T.		ATTORNEY: A.E. Ivey	
NO	NAMES	AGE	SEX
1	Sarah M Lockhart	31	female
2	W.A. Lockhart	11	"

Cherokee Citizenship Commission Docket Books
(1880-84, 1887-89) Volume IV
Tahlequah, Cherokee Nation

3	Martha Lockhart	7	female
4	Ada Lockhart	3	"
5	Lushion Lockhart	1	male

ANCESTOR: Mrs. Badson

Rejected Aug 28th 1889

Office Commission on Citizenship
Cherokee Nation Ind Ter
Tahlequah Aug 28th 1889

The above case having been submitted by Attorney without evidence the Commission decide that the claimant Sarah M Lockhart age 31 yrs and her sons W.A. Lockhart age 11 yrs, Lushion Lockhart age 1 yr and Daughters Martha Lockhart age 7 yrs, Ada Lockhart age 3 yrs are not of Cherokee blood. P.O. Claremore I.T.

Attest
  D.S. Williams
  Asst Clk Com.

Will.P. Ross
Chairman
J.E. Gunter Com

LONG

DOCKET #1692
CENSUS ROLLS 1835

APPLICANT FOR CHEROKEE CITIZENSHIP

POST OFFICE: Salisaw[sic] C.N.		ATTORNEY: Ivey and Welch	
NO	NAMES	AGE	SEX
1	Angelina Long	38	female
2	Sherman Long	22	male
3	Jesse Long	16	"
4	Mary Long	12	female
5	Martha Long	12	"
6	Robert Long	10	male
7	Nancy Long	9	female
8	Jonah Long	1	male
9	Margaret Long	4	female

ANCESTOR: *(Illegible)* Bailey

Rejected Aug 29th 1889

Office Commission on Citizenship
Cherokee Nation Ind Ter
Tahlequah Aug 29th 1889

Cherokee Citizenship Commission Docket Books
(1880-84, 1887-89) Volume IV
Tahlequah, Cherokee Nation

The above named case Ivey & Welch Attorneys for claimants come before the Commission for final hearing without evidence. The Commission therefore decide that Angelina Long age 38 yrs and her children Sherman Long age 22 yrs, Jesse Long age 16 yrs, Mary Long age 12 yrs and Martha Long age 12 yrs (twins), Robert Long age 9 yrs, Nancy Long age 7 yrs, Jonah Long 1 and Margaret Long age 4 yrs are not of Cherokee blood and not entitled to citizenship in the Cherokee Nation. P.O. Salisaw Cher. Nat.

Attest
   D.S. Williams
   Asst Clk Com.

Will.P. Ross Chairman
J.E. Gunter Com

LANDON

DOCKET #1693
CENSUS ROLLS 1835 to 52

APPLICANT FOR CHEROKEE CITIZENSHIP

	POST OFFICE: Carr Mo		ATTORNEY: A.E. Ivey
No	NAMES	AGE	SEX
1	Clarissa Landon	34	female
2	E.C. Landon	12	male
3	Daniel Landon	11	"
4	Florence Landon	4	female
5	Sarah Landon	2	"

ANCESTOR: Lucy Bryant

Rejected Aug 29th 1889

Office Commission on Citizenship
Cherokee Nation Ind Ter
Tahlequah Aug 29th 1889

The above named case having been submitted by Attorney for claimant without proof. The Commission decide that Clarissa Landon or Lerndon age 34 yrs and her sons E.G. Lerndon age 14 yrs and Daniel Lerndon age 11 yrs and her daughters Florence Lerndon age 4 yrs and Sarah E Lerndon age 2 yrs are not of Cherokee blood. P.O. Carr Mo.

Attest
   D.S. Williams
   Asst Clk Com.

Will.P. Ross Chairman
J.E. Gunter Com

Cherokee Citizenship Commission Docket Books
(1880-84, 1887-89) Volume IV
Tahlequah, Cherokee Nation

LAWRENCE

DOCKET #1694
CENSUS ROLLS 1835 to 52

APPLICANT FOR **CHEROKEE CITIZENSHIP**

POST OFFICE: Carr Mo		ATTORNEY: A.E. Ivey	
NO	NAMES	AGE	SEX
1	Richard Lawrence	53	male

ANCESTOR: Lucy Bryant

Rejected Aug 29th 1889

Office Commission on Citizenship
Cherokee Nation Ind Ter
Tahlequah Aug 29th 1889

The above application was submitted by claimant's Attorney A.E. Ivey without evidence therefore we decide that applicant Richard Lawrence age 53 yrs is not a Cherokee by blood. P.O. Carr Mo

Will.P. Ross
Chairman

Attest
D.S. Williams
Asst Clk Com.

J.E. Gunter Com

LAWRENCE

DOCKET #1695
CENSUS ROLLS 1835 to 52

APPLICANT FOR **CHEROKEE CITIZENSHIP**

POST OFFICE: Carr, Mo		ATTORNEY: A.E. Ivey	
NO	NAMES	AGE	SEX
1	Samuel Lawrence	56	male
2	Robert Lawrence	17	"
3	Ida Lawrence	14	female
4	Alex Lawrence	3	male
5	Susan Lawrence	2	female
6	Randolph Lawrence	4 m	male

ANCESTOR: Lucy Bryant

Rejected Aug 29th 1889

Cherokee Citizenship Commission Docket Books
(1880-84, 1887-89) Volume IV
Tahlequah, Cherokee Nation

Office Commission on Citizenship
Cherokee Nation Ind Ter
Tahlequah Aug 29th 1889

The above application was submitted by claimant's Attorney A.E. Ivey without evidence we decide that applicant Samuel Lawrence age 56 yrs and his children Robt Lawrence age 17 yrs, Ida Lawrence age 14 yrs, Alex Lawrence, Susan Lawrence age 2 yrs, Randolph Lawrence age 4 months are not Cherokees by blood and not entitled to citizenship in the Cherokee Nation. P.O. Carr Mo.

Attest
   D.S. Williams
   Asst Clk Com.

Will.P. Ross
   Chairman
J.E. Gunter Com

LAWRENCE

DOCKET #1696
CENSUS ROLLS 1835 to 1852

APPLICANT FOR CHEROKEE CITIZENSHIP

POST OFFICE: Carr Mo		ATTORNEY: A.E. Ivey	
NO	NAMES	AGE	SEX
1	William Lawrence	2	male

ANCESTOR: Lucy Bryant

Rejected Aug 29th 1889

Office Commission on Citizenship
Cherokee Nation Ind Ter
Tahlequah Aug 29th 1889

The above application was submitted by claimant's Attorney A.E. Ivey without evidence. Therefore we decide that applicant William Lawrence age 2 yrs is not a Cherokee by blood & not entitled to citizenship in the Cherokee Nation. P.O. Carr Mo.

Attest
   D.S. Williams
   Asst Clk Com.

Will.P. Ross
   Chairman
J.E. Gunter Com

Cherokee Citizenship Commission Docket Books
(1880-84, 1887-89) Volume IV
Tahlequah, Cherokee Nation

LAWRENCE

DOCKET #1697
CENSUS ROLLS 1835 to 1852

APPLICANT FOR **CHEROKEE CITIZENSHIP**

POST OFFICE: Rome, Mo.		ATTORNEY: A.E. Ivey	
No	NAMES	AGE	SEX
1	John Lawrence	51	male
2	Mariah Lawrence	19	female
3	Louisa Lawrence	16	"
4	Sarah Lawrence	24	"

ANCESTOR: Lucy Bryant

Office Commission on Citizenship
Cherokee Nation Ind Ter
Tahlequah August 30th 1889

This case having been submitted by the Attorney A.E. Ivey without evidence the Commission decide that John Lawrence age fifty one years and his children Mariah Lawrence age 19 years, Louisa Lawrence age 16 years, and Sarah Lawrence age 24 years are not Cherokees by blood and not entitled to Cherokee citizenship.

Attest
  EG Ross
    Clerk Commission

Will.P. Ross
    Chairman
J.E. Gunter   Com

LANDRETH

DOCKET #1698
CENSUS ROLLS 1835 to 1852

APPLICANT FOR **CHEROKEE CITIZENSHIP**

POST OFFICE: Van Buren Ark		ATTORNEY: Ivey and Welch	
No	NAMES	AGE	SEX
1	Zacharia Landreth	37	male
2	Malinda Landreth	4	female

ANCESTOR: William Friends

Rejected Aug 29th 1889

Office Commission on Citizenship
Cherokee Nation Ind Ter
Tahlequah Aug 29th 1889

Cherokee Citizenship Commission Docket Books
(1880-84, 1887-89) Volume IV
Tahlequah, Cherokee Nation

The above application was submitted by claimant's Attorney A.E. Ivey without evidence. Therefore we decide that applicant Zacharia Landreth age 57 yrs and his child Malinda Landreth age 4 yrs are not Cherokees by blood. P.O. Van Buren Ark.

                              Will.P. Ross
Attest   Chairman
  D.S. Williams   J.E. Gunter   Com
  Asst Clk Com.

LAWRENCE

DOCKET #1699
CENSUS ROLLS 1835 to 1852

	POST OFFICE: Carr Mo	APPLICANT FOR CHEROKEE CITIZENSHIP ATTORNEY: A.E. Ivey	
No	NAMES	AGE	SEX
1	Randolph Lawrence	24	male

ANCESTOR: Lucy Bryant

                        Office Commission on Citizenship
                            Cherokee Nation Ind Ter
                           Tahlequah August 29th 1889

The above application was submitted without evidence by claimant's Attorney A.E. Ivey. Therefore we decide that claimant Randolph Lawrence age 24 yrs is not a Cherokee by blood. P.O. Carr Mo

                              Will.P. Ross
Attest   Chairman
  D.S. Williams   J.E. Gunter   Com
  Asst Clk Com.

LAWRENCE

DOCKET #1700
CENSUS ROLLS 1835 to 1852

	POST OFFICE: Rome, Mo	APPLICANT FOR CHEROKEE CITIZENSHIP ATTORNEY: A.E. Ivey	
No	NAMES	AGE	SEX
1	Randolph Lawrence	70	male
2	G.G. Lawrence	18	"

Cherokee Citizenship Commission Docket Books
(1880-84, 1887-89) Volume IV
Tahlequah, Cherokee Nation

3	Margaret Lawrence	16	female
4	Louisa M Lawrence	10	"

ANCESTOR: Lucy Bryant

Rejected Aug 29th 1889

Office Commission on Citizenship
Cherokee Nation Ind Ter
Tahlequah Aug 29th 1889

The above application was submitted by claimant's Attorney A.E. Ivey without evidence. Therefore we decide that applicant Randolph Lawrence age 70 yrs and children G.G. Lawrence age 18 yrs, Margaret Lawrence age 16 yrs, Louisa Lawrence age 10 yrs are not Cherokees by blood.

Will.P. Ross
Chairman
Attest
D.S. Williams   J.E. Gunter   Com
Asst Clk Com.

LAYCOCK

DOCKET #1701
CENSUS ROLLS 1835 to 1852

APPLICANT FOR CHEROKEE CITIZENSHIP

POST OFFICE: Jacksboro Tex		ATTORNEY: A.E. Ivey	
No	NAMES	AGE	SEX
1	S.E. Laycock	28	female
2	Stella Laycock	10	"
3	I.W. Laycock	7	male
4	Thomas Laycock	3	"

ANCESTOR: Zacharia Gunter

Rejected Aug 29th 1889

Office Commission on Citizenship
Cherokee Nation Ind Ter
Tahlequah August 29th 1889

The above application was submitted without evidence. Therefore we decide that applicant Mrs. S.E. Laycock age 28 yrs and her children Stella Laycock age 10 yrs, I.W. Laycock age 7 yrs, Thomas Laycock age 3 yrs are not Cherokees by blood. P.O. Jacksboro Texas.

Cherokee Citizenship Commission Docket Books
(1880-84, 1887-89) Volume IV
Tahlequah, Cherokee Nation

Attest
   D.S. Williams
   Asst Clk Com.

Will.P. Ross
Chairman
J.E. Gunter Com

LEWERS

DOCKET #1702
CENSUS ROLLS 1835 to 1852

APPLICANT FOR CHEROKEE CITIZENSHIP

POST OFFICE: Alma Ark		ATTORNEY: A.E. Ivey	
No	NAMES	AGE	SEX
1	Hanson Lewers	32	male
2	Cary Lewers	9	"
3	John Lewers	8	"
4	Joe L. Lewers	6	"
5	Maggie Lewers	4	female

ANCESTOR: John Lewers

Rejected Aug 29th 1889

Office Commission on Citizenship
Cherokee Nation Ind Ter
Tahlequah August 29th 1889

The above application was submitted by claimant's Attorney A.E. Ivey without evidence. Therefore we decide that applicant Harison[sic] Lewers age 32 yrs and children Cary Lewers age 9 yrs, John Lewers age 8 yrs, Joe Lee Lewers age 6 yrs, Maggie Lewers age 4 yrs are not Cherokees by blood.
P.O. Alma Ark.

Attest
   D.S. Williams
   Asst Clk Com.

Will.P. Ross
Chairman
J.E. Gunter Com

Cherokee Citizenship Commission Docket Books
(1880-84, 1887-89) Volume IV
Tahlequah, Cherokee Nation

LARUE

DOCKET #1703
CENSUS ROLLS 1835

APPLICANT FOR **CHEROKEE CITIZENSHIP**

POST OFFICE: Lees Creek, Ark		ATTORNEY: A.E. Ivey	
No	NAMES	AGE	SEX
1	Hariett[sic] Larue	24	female
2	Eugene Larue	4	male
3	Georg.[sic] L. Larue	2	"

ANCESTOR: Martha M Williams

Rejected Aug 30th 1889

Office Commission on Citizenship
Cherokee Nation Ind Ter
Tahlequah Aug 30th 1889

The claimant in the above case in her declaration made before Ben Dicherl[sic] Clerk of the Circuit Court in and for Crawford County State of Arkansas the 28th day of September A.D. 1887, alleges that her Father George L. Williams is a white man residing as she is informed near Childers Station in the Cherokee Nation, and that her mother, the wife of said Williams from whom she derives her Cherokee blood was Martha M. Williams whose maiden name was Martha M. Groff, the daughter of Harriet Groff whose maiden name was Harriet Pilkelton, who was called and recognized as a Cherokee Indian and both of whom died when applicant was about ten years of age. The only evidence in the case is the affidavit of one Wesley Nelson made and taken at the same time as the declaration who simply swears that he is a citizen of Flint District Cherokee Nation and that he believes that Harriet Larue is the person she represents herself to be and that she is at least 1/8 Cherokee from physical appearance, color and complexion. The Commission can not regard such statements as sufficient to establish the Indian descent of claimant. Besides this the name of Martha M. Williams does not appear on the census roll of Cherokees by blood taken and made by the United States in the year 1835. The Commission therefore decide that the claimant Harriet Larue age 24 yrs and sons Eugene Larue age 4 years and George Lafayette Larue are not of Cherokee blood and not entitled to citizenship in the Cherokee Nation. P.O. Lees Creek Arkansas.

Will.P. Ross
Chairman
J.E. Gunter   Com

Attest
D.S. Williams
Asst Clk Com.

Cherokee Citizenship Commission Docket Books
(1880-84, 1887-89) Volume IV
Tahlequah, Cherokee Nation

LAWRENCE

DOCKET #1704
CENSUS ROLLS 1835 to 1852

APPLICANT FOR CHEROKEE CITIZENSHIP

POST OFFICE: Star of the West Ark		ATTORNEY: A.E. Ivey	
NO	NAMES	AGE	SEX
1	Beckey A Lawrence	18	female

ANCESTOR: John Thompson

Rejected Aug 29th 1889

Office Commission on Citizenship
Cherokee Nation Ind Ter
Tahlequah August 29th 1889

The above application was submitted by applicant's Attorney without evidence. Therefore we decide that applicant Beckey A Lawrence age 18 yrs is not a Cherokee by blood. P.O. Star of the West Ark.

Will.P. Ross
Chairman

Attest
D.S. Williams
Asst Clk Com.

J.E. Gunter Com

LOSSON

DOCKET #1705
CENSUS ROLLS 1835 to 1852

APPLICANT FOR CHEROKEE CITIZENSHIP

POST OFFICE: Mulberry Ark		ATTORNEY: A.E. Ivey	
NO	NAMES	AGE	SEX
1	William E. Losson	39	male
2	John W. Losson	10	"
3	Rosa N. Losson	8	female
4	Mary E. Losson	6	"

ANCESTOR: John Rogers

Now on this the 17th day of March, 1888, comes the above case for a final hearing. The parties having made application pursuant to the provisions of an Act of the National Council approved December 8th 1886 – And all the

Cherokee Citizenship Commission Docket Books
(1880-84, 1887-89) Volume IV
Tahlequah, Cherokee Nation

evidence being duly considered and found to be insufficient and unsatisfactory, it is adjudged and declared by the Commission that

William E. Losson, John W. Losson, Rosa N. Losson, and Mary E. Losson not Cherokees and are not entitled to any of the rights, privileges and immunities of Cherokee citizens by blood.

                                      J. T. Adair   Chairman Commission
                                      John E. Gunter   Commissioner
Attest   D.W. Lipe   Commissioner
    C.C. Lipe
        Clerk Com.

The decision in the James C.C. Rogers case found on Book C, page 627, and testimony on Journal pages 325 to 333 governs this case.

LOGAN

DOCKET #1706
CENSUS ROLLS

APPLICANT FOR CHEROKEE CITIZENSHIP

POST OFFICE: Tate Ga		ATTORNEY: A.E. Ivey	
No	NAMES	AGE	SEX
1	James L. Logan	22	male
2	Liba Logan	2	female

ANCESTOR: Lettie Logan

Rejected Aug 29th 1889

                              Office Commission on Citizenship
                                    Cherokee Nation Ind Ter
                                    Tahlequah August 29th 1889

The above application was submitted by claimant's Attorney A.E. Ivey without evidence. Therefore we decide that claimant James L. Logan age 22 yrs and child Liba Logan are not Cherokees by blood. P.O. Tate Ga.

                                          Will.P. Ross
Attest   Chairman
    D.S. Williams   J.E. Gunter   Com
    Asst Clk Com.

Cherokee Citizenship Commission Docket Books
(1880-84, 1887-89) Volume IV
Tahlequah, Cherokee Nation

LANGLEY

DOCKET #1707
CENSUS ROLLS 1851

APPLICANT FOR CHEROKEE CITIZENSHIP

POST OFFICE: Talona Ga		ATTORNEY: A.E. Ivey	
NO	NAMES	AGE	SEX
1	John A. Langley	22	male
2	William T. Langley	3	"
3	Collumbus[sic] Langley	2	"
4	Edwin T. Langley	1	"

ANCESTOR: Albert Langley

Rejected Aug 29th 1889

                    Office Commission on Citizenship
                    Cherokee Nation Ind Ter
                    Tahlequah Aug 29th 1889

The above application was submitted by claimant's Attorney A.E. Ivey without evidence. Therefore we decide that applicant John Langley age 22 yrs, William T Langley age 3 yrs, Columbus Langley age 2 yrs, Edwin Langley age 1 yr are not Cherokees by blood. Post Office Talona Ark[sic].

                    Will.P. Ross

Attest   Chairman
   D.S. Williams   J.E. Gunter   Com
   Asst Clk Com.

LANGLEY

DOCKET #1708
CENSUS ROLLS 1851

APPLICANT FOR CHEROKEE CITIZENSHIP

POST OFFICE: Talking Rock Ga		ATTORNEY: A.E. Ivey	
NO	NAMES	AGE	SEX
1	Elizabeth T. Langley	24	female

ANCESTOR: William Gibson

Rejected Sept 16th 1889

                    Office Commission on Citizenship
                    Cherokee Nation Ind Ter
                  Tahlequah Sept. 16th 1889

Cherokee Citizenship Commission Docket Books
(1880-84, 1887-89) Volume IV
Tahlequah, Cherokee Nation

The above case was filed on the 3rd day of Oct. 1887. And it being called and was set for Sept. 16th 1889 for a final hearing and according to the time set the case was again called and no one responding and there being no evidence on file in support of the application the Commission are of the opinion and so decide that Elizabeth T. Langley age 24 yrs is not a Cherokee by blood.
Post Office Talking Rock Ga.

                                    Will.P. Ross
Attest   Chairman
  D.S. Williams   R. Bunch   Com
  Asst Clk Com.   J.E. Gunter   Com

LANGLEY

DOCKET #1709
CENSUS ROLLS 1852

APPLICANT FOR CHEROKEE CITIZENSHIP

POST OFFICE: Town Creek Ga		ATTORNEY: A.E. Ivey	
NO	NAMES	AGE	SEX
1	John L. Langley	33	male
2	Annie Langley	33	female
3	Alfred A. Langley	12	male
4	Rebecca J Langley	9	female
5	Columbus C Langley	5	male
6	Kissiah Langley	3	female

ANCESTOR: Andrew J Langley

Rejected Sept 16th 1889

                              Office Commission on Citizenship
                                   Cherokee Nation Ind Ter
                                    Tahlequah Sept. 16th 1889

The above case was filed on the 3rd day of Oct. 1887 and being called was set for Sept. 16th 1889 for a hearing and according to the time set the case was again called but no one responding and there being no evidence on file in support of application the Commission are of the opinion and they so decide that John L. Langley age 33 yrs and Annie Langley mother 33 yrs, Alfred A. son 12 yrs, Rebecca J Daughter 9 yrs, Columbus C. son 5 yrs, Kissiah Langley 3 yrs Daughter, are not Cherokees by blood. P.O. Town Creek Ga.

Attest   Will.P. Ross
  D.S. Williams   Chairman
  Asst Clk Com.   J.E. Gunter   Com

Cherokee Citizenship Commission Docket Books
(1880-84, 1887-89) Volume IV
Tahlequah, Cherokee Nation

LEACH

DOCKET #1710
CENSUS ROLLS 1851

APPLICANT FOR **CHEROKEE CITIZENSHIP**

POST OFFICE: Floyd Springs Ga		ATTORNEY: A.E. Ivey	
No	NAMES	AGE	SEX
1	Lizzie J Leach	26	female
2	Rilla J Leach	8	"
3	Lillie Leach	6	"
4	Martha Leach	3	"
5	John Leach	2	male

ANCESTOR: Jane Gravitt

Rejected Oct 4th 1889

Office Commission on Citizenship
Cherokee Nation Ind Ter
Tahlequah Oct. 4th 1889

The applicant[sic] in the above case was submitted by Atty for applicant A.E. Ivey for the action of the Commission on the 6th day of March. The evidence not be sufficient to the Commission their decision has been with held awaiting evidence for the proper identification of Lizzie J Leach as being related to one Jane Gravitt whom she alleges as her ancestor, but it having not been furnished, the Commission therefore decide that Lizzie J. Leach age 26 yrs and the following children, Rilla J. Leach 8 yrs & Lillie Leach Female 6 yrs, Martha Leach 3 yrs Daughter, John Leach male 2 yrs are not Cherokees by blood. P.O. Floyd Springs Ga.

Attest
D.S. Williams
Asst Clk Com.

Will.P. Ross
Chairman
J.E. Gunter
Com.

Cherokee Citizenship Commission Docket Books
(1880-84, 1887-89) Volume IV
Tahlequah, Cherokee Nation

LOONEY

DOCKET #1711
CENSUS ROLLS 1835 to 1852

APPLICANT FOR **CHEROKEE CITIZENSHIP**

POST OFFICE: Dennison[sic] Tex		ATTORNEY: A.E. Ivey	
No	NAMES	AGE	SEX
1	John F. Looney	52	male
2	E.W. Looney	20	"
3	W.G. Looney	18	"
4	Cora Looney	15	female
	Orville Looney	12	male
6	Lillian Looney	9	female

ANCESTOR: Elizabeth Looney

Office Commission on Citizenship
Tahlequah I.T. Aug 30th 1889

The above case was called and submitted by A.E. Ivey without evidence. The Commission decide that John F. Looney age 52 years and the following children E.W. Looney age 20 years, W.G. Looney age 18 years, Cora Looney age 15 years, Orville Looney age 12 years and Lillian Looney age 9 years are not Cherokees by blood and are not entitled to citizenship in the Cherokee Nation.

Attest
  EG Ross
    Clerk Commission

      Will.P. Ross
        Chairman
      J.E. Gunter Com

LOONEY

DOCKET #1712
CENSUS ROLLS 1835 to 1852

APPLICANT FOR **CHEROKEE CITIZENSHIP**

POST OFFICE: Dennison[sic] Tex		ATTORNEY: A.E. Ivey	
No	NAMES	AGE	SEX
1	L.A. Looney	46	male
2	Etta Looney	15	female
3	Hugh Looney	7	male

ANCESTOR: Elizabeth Looney

Cherokee Citizenship Commission Docket Books (1880-84, 1887-89) Volume IV
Tahlequah, Cherokee Nation

Office Commission on Citizenship
Tahlequah I.T. Aug 30th 1889

The above case was called and submitted by Atty A.E. Ivey without evidence the Commission decide that L.A. Looney age 46 yrs and the following children Etta Looney age 15 yrs and Hugh Looney age 7 yrs are not Cherokees by blood.

Attest   Will.P. Ross
   EG Ross   Chairman
     Clerk Commission   J.E. Gunter   Com

LEE

DOCKET #1713
CENSUS ROLLS 1835 to 52

APPLICANT FOR CHEROKEE CITIZENSHIP

POST OFFICE: Lancaster Ark		ATTORNEY: A.E. Ivey	
No	NAMES	AGE	SEX
1	Annie R Lee		
2	Nettie Lee		
3	Martha Lee		
4	Ora Lee		
5	Viola Lee		
6	William Lee		

ANCESTOR: Lawrence Slaughter

Office Commission on Citizenship
Tahlequah August 30th 1889

The above case was called and and[sic] submitted by Attorney without evidence. The Commission therefore decide that Annie R. Lee age 35 years and the following children Nettie Lee age 13 years, Martha Lee age 11 years, Ora Lee age 5 years, Viola Lee age 3 years and William Lee age 1 year are not Cherokees by blood and not entitled to Citizenship in the Cherokee Nation.

Attest
   EG Ross   Will.P. Ross
     Clerk Commission   Chairman
                             J.E. Gunter   Com

Cherokee Citizenship Commission Docket Books
(1880-84, 1887-89) Volume IV
Tahlequah, Cherokee Nation

HARMON

DOCKET #1714
CENSUS ROLLS 1835 to 1852

APPLICANT FOR CHEROKEE CITIZENSHIP

POST OFFICE: Pittsburk[sic] Kans		ATTORNEY: A.E. Ivey	
No	NAMES	AGE	SEX
1	Mary Harmon	46	female

ANCESTOR: James Smith

See decision in this case in that of Margaret A Puffer in Book "C" Page 434 – Adverse to claimant.

        Cornell Rogers
        Clk Com on Citizenship
Office Com on Citizenship
Tahlequah I.T. Sept. 24th 1888

LUCAS

DOCKET #1715
CENSUS ROLLS 1835

APPLICANT FOR CHEROKEE CITIZENSHIP

POST OFFICE: Bloomfield Ark		ATTORNEY: J.M. Bell	
No	NAMES	AGE	SEX
1	Nancy Lucas	60	female

ANCESTOR: Almon Guinn

        Office Commission on Citizenship
        Cherokee Nation Ind Ter
        Tahlequah Aug 30th 1889

  The above case was called and submitted by A.E. Ivey Attorney without evidence. The Commission decide that Nancy Lucas age sixty years is not a Cherokee by blood and are[sic] not entitled to Citizenship in the Cherokee Nation.

Attest   Will.P. Ross
  EG Ross   Chairman
    Clerk Commission   J.E. Gunter   Com

Cherokee Citizenship Commission Docket Books (1880-84, 1887-89) Volume IV
Tahlequah, Cherokee Nation

LIPSICOMB

DOCKET #1716
CENSUS ROLLS 1835

APPLICANT FOR CHEROKEE CITIZENSHIP

Post Office: Dyer, Crawford Co Ark		Attorney: A.E. Ivey	
No	NAMES	AGE	SEX
1	Elizabeth Lipsicomb	44	female
2	W.M.A. Hayes	7	male
3	Hattie Hays[sic]	5	female

ANCESTOR: John Rogers

Now on this the 17th day of March 1888, comes the above case for a final hearing. The parties having made application pursuant to the provisions of an Act of the National Council approved December 8th 1886, and all the evidence being duly considered and found to be insufficient and unsatisfactory, it is adjudged and declared by the Commission that

Elizabeth Lipsicomb, W.M.A. Hayes and Hattie Hayes, not Cherokees and are not entitled to the rights, privileges and immunities of Cherokee citizens by blood.

        J. T. Adair Chairman Commission
        John E. Gunter Commissioner
Attest   D.W. Lipe Commissioner
 C.C. Lipe
   Clerk Com.

The decision in the James C.C. Rogers case found in Book C, page 627, and testimony on Journal pages 325 to 333 governs this case.

LEMDON

DOCKET #1717
CENSUS ROLLS 1835 to 1852

APPLICANT FOR CHEROKEE CITIZENSHIP

Post Office: Carr Mo		Attorney: A.E. Ivey	
No	NAMES	AGE	SEX
1	Martha Lemdon	23	female
2	William E. Lemdon	2	male
3	John R. Lemdon	6 m	"

ANCESTOR: Lucy Bryant

Cherokee Citizenship Commission Docket Books
(1880-84, 1887-89) Volume IV
Tahlequah, Cherokee Nation

Office Commission on Citizenship
Cherokee Nation Ind Ter
Tahlequah Aug 30th 1889

The above case was called and submitted by Attorney A.E. Ivey without evidence. The Commission therefore decide that Martha Lendon[sic] age 23 yrs and the following children William E Lemdon age 2 yrs and John R. Lemdon age 6 months are not Cherokees by blood.

Attest
   EG Ross
      Clerk Commission

Will.P. Ross
      Chairman
J.E. Gunter   Com

LASSITER

DOCKET #1718
CENSUS ROLLS 1835 to 1852

APPLICANT FOR CHEREOKEE CITIZENSHIP

POST OFFICE: Westfield Ind		ATTORNEY: Wm A. Thompson	
NO	NAMES	AGE	SEX
1	John M Lassiter	33	male

ANCESTOR: Elizabeth Dunbar

Office Commission on Citizenship
Cherokee Nation Ind Ter
Tahlequah Aug 30th 1889

The above case was called and submitted by Attorney A E Ivey without evidence. The Commission decide that John M Lassiter age 33 years is not a Cherokee by blood and are[sic] not entitled to citizenship in the Cherokee Nation.

Attest
   EG Ross
      Clerk Commission

Will.P. Ross
      Chairman
J.E. Gunter   Com

Cherokee Citizenship Commission Docket Books
(1880-84, 1887-89) Volume IV
Tahlequah, Cherokee Nation

LACOCK

DOCKET #1719
CENSUS ROLLS 1835 to 1852

APPLICANT FOR CHEROKEE CITIZENSHIP

POST OFFICE: Morrisville Mo		ATTORNEY: A.E. Ivey	
No	NAMES	AGE	SEX
1	Mary Lacock	30	female
2	Robert T. Acock[sic]	10	male
3	Loulie F. Acock[sic]	8	female
4	Cassie B. Acock[sic]	4	male
5	Charles F. Acock[sic]	1	"

ANCESTOR: Daniel Pritchet

Office Commission on Citizenship
Cherokee Nation Ind Ter
Tahlequah Aug 30th 1889

The above case was this day submitted by A.E. Ivey Attorney for claimant without evidence. The Commission therefore decide that Mrs. Mary Lacock age 30 years, Robert T. Lacock age 10 years, Cassie B. Lacock, age 4 years, Charles F. Lacock age 1 year and daughter Loulie F. Lacock are not of Cherokee blood. Post Office Morrisville Mo.

Attest
    EG Ross
        Clerk Commission

Will.P. Ross
        Chairman
J.E. Gunter Com

LAWRENCE

DOCKET #1720
CENSUS ROLLS

APPLICANT FOR CHEROKEE CITIZENSHIP

POST OFFICE: Dallas Ga		ATTORNEY: A.E. Ivey	
No	NAMES	AGE	SEX
1	Eliza A. Lawrence	19	female
2	Ellen E. Lawrence	3	"
3	Lou E Lawrence	1	"

ANCESTOR: John Tidwell

We the Commission on Citizenship after examining the evidence in the above case, also the census rolls of 1851, taken East of the Mississippi River,

Cherokee Citizenship Commission Docket Books
(1880-84, 1887-89) Volume IV
Tahlequah, Cherokee Nation

find that applicant is the grand daughter of John Tidwell who was a half breed Cherokee Indian.

Therefore we the Commission unanimously agree and decide that Eliza A. Lawrence and her daughters, Ellen E. and Lou E. Lawrence are Cherokees by blood, and are hereby re-admitted to all the rights and privileges of Cherokee citizens by blood.

        J. T. Adair Chairman Commission
        D.W. Lipe Commissioner
        H.C. Barnes Commissioner

Office Com on Citizenship
 Tahlequah I.T. Sept 21st 1888

LONDON

DOCKET #1721
CENSUS ROLLS 1835

APPLICANT FOR CHEROKEE CITIZENSHIP

POST OFFICE: Alma Ark		ATTORNEY: A.E. Ivey	
NO	NAMES	AGE	SEX
1	Julia London	25	female
2	Jessie London	2	"

ANCESTOR: John Chambers

       Office Commission on Citizenship
        Tahlequah I.T. Aug 30th 1889

The above case was submitted this day without evidence. The Commission therefore decide that Julia London age twenty five years and her daughter Jessie London age two years are not of Cherokee blood.
Attest   Will.P. Ross
 EG Ross   Chairman
  Clerk Commission   J.E. Gunter Com

Cherokee Citizenship Commission Docket Books
(1880-84, 1887-89) Volume IV
Tahlequah, Cherokee Nation

LINALY

DOCKET #1722
CENSUS ROLLS

APPLICANT FOR **CHEROKEE CITIZENSHIP**

POST OFFICE: Pomona, N.C.		ATTORNEY: L.B. Bell	
NO	NAMES	AGE	SEX
1	John Van Linaly		male

ANCESTOR: Sarah Morgan

The Commission decide against John Vann Linaly in the above case. See case of John Scott Docket 1584, Book D, Page 70. P.O. Pomona N.C.

Will.P. Ross
Chairman
J.E. Gunter Com

SENSBAUGH

DOCKET #1723
CENSUS ROLLS

APPLICANT FOR **CHEROKEE CITIZENSHIP**

POST OFFICE: Decatur, Tex		ATTORNEY: C.H. Taylor	
NO	NAMES	AGE	SEX
1	Mary P. Sensbaugh	27	female
2	Zephin O. Sensbaugh	7	"
3	James S Sensbaugh	5	male
4	Maud Sensbaugh	3	female

ANCESTOR: Mary Ray nee Taylor

Rejected Sept 16th 1889

Office Commission on Citizenship
Cherokee Nation Ind Ter
Tahlequah Sept 16th 1889

The above case was called three times and no response from applicant or by Atty and there being no evidence in support of claim the Commission therefore decide that Mary P. Sensbaugh age 27 yrs and the following children Zephin O. Female 7 yrs, James S. male 5 yrs, and Maud Sensbaugh Female 3 yrs are not Cherokees by blood.

Cherokee Citizenship Commission Docket Books
(1880-84, 1887-89) Volume IV
Tahlequah, Cherokee Nation

Attest
   D.S. Williams
   Asst Clk Com.

Will.P. Ross   Chairman
J.E. Gunter   Com

LINDLEY

DOCKET #1724
CENSUS ROLLS

APPLICANT FOR CHEROKEE CITIZENSHIP

POST OFFICE: Hoyt Kans		ATTORNEY: L.B. Bell	
NO	NAMES	AGE	SEX
1	Edward A Lindley		male

ANCESTOR: Sarah Morgan

The Commission decide against claimant. See decision in the case of ~~Andrew~~ John Scott ~~Meredith~~ Docket ~~2180~~ 1584 Book D ~~E~~, Page ~~26~~70 and John Henly Docket 1250, Book C Page 376.

Will.P. Ross   Chairman
John E. Gunter   Com

LINDLY

DOCKET #1725
CENSUS ROLLS

APPLICANT FOR CHEROKEE CITIZENSHIP

POST OFFICE: Union Store[sic] Kans		ATTORNEY: L.B. Bell	
NO	NAMES	AGE	SEX
1	Albert G. Lincly		male

ANCESTOR: Sarah Morgan

Rejected July 2nd 1889

Adversely

   See decision of Commission in the case of John R. Henly Docket 553, Book B, Page 266.

Attest
   D.S. Williams
   Asst Clk Com.

Will.P. Ross   Chairman
J.E. Gunter   Com

Cherokee Citizenship Commission Docket Books
(1880-84, 1887-89) Volume IV
Tahlequah, Cherokee Nation

LORRONCE

DOCKET #1726
CENSUS ROLLS

APPLICANT FOR CHEROKEE CITIZENSHIP

POST OFFICE: Oskaloosa Iowa		ATTORNEY: L.B. Bell	
No	NAMES	AGE	SEX
1	Mary S.A. Lorronce	57	female
2	Anna J Lorronce	23	"
3	Albert Lorronce	15	male

ANCESTOR: Martha Elmore

The Commission decide against claimant. See decision in case Lible J Bogue, Docket 2183, Book E, Page 29.

Will.P. Ross
Chairman
J.E. Gunter   Com

LEWELLEN

DOCKET #1727
CENSUS ROLLS 1835 to 1852

APPLICANT FOR CHEROKEE CITIZENSHIP

POST OFFICE: Joplin Mo		ATTORNEY: L.S. Sanders	
No	NAMES	AGE	SEX
1	William C Lewellen	50	male

ANCESTOR: Dicy Lewellen

See decision in this case in the Dicey Llewellyn case in Book "B" page 221. Adverse.

Cornell Rogers
Clerk Com.

August 29th '88.

Cherokee Citizenship Commission Docket Books
(1880-84, 1887-89) Volume IV
Tahlequah, Cherokee Nation

LORRONCE

DOCKET #1728
CENSUS ROLLS

APPLICANT FOR CHEROKEE CITIZENSHIP

POST OFFICE: Oskoloosa[sic] Iowa		ATTORNEY: L.B. Bell	
No	NAMES	AGE	SEX
1	William A Lorronce	26	male

ANCESTOR: Martha Elmore

The Commission decide against claimant. See decision in case Lible J Bogue, Docket 2183, Book E, Page 29.

Will.P. Ross
Chairman
J.E. Gunter   Com

LAWRENCE

DOCKET #1729
CENSUS ROLLS 1835

APPLICANT FOR CHEROKEE CITIZENSHIP

POST OFFICE: Blue Springs Mo		ATTORNEY: Boudinot and Rasmus	
No	NAMES	AGE	SEX
1	John Lawrence	28	male

ANCESTOR: Jack West & Martha Hill

Rejected Aug 29th 1889

Office Commission on Citizenship
Cherokee Nation Ind Ter
Tahlequah Aug 29th 1889

The above case was called and submitted by Atty Rasmus &Boudinot without evidence. The Commission decide that John Lawrence age 28 yrs is not a Cherokee by blood.

Will.P. Ross
Chairman
Attest
D.S. Williams   J.E. Gunter   Com
Asst Clk Com.

Cherokee Citizenship Commission Docket Books
(1880-84, 1887-89) Volume IV
Tahlequah, Cherokee Nation

LANGLEY

DOCKET #1730
CENSUS ROLLS 1835 to 1852

APPLICANT FOR CHEROKEE CITIZENSHIP

POST OFFICE: Talking Rock Ga	ATTORNEY: Boudinot and Rasmus		
No	NAMES	AGE	SEX
1	Albert Langley	33	male

ANCESTOR: Sally Langley

Re-admitted Sept 23rd 1889

Office Commission on Citizenship Cher Nat Ind Ter
Tahlequah Sept 3rd 1889

The application in the above case was filed the 4th day of October A.D. 1887. From the testimony produced it appears that the applicant Albert Langley who has died since filing his application was son of one Sally Langley nee Sally Hubbard who was the daughter of one Nelly Wilkerson and from whom applicant derived his Cherokee blood and whose name will be found on the census roll of 1851. It is also proven that the before named Albert Langley deceased was the Father of William Langley who was born about 1856, John Albert Langley was born about one year later and Warner Langley who was born about a year after John Albert. Albert Langley deceased had a step daughter by his first wife named Annie Scott who was white. The name of Albert Langley being found on the roll of Cherokees by blood taken by the United States in 1851, the Commission therefore decide that her[sic] children William Langley, John Albert Langley and Warner Langley aged respective about thirty three, thirty two and thirty years, are of Cherokee blood and entitled to re-admission to citizenship in the Cherokee Nation.

Will.P. Ross
Chairman
Attest D.S. Williams   J.E. Gunter   Com
Asst Clk Com.

Cherokee Citizenship Commission Docket Books
(1880-84, 1887-89) Volume IV
Tahlequah, Cherokee Nation

LANGLEY

DOCKET #1731
CENSUS ROLLS 1835 to 1852

APPLICANT FOR **CHEROKEE CITIZENSHIP**

POST OFFICE: Haska[sic] Texas		ATTORNEY: Boudinot and Rasmus	
NO	NAMES	AGE	SEX
1	Sadie H Langley	18	female

ANCESTOR: Josiah Langley

Office Commission on Citizenship
Cherokee Nation Ind Ter
Tahlequah Aug 28th 1889

The application in the above case was filed on the 4th day of October A.D. 1887. The testimony of Mrs. Annie Leach and Mrs. Francis Tipton recognized citizens of the Nation by blood and residents of Tahlequah District taken before the Commission Aug 21st A.D. 1889 proves that they had a full brother by the name of Josiah Langley who died about 20 years since in Arkansas. There is however no identification of Sadie H. Langley the applicant as the daughter of said Josiah Langley.

The Commission thefore[sic] decide that Sadie H. Langley has not proven herself to be of Cherokee blood and is not entitled to Citizenship in the Cherokee Nation.

Attest   Will.P. Ross
    EG Ross   Chairman
       Clerk Commission   J.E. Gunter   Com

LATTA

DOCKET #1732
CENSUS ROLLS 1835 to 1852

APPLICANT FOR **CHEROKEE CITIZENSHIP**

POST OFFICE: Wau-hil-leu, I.T.		ATTORNEY: L.S. Sanders	
NO	NAMES	AGE	SEX
1	Thomas Latta	40	male

ANCESTOR: Francis Latta

Cherokee Citizenship Commission Docket Books
(1880-84, 1887-89) Volume IV
Tahlequah, Cherokee Nation

Office Commission on Citizenship
Cherokee Nation Ind Ter
Tahlequah Aug 30th 1889

This case having been submitted by the Attorneys without evidence the Commission decide that Thomas Latta age 40 years is not of Cherokee blood and not entitled to citizenship in the Cherokee Nation.

Attest
  EG Ross
    Clerk Commission

Will.P. Ross
  Chairman
J.E. Gunter Com

LARNE

DOCKET #1733
CENSUS ROLLS 1835 to 1852

APPLICANT FOR CHEROKEE CITIZENSHIP

POST OFFICE: Clarksville Ark		ATTORNEY: Boudinot and Rasmus	
NO	**NAMES**	**AGE**	**SEX**
1	M.A. Larne	17	female

ANCESTOR: Barsheba Goodrich

Office Commission on Citizenship
Cherokee Nation Tahlequah
June 20, 1889

There being no evidence in support of the above named case the Commission decide that M.A. Larne aged 17 years is not a Cherokee by blood.

Attest
  EG Ross
    Clerk Commission

Will.P. Ross
  Chairman
J.E. Gunter Com

Cherokee Citizenship Commission Docket Books
(1880-84, 1887-89) Volume IV
Tahlequah, Cherokee Nation

LEWIS

DOCKET #1734
CENSUS ROLLS 1835

APPLICANT FOR CHEROKEE CITIZENSHIP

POST OFFICE: Afton I.T.		ATTORNEY: H.T. Landrum	
NO	NAMES	AGE	SEX
1	Laura Lewis	24	female

ANCESTOR: John Ward

Office Commission on Citizenship
Cherokee Nation Ind Ter
Tahlequah Aug 30th 1889

This case having been submitted (submitted)[sic] by the Attys without evidence the Commission decide that Laura Lewis age 24 years is not a Cherokee by blood and not entitled to Cherokee Citizenship.
Attest   Will.P. Ross
  EG Ross   Chairman
    Clerk Commission   J.E. Gunter   Com

LATTA

DOCKET #1735
CENSUS ROLLS 1835 to 1852

APPLICANT FOR CHEROKEE CITIZENSHIP

POST OFFICE: Wau-hil-la I.T.		ATTORNEY: L.S. Sanders	
NO	NAMES	AGE	SEX
1	R.J. Latta	24	male

ANCESTOR: Francis Latta

Office Commission on Citizenship
Tahlequah Aug 30th 1889

This case having been submitted by the Attorneys without evidence the Commission decide that R.J. Latta age 24 years is not a Cherokee by blood and not entitled to Cherokee Citizenship.
Attest   Will.P. Ross
  EG Ross   Chairman
    Clerk Commission   J.E. Gunter   Com

Cherokee Citizenship Commission Docket Books
(1880-84, 1887-89) Volume IV
Tahlequah, Cherokee Nation

LEE

DOCKET #1736
CENSUS ROLLS 1835 to 52

APPLICANT FOR **CHEROKEE CITIZENSHIP**

POST OFFICE: Evansville Ark		ATTORNEY:	
NO	NAMES	AGE	SEX
1	William Lee	40	male

ANCESTOR: William Lee

        Office Commission on Citizenship
        Cherokee Nation Ind Ter
        Tahlequah Aug 30th 1889

  This case having been submitted by the Attorneys without evidence the Commission decide that William Lee age 40 years is not a Cherokee Indian by blood and not entitled to Cherokee Citizenship.

Attest   Will.P. Ross
 EG Ross   Chairman
   Clerk Commission   J.E. Gunter   Com

LEGRAND

DOCKET #1737
CENSUS ROLLS 1835 to 52

APPLICANT FOR **CHEROKEE CITIZENSHIP**

POST OFFICE: Echo, I.T.		ATTORNEY: L.S. Sanders	
NO	NAMES	AGE	SEX
1	Cordelia E. Legrand	28	female
2	Hescuba Legrand	4 m	"

ANCESTOR: Malissa Foust

        Office Commission on Citizenship
        Cherokee Nation Ind Ter
        Tahlequah Aug 30th 1889

  This case having been submitted by the Attorneys without evidence the Commission decide that Cordelia E Legrand age twenty eight years and her daughter Heccuba[sic] Legrand are not Cherokees by blood. Post Office Echo I.T.

Cherokee Citizenship Commission Docket Books
(1880-84, 1887-89) Volume IV
Tahlequah, Cherokee Nation

Attest   Will.P. Ross
   EG Ross   Chairman
    Clerk Commission   J.E. Gunter   Com

LEWELLEN

DOCKET #1738
CENSUS ROLLS 1835 to 52

APPLICANT FOR CHEROKEE CITIZENSHIP

POST OFFICE: Joplin Mo.		ATTORNEY: L.S. Sanders	
No	NAMES	AGE	SEX
1	Vincent B. Lewellen	52	male

ANCESTOR: Dicy Lewellen

See decision in this case in the Dicey Llewellyn case in Book "B" page 221 – Adverse.

                                             Cornell Rogers
                                                  Clerk Com.

August 29th '88.

LEWELLEN

DOCKET #1739
CENSUS ROLLS 1835 to 52

APPLICANT FOR CHEROKEE CITIZENSHIP

POST OFFICE: Joplin, Mo.		ATTORNEY: L.S. Sanders	
No	NAMES	AGE	SEX
1	James L Lewellen		

ANCESTOR: Dicy Lewellen

See decision in this case in the Dicey Llewellyn case in Book "B" page 221 – Adverse.

                                             Cornell Rogers
                                                  Clerk Com.

August 29th '88.

Cherokee Citizenship Commission Docket Books
(1880-84, 1887-89) Volume IV
Tahlequah, Cherokee Nation

JOHNSON

DOCKET #1740
CENSUS ROLLS 1835 to 1852

APPLICANT FOR CHEROKEE CITIZENSHIP

POST OFFICE: Joplin Mo		ATTORNEY: L.S. Sanders	
No	NAMES	AGE	SEX
1	Rebecca J Johnson	36	female
2	Amanda Johnson		"
3	Robt Johnson		male
4	Mitchell Johnson		"
5	Dica Johnson		
6	Mary Johnson		female

ANCESTOR: Dicy Lewellen

See decision in this case in the Dicey Llewellyn case in Book "B" page 221 – Adverse.

Cornell Rogers
Clerk Com.

August 29th '88.

LOVELADY

DOCKET #1741
CENSUS ROLLS 1835 to 52

APPLICANT FOR CHEROKEE CITIZENSHIP

POST OFFICE: Evans, Col		ATTORNEY: L.S. Sanders	
No	NAMES	AGE	SEX
1	Martha J Lovelady	47	female
2	Charles H Lovelady	18	male
3	Mary L. Lovelady	16	female
4	William T. Lovelady	6	male

ANCESTOR: Emeline Boatright

Office Commission on Citizenship
Tahlequah I.T. Aug 30th 1889

This case having been submitted by the Attorneys without evidence the Commission decide that Martha J. Lovelady age 47 years and her children Charles Henry age 18 years, Mary L. age 16 years, William T. Lovelady age 6 years are not Cherokees by blood.

Cherokee Citizenship Commission Docket Books
(1880-84, 1887-89) Volume IV
Tahlequah, Cherokee Nation

Attest
  EG Ross
    Clerk Commission

Will.P. Ross
  Chairman
  J.E. Gunter   Com

LAWRENCE

DOCKET #1742
CENSUS ROLLS

APPLICANT FOR **CHEROKEE CITIZENSHIP**

POST OFFICE: Polo[sic] Ark		ATTORNEY: C.H. Taylor	
No	NAMES	AGE	SEX
1	Richard Lawrence	52	male
2	William Lawrence	26	"
3	Randolph Lawrence	22	"

ANCESTOR: Arch Coody

Office Commission on Citizenship
Tahlequah I.T. Aug 30th 1889

This case having been submitted by the Attorneys without evidence the Commission decide that Richard Lawrence age 52 yrs, William Lawrence age 26 yrs Randolph Lawrence age 22 yrs are not Cherokees by blood.

Attest
  EG Ross
    Clerk Commission

Will.P. Ross
  Chairman
  J.E. Gunter   Com

LAWRENCE

DOCKET #1743
CENSUS ROLLS

APPLICANT FOR **CHEROKEE CITIZENSHIP**

POST OFFICE: Polo[sic] Ark		ATTORNEY: C.H. Taylor	
No	NAMES	AGE	SEX
1	John Lawrence	50	male
2	Sarah Lawrence	25	female
3	Malinda Lawrence	23	"
4	Martha Lawrence	20	"
5	Morah Lawrence	16	"
6	Louisa Lawrence	14	"

ANCESTOR: Arch Coody

Cherokee Citizenship Commission Docket Books
(1880-84, 1887-89) Volume IV
Tahlequah, Cherokee Nation

Office Commission on Citizenship
Cherokee Nation Ind Ter
Tahlequah Aug 30th 1889

This case having been submitted by Attorney without evidence the Commission decide that John Lawrence age 50 years and his children Sarah age 25 years, Malinda age 23 years, Martha age 20 years, Morah age 16 years and Louisa Lawrence are not Cherokees by blood.

Attest   Will.P. Ross
   EG Ross   Chairman
       Clerk Commission   J.E. Gunter   Com

LAWRENCE

DOCKET #1744
CENSUS ROLLS

APPLICANT FOR **CHEROKEE CITIZENSHIP**

	POST OFFICE: Carr, Mo	ATTORNEY: C.H. Taylor	
No	NAMES	AGE	SEX
1	T.R. Lawrence	44	male
2	James J Lawrence	23	"
3	D.B. Lawrence	14	"

ANCESTOR: Arch Coody

Office Commission on Citizenship
Tahlequah I.T. Aug 30th 1889

This case having been submitted by the Attys without evidence the Commission decide that T.R. Lawrence age 44 years and is children James J Lawrence aged 23 years, and D.B. Lawrence aged 14 years are not Cherokees by blood.

Attest   Will.P. Ross
   EG Ross   Chairman
       Clerk Commission   J.E. Gunter   Com

Cherokee Citizenship Commission Docket Books
(1880-84, 1887-89) Volume IV
Tahlequah, Cherokee Nation

LABOYTAUX

DOCKET #1745
CENSUS ROLLS

APPLICANT FOR **CHEROKEE CITIZENSHIP**

POST OFFICE: New Castle Ind		ATTORNEY: L.B. Bell	
No	NAMES	AGE	SEX
1	Electa Laboytaux	26	female
2	Electa Laboytaux, Jr	13	"

ANCESTOR: Ann Crews

The Commission decide against claimant. See decision in the case of Andrew Meredith Docket 2180 Book E, Page 26 and John Henly Docket 1250, Book C Page 376.

Will.P. Ross   Chairman
John E. Gunter   Com

LITTLE

DOCKET #1746
CENSUS ROLLS 1835 to 1852

APPLICANT FOR **CHEROKEE CITIZENSHIP**

POST OFFICE: Wau-hil-lau I.T.		ATTORNEY: Boudinot and Rasmus	
No	NAMES	AGE	SEX
1	Nancy D Little	26	female
2	Julia L Little	9	"
3	Robert S. Little	8	male
4	Benj F. Little	7	"
5	May R Little	4	female
6	Cottillia E Little	3	"
7	Ansel Z. Little	1	male

ANCESTOR:

Commission on Citizenship.

CHEROKEE NATION, IND. TER.

Tahlequah, August 31st 1889

Cherokee Citizenship Commission Docket Books
(1880-84, 1887-89) Volume IV
Tahlequah, Cherokee Nation

Nancy D. Little
vs   Application for Cherokee Citizenship
The Cherokee Nation

The application in the above case was filed on the 1st day of October, 1887, the claimant alleging that she is the daughter of one Reuben Jackson ~~who~~ and the grand daughter of one Sandy Jackson whose name she believes was enrolled on the census rolls of Cherokees by blood taken and made by the United States in the years 1835-48-51-52. In support of the above case is offered the affidavit of one James T. Gardenhire taken the 15th day of January 1881 before W.C. Laffery a Justice of the Peace in Hamilton County, State of Tennessee. This affiant is objected to by Attorney for the Nation because it does not fall within the rule requiring the credibility of affiant to be *(illegible)* by the office before whom they are taken, the objection is sustained but the affidavit is not material as it is based entirely upon ~~what~~ hearsay in regard to Sandy Jackson. There is also presented the affidavit of Rheuben[sic] Smith who makes his mark with one attesting witness before W.E. Newbold, N.P. on the 3rd day of August 1881 in Logan County State of Arkansas, and who represents that he was born near Qualla Town in North Carolina in 1805. He swears that he was personally acquainted with Sandy Jackson and "knew him to be a Cherokee Indian by action, complexion and conduct with the Indians" and that he was "drowned in the old Madison Mile pond" which is now in Sequachie[sic] County, Tennessee and that he also knew Reuben Jackson to be the son of Sandy Jackson. This affidavit was objected to on the ground as the preceding one and the objection was sustained. There are also presented the affidavit of William C. Laffery and G.W. Laffery made the 10th day of June 1882 before L.M. Clark, Clk. County Court of Hamilton County, State of Tennessee identifying claimant as the daughter of Reuben Jackson. On the 25th day of October 1888, before the Commission on Citizenship Wat Christie swears that he knew one Sandy Jackson about 60 years before at Ross' Landing in the Old Cherokee Nation, but did not know where he lived nor anything about his kinsfolk, but he was a Cherokee and heard that he was drowned in the Tennessee below Calhoun, Tennessee. He did not know Reuben Jackson. He thinks Sandy Jackson lived about Cleveland. The Cherokees called him Jackson "Littledeer" and does not think he spoke English and was about 30 years old when he knew him. Did not know what the whites called him.

~~Although~~, These statements show that Sandy Jackson and his son Reuben Jackson were probably alive ~~when~~ and in the Cherokee Country at the time the census of Cherokees by blood was taken by the United States in the year 1835

Cherokee Citizenship Commission Docket Books
(1880-84, 1887-89) Volume IV
Tahlequah, Cherokee Nation

and that Reuben Jackson was also alive at the date of 1852 and if known to be and recognized as Cherokees their names would have been entered on one of them but neither the name of Sandy Jackson, Reuben Jackson nor Jackson "Littledeer" is to be found. The Commission therefore decide that that[sic] Nancy D Little age 26 yrs and her daughter Julia L age 9 yrs, Mary R. age 4 yrs & Cotillia age 3 yrs and her sons Robert E. 8 yrs, Benj. F. 7 yrs & Ansel Z. Little 1 yr are not of Cherokee blood. P.O. Wau-hil-lab[sic] Ind. Ter. (over)

Will.P. Ross
Chairman
J.E. Gunter   Com

LOGAN

DOCKET #1747
CENSUS ROLLS 1835

APPLICANT FOR CHEROKEE CITIZENSHIP

	POST OFFICE: McKinney Tex	ATTORNEY: Wm A. Thompson	
NO	NAMES	AGE	SEX
1	Mary E Logan		female
2	Flossie Logan	12	female
3	Jeane Logan	11	"
4	Willie Logan	9	male
5	Harry Logan	7	"
6	Stewart Logan	3	"
7	Elizabeth Logan	1	female

ANCESTOR: Jack McGarrah

Office Commission on Citizenship
Cherokee Nation June 26, 1889

There being no evidence in support of the above named case the Commission decide that Mary E Logan and the following children Flossie female age 12 years, Jeane female aged 11 years, Willie male aged 9 years, Harry male aged 7 years, Stewart male aged 3 years and Elizabeth Logan female aged one year are not Cherokees by blood. Post Office McKinney Texas.
Attest   Will.P. Ross
   EG Ross   Chairman
      Clerk Commission   J.E. Gunter   Com

Cherokee Citizenship Commission Docket Books
(1880-84, 1887-89) Volume IV
Tahlequah, Cherokee Nation

LATTY

DOCKET #1748
CENSUS ROLLS 1835 to 1852

APPLICANT FOR **CHEROKEE CITIZENSHIP**

POST OFFICE: Wau-hil-lau, I.T.		ATTORNEY: L.S. Sanders	
NO	NAMES	AGE	SEX
1	James M. Latty	42	male
2	Rosa B. Latty	13	female
3	Napoleon Latty	10	male
4	Lewis Latty	7	"
5	Jefferson Latty	4	"
6	Modison[sic] Latty	1	"

ANCESTOR: Francis Latty

Office Commission on Citizenship Tahlequah I.T. Oct. 24th 1888

Now on this, the above written date comes this case up for final hearing, it having been regularly submitted by Plaintiffs' Attorney. The application in this case alleges that one Francis Latty is the grand mother of the applicant, and that she is of Cherokee blood, and that her name will appear on some of the rolls of Cherokees. We, the Commission on Citizenship, have examined carefully the rolls laid down in the 7th Sec. of Act of Dec. 8th 1886 in relation to citizenship and fail to find the name of Francis Latty enrolled thereon, hence we are of the opinion that James M. Latty and his 5 children, viz: Rosa B. – Napoleon – Lewis – Jefferson and Madison Latty are not Cherokees by blood, and are not entitled to any of the privileges of citizens of the Cherokee Nation, and are intruders upon the public domain of the same. – In the absence of the fact that the said rolls do not contain the name of their alleged Cherokee ancestor, we deem it not important to recount the testimony.

                                      J. T. Adair   Chairman Commission
                                      D.W. Lipe   Commissioner
                                      H.C. Barnes Commissioner

Cherokee Citizenship Commission Docket Books
(1880-84, 1887-89) Volume IV
Tahlequah, Cherokee Nation

LEACH

DOCKET #1749
CENSUS ROLLS 1835 to 1852

APPLICANT FOR CHEROKEE CITIZENSHIP

POST OFFICE: Mayfield Ky		ATTORNEY: Boudinot and Rasmus	
NO	NAMES	AGE	SEX
1	Thomas Goodrich Leach	26	male

ANCESTOR: Barsheba Goodrich

Office Commission on Citizenship
Cherokee Nation June 20th 1889

There being no evidence in support of the above named case the Commission decide that Thomas Goodrich Leach is not a Cherokee by blood. Post Office Mayfield Ky.

Attest   Will.P. Ross
  EG Ross   Chairman
    Clerk of Commission   J.E. Gunter Com

LEWELLEN

DOCKET #1750
CENSUS ROLLS

APPLICANT FOR CHEROKEE CITIZENSHIP

POST OFFICE:		ATTORNEY: L.S. Sanders	
NO	NAMES	AGE	SEX
1	Steve Lewellen	48	male
2	Alfred B. Lewellen	8	"
3	Cordoro D. Lewellen	6	"

ANCESTOR: Nancy Bennum

See decision in this case in the Dicey Llewellyn case in Book "B" page 221 – Adverse.

                         Cornell Rogers
                                Clerk Com.
August 29th '88.

Cherokee Citizenship Commission Docket Books
(1880-84, 1887-89) Volume IV
Tahlequah, Cherokee Nation

LONG

DOCKET #1751
CENSUS ROLLS 1835 to 1852

APPLICANT FOR CHEROKEE CITIZENSHIP

POST OFFICE: Webbers Falls I.T.		ATTORNEY: Wm A. Thompson	
No	NAMES	AGE	SEX
1	James E. Long	27	male

ANCESTOR: Robert Rogers

In the matter of the above applicant, who claims to be the son of Fernecy Jane Long, and claiming his Cherokee blood from Robert Rogers, The decision in her (Fernecy J Long) case will apply to this case: he is not a Cherokee by blood and is hereby rejected and declared to be an intruder upon the public domain of the Cherokee Nation, and not entitled to any of the rights and privileges of the Cherokee Nation.

J. T. Adair   Chairman Commission
D.W. Lipe   Commissioner
H.C. Barnes   Commissioner

Office Com on Citizenship
Tahlequah I.T. Sept. 24th 1888.

LEACH

DOCKET #1752
CENSUS ROLLS 1835 to 1852

APPLICANT FOR CHEROKEE CITIZENSHIP

POST OFFICE: Logan Ark		ATTORNEY: Geo O. Buter[sic]	
No	NAMES	AGE	SEX
1	Mary Francis Leach	36	female
2	John A. Leach	14	male
3	Billie West Leach	12	"
4	Arliley[sic] Leach	10	"
5	Arthur Leach	8	"

ANCESTOR: Joe Watts

Rejected Aug 31st 1889

Office Commission on Citizenship
Cherokee Nation Ind Ter
Tahlequah Aug 31st 1889

Cherokee Citizenship Commission Docket Books
(1880-84, 1887-89) Volume IV
Tahlequah, Cherokee Nation

The above case was called and submitted by Atty George O Butler without evidence. The Commission decide that Mary Francis Leach age 36 yrs and the following children John A male 14 yrs, Billie male 12 yrs, Arliley male 10 yrs and Arthur Leach male 7 yrs are not Cherokees by blood and are not entitled to citizenship in the Cherokee Nation. Post Office Logan Ark.

Will.P. Ross
Chairman
Attest
   D.S. Williams   J.E. Gunter Com
   Asst Clk Com.

LAMB

DOCKET #1753
CENSUS ROLLS

APPLICANT FOR **CHEROKEE CITIZENSHIP**

POST OFFICE: Spiceland Ind		ATTORNEY: L.B. Bell	
No	NAMES	AGE	SEX
1	Eoline Dix. Lamb	32	female
2	Geneva Lamb	6	"
3	Virgia Lamb	4	"

ANCESTOR: Martha Elmore

The Commission decide against claimant. See decision in case Lible J Bogue, Docket 2183, Book E, Page 29.

Will.P. Ross
Chairman
J.E. Gunter Com

LOWDEN

DOCKET #1754
CENSUS ROLLS

APPLICANT FOR **CHEROKEE CITIZENSHIP**

POST OFFICE:		ATTORNEY: L.B. Bell	
No	NAMES	AGE	SEX
1	Mary A Lowden	32	female
2	Florence Lowden	8	"
3	Martha I Lowden	6	"

ANCESTOR: Ann Crews

Cherokee Citizenship Commission Docket Books
(1880-84, 1887-89) Volume IV
Tahlequah, Cherokee Nation

The Commission on Citizenship decide against claimant. See decision in the Andrew Meredith case Docket 2180 Book E, Page 26 and John Henly Docket 1250, Book C Page 376.

Will.P. Ross
Chairman
John E. Gunter   Com

LAW

DOCKET #1755
CENSUS ROLLS

APPLICANT FOR **CHEROKEE CITIZENSHIP**

POST OFFICE: Union Town Ark		ATTORNEY: C.H. Taylor	
NO	NAMES	AGE	SEX
1	Robert Law	38	male
2	Martha Law	17	"[sic]
3	Harry Law	15	male
4	George Law	10	"
5	Coley Law	8	female
6	Sissie Law	1	"

ANCESTOR: William Law

Rejected Aug 31st 1889

Office Commission on Citizenship
Cherokee Nation Ind Ter
Tahlequah Aug 31st 1889

The above application was submitted by claimant's Attorney without evidence. Therefore we decide that claimant Robert Law age 38 yrs and children Martha Law age 17 yrs, Harry Law age 15 yrs, George Law age 10 yrs, Caley[sic] Saw[sic] age 8 yrs and Sissie Law age 1 yr. are not Cherokees by blood and not entitled to citizenship in the Cherokee Nation. P.O. Union Town Ark.

Will.P. Ross
Attest   Chairman
   D.S. Williams   J.E. Gunter   Com
   Asst Clk Com.

Cherokee Citizenship Commission Docket Books
(1880-84, 1887-89) Volume IV
Tahlequah, Cherokee Nation

LATTY

DOCKET #1756
CENSUS ROLLS 1835 to 52

APPLICANT FOR CHEROKEE CITIZENSHIP

POST OFFICE: Dickson Ark		ATTORNEY: L.S. Sanders	
No	NAMES	AGE	SEX
1	William Latty	54	male
2	James Latty	20	"
3	Louinda[sic] Latty	16	female

ANCESTOR: Francis Latty

Rejected Aug 31st 1889

Office Commission on Citizenship
Cherokee Nation Ind Ter
Tahlequah Aug 31st 1889

The above case was called and submitted by Atty Rasmus without evidence. The Commission decide that William Latty age 54 yrs and the following children James Latty male 20 yrs and Louinda Latty Female 16 yrs are not Cherokees by blood and are not entitled to citizenship in the Cherokee Nation. Post Office Dickson Ark.

Attest
   D.S. Williams
   Asst Clk Com.

            Will.P. Ross
                        Chairman
J.E. Gunter Com

WRIGHT

DOCKET #1757
CENSUS ROLLS 1835 to 52

APPLICANT FOR CHEROKEE CITIZENSHIP

POST OFFICE: Chester, Crawford Co Ark		ATTORNEY: Wm A. Thompson	
No	NAMES	AGE	SEX
1	William C. Wright	31	male
2	Nora May Wright		female
3	Elmer Wright		male

ANCESTOR: Nancy Mulkee

Office Commission on Citizenship
Cherokee Nation July 3rd 1889

Cherokee Citizenship Commission Docket Books
(1880-84, 1887-89) Volume IV
Tahlequah, Cherokee Nation

There being no evidence in support of the above named case the Commission decide that Wm C. Wright aged 31 years and the following children Nora May Wright Female and Elmer Wright Male are not Cherokees by blood. Post Office Chester, Crawford Co, Ark.

Attest   Will.P. Ross
   EG Ross   Chairman
     Clerk Commission   J.E. Gunter   Com

WALLACE

DOCKET #1758
CENSUS ROLLS 1835 to 52

APPLICANT FOR CHEROKEE CITIZENSHIP

POST OFFICE: Van Buren Ark		ATTORNEY: A.E. Ivey	
No	NAMES	AGE	SEX
1	Hariett Wallace	24	female
2	John Wallace	4	male
3	Martha Wallace	2	female

ANCESTOR: John Azbill

Rejected Aug 31st 1889

                         Office Commission on Citizenship
                               Cherokee Nation Ind Ter
                                 Tahlequah Aug 31st 1889

The above case was called and submitted by A.E. Ivey Atty without evidence. The Commission decide that Hariett Wallace age 24 yrs and the following children John Wallace male 4 yrs and Martha Wallace Female age 2 yrs are not Cherokees by blood and are not entitled to citizenship in the Cherokee Nation. Post Office Van Buren Ark.

                             Will.P. Ross
Attest   Chairman
   D.S. Williams   J.E. Gunter   Com
   Asst Clk Com.

Cherokee Citizenship Commission Docket Books
(1880-84, 1887-89) Volume IV
Tahlequah, Cherokee Nation

WALLACE

DOCKET #1759
CENSUS ROLLS 1835

APPLICANT FOR CHEROKEE CITIZENSHIP

POST OFFICE: White Right Tex		ATTORNEY: A.E. Ivey	
No	NAMES	AGE	SEX
1	Anna Wallace	33	female
2	Maud Wallace	11	"
3	Mabel Wallace	7	"
4	Welch Wallace	5	male

ANCESTOR: John Ross

Commission on Citizenship.

CHEROKEE NATION, IND. TER.

Tahlequah, September 12th 1888

Ann A. Wallace, et al
    (VS)
Cherokee Nation

    The above case consists of the applications of Ann A. Wallace, et al, J.F. Hopper, et al. and Mary K. Hartley, et al. & E.J. Hopper. All residents of White Right, Texas and claiming a Cherokee descent from John Ross, dec'd., Ex. Chief of the Cherokee Nation.

    It is useless to recount the testimony of the applicants in these cases, as they set up the plea in their applications for citizenship that they are the grand children of John Ross, the same who use to own and operate the ferry on the Tennessee river where Chattanooga, Tennessee now stands, and for forty years thereafter, the Principal Chief of the Cherokee Nation claiming that their father was a son of Ex. Chief John Ross, and that his name was John Ross.

    The testimony of Hon. Allen Ross, who is now seventy years old and a son of Ex. Chief John Ross, taken in part of the Cherokee Nation in these cases shows that he had three full brothers, named James, Silas and George W. Ross, all born in the Old Cherokee Nation, and that he had one half brother named John Ross who is now between 30 and 40 years old and that he was born in this Nation, and now lives at Park Hill Cherokee Nation, consequently the foregoing

Cherokee Citizenship Commission Docket Books
(1880-84, 1887-89) Volume IV
Tahlequah, Cherokee Nation

named applicants for Cherokee citizenship could not have been descended from John Ross, the son of Ex. Chief John Ross, who now lives at Park Hill.

We the Commission on Citizenship are of the opinion that Old John Ross had but one son named John, therefore, after hearing the statement of _____ Allen Ross in relation thereto, at once arrive at the conclusion that the applicants could not and did not spring from this man, John Ross, and Ann A. Wallace, Maude Wallace, Mabel Wallace, Welch Wallace, Mary K Hartley, Alice Hartley, Noah Hartley, Viola Hartley, Lilly Hartley, J.F. Hopper, Bill Hopper and Orville Hopper and E.J. Hopper are not Cherokee by blood and not entitled to the rights and privileges of such on account of their blood, and the Commission do hereby so declare.

        J. T. Adair Chairman Commission
        D.W. Lipe Commissioner
        H.C. Barnes Commissioner

WILMETH

DOCKET #1760
CENSUS ROLLS 1835

APPLICANT FOR CHEROKEE CITIZENSHIP

POST OFFICE: McKinney Tex		ATTORNEY: Wm A. Thompson	
No	NAMES	AGE	SEX
1	Claud Wilmeth	21	male
2	Aurela Wilmeth	15	"

ANCESTOR: Jack McGarrah

        Office Commission on Citizenship
        Cherokee Nation June 26, 1889

There being no evidence in support of the above named case the Commission decide that Claud Wilmeth aged 21 years and his brother Aurela Wilmeth aged 15 years are not Cherokees by blood. Post Office McKinney Texas.

Attest   Will.P. Ross
 EG Ross   Chairman
  Clerk Commission   J.E. Gunter Com

Cherokee Citizenship Commission Docket Books
(1880-84, 1887-89) Volume IV
Tahlequah, Cherokee Nation

WILSON
DOCKET #1761
CENSUS ROLLS 1835 to 52

APPLICANT FOR CHEROKEE CITIZENSHIP

POST OFFICE: Mayfield Ky		ATTORNEY: Boudinot and Rasmus	
No	NAMES	AGE	SEX
1	M. Arabella Wilson	34	female
2	Cora Lee Wilson	13	female

ANCESTOR: Barsheba Goodrich

Office Commission on Citizenship
Cherokee Nation June 20th 1889

There being no evidence in support of the above named case the Commission decide that M. Arabella Wilson aged 34 years and her daughter Cora Lee Wilson aged 13 years are not Cherokees by blood.

Attest   Will.P. Ross
  EG Ross   Chairman
    Clerk Commission   J.E. Gunter   Com

WINFIELD
DOCKET #1762
CENSUS ROLLS 1835 to 52

APPLICANT FOR CHEROKEE CITIZENSHIP

POST OFFICE: Fort Smith Ark		ATTORNEY: Boudinot and Rasmus	
No	NAMES	AGE	SEX
1	Sallie E Winfield	44	female
2	Wallie Winfield	16	male
3	George Winfield	9	"

ANCESTOR: Barsheba Goodrich

Office Commission on Citizenship
Cherokee Nation June 20th 1889

There being no evidence in support of the above named case the Commission decide that Sallie E. Winfield aged 44 years and the following children Walter male aged 16 years and George Winfinfield[sic] age 9 years are not Cherokees by blood.

Cherokee Citizenship Commission Docket Books
(1880-84, 1887-89) Volume IV
Tahlequah, Cherokee Nation

Attest
  EG Ross
    Clerk Commission

Will.P. Ross
    Chairman
J.E. Gunter Com

WHITE

DOCKET #1763
CENSUS ROLLS

APPLICANT FOR CHEROKEE CITIZENSHIP

POST OFFICE: Afton I.T.		ATTORNEY: L.B. Bell	
No	NAMES	AGE	SEX
1	Angeline H. White	45	female

ANCESTOR: Ann Crews

The Commission decide against claimant. See decision in the case of Andrew Meredith Docket 2180 Book E, Page 26 and John Henly Docket 1250, Book C Page 376.

                Will.P. Ross
                      Chairman
           John E. Gunter Com

WORTHINGTON

DOCKET #1764
CENSUS ROLLS

APPLICANT FOR CHEROKEE CITIZENSHIP

POST OFFICE: Clarksville Ohio		ATTORNEY:	
No	NAMES	AGE	SEX
1	Rhoda C. Worthington		

ANCESTOR: Martha Elmore

The Commission decide against claimant. See decision in case Lible J Bogue, Docket 2183, Book E, Page 29.

                Will.P. Ross
                Chairman
           J.E. Gunter Com

Cherokee Citizenship Commission Docket Books
(1880-84, 1887-89) Volume IV
Tahlequah, Cherokee Nation

WAKEFIELD

DOCKET #1765
CENSUS ROLLS 1851 & 52

APPLICANT FOR CHEROKEE CITIZENSHIP

POST OFFICE: Valley Town N.C.		ATTORNEY: C.H. Taylor	
NO	NAMES	AGE	SEX
1	Liddy Wakefield	37	female
2	Bettie Wakefield	17	"
3	Ollie Wakefield	15	"
4	Thomas Wakefield	14	male
5	Charley Wakefield	12	"
6	Eddie Wakefield	11	"
7	Albert Wakefield	9	"
8	Kergie Wakefield	7	"
9	Vergie Wakefield	7	female

ANCESTOR: Elizabeth Whitaker

Now on this the 9th day of February, 1888, comes the above case for a final hearing. And the parties having made application pursuant to the provisions of an Act of the National Council approved December 8th 1886, and all the evidence having been duly examined and found to be sufficient and satisfactory to the Commission, it is adjudged and determined by the Commission that Liddy Wakefield – Bettie Wakefield – Ollie Wakefield – Thomas Wakefield – Charley Wakefield – Eddie Wakefield – Albert Wakefield – Kergie Wakefield and Vergie Wakefield, are Cherokees by blood and they are hereby re-admitted to all the rights, privileges and immunities of Cherokee citizens by blood.

And a certificate of said decision of the Commission and of re-admission was made and furnished said parties accordingly and certificate issued.

J. T. Adair   Chairman Commission
John E. Gunter   Commissioner
                  Commissioner

Attest
   C.C. Lipe
       Clerk Commission

Cherokee Citizenship Commission Docket Books
(1880-84, 1887-89) Volume IV
Tahlequah, Cherokee Nation

WILKS

DOCKET #1766
CENSUS ROLLS 1835

APPLICANT FOR CHEROKEE CITIZENSHIP

POST OFFICE: Hindsville Ark		ATTORNEY: C.H. Taylor	
NO	NAMES	AGE	SEX
1	Lofelia Wilks	28	female
2	Garland Phillips	10	male
3	A.W. Wilks	8	female
4	Callett Wilks	4	male
5	Ora T Wilks	2	female

ANCESTOR: Feraby Vaughn

Office Commission on Citizenship
Cherokee Nation Ind Ter
Tahlequah July 2, 1889

There being no evidence in support of the above named case the Commission decide that Lofelia Wilks and the following named children Garland age 10 years, A.W. female aged 8 years, Callet[sic] aged 4 years, and Ora T. Wilks female aged 2 years are not Cherokees by blood.

Attest   Will.P. Ross
   EG Ross   Chairman
      Clerk Commission   J.E. Gunter   Com

WILLIAMS

DOCKET #1767
CENSUS ROLLS 1835 to 52

APPLICANT FOR CHEROKEE CITIZENSHIP

POST OFFICE: Natural dam Ark		ATTORNEY: J.E. Welch	
NO	NAMES	AGE	SEX
1	Fannie Williams	32	female

ANCESTOR: Larkin Moten

Office Commission on Citizenship
Cherokee Nation Ind Ter
Tahlequah Sept 2nd 1889

Cherokee Citizenship Commission Docket Books
(1880-84, 1887-89) Volume IV
Tahlequah, Cherokee Nation

The above case was called three times and no answer by Attorney or by applicant, the Commission decide that Fannie Williams age 32 years is not a Cherokee by blood. Post Office Natural Dam Ark.

Attest   Will.P. Ross
   EG Ross   Chairman
    Clerk Commission   J.E. Gunter   Com

WILSON

DOCKET #1768
CENSUS ROLLS 1835 to 52

APPLICANT FOR CHEROKEE CITIZENSHIP

POST OFFICE: Harmony Ark		ATTORNEY: Boudinot and Rasmus	
NO	NAMES	AGE	SEX
1	Hughey Wilson	4 m	male

ANCESTOR: Louisa Brown

Rejected Sept 16th 1889

Office Commission on Citizenship
Cherokee Nation Ind Ter
Tahlequah Sept 16th 1889

The Commission reject applicant in the above case. See decision in the Nancy V. Thompson case, Docket 1922, Book D, Page 408 and Amanda Hooley case Docket 1147 Book C, Page 272.

                                    Will.P. Ross
Attest   Chairman
  D.S. Williams   J.E. Gunter   Com
  Asst Clk Com.

WARD

DOCKET #1769
CENSUS ROLLS 1835 to 52

APPLICANT FOR CHEROKEE CITIZENSHIP

POST OFFICE: Clarksville Ark		ATTORNEY: Boudinot and Rasmus	
NO	NAMES	AGE	SEX
1	William W Ward	39	male
2	Mabel E Ward	8	female
3	Margaret E Ward	3	"

Cherokee Citizenship Commission Docket Books
(1880-84, 1887-89) Volume IV
Tahlequah, Cherokee Nation

4	Melvin E Ward	1	male

ANCESTOR: Louisa Brown

Rejected Sept 16th 1889

        Office Commission on Citizenship
         Cherokee Nation Ind Ter
         Tahlequah Sept 16th 1889

The Commission decide against the above applicant & Family. See decision in the case of Amanda E. Hooley same ancestors, Docket 1147, Book C, Page 272.

        Will.P. Ross
Attest   Chairman
 D.S. Williams   J.E. Gunter Com
 Asst Clk Com.

WARD

DOCKET #1770
CENSUS ROLLS 1835 to 52

APPLICANT FOR CHEROKEE CITIZENSHIP

POST OFFICE: Clarksville Ark		ATTORNEY: Boudinot and Rasmus	
NO	**NAMES**	**AGE**	**SEX**
1	Augustus M. Ward	21	male

ANCESTOR: Louisa Brown

Rejected Sept 16th 1889

        Office Commission on Citizenship
         Cherokee Nation Ind Ter
         Tahlequah Sept 16th 1889

The Commission decide against the above applicant, same ancestor as that of Amanda E. Hooley See decision Docket 1147, Book C, Page 272.

        Will.P. Ross
Attest   Chairman
 D.S. Williams   J.E. Gunter Com
 Asst Clk Com.

Cherokee Citizenship Commission Docket Books
(1880-84, 1887-89) Volume IV
Tahlequah, Cherokee Nation

WILSON

DOCKET #1771
CENSUS ROLLS 1835 to 52

APPLICANT FOR CHEROKEE CITIZENSHIP

POST OFFICE: Harmony Ark		ATTORNEY: Boudinot and Rasmus	
NO	NAMES	AGE	SEX
1	William L Wilson	31	male
2	Harlow S Wilson	10	"
3	Minnie M Wilson	8	female
4	Lee Wilson	6	"
5	Maggie Wilson	4	"
6	Sally Wilson		"

ANCESTOR: Louisa Brown

Rejected Sept 16th 1889

Office Commission on Citizenship
Cherokee Nation Ind Ter
Tahlequah Sept 16th 1889

The Commission decide against the above applicant & Family. See decision in the case of Amanda E. Hooley Docket 1147, Book C, Page 272.

Will.P. Ross
Attest   Chairman
  D.S. Williams   J.E. Gunter   Com
  Asst Clk Com.

WILSON

DOCKET #1772
CENSUS ROLLS 1835 to 52

APPLICANT FOR CHEROKEE CITIZENSHIP

POST OFFICE: Harmony Ark		ATTORNEY: Boudinot and Rasmus	
NO	NAMES	AGE	SEX
1	Charles B Wilson	35	male
2	Gordon P Wilson	12	"
3	Robert G Wilson	10	"
4	Floyd H Wilson	8	"
5	Flora Wilson	6	female
6	Jacob R Wilson	4	male

ANCESTOR: Louisa Brown

Cherokee Citizenship Commission Docket Books
(1880-84, 1887-89) Volume IV
Tahlequah, Cherokee Nation

Rejected Sept 16th 1889

         Office Commission on Citizenship
         Cherokee Nation Ind Ter
         Tahlequah Sept 16th 1889

The Commission decide against the above applicant & Family Same ancestor as that of Amanda E. Hooley See decision Docket 1147, Book C, Page 272.

         Will.P. Ross
Attest   Chairman
 D.S. Williams   J.E. Gunter Com
 Asst Clk Com.

WILSON

DOCKET #1773
CENSUS ROLLS 1835 to 52

APPLICANT FOR CHEROKEE CITIZENSHIP

POST OFFICE: Harmony Ark		ATTORNEY: Boudinot and Rasmus	
NO	NAMES	AGE	SEX
1	Hugh G Wilson		

       ANCESTOR: Louisa Brown

Rejected Sept 16th 1889

The Commission decide against applicant. See decision in the case of Amanda Hooley Docket 1147, Book C, Page 272.

         Will.P. Ross
Attest   Chairman
 D.S. Williams   J.E. Gunter Com
 Asst Clk Com.

Cherokee Citizenship Commission Docket Books
(1880-84, 1887-89) Volume IV
Tahlequah, Cherokee Nation

WINFIELD

DOCKET #1774
CENSUS ROLLS 1835 to 52

APPLICANT FOR CHEROKEE CITIZENSHIP

POST OFFICE: Fort Smith Ark		ATTORNEY: Boudinot and Rasmus	
No	NAMES	AGE	SEX
1	Mollie Winfield	24	female

ANCESTOR: Barsheba Goodrich

Office Commission on Citizenship
Cherokee Nation June 20, 1889

There being no evidence in support of the above named case the Commission decide that Mollie Winfield aged 24 years of Fort Smith Arkansas is not of Cherokee blood. The names of children not given.

Attest   Will.P. Ross
   EG Ross   Chairman
       Clerk Commission   J.E. Gunter   Com

WINFIELD

DOCKET #1775
CENSUS ROLLS 1835 to 52

APPLICANT FOR CHEROKEE CITIZENSHIP

POST OFFICE: Fort Smith Ark		ATTORNEY: Boudinot and Rasmus	
No	NAMES	AGE	SEX
1	Willie Ann Winfield	26	female

ANCESTOR: Barsheba Goodrich

Office Commission on Citizenship
Tahlequah Cherokee Nation
June 20th 1889

There being no evidence in support of the above named case the Commission decide that Willie Ann Winfield, age 26 years are[sic] not Cherokee by blood. Post Office Fort Smith Ark.

Attest   Will.P. Ross
   EG Ross   Chairman
       Clerk Commission   J.E. Gunter   Com

Cherokee Citizenship Commission Docket Books
(1880-84, 1887-89) Volume IV
Tahlequah, Cherokee Nation

WINFIELD

DOCKET #1776
CENSUS ROLLS 1835 to 52

APPLICANT FOR CHEROKEE CITIZENSHIP

POST OFFICE: Fort Smith Ark		ATTORNEY: Boudinot and Rasmus	
No	NAMES	AGE	SEX
1	James S Winfield	28	male

ANCESTOR: Barsheba Goodrich

Office Commission on Citizenship
Cherokee Nation June 20, 1889

There being no evidence in support of the above named case the Commission decide that James S. Winfield aged 28 years is not a Cherokee by blood.

Attest   Will.P. Ross
   EG Ross   Chairman
       Clerk Commission   J.E. Gunter   Com

WILKS

DOCKET #1777
CENSUS ROLLS 1835 to 52

APPLICANT FOR CHEROKEE CITIZENSHIP

POST OFFICE: Fayetteville Ark		ATTORNEY: L.S. Sanders	
No	NAMES	AGE	SEX
1	Mal Wilks	42	male

ANCESTOR: George Cline

Rejected Aug 31st 1889

Office Commission on Citizenship
Cherokee Nation Ind Ter
Tahlequah Aug 31st 1889

The above case was called and submitted by Atty Rasmus without evidence. The Commission decide that Mal Wilks age 42 yrs is not Cherokee by blood and is not entitled to citizenship in the Cherokee Nation. Post Office Fayetteville Ark.

Attest   Will.P. Ross
   D.S. Williams   Chairman
   Asst Clk Com.   J.E. Gunter   Com

Cherokee Citizenship Commission Docket Books
(1880-84, 1887-89) Volume IV
Tahlequah, Cherokee Nation

WOMACK

DOCKET #1778
CENSUS ROLLS 1835

APPLICANT FOR **CHEROKEE CITIZENSHIP**

POST OFFICE: Parris[sic] Tex		ATTORNEY: C.H. Taylor	
No	NAMES	AGE	SEX
1	N.J. Womack	43	female
2	J.L. Womack	9	male
3	M.E. Womack	7	female
4	A.V. Womack	1	male

ANCESTOR: Wm Christy

Rejected Aug 31st 1889

Office Commission on Citizenship
Cherokee Nation Ind Ter

The above case was called and submitted by Atty J.M. Taylor without evidence. The Commission decide that N.J. Womack age 43 yrs and the following children J.L. male age 9 yrs, M.E. Female 7 yrs & A.V. Womack male age 1 yr are not Cherokees by blood and are not entitled to citizenship in the Cherokee Nation. Post Office Parris[sic] Texas.

Attest
   D.S. Williams
   Asst Clk Com.

Will.P. Ross
Chairman
J.E. Gunter Com

WILLIAMS

DOCKET #1779
CENSUS ROLLS 1835

APPLICANT FOR **CHEROKEE CITIZENSHIP**

POST OFFICE: Unionville Ark		ATTORNEY: Ivey and Welch	
No	NAMES	AGE	SEX
1	Mary Williams	27	female
2	William Williams	9	male
3	Minnie Williams	9	female
4	Buck Williams	2	male

ANCESTOR: Oo-yah-sis-tah

277

Cherokee Citizenship Commission Docket Books
(1880-84, 1887-89) Volume IV
Tahlequah, Cherokee Nation

Office Commission on Citizenship
Tahlequah I.T. A Aug 31st 1889

The above case was called and submitted by Attorneys Rasmus and Boudinot without evidence. The Commission therefore decide that Mary Williams age 27 years and the following children William aged 9 years, Minnie aged 9 years, Emmett aged 12 years and Buck Williams aged 2 years are not Cherokees by blood and are not entitled to citizenship in the Cherokee Nation.
Attest
    EG Ross   Will.P. Ross
        Clerk Commission   Chairman
                                          J.E. Gunter   Com

WILMETH

DOCKET #1780
CENSUS ROLLS 1835 to 52

APPLICANT FOR **CHEROKEE CITIZENSHIP**

POST OFFICE: McKinney Tex		ATTORNEY: Wm A. Thompson	
NO	NAMES	AGE	SEX
1	T.C. Wilmeth	34	male
2	Aurelia Wilmeth	16	"
3	Lillia Jones half sister		female
4	Glennie Jones " "		"

ANCESTOR: Jack McGarrah

Office Commission on Citizenship
Cherokee Nation June 26, 1889

There being no evidence in support of the above named case the Commission decide that T.C. Wilmeth aged 34 years and the following children Aurelia aged 16 years, Lillia Jones half sister and Glennie Jones are not Cherokees by blood.
Attest
    EG Ross   Will.P. Ross
        Clerk Commission   Chairman
                                          J.E. Gunter   Com

Cherokee Citizenship Commission Docket Books
(1880-84, 1887-89) Volume IV
Tahlequah, Cherokee Nation

WRIGHT

DOCKET #1781
CENSUS ROLLS 1835 to 52

APPLICANT FOR **CHEROKEE CITIZENSHIP**

POST OFFICE: Chester Ark		ATTORNEY: Wm A. Thompson	
No	NAMES	AGE	SEX
1	James C Wright	57	male
2	Lulu S Wright	15	female

ANCESTOR: Nancy Mulkee

Office Commission on Citizenship
Cherokee Nation July 3rd 1889

There being no evidence in support of the above named case the Commission decide that James C Wright aged 57 years and his daughter Lulu S Wright aged 15 years are not Cherokees by blood. Post Office Chester Ark.
Attest
    EG Ross   Will.P. Ross
        Clerk Commission   Chairman
                                                    J.E. Gunter   Com

WHITLY

DOCKET #1782
CENSUS ROLLS 1835 to 52

APPLICANT FOR **CHEROKEE CITIZENSHIP**

POST OFFICE: Collinsville Tex		ATTORNEY: Boudinot and Rasmus	
No	NAMES	AGE	SEX
1	George F. Whitly		

ANCESTOR: Moton
Rejected Aug 28th 1889

Office Commission on Citizenship
Cherokee Nation Ind Ter
Tahlequah Aug 28th 1889

The above case was this day submitted by Mr. Rasmus Attorney for claimant without evidence. The Commission decide that George F. Whitly age 73 years is not of Cherokee blood. P.O. Collinsville Texas

Cherokee Citizenship Commission Docket Books
(1880-84, 1887-89) Volume IV
Tahlequah, Cherokee Nation

Attest
D.S. Williams
Asst Clk Com.

Will.P. Ross
Chairman
J.E. Gunter   Com

WHITLY

DOCKET #1783
CENSUS ROLLS 1835 to 52

APPLICANT FOR **CHEROKEE CITIZENSHIP**

POST OFFICE: Bowie Tex		ATTORNEY: Boudinot and Rasmus	
NO	NAMES	AGE	SEX
1	Marion Whitley	26	male

ANCESTOR: Morton

Office Commission on Citizenship
Cherokee Nation Aug 28th 1889

The above named case having been submitted by Attorney for claimant without evidence the Commission decide that Marion Whitley 21 yrs old is not of Cherokee blood, names of family not given. P.O. Bowie Texas.

Attest
D.S. Williams
Asst Clk Com.

Will.P. Ross
Chairman
J.E. Gunter   Com

WHITLEY

DOCKET #1784
CENSUS ROLLS 1835 to 1852

APPLICANT FOR **CHEROKEE CITIZENSHIP**

POST OFFICE: Hartford Ark		ATTORNEY: Boudinot and Rasmus	
NO	NAMES	AGE	SEX
1	E.T. Whitley	40	male
2	Susan H Whitley	16	female
3	Lilly J Whitley	15	"
4	John I. Whitley	11	male
5	James E. Whitley	9	"
6	Hiram L. Whitley	7	"
7	Mary E. Whitley	4	female

Cherokee Citizenship Commission Docket Books
(1880-84, 1887-89) Volume IV
Tahlequah, Cherokee Nation

| 8 | | Aldenia Whitley | 2 | " |
| 9 | | Laura A. Whitley | babe | " |

ANCESTOR: Morton

Office Commission on Citizenship
Tahlequah September 2nd 1889

 The above application was called up for final hearing. We find that applicant claims to derive her Cherokee blood through one Morton, whose name claimant believes is enrolled upon some of the census rolls of Cherokees taken in the years 1835, 48, 51, 52. To sustain these allegations, applicant submits as evidence the affidavits of Rebecca Harney taken before a Clerk of Cook County in and for the State of Texas. Also the affidavit of Weidham Whitley taken before the same Clerk.

 All of this evidence is "Exparte" and not sufficient in our minds to establish the claim of applicant, and also the name of applicant's ancestor Morton does not appear upon the census rolls as alleged by claimant. Therefore we decide that applicant E.T. Whitley and children Susan H. Whitley age 16 years, Lilly J. Whitley age 15 years, John T. Whitley age 11 yrs, James E. Whitley age age[sic] 9 yrs, Hiram L. Whitley age 7 yrs, Mary E. Whitley age 2 yrs, Laura A Whitley infant are not Cherokees by blood. P.O. Hartford Ark.

Attest   Will.P. Ross   Chairman
 EG Ross   J.E. Gunter   Com
   Clerk Commission

WHITLEY

DOCKET #1785
CENSUS ROLLS 1835 to 52

APPLICANT FOR **CHEROKEE CITIZENSHIP**

POST OFFICE: Yz[sic], Montage Co, Tex.		ATTORNEY: Boudinot and Rasmus	
NO	NAMES	AGE	SEX
1	H.C. Whitley	44	male

ANCESTOR: Moton

Rejected Aug 28th 1889

Office Commission on Citizenship
Cherokee Nation Ind Ter
Tahlequah Aug 28th 1889

Cherokee Citizenship Commission Docket Books
(1880-84, 1887-89) Volume IV
Tahlequah, Cherokee Nation

Wm F. Rasmus Attorney for claimant in the above named case having submitted the same without evidence the Commission decide that H.C. Whitley age 47 yrs is not of Cherokee blood. P.O. Uz, Montage Co, Texas.

                              Will.P. Ross
Attest   Chairman
   D.S. Williams   J.E. Gunter Com
   Asst Clk Com.

WHITLEY

DOCKET #1786
CENSUS ROLLS 1835 to 52

APPLICANT FOR CHEROKEE CITIZENSHIP

POST OFFICE: Whitesboro, Tex		ATTORNEY: Boudinot and Rasmus	
NO	NAMES	AGE	SEX
1	William Whitley	30	male

ANCESTOR: Moton

Rejected Aug 28th 1889

                        Office Commission on Citizenship
                            Cherokee Nation Ind Ter
                            Tahlequah Aug 28th 1889

The above case was called and submitted by Atty Rasmus without evidence. The Commission decide that William Whitley age 30 yrs is not a Cherokee by blood and are[sic] not entitled to citizenship in the Cherokee Nation. Post Office Whitesboro, Texas.

                              Will.P. Ross
Attest   Chairman
   D.S. Williams   J.E. Gunter Com
   Asst Clk Com.

WHITLEY

DOCKET #1787
CENSUS ROLLS 1835 to 52

APPLICANT FOR CHEROKEE CITIZENSHIP

POST OFFICE: Callisburg, Tex.		ATTORNEY: Boudinot and Rasmus	
NO	NAMES	AGE	SEX
1	John V. Whitley	28	male

ANCESTOR: Morton

Cherokee Citizenship Commission Docket Books
(1880-84, 1887-89) Volume IV
Tahlequah, Cherokee Nation

Rejected Aug 28th 1889

>Office Commission on Citizenship
>Cherokee Nation Ind Ter
>Tahlequah Aug 28th 1889

The above application having been submitted this day by W.F. Rasmus Attorney for claimant without evidence the Commission decide that John V. Whitley age 28 years is not entitled to citizenship in the Cherokee Nation as a Cherokee Indian by blood. P.O. Callisburg Texas.

Will.P. Ross
Chairman

Attest
D.S. Williams
Asst Clk Com.

J.E. Gunter Com

WILSON

DOCKET #1788
CENSUS ROLLS 1835 to 52

APPLICANT FOR CHEROKEE CITIZENSHIP

POST OFFICE:		ATTORNEY: L.B. Bell	
No	NAMES	AGE	SEX
1	Catherine R. Wilson		

ANCESTOR:

The Commission decide against claimant. See decision in the case of Andrew Meredith Docket 2180 Book E, Page 26 and John Henly Docket 1250, Book C Page 376.

Will.P. Ross Chairman
John E. Gunter Com

WILMOUTH

DOCKET #1789
CENSUS ROLLS 1835 to 52

APPLICANT FOR CHEROKEE CITIZENSHIP

POST OFFICE: McKinney Tex		ATTORNEY: Wm A. Thompson	
No	NAMES	AGE	SEX
1	Claud Wilmouth	28	male

ANCESTOR: Jack McGarrah

Cherokee Citizenship Commission Docket Books (1880-84, 1887-89) Volume IV
Tahlequah, Cherokee Nation

Office Commission on Citizenship
Cherokee Nation June 26, 1889

There being no evidence in support of the above named case the Commission decide that Claud Wilmouth aged 28 years is not a Cherokee by blood. Post Office McKinney Texas.
Attest
  EG Ross   Will.P. Ross
    Clerk Commission   Chairman
            J.E. Gunter Com

WOODS

DOCKET #1790
CENSUS ROLLS 1852

APPLICANT FOR CHEROKEE CITIZENSHIP

POST OFFICE: Whitewright Tex		ATTORNEY: John L. Adair	
No	NAMES	AGE	SEX
1	Mrs. J.B. Woods		female

ANCESTOR: Webster

Office Commission on Citizenship
Tahlequah I.T. September 2nd 1889

The above case was called three several times at not less than one hour apart. The Commission therefore decide that Mrs. J.B. Woods is not a Cherokee by blood and is not entitled to citizenship in the Cherokee Nation.
Attest
  EG Ross   Will.P. Ross
    Clerk Commission   Chairman
            J.E. Gunter Com

WINFORD

DOCKET #1791
CENSUS ROLLS 1835 to 52

APPLICANT FOR CHEROKEE CITIZENSHIP

POST OFFICE: Van Buren Ark		ATTORNEY: Boudinot and Rasmus	
No	NAMES	AGE	SEX
1	Alice Winford	33	female

Cherokee Citizenship Commission Docket Books
(1880-84, 1887-89) Volume IV
Tahlequah, Cherokee Nation

2	Eddie Winford	11	male
3	Bolin Winford	8	"
4	William Winford	6	"
5	Haden Winford	5	"
6	Bertie Winford	babe	

Ancestor: Micajah Scott

Rejected Aug 31st 1889

Office Commission on Citizenship
Cherokee Nation Ind Ter
Tahlequah Aug 31st 1889

The above application was submitted by claimant's Attorney W.F. Rasmus at the 3rd calling of the Docket without evidence in support of the application. Therefore we decide that applicant Alice Winfield[sic] age 33 yrs and her children Eddie Winfield[sic] age 11 yrs, Bolin Winfield[sic] age 8 yrs, William Winfield[sic] age 6 yrs, Haden age 5 yrs and Bertie infant are not Cherokees by blood. P.O. Van Buren Ark.

Attest
D.S. Williams
Asst Clk Com.

Will.P. Ross
Chairman
J.E. Gunter   Com

WHITEHEAD

Docket #1792
Census Rolls 1835 to 52

Applicant for CHEROKEE CITIZENSHIP

Post Office: Siloam Springs Ark		Attorney: L.S. Sanders	
No	NAMES	Age	Sex
1	Alma J Whitehead	34	female
2	Thomas L Whitehead	15	male
3	Rebecca A Whitehead	13	female
4	James P. Whitehead	11	male
5	Albert J Whitehead	9	"
6	Charles S Whitehead	7	"
7	Rosa M Whitehead	5	female
8	Fredrick R Whitehead	2	male

Ancestor: Saphrona Davis

Cherokee Citizenship Commission Docket Books
(1880-84, 1887-89) Volume IV
Tahlequah, Cherokee Nation

Office Commission on Citizenship
Tahlequah I.T. Aug 31st 1889

The above application was submitted at the 3rd calling by claimant's Attorney Mr. William F. Rasmus without evidence. Therefore we decide applicant Alma J Whitehead age 34 years and her children to wit, Thomas L age 15 years, Rebecca A age 13 years, James F age 11 years, Albert J age 9 years, Charles S age 7 years, Rosa M age 5 years and Fredrick R. Whitehead are not Cherokees by blood and not entitled to citizenship in the Cherokee Nation.

Attest   Will.P. Ross
   EG Ross   Chairman
       Clerk Commission   J.E. Gunter   Com

WEBB

DOCKET #1793
CENSUS ROLLS 1835 to 52

APPLICANT FOR CHEROKEE CITIZENSHIP

POST OFFICE: Tahlequah I.T.		ATTORNEY: Boudinot and Rasmus	
No	NAMES	AGE	SEX
1	Mary N. Webb	37	female
2	Chas W. Webb	16	male

ANCESTOR: Asa Guinn

Rejected Sept 20th 1889

Office Commission on Citizenship Cher Nat I.T. Tahlequah Sept 20th 1889

The applicant in the above case alleges that she is the daughter of one Asa Guinn whose name she believes was enrolled on the Census rolls of Cherokees by blood taken and made by the United States in the years 1835-48-51&52. In support of her claim is offered the evidence taken in the Bat Guinn case and the statement of Mrs. Nancy Martin who identifies her as her own Neice[sic] and the daughter of Asa Guinn. The evidence in the Bat Guinn case failed to establish the Cherokee blood of the said Bat Guinn and his brother Asa Guinn and as the name of Asa Guinn does not appear on the before named rolls the Commission decide that the claimants Mary N Webb age 37 yrs and her son Charley W. Webb are not of Cherokee blood and not entitled to citizenship in the Cherokee Nation.

Cherokee Citizenship Commission Docket Books
(1880-84, 1887-89) Volume IV
Tahlequah, Cherokee Nation

Will.P. Ross
Attest   Chairman
     D.S. Williams   J.E. Gunter   Com
     Asst Clk Com.

WILSON

DOCKET #1794
CENSUS ROLLS 1835 to 52

APPLICANT FOR CHEROKEE CITIZENSHIP

POST OFFICE: Siloam Springs Ark		ATTORNEY: L.S. Sanders	
NO	NAMES	AGE	SEX
1	Delitha A Wilson	34	female
2	Robert L. Wilson	14	male
3	Emma J Wilson	11	female
4	Jessie M Wilson	7	"
5	Charley E Wilson	5	male

ANCESTOR: John Fox

Rejected Aug 31st 1889

                     Office Commission on Citizenship
                            Cherokee Nation Ind Ter
                            Tahlequah Aug 31st 1889

The above case was called and submitted by Attys' Rasmus & Boudinot without evidence. The Commission decide that Delitha A Wilson age 34 yrs and the following children Robert S. male 14 yrs, Emma J. female 11 yrs, Jessie M female 7 yrs, and Charley E Wilson male 5 yrs are not Cherokees by blood and are not entitled to citizenship in the Cherokee Nation. Post Office Siloam Springs Ark.

                                   Will.P. Ross
Attest   Chairman
     D.S. Williams   J.E. Gunter   Com
     Asst Clk Com.

Cherokee Citizenship Commission Docket Books
(1880-84, 1887-89) Volume IV
Tahlequah, Cherokee Nation

WALKER

DOCKET #1795
CENSUS ROLLS 1835 to 52

APPLICANT FOR CHEROKEE CITIZENSHIP

POST OFFICE: Dallis[sic] City Ill		ATTORNEY: L.S. Sanders	
NO	NAMES	AGE	SEX
1	Thomas H.B. Walker	35	male
2	George M Walker	15	"
3	Sada M.D. Walker	13	female
4	Henry Walker	9	male
5	Mary J Walker	7	female
6	Lula Walker	5	"
7	Oran Walker	2	male

ANCESTOR: Mary Ellen Mead

Office Commission on Citizenship
Cherokee Nation Ind Ter
Tahlequah August 31st 1889

The above claimants were called three times and the case was submitted by Mr. William Rasmus without any evidence in support of the application.

Therefore we decide that applicant Thomas H.B. Walker age 35 years and family George M. Walker age 15 years, Sada M.D. Walker age 13 years, Henry Walker age 9 years, Mary J Walker age 7 years, Lula Walker age 5 years and Oran Walker age 2 years are not Cherokees by blood and not entitled to citizenship in the Cherokee Nation.

Attest   Will.P. Ross
   EG Ross   Chairman
      Clerk Commission   J.E. Gunter   Com

WALKER

DOCKET #1796
CENSUS ROLLS 1835 to 52

APPLICANT FOR CHEROKEE CITIZENSHIP

POST OFFICE: Edmonds, Ill		ATTORNEY: L.S. Sanders	
NO	NAMES	AGE	SEX
1	John B.W. Walker	37	male
2	Ella Walker	9	female

Cherokee Citizenship Commission Docket Books
(1880-84, 1887-89) Volume IV
Tahlequah, Cherokee Nation

3	Johnie Walker	7	male
4	Oren F Walker	1	"

ANCESTOR: Mary Ellen Mead

Rejected Aug 31st 1889

> Office Commission on Citizenship
> Cherokee Nation Ind Ter
> Tahlequah Aug 31st 1889

The above case was called and submitted without evidence by Attys Rasmus & Boudinot. The Commission now decide that John B.W. Walker age 37 yrs and the following children Ella Walker female 9 yrs, Johnie male 7 yrs, and Oren F. Walker male age 1 yr are not Cherokees by blood and are not entitled to citizenship in the Cherokee Nation. Post Office Edmonds Ill.

Attest
D.S. Williams
Asst Clk Com.

Will.P. Ross
Chairman
J.E. Gunter   Com

WASSON

DOCKET #1797
CENSUS ROLLS

APPLICANT FOR **CHEROKEE CITIZENSHIP**

POST OFFICE: Sumner Co, Kans		ATTORNEY: L.B. Bell	
No	NAMES	AGE	SEX
1	Henry Wasson	30	male

ANCESTOR: Ann Crews

The Commission decide against claimant. See decision in the case of Andrew Meredith Docket 2180 Book E, Page 26 and John Henly Docket 1250, Book C Page 376.

Will.P. Ross   Chairman
John E. Gunter   Com

Cherokee Citizenship Commission Docket Books
(1880-84, 1887-89) Volume IV
Tahlequah, Cherokee Nation

WINN

DOCKET #1798
CENSUS ROLLS 1835 to 52

APPLICANT FOR **CHEROKEE CITIZENSHIP**

POST OFFICE: McKinney Tex		ATTORNEY: Wm A. Thompson	
No	NAMES	AGE	SEX
1	S.C. Winn	35	female
2	Effie Winn	10	"
3	Hattie Winn	7	"
4	Mattie Winn	6	"
5	Mounie Winn	1	"

ANCESTOR: Johnny Bryant

Office Commission on Citizenship
Tahlequah Ind Ter
September 2nd 1889

The above case was called three several times not less than one hour apart and no response from applicant or by Atty the Commission therefore decide that S.C. Winn age 35 years and the following children Effie age 10 years, Hattie age 7 years, Mattie age 6 years and Mounie Winn age 1 year are not Cherokees by blood and are not entitled to citizenship in the Cherokee Nation.

Attest

EG Ross
Clerk Commission

Will.P. Ross
Chairman
J.E. Gunter Com

WILSON

DOCKET #1799
CENSUS ROLLS 1835 to 52

APPLICANT FOR **CHEROKEE CITIZENSHIP**

POST OFFICE: Fayetteville, Ark		ATTORNEY: L.S. Sanders	
No	NAMES	AGE	SEX
1	William Wilson	45	male

ANCESTOR: George Cline

Rejected Sept 2nd 1889

Office Commission on Citizenship
Cherokee Nation Ind Ter
Tahlequah Sept 2nd 1889

Cherokee Citizenship Commission Docket Books
(1880-84, 1887-89) Volume IV
Tahlequah, Cherokee Nation

The above case was called 3 several times not less than one hour at intervals and no response from applicant or by Atty. The Commission therefore decide that Wm Wilson age 45 yrs is not a Cherokee by blood. P.O. Fayetteville Ark.

Attest
    D.S. Williams
    Asst Clerk Commission

Will.P. Ross
Chairman
J.E. Gunter Com

WALKER

DOCKET #1800
CENSUS ROLLS 1835 to 52

APPLICANT FOR CHEROKEE CITIZENSHIP

POST OFFICE: Siloam Springs, Ark		ATTORNEY: L.S. Sanders	
No	NAMES	AGE	SEX
1	Joseph H. Walker	43	male
2	Mary E Walker	20	female
3	Charles H. Walker	18	male
4	Joseph E. Walker	16	"
5	George F. Walker	13	"
6	Norah E. Walker	10	female
7	Margaret E. Walker	6	"
8	Bessie L. Walker	1	"

ANCESTOR: Margaret Walker

Rejected Sept 2nd 1889

Office Commission on Citizenship
Cherokee Nation Ind Ter
Tahlequah Sept 3rd 1889

The above named applicant was called 3 times & no answer & there being no evidence on file in support of the application, we decide that applicant Joseph H. Walker age 43 yrs. and children viz: Mary Ellen Walker age 20 yrs, Charles H. Walk[sic] age 18 yrs, Joseph E. Walker age 16 yrs, George F. Walker age 13 yrs, Noah[sic] Edna Walker age 10 yrs, Margaret E. Stella Walker age 6 yrs & Bessie L. Walker age 1 yr. are not Cherokees by blood. P.O. Siloam Springs Ark.

Attest
    D.S. Williams
    Asst Clk Com.

Will.P. Ross
Chairman
J.E. Gunter Com

Cherokee Citizenship Commission Docket Books
(1880-84, 1887-89) Volume IV
Tahlequah, Cherokee Nation

WELCH

DOCKET #1801
CENSUS ROLLS 1851 & 52

APPLICANT FOR **CHEROKEE CITIZENSHIP**

POST OFFICE: Marble, N.C.		ATTORNEY: C.H. Taylor	
NO	NAMES	AGE	SEX
1	James B. Welch	16	male

ANCESTOR: Loyd Welch

We the Commission on Citizenship after a careful examination of all the testimony in the case of James B. Welch, and the peculiar circumstances attending case, render it necessary that the Commission shall male an explanation of the reasons which have controled[sic] it in rendering up judgment. It appears from the testimony the applicant is the son of a white woman, who had not been married to Lloyd Welch, the alleged father of applicant. It also appears that this white woman had other children born to her before and after the applicant, all of whom are said to be white. It is in proof that the mother of the applicant testified before a Court in North Carolina that said Lloyd Welch was the father of applicant, and that Mr. Welch did acknowledge him as such, and did at his death will his estate to the applicant; it further appears that said applicant is now at school in the state of North Carolina, sharing the benefits of an educational fund set apart for the educating of orphans and indigents among the North Carolina tribe of Cherokees. While the testimony in behalf of applicant is apparently and sufficiently conclusively as to his Cherokee blood, we deem it best in making up our opinion concerning applicants of this character to with-hold our approval, in doing so, we are guided by the decision of William Siler in similar cases when taking the census of Cherokees East in the year 1851, who in every instance refused to enroll illegitimate children born of white women.

              John E. Gunter Commissioner
              D.W. Lipe Commissioner

  J. T. Adair Chairman Commission dissenting from above opinion

Cornell Rogers
 Clerk

Cherokee Citizenship Commission Docket Books
(1880-84, 1887-89) Volume IV
Tahlequah, Cherokee Nation

WILSON

DOCKET #1802
CENSUS ROLLS 1835 to 52

APPLICANT FOR CHEROKEE CITIZENSHIP

POST OFFICE: Ennis Texas		ATTORNEY: Wm A. Thompson	
No	NAMES	AGE	SEX
1	Alice Wilson	30	female
2	Winnie Wilson	14	"
3	Maggie Wilson	12	"

ANCESTOR: Jack McGarrah

Office Commission on Citizenship
Cherokee Nation June 26, 1889

There being no evidence in support of the above named case the Commission decide that Alice Wilson aged thirty years and the following children Winnie aged fourteen years and Maggie Wilson aged 12 years are not Cherokees by blood. Post Office Ennis Texas.

Attest   Will.P. Ross
   EG Ross   Chairman
      Clerk Commission   J.E. Gunter Com

WARD

DOCKET #1803
CENSUS ROLLS

APPLICANT FOR CHEROKEE CITIZENSHIP

POST OFFICE: Afton I.T.		ATTORNEY: L.B. Bell	
No	NAMES	AGE	SEX
1	P.E. Ward		

ANCESTOR: Mary Crews

The Commission decide against claimant. See decision in the case of Andrew Meredith Docket 2180 Book E, Page 26 and John Henly Docket 1250, Book C Page 376.

Will.P. Ross   Chairman
John E. Gunter   Com

Cherokee Citizenship Commission Docket Books
(1880-84, 1887-89) Volume IV
Tahlequah, Cherokee Nation

WASSON

DOCKET #1804
CENSUS ROLLS

APPLICANT FOR CHEROKEE CITIZENSHIP

POST OFFICE: Westfield Ind		ATTORNEY: L.B. Bell	
No	NAMES	AGE	SEX
1	Charles Wasson	28	male

ANCESTOR: Ann Crews

The Commission decide against claimant. See decision in the case of Andrew Meredith Docket 2180 Book E, Page 26 and John Henly Docket 1250, Book C Page 376.

                                Will.P. Ross   Chairman
EG Ross   John E. Gunter   Com
    Clerk Com

WOODARD

DOCKET #1805
CENSUS ROLLS

APPLICANT FOR CHEROKEE CITIZENSHIP

POST OFFICE: Afton I.T.		ATTORNEY: L.B. Bell	
No	NAMES	AGE	SEX
1	Elizabeth D. Woodard	36	female

ANCESTOR: Ann Crews

The Commission decide against claimant. See decision in the case of Andrew Meredith Docket 2180 Book E, Page 26 and John Henly Docket 1250, Book C Page 376.

                                Will.P. Ross   Chairman
EG Ross   John E. Gunter   Com
    Clerk Com

PAYNE

DOCKET #1806
CENSUS ROLLS

APPLICANT FOR CHEROKEE CITIZENSHIP

POST OFFICE: Ft. Smith, Ark		ATTORNEY:	
No	NAMES	AGE	SEX
1	Mrs. S.H. Payne	50	female

Cherokee Citizenship Commission Docket Books
(1880-84, 1887-89) Volume IV
Tahlequah, Cherokee Nation

2	Mrs. Mary L Morgan	33	"
3	Gabriel L Payne	31	male
4	Houston J Payne	23	"
5	Gunter M Payne	20	"
6	Okla E Payne	17	female

ANCESTOR:

Charged with fraud and bribery in obtaining Cherokee Citizenship.

Cherokee Nation
VS.
Mrs. Martha A. Payne

Charged with obtaining her citizenship through fraud and bribery.

Under an Act of the National Council approved December 8th 1886, creating and authorizing the Commission on Citizenship to summon certain parties therein named to appear and answer the complaint of the Nation, charging said parties with having obtained their citizenship in the Cherokee Nation through fraud and bribery, and show cause why the decrees of former Courts should not be set aside on account of fraud having been practiced in obtaining the same.

Mrs. S.H. Payne was duly summoned to appear before the Commission on the 5th day of July 1887. It appears that Mrs. Martha A. Payne, wife of Dr. S.H. Payne, deceased, and her family together with Eudora Cobb and family, did procure a decision of the Supreme Court of this Nation on May 21st 1871, then sitting as a Commission to try and determine applicants for citizenship, admitting them to rights of Cherokees.

It appears from the testimony of Sophia Pigeon that the grand father of Mrs. S.H. Payne was one Starling Gunter, who it is alleged was one of the sons of Old John Gunter, a white man, who resided at Gunters Landing, on the Tennessee river, in the Old Nation, and further, that Sarah L. Gunter was the daughter of Starling Gunter, who was the mother of Mrs. Martha A. Payne. The testimony of Ann Hughs is substantially the same as that of Sophia Pigeon.

The testimony of Jennie Pigeon shows that she had a talk with Anne Bigfeather, and she (Anne Big-feather) told her that she knew Starling and Charles Gunter, and that they were children of one of the Gunters by a Cherokee woman, and that when those boys, Starling and Charles, were quite small that their mother died and that they were taken by their white kin into the states, and

Cherokee Citizenship Commission Docket Books
(1880-84, 1887-89) Volume IV
Tahlequah, Cherokee Nation

remained out of the Nation until they were grown, when they would go into the Nation and remain a short time, returning to the states, somewhat after the fashion of *(illegible)*, and that she knew Starling Gunter after he was married and that one of his daughters married a white man, and from what she had heard, was fully satisfied that Mrs. Martha A Payne was the grand-daughter of Starling Gunter by this marriage of his daughter, above spoken of.

The reason that was given why Mrs. Schrimsher and Mrs. Lipe did not know Starling Gunter, was that he lived about 60 or 70 miles from them.

The evidence of Defendants is not complete, as some of the papers upon which the decision was made by the Supreme Court, sitting as a Commission on the 31st day of May 1871, are not among the papers submitted to this Commission, but the important and really valuable ones to the Defendant in establishing their case in 1871 are here as evidence and have been examined thoroughly.

There was no motion made by Defendants' Attorney to exclude the remaining testimony in this case on account of it not all being in proof before this Commission upon which to base an opinion.

The testimony of Wm P. Ross in this case is important, he states that he is 68 years old, and was born where Chattanooga now stands, at that time in the Old Cherokee Nation. Mr. Ross was born about the year 1820, and was even a conspicuous man among the Cherokees, both East and West of the Mississippi river. His testimony further shows that he was about 17 or 18 years old when he came to this Country in the year 1837, and that he was well acquainted with the Gunters in the Old Nation. That the children of John Gunter, Sen. were Samuel, Edward, John, Mrs. Blackburn whose given name was Patsey; Mrs. Schrimsher, whose given name was Elizabeth; and Mrs. Lipe whose given name was Catharine. He further says that the above named persons were all the children that Old John Gunter had, that he knew of, and that he does not know that John Gunter, Jr. was ever married or had descendants, and that Samuel Gunter was the oldest son of John Gunter, Sen. who if now living would be over one hundred years old.   From Mr. Ross' statement, we draw the conclusion at once that he was well and intimately acquainted with the Gunter family.

The testimony of John L. McCoy shows: that he is about 75 years old, and that he was Interpreter for a United States enrolling Agent in the year 1835, preparatory to removing the Cherokees from their homes in the Old Nation to

Cherokee Citizenship Commission Docket Books
(1880-84, 1887-89) Volume IV
Tahlequah, Cherokee Nation

this Country, and that his father married into the Gunter family, and that he knew them, well and intimately, and that Samuel Gunter was the oldest son of John Gunter, Sen. who if now living would be about one hundred years old, and that John Gunter, Jr. never married in the Old Nation, but had a wife after he came to this Country, and from this marriage there was no issue, and that he was well acquainted with the people in the section of country in the Old Nation where his Aunt Sophia Pigeon lived, and that there was no Gunter family lived near her. He further states that he never heard of Old John Gunter having two sons by the names of Charles and Starling Gunter by a woman named Maria, previous to his marriage with Katy, nor that he was ever married before, and that he went to Gunters Landing on the Tennessee river in the year 1817, and lived in the Gunter family up to the year 1823.

The testimony of Thomas Ballard, shows that George Johnson was the Attorney in this case before the Court in 1871, at the time of the admission of S.H. Payne family an Eudora Cobb family to Cherokee citizenship and that in the year 1874 or 1876 that George Johnson was a candidate in Sequoyah District for a seat in the Senate branch of the Nation Council and that he was not elected according to the footings of the Election Returns, and that he came to the conclusion that he was defeated on account of illegal votes being case, and employed Thomas Ballard and one Jeremiah to hunt up the illegal votes, but told them that they need not go down on the river for that purpose, as the parties Paynes & Bells were there (in the Cherokee Nation) at his investigation and that he would not molest them, that he would leave that for others to do.

The evidence of D.W. Bushyhead shows: that about the year 1874, he heard Jennie Pigeon talking to several men who were standing by, near the Capital doorway about a paper, presumably her affidavit in this case in 1871, and that when asked why she signed it, she said that she did not know what was in it, and that she did so to please George Johnson, who promised her Thirty Dollars to do so. She was very destitute and one of the principal witnesses in this case.

The definition of the word fraud according to Webster, is "deception deliberately practiced with a view to gaining an unlawful or unfair advantage: artifice by which the right or interest to another is injured."

In making up our opinion in this case, we have done so hesitatingly, not but that we were convinced beyond a reasonable doubt that fraud had been practiced in the court at the time of admitting Dr. S.H. Payne, et al, but in

Cherokee Citizenship Commission Docket Books
(1880-84, 1887-89) Volume IV
Tahlequah, Cherokee Nation

deference to the Court and the parties conserned[sic] herein. It must constantly be borne in mind in investigating the rights of parties claiming citizenship in this Nation, that the right of re-admission rests solely upon blood. Therefore witnesses testifying in behalf of claimants, whose Cherokee blood has become attenuated that it is difficult to trace, the parties so testifying should be scrutinized closely as to their opportunity of knowing the facts about which they testify. This is a correct principle in law, and a disregard of it will often lead Courts and juries into error in making up opinions or rendering verdicts.

The Pigeon women were what is known as full blood Cherokees, speaking only the language of their people. They were Cherokees of a past generation, always in indigent circumstances so far as known, and never living anywhere else than among their people. The opportunity for knowing things beyond their immediate neighborhood in which they lived, must in the very nature of things have been exceedingly meager. The testimony shows conclusively that Sophia Pigeon and Samuel Gunter, son of John Gunter, Sen. must have been about the same age, but in all probability Samuel was the oldest. Starling and Charles Gunter whom it is alleged were the sons of Old John Gunter, if his sons at all, must have been considerably older than Samuel Gunter and consequently much older than Sophia Pigeon; therefore we cannot attach any importance under the circumstances surrounding her at that remote period, when she testifies to relationship existing between parties before she was born. It is not claimed by the defendants in this case that they had ever resided in this Nation until a short time previous to their admission in 1871. The certainly did not live in the Old Nation East, in the year 1835, for the census rolls of that year would certainly show it if they had, provided they were Cherokees; consequently the Commission under all the circumstances, cannot believe it even possible that any of the old women who testified in defendants behalf originally, could have identified Mrs. Martha A. Payne as being the grand-daughter of Starling Gunter, admitting him to be of Indian descent.

Why these defendants did not procure their evidence in 1871 from among the Gunters, the descendants of Old John Gunter, instead of hunting their witnesses from among the ignorant and needy of this people, is inexplicable to this Commission, and raises in the minds of its members, a strong presumption that they resorted to illegal strategem[sic] when obtaining citizenship in 1871.

It will be noticed by examination of the affidavits of the Pigeon women, Anna Hughs and Big-feather, who is made to testify through Jennie Pigeon, that dates, locations and ages of affiants or the claimants are conspicuously absent.

Cherokee Citizenship Commission Docket Books
(1880-84, 1887-89) Volume IV
Tahlequah, Cherokee Nation

The only instance to the contrary, is mentioned by Big-feather where she is made to say, Starling and Charles Gunter were back and forth to the states [what states] up to the time the Cherokees left the Old Nation.

With the authenticated census rolls of Cherokees taken by U.S. Agents in the year 1835 before this Commission, with the certificates of these Agents attached thereto, certifying that said rolls are a complete census of all Cherokees residing the geographical limits of the states of Tennessee, North Carolina, Georgia and Alabama, it is evident to this Commission that Big-feather did not state what Jennie Pigeon says she stated, or if stated by her, was erroneous.

One other circumstance connected herewith, worthy of serious consideration, and that is: George Johnson was one of the Attorneys for the defendants in 1871 and seems to have been principally instrumental in procuring testimony for the claimants at that time.

All of the affidavits heretofore mentioned on part of the defendants are wholly ex-parte, taken by this Attorney, deeply interested in the success of his clients. The testimony of Mr. Bushyhead fully demonstrated the corrupt methods resorted to by this Attorney in obtaining the citizenship of these defendants.

This Commission in summing up and weighing all the facts and circumstances connected with this case, are unanimously of the opinion - : first, that Starling Gunter, the alleged ancestor of defendants was not a Cherokee by blood; secondly, bribery was practiced in procuring evidence in 1871 when defendants were admitted to citizenship in this Nation; therefore we the Commission declare null and void the decrees of a former Court granting citizenship to defendants, to wit: Martha A. Payne and her children, Gabriel L Llewellyn Morgan, nee Payne, Houston J, Gunter M. and Okla E. Payne.

                        J. T. Adair   Chairman Com on Citizenship
                        John E. Gunter Commissioner
                        D.W. Lipe   Commissioner

Office Commission on Citizenship
Tahlequah I.T. March 2nd A.D. 1888

Cherokee Citizenship Commission Docket Books
(1880-84, 1887-89) Volume IV
Tahlequah, Cherokee Nation

WALDEN

DOCKET #1807
CENSUS ROLLS 1835 to 1852

APPLICANT FOR **CHEROKEE CITIZENSHIP**

POST OFFICE: Oklahoma I.T.		ATTORNEY: A.E. Ivey	
No	NAMES	AGE	SEX
1	J.M. Walden	41	male
2	Albert Walden	14	"
3	George W. Walden	12	"
;	Margaret E Walden	10	female
5	Oscar F Walden	8	male
6	Lidia J Walden	6	female
7	Jeremiah Walden	8 m	male

ANCESTOR: John Thompson

Rejected Sept 2nd 1889

Office Commission on Citizenship
Cherokee Nation Ind Ter
Tahlequah Sept 2nd 1889

The application in the above case alleges that he derives his Cherokee blood from one John Thompson whose name he believes will be found on the census rolls of Cherokees by blood taken and made by the United States in the years 1835 – 52. James Young age 76 yrs and Benjamin Stephens age 74 yrs in exparte affidavits taken before John M. Somerville Clk of Circuit Court of Howard County, State of Arkansas on the 21st day of October 1887. Swear that John M. Walden is the son of John and Nancy Walden, that Nancy Walden was the daughter of Millie Young whose Father was John Thompson a half blood Cherokee Indian but from what source they derive their knowledge is not states[sic]. It does not appear that the applicant has at any time resided among the Cherokee people or that he has enjoyed or sought to enjoy any Cherokee rights or privileges *(illegible)* residing in Arkansas on the borders. Nor is the name of John Thompson to be found on the census rolls of Cherokees taken as before stated in the years 1835-52. The Commission therefore decide that John M Walden age 41 yrs and his children Albert Walden 14 yrs, George W. Walden 12 yrs, Margaret E. Walden 10 yrs, Oscar F. Walden 8 yrs, Lidia J Walden 6 yrs, and Jeremiah Walden 8 months of age are not of Cherokee blood and not entitled to citizenship in the Cherokee Nation. P.O. Ok-la-ho-ma Ind. Ter.

Cherokee Citizenship Commission Docket Books (1880-84, 1887-89) Volume IV
Tahlequah, Cherokee Nation

Will.P. Ross
Chairman
J.E. Gunter   Com

Attest
   D.S. Williams
   Asst   Clk   Com.

WALDEN

DOCKET #1808
CENSUS ROLLS 1835

APPLICANT FOR **CHEROKEE CITIZENSHIP**

POST OFFICE: Oklahoma I.T.		ATTORNEY: A.E. Ivey	
NO	NAMES	AGE	SEX
1	George Walden	31	male
2	Sherman Walden	20	"
3	Mary R. Walden	18	female

ANCESTOR: John Thompson

Rejected Sept 2nd 1889

Office Commission on Citizenship
Cherokee Nation Ind Ter
Tahlequah Sept. 2nd 1889

The above case was called 3 several times not less than one hour at intervals and no response from applicant or by Atty the Commission therefore decide that George Walden age 31 yrs and the following children Sherman Walden male age 20 yrs Brother, Mary R. Walden female age 18 yrs Sister, are not Cherokees by blood. Post Office Ok-la-ho-ma I.T.

Will.P. Ross
Chairman
J.E. Gunter   Com

Attest
   D.S. Williams
   Asst   Clk   Com.

WHITINGTON

DOCKET #1809
CENSUS ROLLS 1835 to 1852

APPLICANT FOR **CHEROKEE CITIZENSHIP**

POST OFFICE: Van Buren Ark		ATTORNEY: A.E. Ivey	
NO	NAMES	AGE	SEX
1	Sarah E Whitington	30	female

Cherokee Citizenship Commission Docket Books
(1880-84, 1887-89) Volume IV
Tahlequah, Cherokee Nation

2	Sarah F Whitington	9	"
3	John R Whitington	8	male
4	William L Whitington	6	"
5	Herschal Whitington	4	"
6	Rosa B. Whitington	3	female
7	Logan Whitington	2	male
8	Lulu Whitington	1	female

ANCESTOR: Fannie Little, Whore[sic]

Rejected Sept 2nd 1889

Office Commission on Citizenship
Cherokee Nation Ind Ter
Tahlequah Sept 2nd 1889

The above case was called 3 several times not less than one hour at intervals. The Commission decide that Sarah E Whitington age 30 yrs and Sarah Frances Female 9 yrs, John Rance male 8 yrs, William Lafayette male 6 yrs, Herschal 4 yrs, Rosa Bell 3 yrs, Logan 2 yrs and Lulu Whitington 1 yr are not Cherokees by blood. P.O. Van Buren Ark.

Attest
   D.S. Williams
   Asst Clk Com.

Will.P. Ross
Chairman
J.E. Gunter Com

WILLIAMS

DOCKET #1810
CENSUS ROLLS

APPLICANT FOR **CHEREOKEE CITIZENSHIP**

POST OFFICE: Canesauga[sic] Ga		ATTORNEY: A.E. Ivey	
NO	NAMES	AGE	SEX
1	Joseph B. Williams	23	male
2	Maud J Williams	2	female

ANCESTOR: John A. Williams

Rejected Sept 2nd 1889

Office Commission on Citizenship
Cherokee Nation Ind Ter
Tahlequah Sept 2nd 1889

The above case was called 3 several times not less than one hour at intervals and no response from applicant or by Atty the Commission decide that Joseph B.

Cherokee Citizenship Commission Docket Books
(1880-84, 1887-89) Volume IV
Tahlequah, Cherokee Nation

Williams age 23 yrs and his daughter Maud J. Williams Female age 2 yrs are not Cherokees by blood. P.O. Conesauga[sic] Ga.

                                        Will.P. Ross
Attest   Chairman
  D.S. Williams   J.E. Gunter   Com
  Asst Clk Com.

WEIR

DOCKET #1811
CENSUS ROLLS 1835

APPLICANT FOR CHEROKEE CITIZENSHIP

POST OFFICE: Berryville Ark		ATTORNEY: A.E. Ivey	
No	NAMES	AGE	SEX
1	Elmina Weir	44	female
2	J.W. Abrams	24	male
3	Manerva J. Weir	20	female
4	M.L. Weir	17	"
5	J.T. Weir	6	male
6	Birdie Weir	3	female

ANCESTOR: Hiram Bryant

Now on this the 26th day of June 1888, comes the above case up for final hearing, it being one of eleven cases claiming a descent from Hiram Bryant. The decision in this case will be found on this Book page 311, testimony will be found in the Rachel Wilder & Isaac [sic] cases, found on Record pages 74 to 81 – Adverse to claimants.

                        J T Adair   Chairman Commission
                        D.W. Lipe   Commissioner

WALKER

DOCKET #1812
CENSUS ROLLS

APPLICANT FOR CHEROKEE CITIZENSHIP

POST OFFICE: Talking Rock Ga		ATTORNEY: A.E. Ivey	
No	NAMES	AGE	SEX
1	Jane C Walker	36	female
2	Elisa[sic] A. Walker	9	"
3	James Walker	6	male

Cherokee Citizenship Commission Docket Books
(1880-84, 1887-89) Volume IV
Tahlequah, Cherokee Nation

4	Salina C Walker	4	female

ANCESTOR: William Gibson

Rejected Sept 2nd 1889

Office Commission on Citizenship
Cherokee Nation Ind Ter
Tahlequah Sept 2nd 1889

The above case was called 3 several times not less than one hour at intervals and no response from applicant or by Atty. The Commission therefore decide that Jane C Walker age 36 yrs and the following children Eliza A. Female 9 yrs, James male 6 yrs and Salina C. Walker Female 4 yrs are not Cherokees by blood. Post Office Talking Rock Ga.

Attest
    D.S. Williams
    Asst Clk Com.

Will.P. Ross
Chairman
J.E. Gunter Com

WILLIAMS

DOCKET #1813
CENSUS ROLLS

APPLICANT FOR CHEROKEE CITIZENSHIP

POST OFFICE: Canesauga[sic] Ga		ATTORNEY: A.E. Ivey	
No	NAMES	AGE	SEX
1	John A. Williams	74	male
2	Andrew C. Williams	27	"
3	Isaac C Williams	24	"

ANCESTOR: William Williams

Rejected Sept 2nd 1889

Office Commission on Citizenship
Cherokee Nation Ind Ter
Tahlequah Sept 3rd 1889

The above case was called 3 times not less than one hour at intervals and no response from applicant or by Atty. The Commission therefore decide that John A Williams age 74 yrs and the following children, Andrew C. Williams male 27 yrs, Isaac C. Williams age 24 yrs are not Cherokees by blood.
P.O. Canesauga[sic] Ga.

Cherokee Citizenship Commission Docket Books
(1880-84, 1887-89) Volume IV
Tahlequah, Cherokee Nation

Attest
D.S. Williams
Asst Clk Com.

Will.P. Ross
Chairman
J.E. Gunter Com

WILHITE

DOCKET #1814
CENSUS ROLLS 1835

APPLICANT FOR CHEROKEE CITIZENSHIP

POST OFFICE: Berryville Ark		ATTORNEY: A.E. Ivey	
NO	NAMES	AGE	SEX
1	Nancy Wilhite	25	female
2	Joseph Wilhite	6	male
3	Mary C Wilhite	4	female

ANCESTOR: Hiram Bryant

Now on this the 26th day of June 1888, comes the above case up for final hearing, it being one of eleven cases claiming a descent from Hiram Bryant. The evidence in this case will be found on Record pages 74 to 81 in the Rachel Wilder & Isaac Terry cases.

Decision will be found in case of Rachel Wilder in this Book on page 311– Adverse to claimants.

J T Adair   Chairman Commission
D.W. Lipe   Commissioner

WELLS

DOCKET #1815
CENSUS ROLLS

APPLICANT FOR CHEROKEE CITIZENSHIP

POST OFFICE: Alma Ark		ATTORNEY: A.E. Ivey	
NO	NAMES	AGE	SEX
1	Sarah Wells	45	female
2	James M. Wells	19	male
3	Rosa G. Wells	15	female
4	Moses M. Wells	13	male
5	Harvey W. Wells	12	"

ANCESTOR: S. Ramsey

Cherokee Citizenship Commission Docket Books
(1880-84, 1887-89) Volume IV
Tahlequah, Cherokee Nation

Rejected Sept 2nd 1889

                    Office Commission on Citizenship
                    Cherokee Nation Ind Ter
                    Tahlequah Sept 2nd 1889

The above applicant was called 3 times & no answer & there being no evidence on file in support of the application, We decide that applicant Sarah Wells age 45 yrs and children James W. Wells age 19 yrs, Rosa G. Wells age 15 yrs, Moses M. Wells age 13 yrs and Harvey W. Wells age 12 yrs are not Cherokees by blood. P.O. Alma Ark.

                    Will.P. Ross
Attest   Chairman
   D.S. Williams   J.E. Gunter   Com
   Asst Clk Com.

WHITINGTON

DOCKET #1816
CENSUS ROLLS 1835

APPLICANT FOR CHEROKEE CITIZENSHIP

POST OFFICE: Terry Town Ark		ATTORNEY: A.E. Ivey	
NO	NAMES	AGE	SEX
1	Harriett L Whitington	33	female
2	Sarah E. Whitington	14	"
3	Wm. T. Whitington	11	male
4	Mary E. Whitington	8	female
5	Stella M. Whitington	6	"
6	Fanny A. Whitington	4	"

ANCESTOR: Mima Franklin

Now on this the 9th day of January 1888, comes the above case up for final hearing. The applicants having made application pursuant to the provisions of an Act of the National Council approved Dec 8th 1886, and all the evidence being duly considered in the <u>Mary A</u>. Couch case, which is a list one of all cases claiming a direct lineage from Mima Edwards, it is adjudged and determined by the Commission that Harriett L Whittington[sic], Sarah E. – Wm T. – Mary E. – Stella M. and Fanny A. Whittington[sic] are not Cherokees by blood, and not entitled to the rights & privileges of such.

Cherokee Citizenship Commission Docket Books
(1880-84, 1887-89) Volume IV
Tahlequah, Cherokee Nation

The decision in the Mary A Couch case which will be found on Page 100 of Docket "A", governs this case.

                J T Adair   Chairman Commission
                D.W. Lipe   Commissioner

WALDEN

DOCKET #1817
CENSUS ROLLS 1835 to 1852

APPLICANT FOR CHEROKEE CITIZENSHIP

POST OFFICE: Galena Ark.		ATTORNEY: A.E. Ivey	
No	NAMES	AGE	SEX
1	James Walden	34	male
2	Jasper Walden	10	"
3	J.W. Walden	8	"
4	Jno Walden	4	"

ANCESTOR: John Thompson

Rejected Sept 2nd 1889

                    Office Commission on Citizenship
                    Cherokee Nation Ind Ter
                    Tahlequah Sept. 3rd 1889

The above case was called 3 several times not less than one hour at intervals and no response from applicant or by Atty. The Commission therefore decide that Jas Walden age 34 yrs and the following children Jasper male 10 yrs, J.W. male 8 yrs, and Jno Walden male age 4 yrs are not Cherokees by blood. P.O. Galena Ark.

                Will.P. Ross
Attest   Chairman
  D.S. Williams   J.E. Gunter Com
  Asst Clk Com.

WELCH

DOCKET #1818
CENSUS ROLLS 1835 to 1852

APPLICANT FOR CHEROKEE CITIZENSHIP

POST OFFICE: Claremore I.T.		ATTORNEY: L.B. Bell	
No	NAMES	AGE	SEX
1	S.L. Welch	23	female

Cherokee Citizenship Commission Docket Books (1880-84, 1887-89) Volume IV
Tahlequah, Cherokee Nation

2	E.L. Welch	5	"
3	Mary Welch	3	"
4	Charley Welch	1	male

ANCESTOR: Mrs. Bradson

Rejected Sept 2nd 1889

                                    Office Commission on Citizenship
                                    Cherokee Nation Ind Ter
                                    Tahlequah Sept 2nd 1889

The above case was called 3 several times not less than one hour at intervals and no response from applicant or by Atty. The Commission therefore decide that SL. Welch age 23 yrs and the following children E.L. Female 5 yrs, Mary Welch Female 3 yrs, & Charley Welch male 1 yr are not Cherokees by blood. P.O. Claremore I.T.

                                          Will.P. Ross
Attest   Chairman
    D.S. Williams   J.E. Gunter   Com
    Asst Clk Com.

WHITE

DOCKET #1819
CENSUS ROLLS 1851

APPLICANT FOR CHEROKEE CITIZENSHIP

POST OFFICE: *(Illegible)* Ga.		ATTORNEY: A.E. Ivey	
NO	NAMES	AGE	SEX
1	Mary White	40	female
2	Sarah White	19	"
3	Martha L White	17	"
4	William J White	15	male
5	James A. White	13	"
6	Thomas J. White	11	"
7	George W. White	9	"
8	Lewis R. White	7	"
9	Walter P. White	5	"
10	Mary P. White	2	female

ANCESTOR: John Tidwell

We the Commission on Citizenship after carefully examining the above entitles case of Mary White and her nine children, find them to be descendants

Cherokee Citizenship Commission Docket Books
(1880-84, 1887-89) Volume IV
Tahlequah, Cherokee Nation

of John Tidwell, whose case came up before this Commission and found to be a Cherokee by blood, and from the proof submitted, connecting Mary White and her nine children, viz: Sarah E., Martha L., William J., James A., Thomas J., George W., Lewis A., Walter P. and Mary P. White are Cherokees by blood and are hereby re-admitted to all the rights and privileges of Cherokee citizens by blood.

          J. T. Adair   Chairman Commission
          D.W. Lipe   Commissioner
          H.C. Barnes   Commissioner

Office Com on Citizenship
Tahlequah I.T. Sept 21st 1888.

WARDEN

DOCKET #1820
CENSUS ROLLS 1835 to 1852

APPLICANT FOR CHEROKEE CITIZENSHIP

POST OFFICE: Blue Jacket I.T.		ATTORNEY: A.E. Ivey	
No	NAMES	AGE	SEX
1	Mary A. Warden	26	female
2	Octavey J Warden	5	"

ANCESTOR: Isom Sizemore

Rejected Sept 2nd 1889

         Office Commission on Citizenship
         Cherokee Nation Ind Ter
         Tahlequah Sept 2nd 1889

The above case was called 3 several times not less than one hour at intervals and no response from applicant or by Atty. The Commission therefore decide that Mary A. Warden age 26 yrs and her child Octavey J Warden Female age 5 yrs are not Cherokees by blood. P.O. Blue Jacket I.T.

         Will.P. Ross
Attest   Chairman
   D.S. Williams   J.E. Gunter   Com
   Asst Clk Com.

Cherokee Citizenship Commission Docket Books
(1880-84, 1887-89) Volume IV
Tahlequah, Cherokee Nation

WILLIS

DOCKET #1821
CENSUS ROLLS 1835 to 1852

APPLICANT FOR CHEROKEE CITIZENSHIP

POST OFFICE: Vinita C.N.		ATTORNEY: A.E. Ivey	
No	NAMES	AGE	SEX
1	Annie Willis	27	female

ANCESTOR: John Willis

Rejected Sept 2nd 1889

Office Commission on Citizenship
Cherokee Nation Ind Ter
Tahlequah Sept 2nd 1889

The above case was called 3 several times not less than one hour at intervals and no response from applicant. The Commission decide that Annie Willis age 27 yrs is not a Cherokee by blood. Post Office Vinita I.T.

Attest
   D.S. Williams
   Asst Clerk Commission

Will.P. Ross
   Chairman
J.E. Gunter   Com

WISHAN

DOCKET #1822
CENSUS ROLLS 1835 to 1852

APPLICANT FOR CHEROKEE CITIZENSHIP

POST OFFICE: Blue Jacket Ind. Ter.		ATTORNEY: A.E. Ivey	
No	NAMES	AGE	SEX
1	Martha J Wishan	21	Female

ANCESTOR: Joel Sizemore

Rejected Sept 2nd 1889

Office Commission on Citizenship
Cherokee Nation Ind Ter
Tahlequah Sept 2nd 1889

The above applicant was called 3 times & no answer and there being no evidence on file in support of the application. We decide that applicant Martha J Wishen[sic] age 21 yrs is not a Cherokee a blood. P.O. Blue Jacket I.T.

Cherokee Citizenship Commission Docket Books
(1880-84, 1887-89) Volume IV
Tahlequah, Cherokee Nation

Attest
   D.S. Williams
    Asst Clk Com

Will.P. Ross
   Chairman
J.E. Gunter Com

WOOTEN

DOCKET #1823
CENSUS ROLLS

APPLICANT FOR CHEROKEE CITIZENSHIP

POST OFFICE: Blue Jacket Ind. Ter.		ATTORNEY: A.E. Ivey	
NO	NAMES	AGE	SEX
1	Eliza Emma Wooten	25	Female

ANCESTOR: Joel Sizemore

Rejected Sept 2nd 1889

               Office Commission on Citizenship
               Cherokee Nation Ind Ter
               Tahlequah Sept 2nd 1889

The above case was called 3 several times not less than one hour at intervals and no response from applicant or by Atty. The Commission decide that Eliza Emma Wooten age 25 yrs is not a Cherokee by blood. P.O. Blue Jacket I.T.

Attest
   D.S. Williams
    Asst Clerk Commission

Will.P. Ross
   Chairman
J.E. Gunter Com

WALLACE

DOCKET #1824
CENSUS ROLLS 1835 to 1852

APPLICANT FOR CHEROKEE CITIZENSHIP

POST OFFICE: Mulberry Station Ark		ATTORNEY: A.E. Ivey	
NO	NAMES	AGE	SEX
1	Mary F. Wallace	28	Female
2	Florence E Wallace	6	"
3	Mumdum Wallace	Infant	"

ANCESTOR: John Rogers

Cherokee Citizenship Commission Docket Books
(1880-84, 1887-89) Volume IV
Tahlequah, Cherokee Nation

Now on this the 17th day of March 1888, comes the above case for a final hearing. The parties having made application pursuant to the provisions of an Act of the National Council approved December 8th 1886, and all the evidence being duly considered and found to be insufficient and unsatisfactory it is adjudged and determined by the Commission that

    Mary F. Wallace, Florence E Wallace and Mundum[sic] Wallace not Cherokees and are not entitled to the rights, privileges and immunities of Cherokee citizens by blood.

	J. T. Adair Chairman Commission
	John E. Gunter Commissioner
Attest	D.W. Lipe Commissioner
C.C. Lipe	
Clerk Com.	

The decision in the James C.C. Rogers case found in Book C, page 627, and testimony on Journal pages 325 to 333 governs this case.

WILDER

DOCKET #1825
CENSUS ROLLS 1835

APPLICANT FOR CHEROKEE CITIZENSHIP

POST OFFICE: Viola Mo		ATTORNEY: A.E. Ivey	
NO	NAMES	AGE	SEX
1	Rachael Wilder	69	Female

ANCESTOR: Hiram Bryant

Rachel Wilder, et al.
    (VS)   Applicants for Cherokee Citizenship
Cherokee Nation

Now on this the 26th day of June 1888, comes the above entitled case up for final disposition, it being submitted by Plaintiffs' Attorney, Mr. Hitchcock, regularly and in conformity to law. The evidence of Rachel Wilder, the elder of eleven who have application on file in this office, claiming a lineal descent from one Hiram Bryant, their alleged Cherokee ancestor, shows, that she is 70 years old, and that she lives in the state of Missouri, and that she is the daughter of Hiram Bryant, but fails to show ~~his~~ whose son he was, or if he ever had a sister Lucy; and further, that she has nine children, eight by her second husband Mr.

Cherokee Citizenship Commission Docket Books
(1880-84, 1887-89) Volume IV
Tahlequah, Cherokee Nation

Terry and one by her first husband Mr. Watson, and that she was always taught to believe that she was of Cherokee Indian descent.

The testimony of <u>John T. Moulder</u> shows, that he was well acquainted with Isaac Terry, a son of Rachel Wilder, and that he derives his Cherokee blood from his mother, Rachel Wilder, and she from her father, Hiram Bryant, who lived in the Old Cherokee Nation, and that the name of applicants ancestors appears upon some of the old rolls of Cherokees, and that Hiram Bryant had a sister Lucy Bryant, who also lived in the Old Cherokee Nation, and that Hiram Bryant removed from the Old Cherokee Nation to Kentucky about 55 years ago. The testimony of <u>C.W. Warren</u>, a resident of Stone County, state of Missouri, is in the whole substantially the same as that of John T. Moulder, even to the extent of mentioning that Hiram Bryant had a sister Lucy Bryant. The testimony of D.H. Garrett is also substantially and nearly <u>verbatim</u> the same language as that of John T. Moulder and C.W. Warren. This is the testimony of applicants as touches their claim to Cherokee Indian descent.

You will at once see that Rachel Wilder, who is 70 years old, fails to show that her father ever had a sister Lucy, and the presumption is with the Commission, if Hiram Bryant ever had such a sister, she being her niece, would have set the fact forth, so as to strengthen as far as possible her claim to Cherokee citizenship. She was related to her father's kindred by blood, and certainly had a better opportunity than others, of knowing of her own blood relations than those who were not so connected, she being a woman, according to the testimony of C.W. Warren, John T. Moulder and D.H. Garrett about 15 years old when she, with her father, Hiram Bryant, removed from the Old Nation and went to the state of Kentucky, about 55 years ago. This may have been, however, an omission on her part.

The Census and Pay rolls of Cherokees taken in the Old Nation, mentioned in the 7th Sec. of the law creating and empowering this Commission, were offered as testimony by Hon. R.L. Wyly, Nation's Attorney.

The name of Lucy Bryant does appear upon the roll of Reservees taken in the Old Nation under the treaty of 1817, with only one in family, and under the heads of "Remarks" noted <u>Widow</u>, which at once conveys the impression to the minds of the Commission that her maiden name must have been other than Bryant. This though is only to show that we have treated this case with, together with all our findings in similar ones, all fairness and consideration, for this roll is not one mentioned in the 7th Sec. of the law referred to, under which, and which

Cherokee Citizenship Commission Docket Books
(1880-84, 1887-89) Volume IV
Tahlequah, Cherokee Nation

alone, applicants for Cherokee citizenship can be re-admitted to citizenship in this Nation by this Commission.

There was no efforts made by the Plaintiffs in this case to show that they ever participated or were ever in any way beneficiaries of any of the benefits growing out of the treaties between the Cherokee Nation and the United States. These parties left the Old Nation according to the evidence contained herein, some two or three years prior to the taking of the Census Rolls of Cherokees in the year 1835, and as a matter of course, admitting them to be Cherokees, could not be found on this roll, or on subsequent ones, as there is no evidence that they ever returned to the Country that once comprised the "Old Nation".

We have searched the rolls referred to and fail to find the name of Hiram Bryant or any of the applicants enrolled thereon, and the Commission under the law, declares that Rachel Wilder, Isaac Terry, Joseph R. Terry, Wm Terry, Elizabeth Terry, John Terry, Dora Bell Terry, Wiley C. Terry, Robert Terry, A.M. Terry, Maude Terry, John Terry, Lucretia O. Terry, Rachel C. Terry, Miles Terry, Rosetta Terry, N.B. Terry, Pearly Terry, Effie Terry, Ada Terry, Samuel Terry, Jr., John Terry, Calvin Terry, Russell D. Terry, Joseph Terry, Malvara Staups, Nancy Staups, Rachel Staups, Wm Staups, Gordon Staups, Nancy Wilhite, Joseph Wilhite, Mary C. Wilhite, Samuel Hatton, Sam B, Hatton, N.L. Hatton, N.S.G. Hatton, Mary E. Hatton, Wm L. Hatton, Almedia J. Hatton, Elmina Weir, J.W. Albanus, Manerva J. Weir, M.L. Weir, J.T. Weir, and Birdie Weir, are not Cherokees by blood and are not entitled to any of the rights, privileges and immunities of Cherokee citizens by virtue of such blood.

The above parties are now residents of Missouri, Arkansas and New Mexico.

        J T Adair   Chairman Commission
        D.W. Lipe Commissioner

WHEELER

DOCKET #1826
CENSUS ROLLS 1835 to 1852

APPLICANT FOR CHEROKEE CITIZENSHIP

POST OFFICE: Altamont, Kansas		ATTORNEY: A.E. Ivey	
NO	NAMES	AGE	SEX
1	Lucinda K Wheeler	33	Female
2	Ada E. Wheeler	10	"

Cherokee Citizenship Commission Docket Books
(1880-84, 1887-89) Volume IV
Tahlequah, Cherokee Nation

3	Reubin A. Wheeler	8	Male
4	Charles F. Wheeler	2	"

ANCESTOR: John E Elliott   Mrs. Mayfield

Rejected Sept 2nd 1889

                        Office Commission on Citizenship
                        Cherokee Nation Ind Ter
                        Tahlequah Sept 2nd 1889

The above case was called 3 times not less than one hour at intervals and no response from applicant or by Atty. The Commission therefore decide that Lucinda R. Wheeler age 33 yrs and the following children Ada E. Female 10 yrs, Reubin male 8 yrs and Charles F. Wheeler male 2 yrs are not Cherokees by blood. P.O. Altamount[sic] Kansas.

                        Will.P. Ross
Attest   Chairman
   D.S. Williams   J.E. Gunter   Com
   Asst Clk Com.

WARD

DOCKET #1827
CENSUS ROLLS 1851

APPLICANT FOR CHEROKEE CITIZENSHIP

POST OFFICE: Ellijay Georgia		ATTORNEY: A.E. Ivey	
No	NAMES	AGE	SEX
1	Charles J Ward	20	Male

ANCESTOR: John Ward

Rejected Sept 2nd 1889

                        Office Commission on Citizenship
                        Cherokee Nation Ind Ter
                        Tahlequah Sept 2nd 1889

The above case was called 3 several times not less than one hour apart and no response from applicant or by Atty. The Commission decide that Charles J. Warden[sic] age 20 yrs is not a Cherokee by blood. P.O. Ellijay Ga.

                        Will.P. Ross
Attest   Chairman
   D.S. Williams   J.E. Gunter   Com
   Asst Clk Com.

Cherokee Citizenship Commission Docket Books (1880-84, 1887-89) Volume IV
Tahlequah, Cherokee Nation

WAFFORD

DOCKET #1828
CENSUS ROLLS 1835 to 1852

APPLICANT FOR **CHEROKEE CITIZENSHIP**

POST OFFICE: Little River Texas		ATTORNEY: A.E. Ivey	
NO	NAMES	AGE	SEX
1	M. L. Wafford	40	Male

ANCESTOR: Wofford

Rejected Sept 2nd 1889

Office Commission on Citizenship
Cherokee Nation Ind Ter
Tahlequah Sept 3rd 1889

The above applicant was called 3 times & no answer & there being no evidence on file in support of the application we decide that applicant M.L. Wofford[sic] age 40 yrs and his 3 children are not Cherokees by blood. P.O. Little River Texas.

	Will.P. Ross
Attest	Chairman
D.S. Williams	J.E. Gunter Com
Asst Clerk Commission	

WALDEN

DOCKET #1829
CENSUS ROLLS 1835 to 1852

APPLICANT FOR **CHEROKEE CITIZENSHIP**

POST OFFICE: Galena Ark		ATTORNEY: A.E. Ivey	
NO	NAMES	AGE	SEX
1	John T. Walden	30	male
2	Nancy Ann Walden	8	female
3	John B. Walden	6	male
4	George T. Walden	4	"
5	Andrew Walden	2	"

ANCESTOR: John Thompson

Rejected Sept. 2nd 1889

Cherokee Citizenship Commission Docket Books
(1880-84, 1887-89) Volume IV
Tahlequah, Cherokee Nation

>Office Commission on Citizenship
>Cherokee Nation Ind Ter
>Tahlequah Sept 2nd 1889

The Commission in the above case decide that John T. Walden age 30 yrs and his daughter Nancy Ann Walden 8 yrs and sons John B. Walden 6 yrs, George T. Walden 4 yrs and Andrew Walden 2 yrs are not of Cherokee blood because no proof accompanies their application and because the name of John Thompson is not found on the census rolls of Cherokees by blood taken by the United States in the years 1835-52. See decision in case of John M. Walden Docket 1807, Book D, Page 273. P.O. Galena Arkansas.

Attest	Will.P. Ross Chairman
D.S. Williams Asst Clk Com.	J.E. Gunter Com

WILLS

DOCKET #1830
CENSUS ROLLS 1835 to 48

APPLICANT FOR CHEROKEE CITIZENSHIP

POST OFFICE: Alma Ark		ATTORNEY: A.E. Ivey	
NO	NAMES	AGE	SEX
1	Samuel Wills	24	male

ANCESTOR: Samuel Ramsey

Rejected Sept 2nd 1889

>Office Commission on Citizenship
>Cherokee Nation Ind Ter
>Tahlequah Sept 2nd 1889

The above case was filed on the 5th day of Oct. 1887 and was called 3 several times for a final hearing and no response from applicant or by Atty, the Commission therefore decide that Samuel Wills age 24 yrs is not a Cherokee by blood. P.O. Ok-la-ho-ma I.T.

Attest	Will.P. Ross Chairman
D.S. Williams Asst Clerk Commission	J.E. Gunter Com

Cherokee Citizenship Commission Docket Books
(1880-84, 1887-89) Volume IV
Tahlequah, Cherokee Nation

WILLIAMS

DOCKET #1831
CENSUS ROLLS 1835 to 1852

APPLICANT FOR CHEROKEE CITIZENSHIP

POST OFFICE: Lancaster Ark		ATTORNEY: A.E. Ivey	
No	NAMES	AGE	SEX
1	Sarah Williams	39	female
2	Mollie Williams	12	"
3	Dilana M. Williams	9	"
4	Silas B. Williams	7	male
5	Nancy C. Williams	1	female

ANCESTOR: David Brank

Rejected Sept 2nd 1889

Office Commission on Citizenship
Cherokee Nation Ind Ter
Tahlequah Sept 2nd 1889

The above applicant was called 3 times & no answer either in person or Attorney & there being no evidence on file in support of the application we decide that applicant Sarah Williams age 39 yrs and her children Mollie C. Williams age 12 yrs, Delana M. Williams age 9 yrs Silas B. Williams age 7 yrs and Nancy C. Williams age 1 yr are not Cherokees by blood. P.O. Lancaster Ark.

	Will.P. Ross
Attest	Chairman
DS Williams	J.E. Gunter Com
Asst Clk Com.	

WILLIAMSON

DOCKET #1832
CENSUS ROLLS 1835 to 1852

APPLICANT FOR CHEROKEE CITIZENSHIP

POST OFFICE: Vinita C.N.		ATTORNEY: A.E. Ivey	
No	NAMES	AGE	SEX
1	Elizabeth Williamson	48	female

ANCESTOR: Henry Hines

Cherokee Citizenship Commission Docket Books
(1880-84, 1887-89) Volume IV
Tahlequah, Cherokee Nation

Office Commission on Citizenship
Cherokee Nation Ind Ter
Tahlequah Sept 2nd 1889

The above case was called 3 several times not less than one hour at intervals and no response from applicant or by Atty. The Commission therefore decide that Elizabeth Williams[sic] age 48 yrs is not a Cherokee by blood. Post Office Vinita I.T.

Will.P. Ross
Attest   Chairman
  D.S. Williams   J.E. Gunter   Com
  Asst   Clerk Commission

WALLACE

DOCKET #1833
CENSUS ROLLS 1835 to 1852

APPLICANT FOR **CHEROKEE CITIZENSHIP**

POST OFFICE: Evansville Ark		ATTORNEY: A.E. Ivey	
NO	NAMES	AGE	SEX
1	Mary A Wallace	26	female
2	Pearly Wallace	5	"
3	Mattie M Wallace	3	"
4	James D. Wallace	3	male
5	Lizzie J Wallace	8 m	female

ANCESTOR: Ben & Polly Cross, nee Brown

Commission On Citizenship
Cherokee Nation
Tahlequah Oct 27th 1889.

Mary A. Wallace
    vs   Application for Cherokee Citizenship
The Cherokee Nation

The applicant in the above case alleges that she is the grand daughter of Benjamin and Polly Cross nee Polly Brown whose name she believe s was duly enrolled on the census rolls of Cherokees by blood taken by the United States in the years 1835-52. Before the Commission on Citizenship July 12th 1888 the applicant Mrs. Mary A. Wallace states that she is 26 years of age and has four

Cherokee Citizenship Commission Docket Books
(1880-84, 1887-89) Volume IV
Tahlequah, Cherokee Nation

children by her husband, Wallace who is a white man, viz: Pearly Preston Wallace, Minta[sic] May Wallace and James Day Wallace (twins) and Lizzie Jane Wallace aged respectively 6, 4, and 2 yrs. And that there are also living with her family five children of her husband by a previous marriage with a white woman and who are white viz: Cora, Lilla, Bella, Leander, Lovely F. and Walter Wallace.

The evidence introduced in the case covers the statements of several witnesses in favor of the claimant and also of the Cherokee Nation. The Commission have given these statements careful consideration altho[sic] the greater portion of the former were taken exparte in the state and fail to fall within the rule governing the introduction of such papers which requires the affidavits of persons living in the Nation to be taken before the Commission in person unless witnesses are physically unable to appear and there on proper notification to Attorneys who may desire to have the privileges of cross examination. Such is said to have been the condition of several of the witnesses whose affidavits were made exparte in Washington County state of Arkansas, before T.B. Green a Notary Public on the 7th day of March, the 3rd day of July 1888 in *(illegible)* of applicant. The former are those of Benjamin Harrison, 76 years old, Mrs. Elizabeth Harrison 65 years of age, W.H. Harrison 47 years and Hiram Harrison 45 years all residents of Dutch Mills Arkansas. Benj. Harrison and Elizabeth Harrison became acquainted with Benjamin Cross and his wife about 1838 at a crossing of Grand River Mo. knows as the "Cherokee Crossing" and they had gone there from Tennessee in 1836 or 7. They claimed to be Cherokees. Benjamin Cross claiming to be 1/4 blood. The identification of Mary A. Wallace as the daughter of James Cross and Benjamin her grand father daughter of Benjamin Cross by the Harrison family is *(illegible)* but their knowledge of their her Cherokee blood is not of a personal character. They know only what they claim to have heard from the Crosses themselves or from neighborhood reports. The other witnesses for claimant were Mrs. Charlotte Collins, Mrs. Jane Freeman, Cinda Adair, Ruth Collins and Eliza Dougherty or "Dorhity" – none of whom knew the claimant more than a few months prior to the date of their statements and after her arrival in the Nation their identification of her *(illegible)* chiefly upon her own stat declarations. Mrs Eliza Dorhity of Going Snake District Cherokee Nation 88 yrs old, in her statement July 3rd 1888 before the Notary Public named above says that she has known claimant about nine months and was told by her that she was the daughter of Jim Cross and grand daughter of Benj and Polly Cross. She derives other information in regard to the Crosses from Benjamin Harrison before named and believes that they were the same persons who left Tennessee and that Polly Cross was the daughter

Cherokee Citizenship Commission Docket Books
(1880-84, 1887-89) Volume IV
Tahlequah, Cherokee Nation

of her Uncle John Brown and a white woman named Ruth Creel whom he had taken from a white man by the name of Creek and kept as one of two wives in his own yard. His lawful wife was part Cherokee. He testifies that Brown raised four or five children by the woman Creel one of whom was named Polly and a boy named William and that she was well acquainted with their children but left her home East in 1833 and *(illegible...)* afterwards. Her mother with whom she came to this country she states told her that Polly Brown married a quarter blood Cherokee and moved to Carroll County Mo. but does not state the year and believes that claimant is her relative and so acknowledged. The statements of the other witnesses named are not material to the main *(illegible)* nor are the statements of Thomas Starr and James Crittenden further than that they corroborate the fact that John Brown had more than one wife one of them was white and that he had families by them. The most important witness however in the case is is[sic] Dr. D.D. Thornton of Delaware District Cherokee Nation and whose affidavit was taken by in the presence of the Attorney for the Nation and of Mr. Wallace the husband of Mrs. Mary A. Wallace at Vinita by D.S. Williams a Clerk of the Commission on the 9th day of October *(illegible...)* Dr. Thornton swears that he is in his 70th year that he is a citizen of the Nation by intermarriage and that he has been in this Country about 41 years, that he married his wife Elizabeth daughter of John Brown and his lawful wife Elizabeth Brown in the state of Tennessee in the year 1845. John Brown had two wives one was white by the name of Creel and one son by her named William. He also had two daughters by *(illegible)* Cherokee wife, Elizabeth. Wife of witness a half-sister Ailsey and who was also a *(illegible)* of John Brown by a Cherokee woman who married a Holmes. John Brown has sons also named *(Name Illegible)*, John Brown, Robert Brown, James Brown and Thomas Brown but not by the Creel woman. He has heard of a Polly Brown, who is said to be a Cherokee but she is not of the family of John Brown of whom he speaks. Witness was acquainted with John Brown and his family in the Old Nation in Tennessee from his boyhood and he never had any other children by the Creel woman other than William Brown died where he lived near the Tennessee River at the mouth of what is called the "Lookout Valley". He knew the Creel woman back in Tennessee. John Brown was dead when witness left there but she was still living and only had one child and he thinks the only one she ever had and Brown left her on his place where she died. Elizabeth Brown died in Cherokee Nation. In addition to this statement while the name of John Brown is found on the Census Rolls of Cherokees by blood taken in 1835 the names of Benjamin Cross and Polly Cross nee Brown both of whom it is alleged were of Cherokee Indian descent and who did not leave the Eastern Nation until 1836 or 1837 are not so found nor are they found on the

Cherokee Citizenship Commission Docket Books
(1880-84, 1887-89) Volume IV
Tahlequah, Cherokee Nation

Silar roll of 1852 named in the application. The Commission therefore decide that the applicant Mary A Wallace the wife of Lee P. Wallace and her children named above are not of Cherokee blood. P. Office Evansville Ark.

                        Will.P. Ross
                                Chairman
                       Rabbit Bunch
                       J.E. Gunter   Com

WARDLON

DOCKET #1834
CENSUS ROLLS 1835 to 1852

APPLICANT FOR CHEROKEE CITIZENSHIP

POST OFFICE: Rogers Ark		ATTORNEY: A.E. Ivey	
NO	NAMES	AGE	SEX
1	Alice Wardlon	16	female

ANCESTOR: Mary S. Bell

Rejected Sept 2nd 1889

                          Office Commission on Citizenship
                              Cherokee Nation Ind Ter
                              Tahlequah Sept. 2nd 1889

The above case was called 3 times not less than one hour at intervals for a final hearing and no response from applicant or by Atty. The Commission therefore decide that Alice Wardlon nee Reeves age 16 yrs is not a Cherokee by blood. P.O. Rogers Ark.

                          Will.P. Ross
Attest   Chairman
   D.S. Williams   J.E. Gunter   Com
   Asst Clk Com.

Cherokee Citizenship Commission Docket Books
(1880-84, 1887-89) Volume IV
Tahlequah, Cherokee Nation

WELLS

DOCKET #1835
CENSUS ROLLS 1835 to 1852

APPLICANT FOR CHEROKEE CITIZENSHIP

POST OFFICE: Dyer, Crawford Co Ark	ATTORNEY: A.E. Ivey	
NO	NAMES	AGE	SEX
1	Thomas H Wells	28	male

ANCESTOR: John Rogers

Now on this the 17th day of March 1888, comes the above case for a final hearing. The parties having made application pursuant to the provisions of an Act of the National Council approved December 8th 1886, and all the evidence being duly considered and found to be insufficient and unsatisfactory, it is adjudged and declared by the Commission that

Thomas H. Wells is not a Cherokee and he is not entitled to the rights, privileges and immunities of Cherokee citizens by blood.

                        J. T. Adair   Chairman Commission
                        John E. Gunter   Commissioner
Attest   D.W. Lipe   Commissioner
   C.C. Lipe
      Clerk Com.

The decision in the James C.C. Rogers case found in Book C, page 627, and testimony on Journal pages 325 to 333 governs this case.

MABRY

DOCKET #1836
CENSUS ROLLS 1835 to 1852

APPLICANT FOR CHEROKEE CITIZENSHIP

POST OFFICE: Webbers Falls I.T.	ATTORNEY: A.E. Ivey	
NO	NAMES	AGE	SEX
1	Belle Mabry ~~C.H. Taylor Wilkerson~~	28	male[sic]

ANCESTOR: Uriah Wilkerson

Rejected June 29th 1889

Cherokee Citizenship Commission Docket Books
(1880-84, 1887-89) Volume IV
Tahlequah, Cherokee Nation

Now on this the 29th day of January, comes this case for final hearing the same having been submitted to the Commission on Citizenship created by the Act of December 8th 1886 by the Attorneys for the Plaintiff and the defendant with the evidence on the 29th day of September 1888 but not decided by said Commission under the provision of the Act of December 4th 1888 creating a Commission on citizenship, it is made the duty of the Commission to determine all cases not decided by the Commission created by the Act of December 8th 1886. In obedience to the requirement of law this undersigned Commission having taken into consideration all the evidence submitted directly or by reference and having failed to find the name of Uriah Wilkerson on the rolls of either 1835 or 1852 or any other roll named in the 7th Section of the before named Act of 1886 nor do they find the name of the mother of George W. Wilkerson on the rolls of 1851. Further the evidence submitted fails in the opinion of the Commission to establish the identity of George W. Wilkerson, the Father of Plaintiff Belle Mabry as the son of the before named Uriah Wilkerson, it is adjudged and determined by the Commission that therefore by the Commission that ~~Charles H. Wilkerson~~ Belle Mabry is not a Cherokee by blood and is hereby rejected and declared to be an intruder.

This 29th day of Jan 1889

Will.P. Ross   Char Commission
(Cherokee letters)
D.S. Williams   Asst Clk Com.

WHITFORD

DOCKET #1837
CENSUS ROLLS 1835 to 1852

APPLICANT FOR CHEROKEE CITIZENSHIP

POST OFFICE: Greenwood Ark		ATTORNEY: A.E. Ivey	
NO	NAMES	AGE	SEX
1	W.P. Whitford	39	Female

ANCESTOR: Mary Smith

Rejected Sept 2nd 1889

Office Commission on Citizenship
Cherokee Nation Ind Ter
Tahlequah Sept 3rd 1889

The above applicant was called 3 times & no answer and there being no evidence on file in support of the application we decide that claimant W.P. Whitford age 39 yrs and children, Thomas Whitford age 19 yrs, William

Cherokee Citizenship Commission Docket Books
(1880-84, 1887-89) Volume IV
Tahlequah, Cherokee Nation

Whitford age 14 yrs, John Whitford age 11 yrs, Lula Whitford age 5 yrs, Fredrick Whitford age 3 yrs are not Cherokees by blood. P.O. Greenwood Ark.

Attest
   D.S. Williams
   Asst Clk Com

Will.P. Ross
Chairman
J.E. Gunter Com

WELCH

DOCKET #1838
CENSUS ROLLS 1852

APPLICANT FOR CHEROKEE CITIZENSHIP

POST OFFICE: Weatherford Tex		ATTORNEY: J.E. Welch	
NO	NAMES	AGE	SEX
1	James & E.A. Welch	14 & 16	Male

ANCESTOR: Edward Welch

Rejected Sept 2nd 1889

Office Commission on Citizenship
Cherokee Nation Ind Ter
Tahlequah Sept 3rd 1889

The above applicant was called 3 times & no answer either in person or by Attorney, and no evidence on file in support of the application we decide that claimants Jas & E.A. Welch age 14 & 16 yrs are not Cherokees by blood. P.O. Weatherford Tex.

Attest
   D.S. Williams
   Asst Clk Com.

Will.P. Ross
Chairman
J.E. Gunter Com

WHEDDEN

DOCKET #1839
CENSUS ROLLS 1835

APPLICANT FOR CHEROKEE CITIZENSHIP

POST OFFICE: Salina Ind. Ter.		ATTORNEY: C.H. Taylor	
NO	NAMES	AGE	SEX
1	Susan M Whidden	52	Female

ANCESTOR: John Riley

Cherokee Citizenship Commission Docket Books
(1880-84, 1887-89) Volume IV
Tahlequah, Cherokee Nation

Rejected Sept 2nd 1889

>Office Commission on Citizenship
>Cherokee Nation Ind Ter
>Tahlequah Sept 2nd 1889

The claimant in this case was notified that on this day some disposition would be made of her application for Citizenship, and she failed to offer any evidence or testimony in support of her claim. The Commission therefore decide that Susan M. Whedden age 52 yrs is not a Cherokee by blood and not entitled to Citizenship. P.O. Salina I.T.

                        Will.P. Ross
Attest   Chairman
   D.S. Williams   J.E. Gunter   Com
   Asst Clk Com.

WILLIAMS

DOCKET #1840
CENSUS ROLLS 1835

APPLICANT FOR CHEROKEE CITIZENSHIP

POST OFFICE: Miland[sic] Tenn		ATTORNEY: C.H. Taylor	
NO	NAMES	AGE	SEX
1	Mary Williams	31	Female

ANCESTOR: John Bryant

Rejected March 22nd 1889

<u>Adverse</u>

Embraced in decision on page 431.
Book B. in the Aaron Bellew case
Rendered 22nd day of March 1889.

                    Will.P. Ross
                    Chairman Com
             John E. Gunter   Com
Office Com on Citz.
Tahlequah I.T. March 22nd 1889
              D.S. Williams
                Clk Com.

Index

ABEL
  Charles F 103
  E B 103
  Leonard J 103
  Lucinda E 103
  Mary M 103
  Walter L 103
ABRAMS
  J W 303
ACOCK
  Cassie B 240
  Charles F 240
  Loulie F 240
  Robert T 240
ADAIR
  Cinda 320
  J T 4, 9, 10, 17, 28, 31, 32, 33, 83, 89, 103, 109, 110, 117, 124, 139, 140, 143, 144, 148, 153, 160, 172, 173, 175, 179, 210, 216, 217, 218, 231, 238, 241, 258, 260, 266, 269, 292, 299, 303, 305, 307, 309, 312, 314, 323
  John L 284
  John T 102
  Walter S 102
ADDINGTON
  Loucinda 207
AKINS
  J H 202
ALBANUS
  J W 314
ASHLEY 62
ATWOOD
  Mary 5
AZBELL
  John 151
AZBILL
  John 264

BADSON
  Mrs 221
BAILEY
  (Illegible) 221
BAIN
  Agnes 165
BALLARD
  Martha 141
  Thomas 297
BARNES
  H C ..28, 124, 143, 153, 160, 210, 241, 258, 260, 266, 309
  Patsey 176
  Patsy 176
BEAMER
  John 70, 186
BEAN
  Joe 137
  Sarah 145
BELL
  Caroline 42
  J M 13, 111, 237
  L B 8, 48, 59, 74, 85, 87, 120, 125, 131, 132, 133, 134, 153, 155, 156, 163, 166, 167, 168, 169, 190, 242, 243, 244, 245, 255, 261, 268, 283, 289, 293, 294, 307
  Mary S 104, 144, 215, 322
BELLEW
  Aaron 326
BELLS 297
BENNUM
  Nancy 259
BIG-FEATHER 298, 299
  Anne 295
BIRCHFIELD
  Sallie 50
BLACKBURN

Edward 296
John 296
Mrs 296
Patsey 296
Samuel 296
BLISS
Rebecca 146
BOATRIGHT
Emeline 252
Emiline 164, 171
BOGUE
Lible J 244, 245, 261, 268
BOHANNON
J H 47
BONDS
Sarah 214
Sarah A ... 191, 192, 193, 208, 212
BOUDINOT
E C 162, 166, 180, 183, 187
Mr 50, 51
BOUDINOT & R 117, 118, 119, 127, 148, 149, 150, 151, 152, 153, 154
BOUDINOT & RASMUS. 6, 7, 19, 46, 49, 51, 65, 68, 84, 86, 89, 90, 91, 92, 110, 112, 114, 116, 179, 186, 187, 188, 189, 245, 246, 247, 248, 255, 259, 267, 271, 272, 273, 274, 275
BOUDINOT AND RASMUS .. 278
BOUDINOT AND RASMUS . 279, 280, 281, 282, 284, 286
BRADSON
Mrs 22, 25, 308
BRANK
David 318
BRITTON
John 153
BROCK
Susan 19

BROWN
Cecil 65
Elizabeth 197, 321
James 321
John 197, 321
Louisa 271, 272, 273, 274
Polly 319, 321
Robert 321
Sela 158, 159
Thomas 197, 321
William 321
BRYANT
Hiram 173, 174, 303, 305, 312, 313, 314
John 131, 180, 326
Johnny 290
Lucy 222, 223, 224, 225, 226, 227, 238, 312, 313
BUNCH
R 67, 233
Rabbit 322
BURGESS
Wm, Sr 186, 187
BUSHYHEAD
D W 297
Mr 299
BUTER
Geo O 260
BUTLER
George O 261

CALDWELL
T 87
CANDERY
Joseph I 70, 71
CASTEN
Levi 178
CHAMBERS
John 241

CHASTIAN
- B F 103
- Benjamin L 103
- Charles 103
- Edward D 103
- G W 103
- Harvey Mc 31
- Harvy Mc 103
- Henry W 103
- A J 103
- James B 103
- Jesse E 31, 103
- Jessie E 31
- John B 103
- John E 103
- John E B 103
- John S 101, 103
- Joseph C 103
- Joseph E 103
- Lafayette G 103
- Laura O L 103
- Leona C 103
- Lillian 103
- Lucinda E 103
- M C 103
- M E 103
- M H 103
- Martha L 103
- Mary E 103
- Mary O 103
- Milo 103
- Milton B 103
- N M 103
- Nancy M 103
- R F 103
- Roder L 103
- T E 103
- Ulyses G 103
- Walter W 103
- William A J 103
- William H 103
- William Leonard 103
- William M 103

CHISHOLM
- Absolom 218, 219
- Tom 219
- William 218, 219
- Wm 218

CHISOLOM
- Solomon 122
- William 218
- Wm 122

CHISOLOW
- Absolum 122
- William 122

CHRISTIE
- Wat 256

CHRISTY
- Ned 203
- Wm 277

CHYSOM
- Wm 135

CHYSON
- Wm 135, 138

CLARK
- L M 256

CLINE
- George 125, 276, 290

CLINTON
- Jeremiah 141
- Leaher 141

COBB
- Eudora 295, 297

COLE
- Mary 70

COLLINS
- Mrs Charlotte 320
- Ruth 320

Index

COODY
- Arch 253, 254
- Daniel 157

COPELAND
- Rachael 46
- Rachel Coplin 46

COPELIN
- Jack 46
- James 47
- Joe 47
- Rachael 47

COPLIN
- Joseph 47
- Rachael 46

CORDERY
- Sally 102

COUCH
- Mary A 83, 172, 175, 306, 307

COWAN
- John 109

CREEK 321

CREEKMORE
- E M 103
- J C 103
- M A 103
- M E 103
- M T 103
- W R 103

CREEL
- Ruth 321

CREWS
- Ann .. 8, 59, 85, 87, 120, 131, 132, 153, 155, 163, 166, 168, 169, 185, 255, 261, 268, 289, 294
- Mary ... 11, 12, 125, 156, 167, 293

CRITENDEN
- Tandy 94

CRITTENDEN
- James 321

- Tandy 95
- Tho 126
- Thos 126

CROSS
- Ben 319
- Benj 320
- Benjamin 319, 320, 321
- James 320
- Jim 320
- Polly 319, 320, 321

DARLEY
- Amanda C 103
- A J 103
- J E 103
- James A 103
- John B F 103
- W B 103
- William M 103
- Wm J J 103

DAVIS
- Saphrona 285

DICKERL
- Ben 229

DORHITY
- Eliza 320

DOUGHERTY
- Eliza 320

DOUGLAS
- J S 46

DUFF
- John A, Sr 19

DUNBAR
- Elizabeth 239

DUNSON
- Mrs 147

EDGLY
- John 97

EDWARDS
  Benjamin Franklin 32
  Henry C 172
  Mima 172, 175, 178, 215, 217
  Silas McDonald 32
ELLIOTT
  John E 315
ELMORE
  Martha 244, 245, 261, 268
  Sarah 74, 133
ELNORA 49
ENGLAND
  Mary 124

FOREMAN
  Bask 113, 114
  Jennie 114
FORMAN
  Annie 8
FOUST
  Malissa 250
FOX
  Cordey 103
  Cynthia C 103
  John 287
  John J 103
  Lucinda M 103
  Martha C 103
FRANKLIN 6
  Mima 83, 174, 175, 306
FREEMAN
  Mrs Jane 320
FRIENDS
  William 225

GARDENHIRE
  James T 256
  Thompson 47
GARRETT

D H 313
GAY
  James B 19
GIBSON
  Ezekiel 204, 206
  Joel 205
  William 232, 304
GOODRICH
  Barsheba .. 7, 65, 91, 92, 111, 112,
    117, 127, 155, 248, 259, 267, 275,
    276
  Bashiba 51
GORHAM
  Lewis 214
GRAVITT
  Jane 234
GREEN
  T B 320
GROFF
  Harriet 229
  Martha M 229
GUINN
  Almon 237
  Asa 286
  Bat 286
GUNTER
  Charles 295, 297, 298, 299
  J E .. 1, 2, 3, 5, 6, 8, 11, 12, 18, 19,
    24, 36, 37, 38, 39, 40, 41, 42, 43,
    44, 45, 47, 48, 50, 51, 53, 54, 55,
    56, 57, 58, 59, 60, 61, 62, 63, 64,
    65, 66, 68, 69, 70, 71, 72, 73, 74,
    75, 76, 77, 78, 79, 80, 81, 82, 83,
    84, 85, 86, 87, 88, 89, 90, 91, 92,
    93, 94, 95, 96, 97, 98, 99, 100,
    104, 105, 106, 107, 108, 109, 111,
    112, 114, 115, 116, 117, 119, 120,
    121, 122, 123, 124, 125, 126, 127,
    128, 129, 130, 131, 132, 133, 134,

135, 136, 137, 138, 141, 142, 143, 145, 146, 147, 149, 150, 151, 152, 154, 155, 156, 157, 158, 159, 160, 161, 162, 165, 166, 167, 168, 170, 171, 172, 174, 175, 176, 177, 178, 180, 181, 182, 183, 184, 185, 186, 187, 188, 189, 190, 191, 192, 194, 195, 196, 197, 198, 199, 200, 201, 202, 203, 204, 205, 207, 209, 211, 213, 214, 215, 219, 220, 221, 222, 223, 224, 225, 226, 227, 228, 229, 230, 231, 232, 233, 234, 235, 236, 237, 239, 240, 241, 242, 243, 244, 245, 246, 247, 248, 249, 250, 251, 253, 257, 259, 261, 262, 263, 264, 266, 267, 268, 270, 271, 272, 273, 274, 275, 276, 277, 278, 279, 281, 282, 283, 284, 285, 286, 287, 288, 289, 290, 291, 293, 301, 302, 303, 304, 305, 306, 307, 308, 309, 310, 311, 315, 316, 317, 318, 319, 322, 325, 326

John, Jr 296, 297
John, Sen 296, 297, 298
John, Sr 296
John E 2, 4, 5, 7, 9, 10, 12, 13, 14, 15, 16, 17, 19, 20, 21, 22, 24, 25, 26, 27, 29, 30, 31, 32, 33, 34, 35, 36, 49, 52, 59, 67, 85, 88, 89, 103, 110, 120, 131, 132, 139, 140, 148, 153, 155, 163, 164, 166, 179, 185, 190, 202, 216, 217, 218, 219, 231, 238, 243, 255, 262, 268, 269, 283, 289, 292, 293, 299, 312, 323
Katy 297
Maria 297
Old John 295, 296, 297, 298
Samuel 296, 297, 298
Sarah L 295

Starling ...295, 296, 297, 298, 299
Zacharia 227

HAINES
James 29
HALE
D W C 81
A E 81
Mrs T E 81
N J 80
W D C 81
W E W 81
W F 81
HANCOCK
Elbert C 68
Leah M 68
HANN
Bennett 72
Bennett H 72
Clay F 72
Cynthia Ann 72
Florence C 72
James F 72
James T 72
Joe 72
Joe W 72
Kate E 72
Lee F 72
Sallie M 72
Wood 72
HANNAH
B F 88, 89
George Ann 88, 89
James A 88, 89
M A 88
M L 89
Mary J 88, 89
W L 88
HARGROVE

K W 27
HARKNESS
  Acy 67
  Benjamin 64, 65, 67
  Edwin L 64, 65
  Elija 67
  Hattie L 67
  Joseph M 67
  Lester 64, 65
  Lucinda 67
  Malissie L 67
  Marion 65, 67
  Maud 67
  Octavia 67
  Sallie T 67
  William H 67
HARMON
  Mary 237
HARNEY
  Rebecca 281
HARP
  Isabella 84
HARRIS
  Mrs Susan 102
HARRISON
  Benj 320
  Benjamin 320
  Hiram 320
  Mrs Elizabeth 320
  W H 320
HARTLEY
  Alice 266
  Lilly 266
  Mary K 265, 266
  Noah 266
  Viola 266
HATTEN
  H F 174
  Hiram F 175

J S 174, 175
Mary J 174, 175
HATTON
  Almedia J 314
  Mary E 314
  N L 314
  N S G 314
  Sam B 314
  Samuel 314
  Wm L 314
HAUKS
  Lizzie 84
HAYDEN
  Alfey 65
  Caroline 65
  Cassie 65
  Etty Mahone 65
HAYES
  Hattie 238
  W M A 238
HAYS
  Hallie 103
  Hattie 238
  W M A 103
HEILMS
  Maggie 58, 59
HENDERSON
  James 83
  John 100
HENLY
  John 8, 11, 12, 59, 85, 88, 120, 125,
    131, 132, 153, 155, 156, 163, 164,
    166, 168, 169, 185, 243, 255, 262,
    268, 283, 289, 293, 294
  John R 74, 133, 243
  Z R 74
HENRY
  Addie M 82
  Chas C 82

Dolph 82
Mary J 82
Mary Jane 82
Nancy Jane 82
Rillie 82
Rillie F 82
Ruby L 82
William 82
Wm 82
HENSLEY
Emma Jane 61, 62
Estella M 61, 62
John W 61, 62
Leubar E 61, 62
HENSON
Elizabeth 69
Henry 69
Richard 181
HERALD
Andrew 70, 71
Fuller M 70, 71
James R 70, 71
Kile 70, 71
Louisa 70, 71
Robert 70, 71
Sarah Jane 70, 71
HERNDON
Ben 73
Benj Z 73
Dora 66
Edward D 66
Felix 73
Geo Henry 66
Harry 73, 74
Hattie 66
James 68, 69
James R 66
Jas R 66
John D 73, 74

Lee 73
Lizzie 74
Loa 68, 69
M E 66
Mack 73
Maggie 68, 69
Mary 73
Merle 68, 69
Nat 73, 74
Noah 69
Norah 68
Sallie B 66
Ula F 66
Willie 73, 74
Wm B 66
HESTER
Benjamin 165
James 199
HIDE
Benjamin 17
HIDER
Berty 70
Mable 70
Mary 69, 70
HIDGON
Mrs 77
HIGHLAND
Charles E 81
Chas E 80
Minnesoto 81
Minnesota 80
Willie H 81
Wm H 80
HILL
Martha 114, 115, 189, 245
HILTON
Silas 24
HINES
Henry 318

HITCHCOCK
Mr 312
HOLMES 197, 321
HOOLEY
Amanda 271, 274
Amanda E 272, 273, 274
HOPPER
Bill 266
E J 265, 266
J F 265, 266
Orville 266
HOSKINS
Marion 85
HOUSE
A B 60, 61
B F 64
C P 60, 61
Calafornia 64
E E 61
F M 60, 61
George 61
Hogosther 60
John 60
John D 64
Lanattia 60
Lee T 64
M F 60, 61
Mansfield 60, 61
Martha 60
Neley E 60, 61
William T 60, 64
Wm H 60
Wm T 64
HOWELL
Andrew Jackson 82
Armento 63
Doly *(Illegible)* 83
Edna Olly 83
George Washington 82

Ida 63
(Illegible) B 83
Joseph Mathew 82
Maggie 83
Martha 63
Robert E Lee 82
Rosa Lee 63
Sarah A 63
William H 63
Wm Edward 83
Wm H 63
Wm Halbert 82
Wm Oscar 82
HUBBARD
Anna 86, 87
Ellen 59
George 86, 87
Jane 86, 87
Lizzie 86, 87
Mattie 86, 87
Sally 246
Sarah 49
HUCKLEBERRY
David 62
David W 62
Emily M 62
Eva W 62
James A 62
Jesse Wage 62
Jessie W 62
Lettia M 62
Lettie M 62
HUDSON
Ada B 78
Amanda 75
Amanda J 75
Andrew J 78
Andrew J, Jr 78
Argal 76, 77

Barbary A 86
Chas F 85
Cleveland 76, 77
David 75
Edward 75, 78, 79, 85
Elmore 76, 77
Fannie 85
Gideon 76, 77
Hamilton 76, 77
James 76, 77
James T 86
Jas F 78
Joseph C 76
Joseph C, Jr 76
Joseph C, Sr 76, 77
Laura 85
Martha 74, 75
Mary A 78
Monroe 76, 77
Walter 75
Washington L 78
William L 79

HUFF
Atwood 87
R B 59

HUGH
Mary 79

HUGHS
Ann 295
Anna 298
Mary 79

HUNTON
Elizabeth 124

HURNDEN
Georgia 71
Leola 71
Lucy 71
Mack 71
W S 71

ICWY
W 32
IVEY
A D 316
A E 1, 2, 3, 4, 5, 6, 9, 10, 11, 12, 20, 21, 22, 23, 24, 25, 26, 27, 28, 29, 30, 31, 33, 34, 35, 37, 38, 40, 41, 42, 61, 62, 63, 74, 75, 77, 78, 80, 81, 82, 83, 84, 85, 86, 88, 93, 94, 95, 96, 97, 98, 99, 100, 104, 105, 106, 108, 109, 110, 136, 139, 140, 141, 142, 143, 144, 145, 146, 147, 151, 171, 172, 173, 174, 175, 176, 177, 178, 181, 191, 192, 193, 194, 195, 196, 198, 199, 203, 204, 205, 206, 207, 208, 209, 210, 211, 212, 213, 214, 215, 216, 217, 219, 220, 222, 223, 224, 225, 226, 227, 228, 230, 231, 232, 233, 234, 235, 236, 237, 238, 239, 240, 241, 264, 265, 300, 301, 302, 303, 304, 305, 306, 307, 308, 309, 310, 311, 312, 314, 315, 317, 318, 319, 322, 323, 324
E A 195, 196
IVEY & WELCH 88, 222
IVEY AND WELCH 221, 225, 277

JACKSON
Reuben 256, 257
Sandy 256, 257
JEREMIAH 297
JOHNSON
Amanda 252
Andrew J 156
Dica 252
Eli 49
Elizabeth Ellen 156
George 297, 299

Mary	252
Mitchell	252
Rebeca Jane	156
Rebecca J	252
Rebecca Jane	156
Rhoda	49
Robt	252

JONES
- Glennie 278
- Lilli 278

KAYS
- Polly 93

KERBY
- Mary 217, 218

KEYS
- Polly 160
- Samuel 159, 160

LABOYTAUX
- Electa 255
- Electa, Jr 255

LACKET
- J W 101, 102
- Sarah 102

LACOCK
- Cassie B 240
- Charles F 240
- Loulie F 240
- Mary 240
- Mrs Mary 240
- Robert T 240

LAFFERY
- G W 256
- W C 256
- William C 256

LAMB
- Eoline Dix 261
- Geneva 261
- Virgia 261

LANDON
- Clarissa 222
- Daniel 222
- E C 222
- Florence 222
- Sarah 222

LANDRETH
- Malinda 225, 226
- Zacharia 225, 226

LANDRUM
- H L 8
- H T 249

LANE
- Moses 195

LANGLEY
- Albert 232, 246
- Alfred A 233
- Andrew J 233
- Annie 233
- Collumbus 232
- Columbus 232
- Columbus C 233
- Edwin 232
- Edwin T 232
- Elizabeth T 232, 233
- John 246
- John A 232
- John Albert 246
- John L 233
- Josiah 247
- Kissiah 233
- Rebecca J 233
- Sadie H 247
- Sally 246
- Warner 246
- William 246
- William T 232

LARNE

Index

M A 248
LARUE
  Eugene 229
  Georg L 229
  George Lafayette 229
  Hariett 229
  Harriet 229
LASSITER
  John M 239
LATTA
  Francis 247
  R J 249
  Thomas 247, 248
LATTY
  Francis 258, 263
  James 263
  James M 258
  Jefferson 258
  Lewis 258
  Louinda 263
  Madison 258
  Modison 258
  Napoleon 258
  Rosa B 258
  William 263
LAW
  Coley 262
  George 262
  Harry 262
  Martha 262
  Robert 262
  Sissie 262
  William 262
LAWRENCE
  Alex 223, 224
  Beckey A 230
  D B 254
  Eliza A 240, 241
  Ellen E 240, 241
  G G 226, 227
  Ida 223, 224
  James J 254
  John 225, 245, 253, 254
  Lou E 240, 241
  Louisa 225, 227, 253, 254
  Louisa M 227
  Malinda 253, 254
  Margaret 227
  Mariah 225
  Martha 253, 254
  Morah 253, 254
  Randolph 223, 224, 226, 227, 253
  Richard 223, 253
  Robert 223
  Robt 224
  Samuel 223, 224
  Sarah 225, 253, 254
  Susan 223, 224
  T R 254
  William 224, 253
LAYCOCK
  I W 227
  S E 227
  Stella 227
  Thomas 227
LEACH
  Arliley 260, 261
  Arthur 260, 261
  Billie 261
  Billie West 260
  John 234
  John A 260, 261
  Lillie 234
  Lizzie J 234
  Martha 234
  Mary Francis 260, 261
  Mrs Annie 247
  Rilla J 234

Thomas Goodrich................ 259
LEE
   Annie R 236
   Martha 236
   Nettie 236
   Ora...................................... 236
   Viola................................... 236
   William...........200, 201, 236, 250
   Wm..................................... 200
LEGRAND
   Cordelia E........................... 250
   Heccuba............................... 250
   Hescuba 250
LEMDON
   John R........................... 238, 239
   Martha 238
   William E 238, 239
LENDON
   Martha 239
LERNDON
   Clarissa............................... 222
   Daniel 222
   E C...................................... 222
   Florence 222
   Sarah E 222
LEVY
   Lorena 218, 219
LEWELLEN
   Alfred B.............................. 259
   Cordoro D........................... 259
   Dicy 244, 251, 252
   James L............................... 251
   Steve 259
   Vincent 251
   William C 244
LEWERS
   Cary 228
   Hanson 228
   Harison 228

Joe L..228
Joe Lee 228
John 228
Maggie 228
LEWIS
   Laura 249
LINALY
   John Van 242
   John Vann 242
LINDLEY
   Edward A 243
LINDLY
   Albert G...............................243
LIPE
   C C ..9, 10, 31, 32, 110, 139, 140, 148, 179, 207, 216, 217, 218, 231, 238, 269, 312
   Catharine 296
   D E 10
   D W ...4, 9, 17, 31, 32, 33, 52, 83, 103, 109, 110, 117, 139, 140, 143, 144, 148, 153, 172, 173, 175, 202, 210, 231, 238, 241, 258, 260, 266, 292, 299, 303, 305, 307, 309, 312, 314, 323
   Mrs 296
LIPSCOMB
   Elizabeth..............................103
LIPSICOMB
   Elizabeth..............................238
LITTLE
   Ansel Z.........................255, 257
   Benj F 255, 257
   Cotillia 257
   Cotillia E 255
   Fannie 302
   Julia L...........................255, 257
   Letitia 35
   Lettitia 198

Mary R	257
May R	255
Nancy D	255, 256, 257
Robert E	257
Robert S	255

"LITTLEDEER"
Jackson 256, 257

LLEWELLYN
Dicey 113, 244, 251, 252, 259

LOCKHART
Ada	221
Lushion	221
Martha	221
Sarah M	220, 221
W A	220, 221

LOGAN
Elizabeth	257
Flossie	257
Harry	257
James L	231
Jeane	257
Lettie	231
Liba	231
Mary E	257
Stewart	257
Willie	257

LONDON
Jessie	241
Julia	241

LONG
Angelina	221, 222
Fernecy Jane	260
James E	260
Jesse	221, 222
Jonah	221, 222
Margaret	221, 222
Martha	221, 222
Mary	221, 222
Nancy	221, 222
Robert	221, 222
Sherman	221, 222

LOONEY
Ada May	219
Allen	219
Charles	219
Cora	235
E W	235
Elizabeth	235
Etta	235, 236
Hugh	235, 236
John F	235
L A	235, 236
Lillian	235
Orville	235
W G	235

LORRONCE
Albert	244
Anna J	244
Mary S A	244
William A	245

LOSSON
John W	103, 230, 231
Mary E	103, 230, 231
Rosa N	103, 230, 231
William	103
William E	230, 231

LOVELADY
Charles H	252
Charles Henry	252
Martha J	252
Mary L	252
William T	252

LOWDEN
Ada Bell	220
Altha C	220
Florene	261
George G	220
Lenora V	220

Leslie H 220
Mackey Jane 220
Macky Jane 220
Martha I 261
Mary A 261
Raymond M 220
LUCAS
Nancy 237
LUCUS
Nancy 182

MABRY
Belle 323, 324
MCCLELLAND
Wm R 49
MCCLINE
Annie 144
MCCOY
Betsy E 3
H A 21, 22
Ida 4
John L 296
L B 22
M E 21, 22
Rosannah 3
S M 21, 22
Sallie 3
Thomas 3
MCCUNE
John 51
Mary 51
MCCUTCHIN
Alphia 5
Flora ? 5
James 5
James R 5
John C 5
Louis 5
Modare 5

Mollie 5
William 5
MCDANIEL
Thos 1
MCDONALD
Geo C 34
Geo P 34
Joles 34
Joohes T 34
Lina M 34
Martha 34
Mary H 34
Mattie S 34
Thomas K 26
W W 25
MCGARRAH
George Henry 18
J C 18
Jack 18, 66, 68, 71, 72, 73, 74, 115,
    180, 183, 202, 257, 266, 278, 283,
    293
Julia 18
Lorance 18
Lucy 18
Mary 18
W D 18
Walter 18
MACKEY
Richard L 220
MCQUINN
Catherine 29
Ivy V 29
James P 29
Jessie 29
John 29
Lora E 29
Louisa 28, 29
Olive 29
MCRAY

Nancy M 33
Ulin L 33
MARCUM
Alfred 19
Thomas 19
MARONEY
Baily R 16, 17
Elizabeth W 17
Florence 16, 17
John L 16, 17
Louiza 17
Martha 16, 17
William H 17
MARSHALL
Allie N 7
Don T 7
Ellen F 30
Geo W 30
John S 6, 7
Myrtle O 7
R C 7
R E 7
Sarah A 6, 7
Thomas W 7
MARTIN
Francis 156
Martha 13
Mrs Nancy 286
MASON
Arch 24
Arnold 24
Dora 24
Lotta 24
Rhoda 24
MASSEY
Jackson 35, 36
James C 35, 36
John R 35, 36
Mary E 35, 36

Rosie D 36
Roxie D 35
Thomas J 35, 36
MAST
M 20
MATHIS
Allen 1, 3
Benjamin 3
Flora B 1, 2
James A 3
James T 3
Jane 1
John M 1, 2
Louisa J 1, 2
Lucinda 1, 2
Mary 141
Nora J 7
Sarah M 3, 7
MAXIE
Hulda L 33, 34
MAYFIELD
Earl 15
Jennie B 15
Joseph H 15
Mrs ..23, 104, 105, 106, 107, 108, 315
Niter 14
Pearl 14
Pearson 14, 15
South M 15
Wm L 14
MAYHEW
H 13, 14
John 13
MAYSON
Arch 24
Arnold 24
Dora 24
Lotta 24

Rebecca 24
Rhoda 24
MEAD
Edna E 16
Elmo M 16
Mary Ellen 16, 288, 289
MEADERS
Delohena 103
Mary 103
MEADORS
Cary 10, 103
Charles 10, 103
Drusilla 9
A J 9
Jessie 9
John D 10, 103
Martha J 10, 103
Nancy D 9
MEADOWS
Delohena 31, 32
A J 103
Jesse 103
Mary E 31, 32
Nancy M Dousilla 103
MEALER
Kindness 20
Miles P 20
MELTON
E L 25
J H 25
Jackson T 22
Lauriny 25
Vivian 25
MEREDITH
Alonzo F 11
Andrew 8, 11, 12, 59, 85, 88, 120,
   125, 131, 132, 156, 163, 164, 166,
   168, 169, 185, 255, 262, 268, 283,
   289, 293, 294

Baby 11
Gracie V 11
Leslie 12
Lillie ? 11
Myrtle M 11
Rosa E 11
Soloman J 11
Wm W 12
MILLER
Arch 184
(Illegible) 123
MILLSAPS
Adelade 17, 18
Benjamin K 17, 18
Desdimony H 17, 18
F M 18
Francis M 17
Malina J 17, 18
Marinda F 17, 18
Mary 17, 18
Nancy T 17, 18
Wesley G 17, 18
William H 17, 18
MITCHEL
Alonzo W 6
Wallace A 6
Walter L 6
William 6
Wm A 6
MOBLEY 62
MOORE
Addie 23, 24
Dora 23
H H 46, 47
Ira G 23, 24
Landan N 23
Landon N 24
Louisa 26
Mary 8

Mary E 23
Sarah 23, 24
MORGAN
Gabriel L Llewellyn 299
Malissa 12
Margaret L 12
Martha A 12
Mrs Mary L 295
Sarah 134, 155, 163, 167, 190, 242, 243
William 12
MORRIS
Andrew F 35
Caledonia A 35
Eliza B 2
James 2
James A 2
James D 35
Joseph D 2
Rachael 47
Rebecca 46
Rose E 2
Sarah M 2
Thomas F 2
William 47
Wm 46, 47
Wm H 35
Wm O 35
MORTON 280, 281, 282
MOSELY
Carter 4
Davis 4
Enoch 4
Hester A J 4
Horatio 4
John 4
Macy 4
Martin 4
Nancy 4

MOSS
Alice 23
Geo H 23
(Illegible) M 23
James B 23
John T 23
Mary Catherine 23
Nancy E 23
MOTEN
Larkin 270
MOTON 279, 281, 282
Hulda 97, 98, 99
Sam 98, 99
Sam'l 97
Wm 50
MOULDER
John T 313
MOUNGER
E J 29, 30
H R 29, 30
I A 29, 30
M P 29, 30
R B 27
MOUNT
W J L 8
MOURNGER
John 27
R B 27
MULKEE
Nancy 263, 279
MUNSON
Wm P 28
MUSGRAVES
James 21
Milly 21
Nancy 21
MYERS
Mrs O T 27

Index

NELSON
  Columbus F 103
  Monroe L 103
  Wesley 229
NEWBOLD
  W E 256

OO-YAH-SIS-TAH 277
ORVIS
  Emeline 187

PANTHER
  Felix 67
PATTERSON
  Howard 49
PAYNE
  Dr S H 295, 297
  Gabriel L 295
  Gabriel L Llewellyn 299
  Gunter M 295, 299
  Houston 295
  Houston J 299
  Martha A 299
  Mrs Martha A 295, 296, 298
  Mrs S H 294, 295
  Okla E 299
  Olka E 295
  S H 297
PAYNES 297
PETITT 101
PHILLIPS
  Garland 270
PIGEON
  Jennie 295, 297, 298, 299
  Sophia 295, 297, 298
PILKELTON
  Harriet 229
POWERS
  Hannah 195

PRICE
  Catharine 161
  Samuel 159
PRITCHET
  Daniel 240
PUFFER
  Margaret A 25, 26, 196, 206, 210, 237

RAGSDALE
  Florence Cullen 137
  Isaac 137
  Loretta Francis 137
  William Thomas 137
  Wm Thomas 137
RALSTON
  Elizabeth 111
  John T 111
  Zachariah 111
RAMSEY
  Charley 136
  Martha 93, 94
  S305
  Samuel 317
  Tina 93
  Tom 136
RANDALL
  Delbirt 145
  Jane 145
  Walter F 145
  Yett 119, 120
RANDOLPH
  Benjamin K 94, 95
  Birdie C 95
  C A 141, 142
  Charles 142
  Ellen 125
  Mary B 95
  Myrtle R 95

Index

Payton 142
Susan C 142
RAPER
   Alexander 96
   Charles, Jr 90
   Charles 89
   Georgia A 96
   Hattie 96
   Jack 96
   James P 89
   Jane 89
   John H 96
   Mora E 89
   Nathaniel 89
   Pearl M 89
   Polly 89
   Samuel D 89
   Thos H 89
   William 96
RASMUS ... 164, 165, 263, 276, 282
   Mr 279
   Mr William 288
   Mr William F 286
   W F 283, 285
   Wm F 282
RASMUS & BOUDINOT 287, 289
RATCLIFF
   Anna M 120
RAY
   Andrew J 120, 121
   B F 137
   B H 118
   Bonnie 133
   Brown 120, 121
   C A 118, 119
   C F 136, 137
   Callen 121
   Carle 133
   Franie L 120, 121

George F 120, 121
George W 134
Green T 132
J P, Sr 118
J T 121
J W, Jr 118
J W, Sr 118
James W 136, 137
John 120, 121
John R 136, 137
Joseph 137
Katy J 120, 121
Lillie B 118, 119
Mary 120, 132, 133, 134, 242
Nancy A 136, 137
P M 136, 137
S E 137
Sallie 118, 119
Savannah T 133
Sis 120, 121
Solomon T 133
Thomas 133
William 121
William J 118
Wm 118
Wm J 118
REACER
   Abraham 129
   J C 129
   John 129
   Lawrance 129
   Lela 129
   Lillie M 129
   Luke 129
   Maud 129
   Willie 129
REASER
   James 128
   John 128

John T 130	**RICKER**	
Lela 130	Celia 97	
Luke 130	Frank 96, 97	
Maud 130	George 96, 97	
Sarah E 128	Margaret 96, 97	
Thomas 128, 130	Martha 96, 97	
Thos 128, 130	Thomas 96, 97	
William M 128	**RICKEY**	
Wm M 128	Dora 97	
REDDEN	**RICKS**	
Clifford 95	Charles 98, 99	
Ruth 95	Grand 98	
Rutha 126	Henryetta 99	
Stella 95	Lena 99	
REESE	Mrs Elizabeth 98	
John 87	Silas 99	
REEVES	**RIFE**	
Alice 322	Infant 94	
Laura 144, 145	Zeda 94	
Martha 144, 145	Zida 126	
Mary C 144, 145	**RIGGLE**	
Nancy 188, 189	Henry 115	
Roasa 144, 145	Jefferson 115	
William 144, 145	**RIGGLES**	
RHEA	Frank 114	
Ella 116	Joe H 114	
Emojean 115, 116	**RIGGS**	
J E 115, 116	Addie May 106	
J L 115, 116	Addison 105	
James F 115, 116	Andrew J 104	
Mary E 115, 116	Charles A 108	
Mrs Ella 115	James W 105, 106	
W A 116	John 107	
W A, Jr 115	John M 106, 107	
RHOADS	Josephine 106, 107	
Nancy E S 103, 140	Landon C H 107	
RICH	Lewis R 105	
Elias C 134	Lundon L 107	
John 129, 130	Nellie M 107	

Rubie L 106
Samuel N 106
Walter A 107
RIGHTES
George A 131
RIGHTS
George A 131
RILEY
John 325
Polly 160
RITTEN
H C 142
J B 143
L A 143
L S 143
R L 142
W R 142
RITTER
H C 142
J B 142
L A 142
R L 142
W R 142
Wm 142
ROADS
Nancy E S 140
ROARK
Martha 125
ROBARDS
C C 113, 114
ROBBINS
Sarah 131
ROBERSON
Nancy 109
Sarah Ann 141
ROBERTS
Alice 146
Allen 122
Allice 146

Bill 122, 123
Blueford 138
Bluford 138
Eli 218
Elijah 122
Francis 218
Frank S 135
Frank T 135
Henry 135, 136
Jim 122, 123
Joe 122
Joe, Jr 122, 123
Joe, Sr 122, 123
John 122, 123
Lady B 135, 136
Lorena 218
Martha Jane 122
Mary 146
Mary Ann 218
Mollie 138
Mose 135
Moses 218
Moses B 135
Mynervia 135
Nancy 146
Tom 122
Victor J 146
William T 138
Wm 146
ROBERTSON
Mary 142, 143
ROBINS
W E 132
ROBINSON
Nancy 109
ROE
Annie 108
Frank 108
Harriett 108

Henrietta 144
Lewis A 108
Mary T..................................... 108
Sol*(Illegible)* B 108
ROGERS
  Benton B................. 103, 110, 147
  Charles.................................... 139
  Charles R 103, 140
  Charles W.............................. 103
  Chas W 100
  Cornell ... 17, 25, 26, 90, 113, 118,
    119, 174, 191, 192, 193, 196, 206,
    208, 210, 212, 214, 237, 244, 251,
    252, 259, 292
  Cynthia M.............................. 111
  Daisy B 100
  Daniel B 103
  A E 138
  Eliza R 103, 138, 139
  Enoch 101, 102
  F C 103
  George 102
  Ham C 100
  Ham L 103
  Henry C 102
  J C 103
  Jackson K 102
  James C C9, 10, 31, 32, 100, 101,
    103, 110, 139, 140, 141, 147, 148,
    231, 238, 312, 323
  James M 103
  James R 110, 111
  John 9, 10, 31, 100, 101, 102, 139,
    140, 147, 230, 238, 311, 323
  John C 100, 103, 139, 140
  John P 102
  Jon 110
  Joseph 102, 103
  Joseph G 139

  Joseph Oceola 103
  L E 110
  Lillie May 100, 103
  Linsey Ann 147
  Linsey Ann E 103, 147
  Lovely 102
  Mary C 103, 110, 147
  Mary M 100, 103
  Mrs Lucinda 143
  Nancy M................................ 111
  Pink 100, 103
  R B 103
  Robert 102, 260
  Rosa 100
  Rose 103
  S C 103
  Samuel M 143
  Sarah F 143
  William.................................. 102
  William E 100, 103
  William M 143
  Wm M 143
ROLAND
  Mary Ann 90
ROREY
  George L 93
  James W 93
  John F 93
  Lee 93
  Samuel I 93
  Sarah E 93
  Sidney 93
ROSS
  Allen 47, 265, 266
  E G 1, 2, 3, 5, 6, 8, 24, 41, 43, 48,
    49, 50, 51, 59, 62, 63, 68, 69, 70,
    82, 83, 84, 85, 86, 88, 89, 90, 92,
    93, 95, 96, 98, 99, 108, 111, 112,
    116, 117, 121, 122, 127, 128, 129,

130, 132, 134, 136, 137, 153, 155, 158, 159, 167, 170, 181, 184, 188, 189, 190, 191, 202, 203, 204, 205, 207, 213, 225, 235, 236, 237, 239, 240, 241, 247, 248, 249, 250, 251, 253, 257, 259, 264, 266, 267, 268, 270, 271, 275, 276, 278, 279, 281, 284, 286, 288, 290, 293
George W 265
James 265
John 265, 266
Leah 68
Malinda 112
Nancy 182
Silas 265
Will E 231
Will P14, 47, 49, 67, 87, 112, 113, 114, 115, 116, 117, 119, 120, 121, 122, 123, 124, 125, 126, 127, 128, 129, 130, 131, 132, 133, 134, 135, 136, 137, 138, 141, 142, 143, 145, 146, 147, 149, 150, 151, 152, 153, 154, 155, 156, 157, 158, 159, 160, 161, 162, 163, 164, 165, 166, 167, 168, 170, 171, 172, 174, 175, 176, 177, 178, 180, 181, 182, 183, 184, 185, 186, 187, 188, 189, 190, 191, 192, 194, 195, 196, 197, 198, 199, 200, 201, 202, 203, 204, 205, 207, 209, 211, 213, 214, 215, 219, 220, 221, 222, 223, 224, 225, 226, 227, 228, 229, 230, 232, 233, 234, 235, 236, 237, 239, 240, 241, 242, 243, 244, 245, 246, 247, 248, 249, 250, 251, 253, 255, 257, 259, 261, 262, 263, 264, 266, 267, 268, 270, 271, 272, 273, 274, 275, 276, 277, 278, 279, 280, 281, 282, 283, 284, 285, 286, 287, 288, 289, 290, 291, 293, 301, 302, 303, 304, 305, 306, 307, 308, 309, 310, 311, 315, 316, 317, 318, 319, 322, 324, 325, 326
Wm P 296
ROUMINE
John C 147
Lillie 147
Mary L 146, 147
ROWCROFT
Mary 133
ROWE
Annie 109
Frank 109
Harriett 109
(Illegible) B 109
Lewis A 109
Mary T 109
ROWLS
Catherine 202
RUCKER
Mary 87
Philip 87
RUSH
Calvin 123
Calvin H 123
Luella 123
Susan Roxanna 123
RUSHING
Anna Bell 91
David H 91, 92
Delva C 91, 92
Geo W 92
George W 92
Henrietta 91, 92
Henry A 92
J W 91, 92
James H 92
James W 91
Lena May 91

Maggie 91, 92	Effie M 127
Mary F 92	Eugene H 116, 117, 119
Mary T 91, 92	George M 127, 128
Myrtle M 92	George W 117
Nancy Mc 91, 92	Guy 127, 128
Robt T 92	John C 117
Thomas L 92	John E 117
W H 112	John W 116
RUSK	M A E 127
Adair Elizabeth 113	Maggie 127
America E 113	Minnie M 117
Eliza E 113	Robert L 116, 117
John M 113	Robert T 127
Lula 113	Russell 116, 117
Mary P 113	Seth 127
Wm D 113	Tresham M 116, 117
RUSSELL	Treshram 90
Brinkey 100	William T . 90, 116, 117, 118, 119
Brinkley 100	William T, Jr 116, 117
James 100	Wm T, Jr 118
John 100	
Nathan 100	**SANDERS**
Samuel 104	Ada B 169, 170
William C 99, 100	Claude G 170
RUTHERFORD	Darcus 192
Alfred P 124	Ellis J 190
Alice 124	Florence 190
Elizabeth 124	*(Illegible)* C 170
John 124	James 192
Joseph R 124	L S14, 15, 16, 17, 50, 70, 113, 123,
Lenora 124	124, 125, 126, 156, 164, 165, 171,
Lenora Wright 124	186, 244, 247, 249, 250, 251, 252,
Lewis W 124	258, 259, 263, 276, 285, 287, 288,
Mary 124	290, 291
Mary England 124	Mary 119, 192
Simonie 124	Milo 163
Wm M 124	Sarah A 187
RYE	Thomas 167
Clarence 117	Willis 190

Wm 192
SAVAGE
  Everett A 195
  Everett Anderson 196
  Sarah E 195, 196
SAW
  Caley 262
SCHRIMSHER
  Elizabeth 296
  Mrs 296
SCOTT
  Adda 149
  Alonza 148
  Aloza 148
  Annie 246
  Charles A 176, 177
  Eliz V 176
  Eliza 150
  Eliza E 150
  Eliza V 177
  Eveline 150
  Francis M 150
  Frank 149
  Geo W 176, 177
  Georgia E 177
  Henry 150
  Isaac 163
  A J 176, 177
  Jane 149
  John 148, 155, 163, 167, 177, 242, 243
  John, Jr 149
  John W 150
  A L M 176
  A L N 176
  Mamie 148
  Marcus D 177
  Mary J 176, 177
  Micajah ... 148, 149, 150, 151, 285

  Micajah, Jr 149
  Nancy 151
  Nannie 149
  Rebecca 149, 150
  Rebecca 2 150
  Robert 154
  Robt S 154
  Sam M 176, 177
  Silvia 154
  Susie 149
  Thomas J 177
  Thos J 176
  Tom 149
  Walter P 176, 177
  Wm C 150
  Zella 148
SEITZE
  Baily B 157
  Clara Jane 157
  Frank M 157
  Henry Bell 157
  J T 157
  Jessie Bryant 157
  Lebron G 157
  William N 157
SELSER
  Martha 160
SENSBAUGH
  James S 242
  Mary P 242
  Maud 242
  Zephin O 242
SETZER
  Polona 215
SHAFER
  E Catherine 156
SHANNON
  Annie 201
  Edward 201

Frank	201	
John C	200, 201	
Luthia	201	
Luthia C	201	
Malisa	201	
Margaret	200	
Morgan	200	

SHEFFIELD
- Bula J 209, 210
- Martha J 209, 210
- Mary A 209, 210

SHELTON
- Amitie V 209
- Anna L 209
- Annie L 209
- Cora B 209
- Cordelia S 209
- Delphia M 209
- John R 209
- Laura M 209
- William M 208, 209
- Wm 209

SHERMAN
- Baby 181
- Cora E 181
- Lizzie 181
- Louisa 186
- Martha 186
- Nancy E 181
- Nettie R 181
- Therissa A 181

SHIBLEY
- Ada 171
- Ada Ann 171
- Hetti Myrtle 164
- Isabelle 164
- Jesse H 171
- Manervia Emaline ... 164
- Mary Edna 171
- Samuel 171
- William Irvin 164

SHOCKEY
- Louisa 187

SHOUSE
- Annie M 182
- Charles A 182
- Elizabeth J 182
- John W 182
- John Wm 182
- Levi L 182
- Maison F 182
- Scott D 182
- Still H 182

SILER
- William 292

SIMPSON
- Catherine 214

SINCLAIR
- Linni 195
- Wm Thomas 195
- Zephamah 195

SIZEMORE
- Alvis Caswell 193
- H H 208
- Isom 193, 208, 309
- Isom F 191
- J Henry 193
- J R 208
- James H 207
- Joel . 191, 192, 212, 214, 310, 311
- L D 191
- Loving J 193
- Manda J 208
- Margaret R 208
- Mary 214
- Noah E 208
- Patience L 208
- Percy Ellen 208

A Reese	193	James S	113
Sarah Ellen	212	Jessie B	171
Wm A	193	John A	206
Wm Sanford	192	John W	113

SLATTON

Lelia 189
Bessie 184
Lester 207
Charles 184
Maggie L 207
Elizabeth 184
Mahala 153, 154
Florence 184
Margaret E 166
James A 184
Mary 324
Nettie 184
Mary A 151, 152
Richard 184
Mary F 171
Wm 184
Mary J 171

SLAUGHTER

Minnie L 165
Lawrance 30
Nancy E 151, 152
Lawrence 173, 236
Nellie M 172

SMART

Nettie 207
Daniel 198
Olan W 189
Edward 198
Ralph N 165
Roxana 198
Randolph N 165
Roxie 198
Rheuben 256

SMITH 198

Robert E 207
Archiles 170
Robert L 207
Augusta W 171
Rosa 210
C J 159
Roxana 199
Daniel 198
Roxie 199
Edward 199
S S 142
Elizabeth 198
Sarah Allice 171
Elizabeth F 186
Sidena Henryetta 171
Emma J 151, 152
Sintha 207
Fleming 151, 152
Thomas 170
Frank 153, 154
Thos 170
George 153, 154
Virgie 151, 152
H 199
Virginia S 207
Harvey 196
Walter H 165
Hasbard H 165
William C 207
J C 158
William 158
James 20, 25, 26, 84, 196, 205, 206, 210, 237
William L 113

SMITHERS

Asa F 178	Alexander 203
Eliza...................................... 178	Alexandra 203
Martha A 178	Ema 203
Matilda 178	Emma 203
Matilda J.............................. 178	Martha 203
Wm A 178	Mary 203
SNODGRASS 80	**STAFFORD**
SOMERVILLE	Caledonia 203, 204
Jno H 197	Cricket 204
John M 300	Eddie 205
SOUTHGATE	Henry H 205
Ethel 165, 166	Isaac F 205
Malissia 166	John M 205
Malissie 165	Lena 203, 204
SPALE	Lou Ella 203, 204
Columbus T 174	Lou Emma 203, 204
John 174	Lougenia 205
Pat... 174	Martha J............................... 205
Robert B 174	Mary J 203, 204
Wm D 174	Nancy 203, 204, 205
SPANKLE	Pete....................................... 204
Daisy 194	Rachiel 203, 204
Henry 194	Rebecca 205
James J 194	William 203, 204
Robert 194	**STAGGS**
Robt...................................... 194	Anderson 152
SPECK	Elliott.................................... 152
Frank 163	George 152
SPELD	Jetty 152
Delilah E 175	John 152
Elizabeth............................... 175	Kableston 152
Henry T 175	Kableton 152
SPINKLE	Luella 152
M 172, 193	Panit 152
Mary 172	**STANLEY**
May 193	J C 169
Moses 211	Susan F 169
Thomas V 172, 193, 194	Wm C 168
SPRINGER	**STAPLER**

Index

J S 52
STARBUCK
   Ann E 167
   Charles E 167
   Lucinda 185
STARNES
   Josephine 200
STARR
   Thomas 321
STAUPS
   Gordon 173, 314
   Malvana 173
   Malvara 314
   Nancy 173, 314
   Rachel 173, 314
   Wm 173, 314
STEELE
   Robert 166, 167
STEELMAN
   Carl F 188
   Carl T 188
   James M 188
   Jesse F 188
   Joel D 189
   John A 188
   Martha J 188
   Mary E 188
   Minty B 188
   Nancy L 188
   Sealey Ella 188
STEPHEN
   Benjamin 38
STEPHENS
   Ada 197
   Benjaman 197
   Benjamin 300
   Elizabeth 197
   George L 196
   J H 196

John 196
John H 197
Martha 196, 197
Mary E 196, 197
Sarah E 196, 197
William 197
STEWART
   Bolen 173, 174
   Charley 162
   Eddie 162
   Elizabeth J 173, 174
   Florence 173, 174
   G M 162
   G W 162
   Jane 162
   Jewell 173, 174
   John 173, 174
   Julia 173, 174
   Laura A 154, 155
   Lizzie N 155
   Lucresy 162
   Minnetta 154, 155
   Nealie 162
   Nealis 162
   Sarah 205
   Sudy 162
   Sue 162
   William 205
   William J 155
STICK
   Hattie 153
STIFF
   Allie 183
   C H 181
   C N 180
   Ezray 183
   Glenn 183
   Jack 183, 184
   Jessie 183

Levi 183
Lou 183
Mary 183
Minnie 183
Ruby 183
S P 202
Sallie 183
STINNETT
Alabama 212
Clay 212
Coosa 212
Cossa 212
E H 213
Early M 213
Forest 212
Inice J 213
James 212, 213
John E 212
John M 213
Louis 212
M E R A 213
Rufus 213
Thomas O 213
Thos O 213
STOCKDALE
Doc 161, 162
Mark 161, 162
Martha 161, 162
STOCKSTON
Daniel 156
James C 156
Rosannah 156
STOKES
Evaline 206, 207
Hattie 206
Hattie N 207
Lyndsy 206, 207
Rhoda 206, 207
STONE

B H 64
STRASNER
Emily 210, 211
Mary 210, 211
Oscar 210, 211
STRONG
William 19
STROUP
Clara B 202
STUDERVANT
Matilda 182, 183
SULLIVAN
Emily 185
May 180
Susan E 180
SUTTON
Caroline 169
Elizabeth More 155
Martha 169
Mary B 168
SWAFORD
Zora C 160
Zorah C 159, 161
SWAN
William B 204

TALLEY
John, Sr. 4
TAYLOR
C H 13, 16, 36, 37, 43, 44, 45, 52,
53, 54, 56, 57, 58, 60, 64, 69, 112,
118, 120, 121, 122, 131, 132, 133,
134, 136, 157, 158, 159, 160, 161,
162, 165, 169, 180, 184, 203, 242,
253, 262, 269, 270, 277, 292, 325,
326
Emily 58
Feraby 58
H 56

Isaac 58
J M 277
John 67
Mary 120, 132, 133, 134, 242
Polly 160
Robin 112
Samuel H 58
Sissie 58
TAYLOR & IVEY 135, 138
TAYLOR AND IVEY 218
TEAGUE 101
TERRY
  Ada 314
  Calvin 314
  Dora Bell 314
  Effie 314
  Elizabeth 314
  Isaac 305, 313, 314
  John 314
  Joseph 314
  Joseph R 314
  Lucretia O 314
  A M 314
  Maude 314
  Miles 314
  Mr 313
  N B 314
  Pearly 314
  Rachel C 314
  Robert 314
  Rosetta 314
  Russell D 314
  Samuel, Jr 314
  Wiley C 314
  Wm 314
THOMAS
  Hannah 90, 116, 118, 119
  Mrs T 193
  Nathan 7, 87

Sally 87
Sarah 172, 194, 211
THOMASON
  Simonie 124
THOMPAON
  Wm A 260
THOMPSON
  Jno 21
  John 38, 39, 40, 210, 230, 300, 301, 307, 316, 317
  Mary 178, 179
  Millie 38
  Nancy Ann 18
  Nancy V 271
  W A 18, 58, 115, 183, 202
  Wm A 66, 71, 72, 73, 129, 130, 166, 182, 239, 257, 263, 266, 278, 279, 283, 290, 293
THORNTON
  Dr 321
  Dr D D 197, 321
TIDWELL
  John .. 33, 210, 240, 241, 308, 309
  Mancel 143
  Mancil 143, 209
  Mandie 33
TINSLEY 218
  Joanna 218
  William 218
TIPTON
  Mrs Francis 247

UNDERWOOD
  James 42, 43
  Luster 42
  Martha 42, 43
  Sarah 43
  Sarana 42
UNDERWOOD, ... 43

USRAY
- Barton 46, 47
- Hugh 46, 47
- Lana 46, 47
- Louisa 46, 47
- Margaret 46, 47
- Winnie 46, 47

VANN 147
- Robbie 166

VAUGH
- George W 36

VAUGHN 63
- Adison M 44
- Allen W 54
- Andrew J 44, 52, 53
- B F 54
- Benjamin 45, 55
- Catherine 44
- Charles J 53
- Christener 44, 45
- Columbus 44
- Cora 37, 52, 53
- Cordelia 37
- Daniel 53
- Dolly 44, 45
- Emma 56
- Feraby..36, 37, 44, 45, 53, 54, 55, 56, 57, 137, 170, 270
- George 44, 45
- George S 57
- George W 36, 52, 53
- Gilford 55
- Grandville 44, 45
- Henry Sr 57
- Isaac, Jr. 56
- Isaac, Sr 56, 57
- James 53
- James D 37
- Jeff 53
- Jennie Ann 54
- Jimmi 57
- John D 37
- John F 44
- John P 55
- Joseph 45
- Kate 45
- Leroy 54
- Manda E 44, 45
- Margaret E 54
- Mark A 45
- Martha 37
- Martha C 43
- Mary A 54
- Molly 37
- Moses 53
- Nancy 37
- Nancy V 37
- O D 54
- Romulus 43
- Sallie 37
- Susan M B H 57
- Thomas 53, 56
- Washington 45
- Wassey 57
- Watkins 57
- Willie 37
- Willie F 37

VESTAL
- Benjamin 48
- David 48
- James M 48
- Jemima 49
- John H 48
- Nathan 48

W P R 111
WADE

William 78
Wm 75, 78, 85, 86
WAFFORD
  M L 316
WAGNER
  Andrew 217
  Emory W 217
  George A 217
  Henry M 216
  James H 217
  John C 215
  Malissa C 217
WAGONER
  Andrew 217
  John C 216
WAKEFIELD
  Albert 269
  Bettie 269
  Charley 269
  Eddie 269
  Kergie 269
  Liddy 269
  Ollie 269
  Thomas 269
  Vergie 269
WALDEN
  Albert 300
  Andrew 316, 317
  George 301
  George T 316, 317
  George W 300
  J M 300
  J W 307
  James 307
  Jas 307
  Jasper 307
  Jeremiah 300
  Jno 307
  John 300

  John B 316, 317
  John M 300, 317
  John T 316, 317
  Lidia J 300
  Margaret E 300
  Mary E 301
  Nancy 300
  Nancy Ann 316, 317
  Oscar F 300
  Sherman 301
WALK
  Charles H 291
WALKER
  Bessie L 291
  Charles H 291
  Elisa A 303
  Eliza A 304
  Ella 288, 289
  George F 291
  George M 288
  Henry 288
  James 303, 304
  Jane C 303, 304
  John B W 288, 289
  Johnie 289
  Joseph E 291
  Joseph H 291
  Lula 288
  Margaret 16, 291
  Margaret E 291
  Margaret E Stella 291
  Mary E 291
  Mary Ellen 291
  Mary J 288
  Noah Edna 291
  Norah E 291
  Oran 288
  Oren F 289
  Sada M D 288

Salina C 304
Thomas H B 288
WALLACE
  Ann A 265, 266
  Anna 265
  Bella 320
  Cora 320
  Florence 103
  Florence E 311, 312
  Hariett 264
  James D 319
  James Day 320
  John 264
  Leander 320
  Lee P 322
  Lilla 320
  Lizzie J 319
  Lizzie Jane 320
  Lovely F 320
  Mabel 265, 266
  Martha 264
  Mary 320
  Mary A 319, 321, 322
  Mary F 103, 311, 312
  Mattie M 319
  Maud 265
  Maude 266
  Minta May 320
  Mr 321
  Mumdamby 103
  Mumdum 311
  Mundum 312
  Pearly 319
  Pearly Preston 320
  Walter 320
  Welch 265, 266
WARD 38, 41
  Augustus M 272
  Charles J 315

  John 249, 315
  Mabel E 271
  Margaret E 271
  Melvin E 272
  P E 293
  William W 271
WARDEN
  Charles J 315
  Mary A 309
  Octavey J 309
WARDLON
  Alice 322
WARREN
  C W 313
WARSAN
  Sarah 123
WASHAM
  M C 8
  Walter 8
WASSON
  Charles 294
  Henry 289
WATERS
  Mike 77
WATSON
  Mr 313
WATTS
  Joe 260
WEBB
  Charley W 286
  Chas W 286
  Mary N 286
WEBSTER 284
WEIR
  Birdie 303, 314
  Elmina 303, 314
  J T 303, 314
  M L 303, 314
  Manerva J 303, 314

WELCH
- Charley 308
- E A 325
- E L 308
- Edward 325
- Geo W 4
- George 88
- J E 159, 161, 170, 270, 325
- James 325
- James B 292
- Jas 325
- Lloyd 292
- Loyd 292
- Mary 308
- S L 307, 308

WELLS
- Columbus C 187, 188
- Harvey W 305, 306
- James M 305
- James W 306
- Moses M 305, 306
- Rosa G 305, 306
- Sarah 305, 306
- Thomas H 323

WEST
- Jack 189, 245
- Jake 114, 115

WHEDDEN
- Susan M 326

WHEELER
- Ada E 314, 315
- Charles F 315
- Lucinda K 314
- Lucinda R 315
- Reubin 315
- Reubin A 315

WHIDDEN
- Susan M 325

WHITAKER
- Elizabeth 269

WHITE
- Angeline H 268
- George W 308, 309
- James A 308, 309
- Lewis A 309
- Lewis R 308
- Martha L 308, 309
- Mary 308, 309
- Mary P 308, 309
- Sarah 308
- Sarah E 309
- Thomas J 308, 309
- Walter P 308, 309
- William J 308, 309

WHITEHEAD
- Albert J 285, 286
- Alma J 285, 286
- Charles S 285, 286
- Fredrick R 285, 286
- James F 286
- James P 285
- Rebecca A 285, 286
- Rosa M 285, 286
- Thomas L 285, 286

WHITFORD
- Fredrick 325
- John 325
- Lula 325
- Thomas 324
- W P 324
- William 324

WHITINGTON
- Fanny A 306
- Harriett L 306
- Herschal 302
- John R 302
- John Rance 302
- Logan 302

Samuel 1	**WOFFORD** 316
Sarah H 48	Liddie 204
William 219, 290	M L 316
William L 273	**WOLFE**
Winnie 293	R M 69, 113
Wm 291	**WOMACK**
WINFIELD	J L 277
Alice 285	M E 277
Bertie 285	N J 277
Bolin 285	A V 277
Eddie 285	**WOODARD**
George 267	Elizabeth D 294
Haden 285	**WOODS**
James S 276	Mrs J B 284
Mollie 275	**WOOTEN**
Sallie E 267	Eliza Emma 311
Wallie 267	**WORTHINGTON**
William 285	Rhoda C 268
Willie Ann 275	**WRIGHT**
WINFINFIELD	Elmer 263, 264
George 267	James C 279
Walter 267	Lenora 124
WINFORD	Lulu S 279
Alice 284	Nora May 263, 264
Bertie 285	William C 263
Bolin 285	Wm C 264
Eddie 285	**WYLY**
Haden 285	R L 313
William 285	
WINN	**YARDEN**
Effie 290	Elizabeth 49, 50
Hattie 290	Richard B 50
Mattie 290	**YEARBERRY**
Mounie 290	Cynthia M R 50
S C 290	Fannie M 50, 51
WISHAN	John G 50, 51
Martha J 310	Lottie A 50, 51
WISHEN	Martha E 50
Martha J 310	Roger E 50, 51

Thos 51	Thomas G 38, 39
Thos N 50	William A 39
Walter C 50, 51	Wm A 39

YORK
    M V 48
YOUNG
    Anderson 40, 41
    Annie B 41
    Cordela 42
    Cordelia 42
    David 38
    Deily 39
    Dill 40
    Eddie 40, 41
    Elisha 37, 38, 39, 40, 41
    Felix 38
    Felix R 38
    Francis 39
    Georgia B 41
    Henry C 37, 38
    Ida 40, 41
    Infant 40, 41
    James 38, 197, 300
    James Lester 52
    Jeremiah 37, 38
    John 38, 40
    John Webster 52
    Joseph S 41
    Larkin 39
    Lillian M 41
    Maggie 38, 39
    Malinda 52
    Mandy 37, 38
    Manin 40, 41
    Margaret J 51
    Micheal 40, 41
    Millie 38, 300
    Nannie May 52
    Robert Andrew 52

www.ingramcontent.com/pod-product-compliance
Lightning Source LLC
Chambersburg PA
CBHW020239030426
42336CB00010B/545